Transformations
of Love

Transformations of Love

The Friendship of
John Evelyn and Margaret Godolphin

FRANCES HARRIS

OXFORD

UNIVERSITY PRESS

OXFORD
UNIVERSITY PRESS

Great Clarendon Street, Oxford OX2 6DP

Oxford University Press is a department of the University of Oxford.
It furthers the University's objective of excellence in research, scholarship,
and education by publishing worldwide in

Oxford New York

Auckland Bangkok Buenos Aires Cape Town Chennai
Dar es Salaam Delhi Hong Kong Istanbul Karachi Kolkata
Kuala Lumpur Madrid Melbourne Mexico City Mumbai Nairobi
São Paulo Shanghai Taipei Tokyo Toronto

Oxford is a registered trade mark of Oxford University Press
in the UK and in certain other countries

Published in the United States
by Oxford University Press Inc., New York

© Frances Harris 2002

British Library Cataloguing in Publication Data
Data available

Library of Congress Cataloging in Publication Data
Data available

ISBN 0-19-925257-2
ISBN 0-19-927032-5 (pbk.)

1 3 5 7 9 10 8 6 4 2

Typeset in Bembo
by Graphicraft Limited, Hong Kong
Printed in Great Britain
on acid-free paper by
Ashford Colour Press Limited,
Gosport, Hampshire

Acknowledgements

I am grateful to the following for allowing me to consult and cite manuscripts from their collections: in the UK: the British Library Board; the National Library of Scotland; the Public Record Office; the Bodleian Library, Oxford; Dorset Record Office (Ilchester MSS); Cornwall Record Office (Rogers and Godolphin MSS); Lincolnshire Record Office and the Earl of Yarborough (Worsley MSS); the University Librarian, University of Sheffield (Hartlib Papers); the Marquess of Bath (Coventry Papers at Longleat House); in the USA: the Library of Congress; the Harry Ransom Humanities Research Center, the University of Texas at Austin; the Houghton Library, Harvard University.

Quotations from John Evelyn, *The Life of Mrs Godolphin*, ed. Harriet Sampson (Oxford University Press, 1939), and *The Diary of John Evelyn*, ed. Esmond de Beer, 6 vols. (Clarendon Press, 1955) are included by permission of Oxford University Press.

My thanks to all those who have shared their knowledge and expertise in particular matters: Paula Backscheider, Patricia Crawford, Guy de la Bédoyère, Andrea Goldsmith, Theodore Hofmann, Michael Hunter, Sarah Hutton, Clyve Jones, Hilton Kelliher, Scot McKendrick, Giles Mandelbrote, Chris Mazeika, Sara Mendelson, Mary Robertson, Isabel Sullivan, Anne Summers, Andrew Walkling, Rachel Weil, Susan Whyman, and Sonya Wynne; and especially to Douglas Chambers, the most generous of Evelyn scholars, and the speakers and participants at the British Library conference in September 2001, who added so much to the understanding of 'John Evelyn and his Milieu'; also to those who helped me with the paintings: Catherine Gordon and Melanie Blake of the Witt Library and Photographic Survey, Courtauld Institute of Art; the staff of the National Portrait Gallery Heinz Library and Archive and the Royal Academy and Victoria and Albert Museum Picture Libraries; Gabriel Naughton, Director of Agnew's, Mr Grevile Bridge and his staff at West Lodge Park, Hadley Wood, and Alicja T. Egbert of the Iris & B. Gerald Cantor Center for Visual Arts at Stanford University, who responded so kindly to my enquiries; and Tabitha Barber, Diana Dethloff, Carol Gibson-Wood, and Catharine MacLeod for guidance in the labyrinth of Restoration portraiture.

I am especially indebted to William Richards and Chris Mazeika for their hospitality at the Master Shipwright's House, Deptford, the last evocative survivor of the historic dockyard; and to Prudence Hartopp, Jane Gore, and Elfrida Roberts for memorable excursions to Wotton, Godolphin, and 'down the river as far as the sea'.

Under the Arts and Humanities Research Board Exchange Scheme I was able to spend the last three months of 2000 on secondment to Royal Holloway, University of London, working on this project in the most congenial environment. Without this the book would have been much longer in the finishing than it has been. I make my most grateful acknowledgements to the AHRB for funding the exchange, to Patricia Crawford, Michael Hunter, Ann Payne, and Alice Prochaska for supporting the application, and to Lyndal Roper and Amanda Vickery, Directors of the Bedford Centre for the History of Women, and their students, who invited me and made it a reality.

Curators at the British Library have magnificent collections to work with. No one could be more fortunate than I am in this respect, or in my colleagues. My affectionate thanks to them, and to my family for all their support.

Contents

List of Illustrations

Abbreviations

BL	British Library
Bray	*Diary and Correspondence of John Evelyn*, ed. William Bray, 4 vols. (1859)
CSP	Public Record Office, *Calendar of State Papers*
CTB	Public Record Office, *Calendar of Treasury Books*
EB	John Evelyn, *Elysium Britannicum*, ed. John Ingram (Philadelphia, 2001)
Hiscock I	W. G. Hiscock, *John Evelyn and Margaret Godolphin* (1951)
Hiscock II	W. G. Hiscock, *John Evelyn and his Family Circle* (1955)
HMC	Historical Manuscripts Commission
JE	John Evelyn
JE, *Diary*	*The Diary of John Evelyn*, ed. Esmond de Beer, 6 vols. (Oxford, 1955)
JE, *Memoires*	John Evelyn, *Memoires for my Grandson*, ed. Geoffrey Keynes (1926)
Keynes, *JE*	Sir Geoffrey Keynes, *John Evelyn: A Study in Bibliophily, with a Bibliography of his Writings*, 2nd edn. (Oxford, 1968)
Life	John Evelyn, *The Life of Mrs Godolphin*, ed. Harriet Sampson (1939)
MB; MG	Margaret Blagge; Margaret Godolphin
ME	Mary Evelyn
Pepys, *Diary*	*The Diary of Samuel Pepys*, ed. Robert Latham and William Matthews, 11 vols. (1971, 1995 paperback)
PF	*Particular Friends: The Correspondence of Samuel Pepys and John Evelyn*, ed. Guy de la Bédoyère (Woodbridge, 1997)
PRO	Public Record Office
RO	Record Office
SG	Sidney Godolphin, afterwards Baron and 1st Earl of Godolphin
Upcott	*The Miscellaneous Works of John Evelyn*, ed. William Upcott (1825)
WJE	*The Writings of John Evelyn*, ed. Guy de la Bédoyère (Woodbridge, 1995)

The editions of Evelyn's *Life of Mrs Godolphin* and *Elysium Britannicum* listed above have been used for citations in the notes, since these now provide the most accessible forms of the texts; but in the body of the work below they are usually referred to with the conventions of unpublished texts ('Life', 'Elysium Britannicum'), to mark the fact that the former was written primarily for manuscript circulation amongst Margaret Godolphin's family and friends, and neither was published for the first time until long after Evelyn's death.

In the notes the place of publication is London except where otherwise stated.

Introduction[1]

'PRAYING is not usual for a Courtier', Margaret Cavendish says in her *Sociable Letters* of 1664, 'Yet those Ladies that are Beautiful are made Saints there, and the men are their Devouts, which offer them Vows, Prayers, Praises and sometimes Thanksgiving . . . Thus you may see many of our Sex are made Saints, though they be Sinners, but they are Sainted for their Beauty, not for their Piety, for their outward Form, not for their inward Grace: Indeed they are worldly Saints, and the Court is their Heaven and Nature their Goddess.'[2] All our assumptions about the Restoration court seem to be confirmed here. We have reached the last degenerate stage of courtly love, in which beauty is worshipped no longer as a sign of grace or virtue, but simply as a preliminary to transgressive sex, in a kind of knowing travesty of conventional piety. Yet the episode I am about to describe strongly suggests that this was not the whole story.

The most controversial aspect of the life of the seventeenth-century diarist John Evelyn has always been his passionate friendship with a maid of honour at the Restoration court: Margaret Blagge, afterwards Mrs Godolphin. In his later years he told the public story of this in his 'Life of Mrs Godolphin', beginning with their first chance encounter in 1669, when she was in her late teens and he a married man much more than twice her age. A notable lay Anglican himself and an intellectual in government service, he was impressed by her devout way of life in so unpromising an environment as the court of Charles II; but it was she who made the first approach towards a closer acquaintance by asking him for help with her financial affairs. Soon, at his instigation, this became a formal pact of spiritual friendship, although she at first took it rather less seriously than he did. Shortly afterwards she resigned her post in the Queen's household, ostensibly to marry the young courtier, Sidney Godolphin (Queen Anne's future Lord Treasurer), to whom she had been engaged for several years, but in reality because she wanted a period of retreat to test her strong

---

[1] This introduction was written last and may be read last.
[2] *Sociable Letters*, 15–16, quoted in Anna Battigelli, *Margaret Cavendish and the Exiles of the Mind* (Lexington, Ky., 1998), 135.

sense of religious vocation. For two years she met regularly with Evelyn for prayer and charitable works, while still debating with herself whether to honour her commitment to marry or dedicate herself to a single religious life. Evelyn was amongst those who finally persuaded her that no such retreat was possible for a young woman alone in Protestant England and that she would do better to pursue her vocation in a godly marriage. But after three years she died in giving birth to her first child and was taken to be buried at her husband's ancestral home in Cornwall, where she had always longed to live. The 'holy friendship', as Evelyn called it, had lasted a bare six years, but he continued to regard it as the most transcendent experience of his long life.

Of course the 'Life of Mrs Godolphin' is not a biography in any modern sense. Its models were Roman Catholic hagiography, the memorial sermon, and puritan 'exemplary lives'.[3] It was intended as a private document, a memorial for her widower and circle of devout friends, and remained so until the nineteenth century, when the manuscript came into the hands of one of Evelyn's descendants, then Archbishop of York, and was published at his instigation in 1847. The Victorians immediately relished this tale of the devout young Anglican woman, a beacon of purity in an ungodly court, of her religious vocation, domestic virtue, and early death in childbirth, and the work ran into several popular editions.[4]

By this time Evelyn's diary and a selection of his letters had also been published, so the main events of his life were known; but his archive, which included the letters and devotional manuscripts on which he had based the 'Life', remained in the hands of his family until it was deposited at Christ Church, Oxford, in the late 1940s. Its custodian there, W. G. Hiscock, used it to interpret the friendship in a very different and post-Freudian light. In two books, *John Evelyn and Margaret Godolphin* (1951) and *John Evelyn and his Family Circle* (1955), he argued that it had actually been a kind of seduction on Evelyn's part; that he tried to prevent the girl from marrying in order to keep her in his power, and had even suppressed or falsified some of the documents afterwards to conceal this from her husband, whose patronage he sought. Evelyn, who appeared so exemplary in his diary, stood revealed as in his way as much a sexual predator as his friend Pepys or the Restoration rakes he professed to despise.

---

[3] *Life*, 115; Bruce Redford, 'Evelyn's *Life of Mrs Godolphin* and the Hagiographical Tradition', *Biography*, 8 (1985), 119–29; Ralph Houlbrooke, *Death, Religion, and the Family in England 1480–1750* (Oxford, 1998), 295–330. For Samuel Clarke's collection of puritan exemplary lives, published in 1683, the year before Evelyn's 'Life' was written, see Jacqueline Eales, 'Samuel Clarke and the "Lives" of Godly Women in Seventeenth-Century England', in W. J. Sheils and D. Wood (eds.), *Women in the Church* (Oxford, 1990), 365–76.

[4] See further Appendix A.

Hiscock's interpretation never fully found favour. His relish in unmasking Evelyn as a liar and a hypocrite was too obvious. His tendency to see Margaret Godolphin's every religious aspiration as a sign of neurosis, only to be cured by her acceptance of a husband and a full sexual relationship, was too crude. The dubiousness of some of his methods was apparent even to those who could not check his sources.[5] In fact his motives were self-consciously iconoclastic in a rather belated Bloomsbury manner. Evelyn as revealed in his diary had become a kind of surrogate eminent Victorian and therefore a legitimate target for debunking. 'On the publication of Evelyn's *Life of Mrs Godolphin*', as Hiscock put it in the preface to his second book, 'the Victorians readily placed the author in the beams of the halo which he had put on the head of his saintly friend.' His purpose was to dislodge both haloes.

In 1995 the Evelyn archive was acquired by the British Library, so that all the documentary evidence he preserved about the friendship is now accessible. At the same time, by a remarkable accident of survival in an unexpected source, the correspondence between Margaret Blagge and Sidney Godolphin of the same period has come to light, providing a perspective on it quite independent of Evelyn's.[6] The material Hiscock brought forward was undeniably interesting and he was right to feel that there was more to the friendship than Evelyn publicly acknowledged. His chief failing was to treat it as a purely personal episode. In fact it belongs, and can only be fully understood in the context of the post-Reformation debate concerning marriage, and the much longer and less studied tradition of intense friendships between men and women in religious settings.

The marriage debate was an old one, much older than the Reformation. Was celibacy more pleasing to God than marriage? Was virginity a more angelic state than carnal love? The precepts of St Paul and the Church Fathers appeared to favour the former and a long neoplatonic tradition seemed to reinforce them. But with the Reformation both humanist and puritan social theory had weighed more heavily in favour of marriage, as a state in which an individual, and especially a woman, could do more good than in a solitary devotional life.[7] In any case there was no longer an institutional environment, as there had been before the Reformation, in which to lead a religious life apart from family ties. A man so inclined might seek a form of collegiate life

---

[5] See further Appendix B.   [6] See further Appendix A: Hammick Papers.
[7] Marina Warner, *Alone of all her Sex: The Myth and Cult of the Virgin Mary* (1976), 74; Margaret R. Sommerville, *Sex and Subjection: Attitudes to Women in Early Modern England* (1995), 251; Margo Todd, *Christian Humanism and the Puritan Social Order* (Cambridge, 1987), 97–115; Anthony Fletcher, 'The Protestant Idea of Marriage in Early Modern England', in A. Fletcher and P. Roberts (eds.), *Religion, Culture and Society in Early Modern Britain* (Cambridge, 1994), 162–3.

in the universities, but for a Protestant woman there was no formal provision of any kind, no prospect apart from marriage. For a young woman such as Margaret Blagge, whose soul, in Evelyn's words, was always 'in the Cloister',[8] this meant a drastic foreclosing of prospects.

The increased importance accorded to marriage did not mean that it was less restrictive for women. For all the renewed emphasis on social utility and companionate relations, prescription and patriarchal authority still prevailed.[9] In fact one effect of Margaret's story is to highlight the poverty of much of the debate about marriage and gender relations at this period, both contemporary and modern. For there was one important non-prescriptive and non-contractual relationship which has received much less attention from historians, even though it made a serious claim at the time to be regarded as more of a sacrament than marriage, and was as open to women as to men; and this was friendship.

In any society of rigidly prescribed and unequal social roles, friendship was likely to be highly valued for the freedoms and emotional satisfactions it offered. Attempts to analyse and define its nature went back to classical and patristic literature and continued through the Middle Ages and into the Renaissance.[10] In Evelyn's day intellectuals as influential and diverse as Francis Bacon, Jeremy Taylor, and Edward Hyde made their contributions, and his own conduct book, 'Oeconomics to a Newly Married Friend', which contrasts friendship and marriage, is the most interesting of all the documents to come from his relationship with Margaret Godolphin. All definitions agreed that friendship was inherently virtuous, or at least that without virtue it was not worthy of the name, but otherwise opinions differed as to its proper scope. Evelyn's invocation as a young man of 'a Friend, a Booke and a Garden' as his ideal was a classic, and in this case rather posturing, statement of Epicurean quiescence;[11] in fact it was the neoplatonic mode which always held the greater significance for him. Originating in the *Symposium* of Plato, this reached its most highly evolved and Christianized form in the Florentine Renaissance, and was made familiar in the courts of Europe through such works as Castiglione's *Book of the Courtier*. In the process the homoeroticism of Plato was transformed into what has been called a 'sublime spiritual eros', by which love for a supremely attractive man

[8] BL Add. MS 78328, pp. 153–4: commonplace notes under 'amicitia'.
[9] For a good recent summary of this debate, see Anne Kugler, 'Constructing Wifely Identity: Prescription and Practice in the Life of Lady Sarah Cowper', *Journal of British Studies*, 40 (2001), 297–9.
[10] E. H. Gombrich, *Symbolic Images* (1972), 139–41; Reginald Hyatte, *The Arts of Friendship: The Idealization of Friendship in Medieval and Early Renaissance Literature* (Leiden, 1994); esp. 1–86.
[11] Michael Hunter, 'John Evelyn in the 1650s', in *Science and the Shape of Orthodoxy* (Woodbridge, 1995), 70.

(or in some versions a woman), stripped of all sensual appetite, could become the pathway to apprehension of, and eventually mystic union with, divine love and beauty.[12] 'Love, that celestial gift, which rests in the soule, & tends to heaven from whence it came, languishes & dies under the feete of a terrestrial beauty, & often ends in feare & despere, in rage & folly,' Evelyn wrote in his commonplace book, 'but friendship is freed of all this.'[13] Love between such friends therefore had the potential to be more significant than any other human relationship; to transform itself into an experience of the divine.

It is not surprising that a good deal of prescriptive writing by the English Protestant clergy was concerned to appropriate this special spiritual status of friendship, at least as it concerned male–female relations, and to contain it within the married state. The companionate marriage, it was said, was or should be the highest form of friendship. But the continued insistence on patriarchal authority was always a stumbling block.[14] It was not easy to see how a relationship whose essence was freedom and equality could really be subsumed into the early modern marriage, which remained essentially a contract for surrendering the independence of one party to another who was deemed to be intrinsically superior. Yet these were not the only voices to listen to. In France the tradition of spiritual friendship continued less interrupted, and by the early seventeenth century had found popular expression in the 'Devout Humanism' of Francis de Sales. This also drew on the neoplatonic tradition, and more specifically on the widely disseminated treatise on spiritual friendship, traditionally attributed to St Augustine but actually by the twelfth-century Cistercian, Aelred of Rievaulx. De Sales's exposition of the connectedness of human and divine love appealed not just to his own countrymen but to Protestants as well and he gave special emphasis to the role of women.[15] In fact it is clear that passionate friendships between men and women who were unconnected by marriage or kinship, centred in shared religious practice, were and are a feature of many sects and periods of Christianity.[16]

[12] Erwin Panofsky; *Studies in Iconology* (New York, 1939), 129–48; Baldesar Castiglione, *The Book of the Courtier*, trans. George Bull (Harmondsworth, 1967), 323–44; Sarah Hutton, 'The Renaissance and the Seventeenth Century: Introduction', in Anna Baldwin and Sarah Hutton (eds.), *Platonism and the English Imagination* (Cambridge, 1994), 71–85.

[13] BL Add. MS 78328, p. 153: commonplace notes under 'amicitia'.

[14] William and Malleville Haller, 'The Puritan Art of Love', *Huntington Library Quarterly*, 5 (1941–2), 235–72; Kugler, 'Constructing Wifely Identity', 298–9.

[15] Terence A. McGoldrick, *The Sweet and Gentle Struggle: Francis de Sales on the Necessity of Spiritual Friendship* (Lanham, Md., 1996), 101–4; Erica Veevers, *Images of Love and Religion: Queen Henrietta Maria and Court Entertainments* (Cambridge, 1989), 21–33; John Spurr, *The Restoration Church of England* (New Haven, 1990), 372–3.

[16] Patrick Collinson, ' "Not Sexual in the Ordinary Sense": Men, Women and Religious Transactions', in *Elizabethan Essays* (1994), 119–50.

There is no need for us to be unduly knowing or condescending about these. De Sales wrote quite frankly of 'the similarity that exists between our spiritual emotions and our physical passions'.[17] The aspect of sublimated sexuality was clearly well understood, and indeed valued by the participants, who never discounted the unruly and subversive nature of sexual passion. We may now take it for granted that passionate sexual love demands physical expression, whatever the consequences if it should arise outside accepted social norms or in competition with other claims, but we may need reminding that this has not always been seen as the only or the best solution. It is clear enough, as Hiscock realized, that at one level Evelyn was 'in love' with Margaret Blagge and knew that he was. The crucial issue was how he dealt with it.

The accessibility of Evelyn's large archive means that we can now more readily understand the complexity of his intellectual make-up. He was a staunch Englishman whose lifelong project was to bring the achievements of the European Renaissance to his own countrymen. He was an unwavering Anglican in the worst of times, for whom the Roman Catholicism he encountered in France as a young man never lost its hold over his imagination and emotions. He was self-fashioned and seen by his contemporaries as the quintessential virtuoso—a gentleman connoisseur with a sensibility attuned to the wonders and not just the mechanics of the natural world. Yet he could protest quite justifiably at the suggestion of dilettantism, for the skills which produced his greatest creative work, the exquisite 'little world' of his garden at Sayes Court in Deptford, were both practical and systematic, and his lifelong project was to make his learning of service of his countrymen and the state. In fact his whole habit of mind was to try to contain and to reconcile oppositions: to be both a courtier and a 'pure squire', ancient and modern, devout layman and Baconian natural philosopher.[18]

Platonic philosophy, with its constant sense of the ideal behind the material appearance and its pervasive system of symbols and correspondences between the higher and lower world, was at the heart of all his thinking. It helped him to find the resolution he always sought between the claims of the

---

[17] Quoted from de Sales's *Treatise of the Love of God*, in Veevers, *Images of Love and Religion*, 24.

[18] A full catalogue of the Evelyn archive is in progress; for a preliminary account, see Theodore Hofmann et al., *John Evelyn in the British Library* (1995), 11–73. T. O'Malley and J. Wolschke-Bulmahn (eds.), *John Evelyn's 'Elysium Britannicum' and European Gardening* (Washington, DC, 1998) has a far wider range than the purely horticultural and provides an excellent introduction to Evelyn's thought. The conference, 'John Evelyn and his Milieu', convened at the British Library, 17–18 September 2001, included contributions on Evelyn's religious and political ideas as well as his connoisseurship; publication of the proceedings is in progress. See also W. E. Houghton, 'The English Virtuoso in the Seventeenth Century', *Journal of the History of Ideas*, 3 (1942), 51–73, 190–219.

active life and the life of the mind and spirit.[19] It made Sayes Court garden not just a horticultural showpiece, but the shadow or representation of paradise or the garden of Eden. And when the time came it also showed him the way, though it was not an easy one, to transform his love for Margaret Godolphin; 'the lover had to deal harshly with his own reprobate desire to despoil the object of his love, struggling perpetually to transmute a mere appetite into something rarer and more deserving. Platonic love is eternal and can have nothing to do with the periodicity of sexual desire.'[20]

The special role accorded to women by neoplatonic philosophy was of course most apparent in courtly society: their beauty and refinement and the love it attracted were seen not just as civilizing influences, but as manifestations of moral worth and virtue. But this was certainly not the only function of women in courts. At a more practical level they were also employed alongside men in the royal household which in the early modern state was at the heart of government. In fact it is now recognized that women could play a significant part in public and political life by this means, at a period when they were apparently excluded by their sex from any formal role.[21] The specific roles open to them would depend on the nature of the court, and this in turn a good deal on the age and personal predilections of the monarch. At the Restoration glamour, confidence, and overt sexuality were at a premium. A new arrival amongst the maids of honour was asked ironically whether she intended to 'set up' as a beauty, a mistress, a wit, or a politician.[22] Margaret Blagge had all the practised courtier's performative skills of wit and display; was one of the nimblest of the 'Spirits that dwell in Fairy-Land', as Evelyn called the denizens of the Restoration court.[23] Yet she still maintained an elaborate devotional life in the heart of Whitehall, and what becomes clear as one explores the Restoration milieu further is that this combination of

[19] Panofsky, *Studies in Iconology*, 138–9; Gombrich, *Symbolic Images*, 152–3; David Stevenson, *The Origins of Freemasonry* (Cambridge, 1988), 79–80.

[20] Germaine Greer, *Slipshod Sybils: Recognition, Rejection and the Woman Poet* (1995), 6.

[21] Sara Mendelson and Patricia Crawford, *Women in Early Modern England* (Oxford, 1998), 370–7. Particular studies of the Tudor and Stuart periods include Barbara Harris, 'Women and Politics in Early Tudor England', *Historical Journal*, 33 (1990), 259–81; Pam Wright, 'A Change in Direction: The Ramifications of a Female Household 1558–1603', in David Starkey et al. (eds.), *The English Court from the Wars of the Roses to the Civil War* (1987), 147–72; Leeds Barroll, 'The Court of the First Stuart Queen', in Linda Levy Peck (ed.), *The Mental World of the Jacobean Court* (Cambridge, 1991), 191–204; Veevers, *Images of Love and Religion*; Sonya Wynne, 'The Mistresses of Charles II and Restoration Court Politics', Ph.D. thesis (Cambridge, 1997); Frances Harris, *A Passion for Government: The Life of Sarah, Duchess of Marlborough* (Oxford, 1991); Robert Bucholz, *The Augustan Court: Queen Anne and the Decline of Court Culture* (Stanford, Calif., 1993).

[22] Quoted in Antonia Fraser, *The Weaker Vessel: Women's Lot in Seventeenth Century England* (1984), 454.

[23] *Life*, 20.

devout piety and worldly display was far from being unique to her. Women played a central role not just in the politics of the court, but in its religious life. For all Pepys's familiar gossip and the tales of Charles II and his mistresses, for all the general sense that this was 'the last truly gay and splendid court in English history',[24] it still remains somewhat dark and unexplored territory. From one point of view it can be seen, and indeed saw itself, as a watershed of modernity, a society which had demystified monarchy and was more concerned with nature's laws than with man's or God's. Yet it was still haunted by the loss of the divinity behind common appearances, of human beauty as the manifestation of the divine, and of the guiding providence which was a consoling sign of God's direct concern with human affairs. The friendship of Evelyn and Margaret Godolphin was not a furtive, isolated, or eccentric episode. It was conducted in terms quite familiar to their contemporaries and in full view of their families and their court circle, who were for the most part supportive and sympathetic. If it seems out of the ordinary to us, this may suggest that the period and the milieu in which it occurred are less easily understood than we have thought.

Feminist history has not always been comfortable in dealing with the evidence of women's spiritual lives.[25] Evelyn, who believed with utter conviction in the social subordination of women and their confinement to private rather than public households, was still convinced of their special redemptive qualities, and of course he was not alone in this. But was it a way of conferring autonomy and power on women, or was it simply another means of enforcing patriarchal norms, of denying their full human status, and devaluing their struggle for self-realization?[26] Margaret Blagge certainly made it clear that she did not want to be seen as an icon of virtue and perfection or a reformer of the court, as Evelyn sought to make her. Although she was concerned to improve herself, she knew she could never be his intellectual equal or take her place in succession to the learned women of the Renaissance courts; 'alas what am I able to pleys you in?', she wrote to him, 'I can't find fault with you nor inform you nor edefy you: and but that you condescend understand what you say; first you hope I am beter then I seem, and you

---

[24] Bucholz, *Augustan Court*, 12; this is part of an admirable short survey of Restoration court culture.

[25] Anne Summers, *Female Lives, Moral States: Women, Religion, and Public Life in Britain 1800–1930* (2000), 67.

[26] For both sides of this debate, see Peter Lake, 'Feminine Piety and Personal Potency: The Emancipation of Mrs Jane Ratcliffe', *Seventeenth Century*, 2 (1987), 143–56; Patricia Crawford, *Women and Religion in England 1550–1720* (1993), 73–5; Collinson, ' "Not Sexual in the Ordinary Sense" ', 126–7; Sommerville, *Sex and Subjection*, 42–3; Anthony Fletcher, *Gender, Sex, and Subordination in England 1500–1800* (New Haven, 1995), 347–8; Greer, *Slipshod Sybils*, 2.

beleev me wiser then in apearance I am; and next if I were non of all this, why because of that you would if possible make me something.' But what she most passionately wanted was not to be made into something, but to know herself: 'The more I know myself, the less I like myself, and yet for the treasuers of the world, I would not but know myself: and I pray I may do so still more and more, till I come to know even as I am known.'[27] This meant first and fore-most being free of the social claims on women, the sense of being constantly observed and regulated, the obligation to be always dedicating herself to others, the subjection to the court and the world of material goods (she complained of female friends who expected her almost to 'live in' shops), and above all the insistence that she had no choice but to marry. Yet she did not long just for self-realization, but in the biblical sense to know herself, 'even as I am known'. Religious aspiration remained at the centre of her life.

Friendship might seem to offer an escape from the constraints of patri-archy, but it still left the possibility of more subtle kinds of psychological exploitation, of masculine preying on female anxieties and conflicts. This of course was the basis of Hiscock's interpretation, but it does not fit the evidence in this case. It was Margaret Blagge and not Evelyn, after all, who initiated the friendship, and for quite self-interested motives of her own. Afterwards she repeatedly and passionately acknowledged the spiritual benefits she received from it, but without masochism or undue dependence; she was equally prepared to tease and on occasion to criticize him sharply, and in the end it was he who showed himself the more insecure of the two. In the same way we find her negotiating the terms of her courtship on remarkably equal terms, sardonically exposing the means by which her lover evaded a full commitment to a devout life and playing so strongly on his guilt at conform-ing to court ways that the conflict she set up in the end brought him to a major breakdown. Impelled by what she called 'that mighty love to the crea-ture', she did eventually accept a godly marriage as the best means Protestant England could offer a woman of reconciling the active and contemplative lives. It brought her great happiness, yet she was aware from the first of how much it constrained her; and of course it had a catastrophic outcome, though one brought about by a random and virulent infective organism and not by any social or cultural agency.

Although Evelyn and Margaret Godolphin differed so widely in age and education, 'never two people', Evelyn's wife remarked, 'were more alike in their way and inclination'; alike in what she called their 'severity', their refusal to be satisfied with the material prospect before them and their need to look

---

[27] BL Add. MS 78307, fo. 13ᵛ: MB to JE, [?11 May 1673].

to something beyond 'and more than all this world contains'.[28] Yet in one essential way they were not alike. Evelyn with his strong life-force, his unquenchable curiosity about the natural world, and his engagement with human society, can be seen as a humanist, a man of the Renaissance. 'Did women have a Renaissance?', it has been asked. Primed with humanist learning, the Renaissance gentleman has been seen as able to move beyond medieval piety and into the modern world 'in ways that were denied to a woman'.[29] Certainly Margaret Godolphin was undereducated, and certainly she seemed to reject secularity and hark back to an older spiritual tradition in which the world and engagement with earthly love were things to renounce. Torn by the conflict between human and divine love, she would sometimes say that she longed for death so that she could be free of these stresses. Yet it is too simple to see them just as the product of female disadvantage. When she died both Evelyn and her husband, for all their worldly engagement, felt themselves drawn after her. 'How delightful is this love dart', Francis de Sales had written, referring to the 'love as strong as death' of the Canticles, 'which wounding us with the incurable wound of heavenly love makes us forever pining and sicke . . . that at length we must yield to death.'[30] In the last resort Margaret Godolphin's influence over both her friend and her husband may have been stronger than theirs over her. ❧

---

[28] BL Add. MSS 78431: JE to ME, 7 July 1675; 78539: ME to Ralph Bohun, 24 Feb. 1675; JE, *The History of Religion*, ed. R. M. Evanson (1850), i. 55.

[29] Joan Kelly, 'Did Women Have a Renaissance?', in *Women, History and Theory* (Chicago, 1984), 30–50; Hilda L. Smith, *Reason's Disciples: Seventeenth-Century English Feminists* (Urbana, Ill., 1982), 48.

[30] Quoted in Stanley Stewart, *The Enclosed Garden: The Tradition and Image in 17th Century Poetry* (Madison, 1966), 146.

Prologue

I N the autumn of 1736 Francis, 2nd Earl of Godolphin, was paying one of his regular visits to his racing stables at Hogmagog near Newmarket when he suffered a fit of giddiness which he feared to be the onset of apoplexy. A physician from nearby Bury St Edmunds, Dr Messenger Monsey, was hastily called in. He found his patient to be a widower in his fifties, of mild and amiable manners and pronounced valetudinarian habits. Although it was doubtful whether he was ever in any real danger, he was quite content to protract his convalescence over several weeks. Monsey was engaged to call frequently, made welcome, and paid well. By the time Godolphin was ready to declare himself recovered the two had become good friends.

Monsey was no ordinary country practitioner.[1] 'If the doctor had lived in the times of allegory he would have had Apollo for his Father and Echo, a nymph of words without meaning, for his mother', one of his friends remarked: 'I cannot imagine what sort of Mortals his parents were, but certainly they were of a peculiar sort.'[2] The son of an eccentric Norfolk clergyman (his curious Christian name came from his mother's family), Monsey had been born in 1694 and so was about fifteen years younger than his patient. He studied at Cambridge, began to practise medicine under the distinguished Sir Benjamin Wrench of Norwich, then set up for himself in small villages on the outskirts of Swaffham, where only the most strenuous activity could gain him a living. In 1725 he improved his circumstances by marrying a well-to-do widow and moving to Bury St Edmunds, 'the Montpelier of Suffolk . . . the town of this part of England, in proportion to its bigness, most thronged with gentry, people of the best fashion and most polite conversation'.[3] Those who lived there were supposed to do so for the pleasure of

---

[1] This account of Monsey is taken from his correspondence in BL Hammick Papers (for which see Appendix A), *A Sketch of the Life and Character of the Late Dr Monsey* (1789); John Taylor, *Records of my Life* (1832), 70–126; J. Cordy Jeaffreson, *A Book about Doctors*, 2nd edn. (1861), 202–7; Reginald Blunt, *Paradise Row* (1906), 148–51; R. W. Ketton-Cremer, *Norfolk Portraits* (1944), 85–95; Kathleen M. Lynch, *A Congreve Gallery* (Cambridge, Mass., 1951), 110–38.

[2] Reginald Blunt, *Mrs Montagu, 'Queen of the Blues'* (1923), i. 250.

[3] Daniel Defoe, *A Tour through the Whole Island of Great Britain*, ed. Pat Rogers (Harmondsworth, 1971), 73–4.

its society, but Monsey did so from sheer necessity. In retirement he enjoyed railling about the difficulties of this part of his life: 'wasn't I a miserable country doctor between twenty-five and thirty years, and is it possible to conceive such a one wouldn't be glad to rest after riding his bones to a jelly almost, and risquing his neck night and day after a parcel of sc[oundre]l l[o]rds, sorry rascals and fantastical pusses who sometimes did and sometimes did not give me something for hearing all their nonsensical complaints, and now and then curing their real ones? Is it nothing to have got rid of the stupidity and slip-sloppery of drivling nurses and conceited chambermaids and waiting women, and, what is worse, the perplexity of obscure cases, the difficulty of relieving plain ones, and the perpetual anxiety and distress of mind about all?'[4] Even at Bury the most energetic practice could not raise his income above £300 a year.

To compensate for his medical drudgery he read widely, but 'principally in the boundless ocean of metaphysics, where so many adventurers wander without rudder, sail or compass'; 'in the intervals of cool reflection he confessed a great part of the unhappiness of his life originated from these unavailing perplexities'.[5] He kept his sanity by buffoonery, deliberately setting out to make himself 'the greatest fool of a witt, and the greatest witt of a fool in the world', pouring scorn on 'all our paltry pretences to wisdom and knowledge', and making a mock epic of the adventures of the goddess Nonsense among the physicians and philosophers in 'crazy, Bedlamite, unconnected prose and poetry'. Yet he retained a bedrock of speculative intelligence and commonsense, and also a capacity for sincere feeling: 'where I love tis with my whole heart. No body can have me by halves.'[6] Francis Godolphin, with his unassuming kindness and decency, was a lovable human being; 'I don't know how it is', Monsey wrote in one of his first bulletins to the Earl's devoted daughter, the Duchess of Newcastle, 'but the small acquaintance I have had with him has given me a strong attachment to him & his welfare'; 'his goodness to me makes me look upon him almost in the same degree of relation with your Grace—I am sure if he was my father I cou'd not feel more anxiety for him than I do.'[7] Godolphin was touched by Monsey's care of him, sympathetic to his circumstances, and entertained by his constant flow of eccentric talk, the perfect foil for his own placid taciturnity.

They renewed their friendship whenever Godolphin visited Newmarket, and within a few years he persuaded Monsey to give up his practice altogether and take up residence in his own house in St James's, as personal

---

[4] Blunt, *Paradise Row*, 149.   [5] Taylor, *Records*, 41.
[6] BL Hammick Papers: Monsey to Mark Hildesley, 28 Feb. 1749; to Charlotte Alexander, 19 Aug. 1764; Blunt, *Mrs Montagu*, i. 67; Ketton-Cremer, *Norfolk Portraits*, 87.
[7] BL Add. MS 33065, fo. 295: Monsey to Duchess of Newcastle, 27 July 1738.

physician, companion, and court jester. To give him some independence the position of physician to Chelsea Hospital was got for him, but with the understanding that he would not have to live in. He thus escaped the drudgery of his practice and at the same time the company of his wife, who, unlike Godolphin's, was still very much alive. It was not a desertion however, but a separation by mutual consent. When Monsey's stepson objected, the doctor simply remarked, 'If he resents my not living with his Mother, it is being concern'd that 2 people don't make one another wretched by living together, that live tolerably easy asunder.'[8] The welfare of their daughter Charlotte, 'dear Charlee', remained the only bond between them. In London Monsey could continue to practise in an undemanding way, treating his friends and their servants without fee and making trips to Chelsea to oversee his charges, while still railling enjoyably at the whims of his leisured patients and the mercenariness of city doctors. 'The great Monsey' was soon a social success in his own right. His Norfolk connections had already given him a familiarity with its great magnates, the Walpoles and the Townshends, and an intimacy with the intellectuals William Windham of Felbrigg and his tutor Benjamin Stillingfleet. Now Stillingfleet drew him into the blue-stocking circle. Soon he was writing excitedly of 'a new friend of mine, a Mrs Montagu, absolutely the cleverest woman I know in the whole Kingdom'. The queen of the blue-stockings in turn hailed him as 'great Physician & admirable quack, most supreme of wits & Mountebanks', and found him 'a good dish at table' whatever the company; 'whether seasoned or candied there are ingredients in you that will hinder you being insipid'.[9]

Monsey remained at Godolphin House until the Earl's death in 1766 at the age of 88. They were an odd couple, but bound together by real affection and mutual gratitude. At the last Monsey came to look on himself as 'one with a chain on his leg', 'a sort of living portmanteau in a lord's coach'; not that Godolphin was ever domineering, but in old age he became more dependent than ever on 'his friend Monsey, as he used to call him', whose company 'he was frequently heard to declare was the solace and comfort of his life'. 'I must be a scoundrel to leave him, and a fool too,' Monsey declared, and he remained until the end 'to take care of him who has shewn such fatherly kindness & concern for me'. When he finally came to vacate his 'sweet room' in Godolphin House after more than a quarter of a century, it was 'the next worst thing to parting with a beloved wife'.[10]

[8] BL Hammick Papers: Monsey to Hildesley, 18 Nov. 1744.
[9] Ibid. Monsey to Hildesley, 14 Feb. 1756; Elizabeth Montagu to Monsey, 29 June 1759.
[10] Ibid : Monsey to Hildesley, 25 Sept. 1752, 20 Mar. 1766; to Elizabeth Montagu, 29 June 1757; to Thomas Simpson, 26 May 1762.

Amongst the possessions he took with him to Chelsea and afterwards bequeathed to his 'dear Charlee', was a small bundle of letters which Godolphin had evidently given him as a keepsake: the courtship letters of his parents, Sidney Godolphin and Margaret Blagge. Monsey was a jackdaw collector of old documents, and the letters of Queen Anne's Lord Treasurer were a historical curiosity. But it was probably his mother's letters which chiefly prompted Francis Godolphin's bequest. In the intricate networks of the East Anglian gentry there were connections over generations between the Monseys and the Blagges, who had once been settled in the area of Bury where Monsey had practised. The bequest marked not just their long friendship, but the kinship they can have known nothing of when it first began.[11] Perhaps Monsey also saw a small manuscript volume with an intricately tooled binding: the presentation copy of John Evelyn's 'Life of Mrs Godolphin' in his own hand, also descended to Francis Godolphin from his father.[12] By the 1760s Evelyn was largely a forgotten figure. His works were out of print and the diaries which restored him to history in the following century were still buried amongst the family papers at Wotton, together with the letters Margaret Godolphin had written to him and the collection of tiny devotional volumes he had painstakingly compiled for her and repossessed after her death. Into the age of enlightenment they preserved a tale as complex as any Monsey had encountered in all his perplexed voyaging on strange seas of thought. ❧

---

[11] BL Add. MSS 19118, fos. 313–4; 19142, fo. 122: Monsey and Blagge pedigrees. See Appendix A for the later history of the letters.

[12] Keynes, *JE*, 248–50 and Plate 14.

I

⸙

The Garden and the River

THE story may begin with John Evelyn's entry in his diary for 28 June 1669: 'To Lond[on] & 30th returned: My Wife being gon a journey of Pleasure downe the River as far as the Sea, with Mrs Howard, & her daughters the Maids of Honor, amongst whom, that excellent creature Mrs Blagge.'[1]

In his own day Evelyn was best known for his writings on forestry and gardening, but now it is this diary for which he is chiefly notable. The more famous journal of his friend Samuel Pepys covers part of the same time-span, and since the two moved in similar circles, some of the same events as well. But Pepys's diary is a vivid, intimate, often scandalous revelation of self during a single decade of his young manhood. Evelyn's is the personal chronicle of the whole of a long, busy, useful, apparently exemplary life in all its external events: journeys, visits, and encounters, crises and rites of passage, curiosities and remarkable occurrences, public and private duties. Part *aide-mémoire*, part casting-up of the spiritual profit and loss of his days, it begins with his earliest recollections and continues, in the wavering spidery hand of extreme old age, until a few weeks before his death in the first years of the new century. Since Evelyn had many abilities and interests and for much of his life moved among the great of his society, the record is a valuable one; but it lacks the intimate detail which Pepys supplies so abundantly. Clearly he chose to omit a great deal from a memoir which he certainly intended should be read by his grand-children, even if he did not foresee its eventual publication. Most notably he makes only glancing and cryptic references in it to the most transforming episode of his life, his relationship with the young woman, 'Mrs Blagge', whom he first mentions in the diary entry above. Yet the inner world of passionate spirituality it discloses is one to which Pepys, in all his copious self-revelation, gives us no access.

[1] JE, *Diary*, iii. 529–30.

At this time Evelyn was in his late forties and his wife a good deal younger: still in her mid-thirties and just recovering from the birth of their last child. Elizabeth Howard and the two teenage daughters who accompanied her on the river voyage were their neighbours at Deptford. The girls' friend Margaret Blagge was at this time not quite 17. In calling her 'Mrs Blagge' Evelyn was giving her the courtesy title accorded all women of respectable status, whether married or not. This first reference to her is a typical diary entry, laconic, abbreviated, unelaborated; simply a reminder to himself of an event which was chiefly worth noting at the time as his wife's first outing after a difficult confinement. It was only in retrospect that it acquired its momentous significance. For the entry also bears tell-tale signs that what we are reading are not the notes he made in his almanac from day to day, but a narrative written up from them with hindsight.[2] He calls both the Howard sisters maids of honour, but in the summer of 1669 only the elder, Dorothy, actually was so. And during this first summer of their acquaintance Evelyn was still eyeing Margaret Blagge from a distance, not at all sure whether she could truly be 'that excellent creature' he afterwards found her.

The boat which took the little group of women on their voyage set out from Deptford or Greenwich. Perhaps it was one of the small private pleasure craft which were common on the river; or, since the Evelyns were friendly with the naval officials who lived nearby, one of the royal yachts, the *Henrietta*, the *Catherine*, or the *Charlotte*, tall-masted, fast, and graceful, sumptuously carved and fitted out within (the young Grinling Gibbons was learning his craft in Deptford at this very time as a carver of the King's ships); on some official errand or sea-trial perhaps, but able to take this little group of friends as a treat. There had been weeks of drought, 'dry burning weather', good for hay-making, and so the cool air of the river was a welcome relief. From Deptford they dropped with the tide down the widening Thames, making their way amongst the crowd of vessels of all shapes and sizes which negotiated the calms, unpredictable shoals, channels, and winding reaches of London's river: the smacks and hoys, the lighters with their loads of timber for the shipyards, the colliers from Newcastle with their topsails able to catch the lightest breeze, the towering East Indiamen with their exotic cargoes, and the small pleasure boats like their own.

Around the windswept marshy tongue of the Isle of Dogs, cropped sparsely by cattle, lay Greenwich, what remained of its despoiled Tudor palace still standing by the waterfront, and beside it Charles II's half-built new

[2] Evelyn made his original diary entries in printed almanacs, which he had bound and interleaved with blank sheets (BL Add. MS 78407: bookseller's bill, 24 July 1661). Some retain the *aide-mémoire* style imposed by the limited space.

one. Evelyn had been consulted about this when the works began, but now they had come to a standstill and were soon to be boarded up and abandoned because there was no money in the Treasury to pay for them. Nor, after the threat of Dutch ships in the Thames two years before, did this ceremonial gateway to the kingdom of a monarch of the seas seem such a good idea after all.[3] Behind it rose the park, newly terraced and planted with avenues, presenting the persevering climber with a panorama which Evelyn pronounced to be (after Constantinople) 'doubtlesse for Citty, river, Ships, Meadows, hill, Woods, & all other distinguishable amenities, the most noble the whole World has to shew'.[4] To east and west lay the river, 'twisting and turning it self up and down' in a dazzle of light, with its constant traffic of vessels large and small; the isolated thickets of naked masts about the docks and boatyards of Deptford, Blackwall, and Rotherhithe merging into one forest below London Bridge. And beyond, overhung by their everlasting pall of smoke, were the roofs and spires of the city, those to the east just rising again from the rubble and ashes of the Great Fire three years before. Beyond, the untouched riverside palaces of the great led westwards to Whitehall and Westminster, where the King lived and Parliament met.

In their passage below Greenwich the women passed the spot where a few years before Evelyn had seen a whale stranded at low water, beleaguered with small boats and shouting crowds, until at last a harpoon was struck deep into its head, 'out of which spouted blood & water, by two tunnells like Smoake from a chimny: & after an horrid grone it ran quite on shore & died';[5] and so on past the East India Company yards and warehouses at Blackwall, with their huge wet-dock where a whole fleet could be laid up safe from weather, tides, and river traffic, and on the opposite bank Deptford's twin royal dockyard at Woolwich, with its deep anchorage and new gun battery hastily set up against the Dutch two years before; past the marshes and fishing villages of the Essex shore and the cornfields, nightingale-haunted copses and chalk spurs of the Kent side, with their lime kilns and grinding windmills; the boatyards, wharves, and rickety waterside clusters of Barking, Erith, Purfleet, and Greenhithe; and so on to Gravesend, 'the door to London by water', environed with market gardens and cherry orchards, a town of many inns, where customs searchers came on board and travellers from the Dover road took ferry every tide for the last stage of their journey up to London. And at last on to the Buoy of Nore where the men of war rode to take on supplies from the Deptford

---

[3] Howard Colvin, *The History of the King's Works*, vol. v (1976), 144–50; Simon Thurley, 'A Country Seat Fit for a King: Charles II, Greenwich and Winchester', in Eveline Cruickshanks and David Starkey (eds.), *The Stuart Courts* (Thrupp, 2000), 214–26.

[4] JE, *Diary*, iii. 85.   [5] Ibid., iii. 214–15.

Yard, and the river merged with the Medway estuary and widened into the
Channel and the open sea. 'The day proved cool, the gale brisk, the air clear',
wrote a cousin of Margaret Blagge's of another such voyage, 'and no inconvenience to molest us, nor wants to trouble our thoughts, neither business to
importune, nor formalities to tease us; so that we came nearer to a perfection
of life there than I was ever sensible of otherwise.'[6]

The Evelyns lived at Sayes Court, a small manor house adjoining 'the
King's Yard' at Deptford, where Mary Evelyn's ancestors had been naval
administrators since the days of Elizabeth. They had come there to make
their home seventeen years before, after many years living out of England.
Even after the execution of Charles I, Mary's father, Sir Richard Browne, had
remained the Stuarts' Resident in Paris, making his house and chapel in the
Faubourg Saint-Germain a refuge for exiled royalists and Anglicans. Evelyn,
the bookish and curious son of a family of Surrey gentry, was a royalist, but a
fastidious one with no military aspirations. Travelling in Europe to avoid the
disturbances in England, he frequented the Brownes' house, noticed the
virtues of their daughter, and though she was so much younger than he, made
her his wife. Five years later, in 1652, they returned to England and settled at
Sayes Court; 'there being now so little appearance of any change for the better',
Evelyn noted in his diary, 'all being intirely in the rebells hands, and this particular habitation, & the Estate contiguous to it . . . very much suffering, for
want of some friend, to rescue it out of the power of the Usurpers'.[7]

Evelyn had been born in the depths of the Surrey countryside. In the little
handwritten volume, 'Instructions Oeconomique', which he presented to
his wife on their marriage, he continued to extoll the virtues of country life.
Yet Sayes Court was no rural retreat. With stout shoes it was only an easy
walk, or an even shorter river journey from London, and on the very boundary of the dockyard, with the tenements of ship-workers reaching to the very
gates. 'I do with all my heart wish for more solitude, who was ever most
averse from being near a great city, [and] designed against it,' Evelyn
protested, 'and yet it was my fortune to pitch here, more out of necessity, and
for the benefit of others, than choice.'[8] He never considered it more than a

---

[6] Roger North, *The Lives of the Norths*, ed. A. Jessopp (1890), iii. 32. For accounts of the Thames,
see Samuel de Sorbière, *A Voyage to England* (1709), 12; Sir Thomas Browne, *Works*, ed. Simon
Wilkin, (1836), i. 135; HMC *Portland MSS*, ii. 276; François Brunet, 'A French Traveller in Charles
II's England', *Cornhill Magazine*, new ser., 20 (Jan.–June 1906), 662; Peter Mundy, *Travels*, ed. R.
C. Temple and L. M. Anstey, Hakluyt Society, 2nd ser., 5 (1936), 158–9; *The Journeys of Celia
Fiennes*, ed. Christopher Morris (1947), 131–2; C. W. Chalklin, *Seventeenth Century Kent* (1965), 89,
148; *The Journal of William Schellincks' Travels in England*, ed. Maurice Exwood and H. L. Lehmann,
Camden Society, 5th ser., 1 (1993), 46–7.

[7] JE, *Diary*, iii. 58–9.   [8] Bray, iii. 73: JE to Jeremy Taylor, 27 Apr. 1656.

temporary expedient and several times in the first decade would talk of a deeper country retirement. In the meantime, however, to one steeped in the ideologies of classical antiquity and the Italian Renaissance, the proximity of London suggested that Sayes Court was not just a small, awkwardly sited manor house, but more properly a 'villa': the name given since the days of Pliny and Horace to the ornamental countryside residence adjacent to the city, to which a jaded citizen could retreat for his pleasure and relaxation.[9]

The debate over the rival virtues of an active public life and a private contemplative existence was an enduring one and Evelyn at first seemed to place himself firmly in the latter camp. Repose and retirement, he insisted on his return to England, were what he most aimed at; 'a Friend, a Booke and a Garden shall for the future perfectly circumscribe my utmost designes'.[10] Yet that assertion from an energetic young man of 32 did not sound quite authentic. It was easy, as Sir Francis Bacon had pointed out, to make rural retirement sound attractive; to make it feel publicly useful and of consequence was another matter. Evelyn could quite truly point out that without the business of the country there would be neither court nor city,[11] but the villa with which he identified Sayes Court had never been self-supporting, much less did it support the court or city. On the contrary it was their satellite, a retreat from the stresses of making one's fortune there. Evelyn, in the disruption of the Civil Wars, had never taken up any profession, never engaged in public life or trade. He had as yet nothing to retire from.

In fact, like many royalists excluded from public life under Cromwell, he was making a virtue of necessity in adopting and celebrating a life of country retirement. Although he could reinforce this with the examples of Epicurus and Horace, it was not an untroubled process. He had been born into a social class of well-to-do county gentry, to whom participation in public life was a birthright, and educated in the humanist ideal of usefulness to his country. He was a compulsively active man and conscious of abilities which might one day make him 'considerable', if he should ever have an opportunity to exercise them. Though he was always reluctant to acknowledge it fully, the city and the court never lost their hold over him. Sayes Court in its proximity to them perhaps suited him better than he was willing to admit.

At its most basic, his industry derived from his sense of sin; the need to fill one's days with useful activity because 'the Devil never leaves the Idle

[9] James Ackerman, *The Villa: Form and Typology of Country Houses* (1990), 9–15, 37.

[10] Quoted in Michael Hunter, 'John Evelyn in the 1650s', in *Science and the Shape of Orthodoxy* (Woodbridge, 1995), 70.

[11] *Public and Private Life in the Seventeenth Century: The Mackenzie–Evelyn Debate*, ed. Brian Vickers (New York, 1986), 92.

unbusied'.[12] The humanists had added their own strictures; so had Bacon—
'in this theatre of man's life it is reserved only for God and Angels to be look-
ers on'—and Evelyn's religious mentor Jeremy Taylor, with his castigation of
the gentry for failing England both politically and spiritually.[13] But Evelyn's
constant sense of being driven also spoke to him of something else: 'a perennial source of perpetual motion to something yet to come, and more than all
this world contains', which was his ultimate argument for the existence of
God.[14] So he suppressed his frustration at the narrow prospect before him and
applied himself to the tasks which presented themselves: his studies, the care
of his family, the improvement of his small estate. There was much to be
done, first of all to the house itself, before he could begin to refer to it, as he
soon began to do deprecatingly, as 'my poor villa'. Low and modestly pro-
portioned, its three flat gables facing south, it stood amid its few sheltering
elms so uncomfortably close to the dockyard wall that it would perhaps have
been sensible, as his father-in-law suggested from Paris, to consider pulling it
down altogether and starting again on a better site overlooking the river. 'But
then', as Evelyn protested, 'the Convenience of such trees & shelter which it
now hath & must then have wanted must have bin parted with: which could
never have donne well: so naked & defenceless, in a place so low and empty
of variety as this is without them'.[15]

It was the typical modernizing of a young couple with their first home: a
new entrance porch with Doric columns, a fine new staircase rising through
the entire height of the house and top-lit by a cupola, several new or enlarged
rooms, two parlours on the ground floor looking into the private garden, a
great chamber overhead, a study for himself with a smaller closet within it,
and a chamber over the porch for the collection of rarities and curiosities he
had acquired on his travels.[16] There was new wainscotting throughout
(Evelyn dated one of his early letters facetiously 'from the Wooden study, in
the Wooden Parlour, of the Wooden house'),[17] and at every turn, at the gates,
threshold, doorways, even the buttery and cellar, it was 'set off with ornaments
and quaint mottoes': invocations of domestic peace and quiet (especially in
contrast to the neighbouring city) and promptings to moral reflection: 'Intret
in has aedes nil nisi tuta quies'; 'Haec urbi vicina juvant, facilesque recessus';

---

[12] JE, *Memoires*, 78.

[13] *Public and Private Life*, ed. Vickers, p. xix; C. John Sommerville, *Popular Religion in Restoration England* (Gainesville, Fla. 1977), 36–7.

[14] JE, *The History of Religion*, ed. R. M. Evanson (1850), i. 55.

[15] BL Add. MS 78221: JE to Sir Richard Browne, 23 Jan. 1654.

[16] BL Add. MS 78628 A: plan and key of Sayes Court, 1653; cf, Colin Platt, *The Great Rebuildings of Tudor and Stuart England* (1994), 165.

[17] BL Add. MS 78298: JE to Sir Samuel Tuke, 24 May 1663.

'magna pars felicitatis est, nosse artem fruendi'.[18] Afterwards, notwithstanding the old elms, Evelyn regretted the decision not to rebuild from scratch; new buildings grafted on to old reminded him of a young and beautiful virgin tied to an 'old, decay'd and doating husband'.[19] But at the time he and his wife were well enough pleased with their first home together.

'He who has a Soule to save, a Family to provide decently for and a severe Accompt to give of his Actions, Needs few Diversions to passe away Time,' Evelyn admonished his grandson many years later.[20] Yet as a young man himself, with all these matters to preoccupy him, he had still felt the need of some recreation. His difficulty was that those which presented themselves gave him no satisfaction, 'because they did not contribute to any improvement of the mind';[21]—with one outstanding exception. Beyond the doorstep of Sayes Court when he first came to live there were only 'a rude Ortchard', the vestiges of the small Tudor house garden, and a field of a hundred acres 'without any hedge'.[22] Formerly pasture for the cattle which supplied the royal household at Greenwich, its very blankness was an invitation. From his childhood Evelyn had had a passion for 'drawing and designing'. By the indulgence of his elder brother he had already made some experiments with garden features, grottoes and fish ponds, at his family home.[23] During his travels in Italy he had studied the great gardens of the Renaissance: Pratolino in Florence, the Villa Aldobrandini at Frascati, the Villa D'Este at Tivoli, the Boboli and Borghese gardens, and in France the royal gardens of the Tuileries, Luxembourg, Saint-Germain-en-Laye, and Fontainebleau. The Paris nurseryman Pierre Morin, whose exquisite small garden was the haunt of horticultural virtuosi, had been his father-in-law's neighbour in the Faubourg Saint-Germain. Creating a garden of his own out of the wasteland on his doorstep was therefore to be his recreation. And if looking back he found gardening 'preferable to all other Diversions whatsoever', it was just because a gardener's work was never done; and yet it was labour 'full of Tranquillity and Satisfaction; Natural and Instructive, and such as (if any) contributes to the most serious Contemplation, Experience, Health, and Longaevity'.[24] In fact it was the perfect reconciliation of the active and contemplative lives which he always sought. For it was not just the making of a garden which

---

[18] BL Add. MS 78613: mottoes for Sayes Court. In translation: 'may nothing enter this house but complete peace'; 'these are pleasing being close to the city and are also easy retreats'; 'a large part of happiness is practising the art of enjoying oneself'.

[19] BL Add. MS 78340: fo. 88ᵛ: 'Husbandry for Sayes Court'; Roland Fréat, *A Parallel between Ancient and Modern Architecture*, trans. by JE (1664), in Upcott, 370.

[20] JE, *Memoires*, 75.   [21] Bray, iii. 317: JE to Lady Sunderland, 4 Aug. 1690.

[22] JE, *Diary*, iii. 80; BL Add. MS 78340, fo. 88ᵛ.   [23] JE, *Diary*, i. 8, 55.

[24] *Kalendarium Hortense* (1664), in *WJE*, 353.

interested him, but the variety of its meanings and purposes. At the same time as he laid out his plot on the ground, he reflected and wrote on every aspect of the process, what he called the 'entire Mysterie' of gardening, from the preparation of the soil (a labour in itself at Sayes Court, since it needed to be mixed liberally with lime, loam, and cow dung before anything would grow well in it), to the recreation of paradise on earth.[25]

Evelyn had been born and nursed in the Surrey hills with their woods, fast-running streams, and sweet air, 'the affection to which kind of solitude I succked in with my very milke'.[26] The unkempt, irregularly shaped, feature-less site amid the riverside mists at Deptford could therefore not have been more alien to him. It tapered towards the river to the north, but stopped short of it, and so just missed the dramatic Thames frontage which would have redeemed all its other disadvantages. What water there was lay in sluggish channels and ponds, more likely to be a nuisance and health hazard than an amenity. The eastern boundary was the ragged diagonal of the dockyard wall. As every garden designer must be, Evelyn was aware that his task was to achieve just that blend of art and nature which suited his particular plot. Some sites were, as he put it, 'naturally artificial' and needed little assistance from art. In others the lack of natural variation at least left the gardener free to develop his design without constraints. Sayes Court, confined by the dockyard boundary, had neither of these advantages. Yet he knew that 'even the most imperfect figure, may, by the Mysteries of Arte and fantsy receive the most gracefull ornaments'; but to work their effect these must retain their mystery. There should be symmetries and correspondences, but these must be subtle. At all costs he was determined to avoid 'those painted and formal projections of our cockney gardens and plotts, which appeare like gardens of past-board and march-pane, and which smell more of paint then of flowers and verdure'.[27] Sayes Court would be princely in conception if not in size, and from the beginning natural verdure was to be Evelyn's greatest delight in gardening, and the source of its most profound meanings.

His first task was to restore the old Tudor house garden, on which the windows of the refurbished parlours and drawing room looked out. This had its origins in the medieval walled garden or the 'giardino segreto' of the Italian villa. There was a fountain in the centre, an arbour in one corner

[25] BL Add. MS 78340, fo. 88ᵛ. The comprehensive work on gardening was of course his 'Elysium Britannicum', begun in the late 1650s but conceived long before; see *EB*, 13.

[26] JE, *Diary*, i. 6.

[27] *EB*, 96–7; Sir Thomas Browne, *Works*, ed. Geoffrey Keynes (1964), iv. 274–5: JE to Browne, [28 Jan. 1659/60]; cf. John Dixon Hunt, 'Evelyn's Idea of a Garden', in T. O'Malley and J. Wolschke-Bulmahn (eds.), *John Evelyn's Elysium Britannicum and European Horticulture* (Washington, DC, 1998), 277.

under the old elms for which he had redeemed the house, and beds of choice flowers and herbs which he could cultivate himself. It was a refuge from the semi-public space of the 'great garden' beyond. But it encompassed much more than this, calling to mind the enclosed garden, the 'hortus conclusus' of the Canticles, an emblem of spiritual containment and completeness, 'wherein all things mysteriously and spiritually are to be found'.[28] 'Noble spirits', added Dr Thomas Browne of Norwich, in a work Evelyn admired, 'contented not themselves with Trees, but by the attendance of Aviaries, Fish Ponds, and all variety of Animals, they made their gardens the Epitome of the earth.'[29] A garden menagerie presented difficulties to all but the most princely of gardeners, but Evelyn did set up an aviary directly opposite his parlour windows. There was also an ornamental glass-fronted beehive, adorned with 'variety of Dials, little Statues and Vanes', a present from the Oxford virtuoso and mathematician, Dr John Wilkins. In it the bees, potent symbols of chastity ('they are so chaste, that they sting those that smell of copulation, and they stall themselves in Virgins Sepulchres', according to one commentator on the wonders of the natural world), and so full of meaning as well for those musing on theories of government or the progress of science, could be observed 'making their honey and combs mighty pleasantly'.[30]

Sir Francis Bacon, whose works had laid down the intellectual programme for Evelyn's generation, went further and recommended that a truly universal garden should contain not merely collections of plants and animals, but a library, a museum, and a laboratory, so as to comprehend all learning.[31] Evelyn had already made provision for his library and cabinet of curiosities in the renovated house, but he reserved the west side of this private garden for his 'elaboratory'. In this impressive building with its twenty-foot pillared portico, the gardener as natural philosopher could practise the arts of 'distilling and extracting of essences, resuscitation of plants, with other rare experiments'. Although its equipment was similar to that in his wife's still-room, it was quite distinct from the domestic offices. Within, several more of Evelyn's favourite mottoes signalled the masculine project of the Baconian scientist: 'Omnia explorate, Meliora retinete' ('explore all things, hold fast to the best', the motto Evelyn also wrote in his books); and 'Amicus Socrates, Amicus Plato, sed magis Amica Veritas': it was by experiment, not just by the received

---

[28] Quoted in Philip Almond, *Adam and Eve in Seventeenth Century Thought* (Cambridge, 1999), 94; cf. Stanley Stewart, *The Enclosed Garden: The Tradition and Image in 17th Century Poetry* (Madison, 1966), 36–45.

[29] 'The Garden of Cyrus', in Browne, *Works*, ed. Keynes, i. 176.

[30] JE, *Diary*, iii. 110; Almond, *Adam and Eve*, 96; EB, 273–87.

[31] Oliver Impey and Arthur McGregor (eds.), *The Origins of Museums* (Oxford, 1985), 1.

wisdom of the ancient philosophers that knowledge progressed and truth was discovered.[32] This was a connoisseur's environment, of one never so immersed in the search for truth that the external trappings ceased to appeal. Although Evelyn had studied chemistry in Paris and planned an English translation of his master's lectures, he was never, unlike his friend Robert Boyle, a true experimental chemist in his own right. The vegetable distillations he produced—spirit of roses or violets—were pleasant applications of its procedures for a gentleman gardener; essentially recreations, as Evelyn was the first to admit, but ones which did 'service to the desiderants of philosophy, which is the only part of learning best illustrated by experiments, and after the study of religion, certainly the most noble and virtuous'.[33]

Another of the inscriptions in the laboratory drew attention to the deeper meaning of Evelyn's whole garden enterprise: 'Omnia in rebus humanis dubia, incerta, suspenda, magisque verisimilia quam vera.' This was a return to the mental world of the platonic philosopher, in which the material environment as perceived by the senses was provisional and imperfect; rather a verisimilitude or a representation of truth than truth itself. In these terms the garden in all its aspects, however beautiful and complete it seemed, was only the shadow of a higher, more perfect, and more durable reality. Over the outer door of the garden laboratory, referring to the purifying and transforming fire of the chemist's furnaces, was inscribed the word 'Purgatorium'. To enter paradise, the great garden which lies beyond, an alchemist in just such a garden laboratory tells his visitor in another of Evelyn's writings, he must first pass through the 'Purgatorium'.[34]

The main compartments of the 'great garden' of Sayes Court lay to the north and west of the house, away from the dockyard and towards the river. Except for the high brick wall which surrounded the whole garden and the enclosed private space next to the house, Evelyn favoured hedges rather than fences for the internal divisions: of lilac, espaliered fruit trees, cypress, and above all holly or alaternus, an evergreen from France with 'hony-breathing blossom' which the bees loved, 'the most beautiful, and useful of Hedges, and Verdure in the world'.[35] Immediately to the west of the private garden lay

---

[32] *EB*, 22; BL Add. MSS 78340, fo. 89: 'Husbandry for Sayes Court'; 78628 A: plan of Sayes Court, 1653; 78613: mottoes for Sayes Court. Add. MS 78345: JE's translation of Le Fèvre's treatise on chemistry, has plans and drawings, partly reproduced in F. Sherwood Taylor, 'The Chemical Studies of John Evelyn', *Annals of Science*, 8 (1952), 285, 290–2, which have close similarities to the ground plan of the garden laboratory on the 1653 plan of Sayes Court.

[33] Bray, iii. 84: JE to Benjamin Maddox, 10 Jan. 1657.

[34] BL Add. MS 78346, fos. 3–9: 'Coelum sanitatis', an alchemical treatise in JE's hand, probably translated and with a preface by him.

[35] *EB*, 95–6; *Sylva* (1664), in *WJE*, 265–6.

the nursery, where he reared the hundreds of plants which were to form his main garden. And to the north of that, separated from the outhouses by a lilac hedge, was the kitchen garden, with its serried beds of vegetables and herbs.[36] This was as much part of Evelyn's project as the garden of pleasure. He took a virtuoso's interest in cooking, preserving, and distilling, as well as in the cultivation of fruit and salad plants. The natural produce of the earth, he could point out, had been the food of prelapsarian man and he traced the golden age of perpetual fruitfulness and peaceful coexistence with animals, celebrated in classical literature, to a lingering memory of that 'paradisian fare'.[37]

Further west, beyond all these domestic areas, was the garden proper, divided according to the Italianate manner into the formal garden and the grove beyond.[38] The patterns of the formal garden, or parterre as it was called in the French fashion, were best appreciated from some elevated point: the upper windows of the house, the artificial mount which Evelyn created in the centre, or the raised terrace walk which separated it from the grove. For this parterre he had a specific model: the Paris garden of Pierre Morin. The nurseryman's specialties were evergreens, especially the alaternus which he had introduced from Provence, and dazzling varieties of tulip, iris, ranunculi, and anemones. His garden was designed to show these off to best advantage. Within a rectangle of walks lined with alaternus was a meticulously clipped oval cypress hedge, and within this, cases of delicate evergreens, orange trees, myrtle and phylaria, and box-edged beds radiating from the fountain in the centre like the petals of a flower. In these were arrayed the flowers from his catalogue.[39] Evelyn had been captivated by this combination of year-round greenery and exotic blooms. Perhaps he also wanted to coax and please his young wife, who left her beloved Paris reluctantly, for he had set out for England with bushels of cypress and alaternus seeds and parcels of bulbs, determined to create his own Deptford 'Morin garden'. Like Morin, he set an oval of cypress within a rectangle lined with alaternus, filling the quadrants with evergreen thickets and private walks. These led into secluded 'cabinets' or arbours, which Mary Evelyn was allowed to embellish with 'emblems' of particular friends. The outer oval was occupied with grass and flower pots and the inner circle with a parterre of twelve flower beds more elaborately

[36] BL Add. MS 78628 A: plan of Sayes Court, 1653.

[37] JE, *Acetaria: A Discourse of Sallets*, ed. Christopher Driver (Totnes, 1996), 74–5; cf. Keith Thomas, *Man and the Natural World* (Harmondsworth, 1984), 17.

[38] John Dixon Hunt, *Garden and Grove: The Italian Renaissance Garden in the English Imagination* (1986), 85.

[29] Prudence Leith-Ross, 'A Seventeenth Century Paris Garden', *Garden History*, 21 (1993), 150–7.

patterned than Morin's, surrounding a mount set about with cypress and surmounted by a sun dial.[40]

At first Evelyn was proud of this creation, which became quickly established, and thought it finer than its original. But within a few years it began to seem less satisfactory to him: trivial, flat and fussy, fit only to give pleasure to women while his greater, slower, and more durable designs were brought to fruition; the planting of trees and groves, when complete would present 'a prospect of a noble & masculine majestie far surpassing those trifling bankes and busy knotts'.[41] A few years more and the box and cypress of the Morin garden and mount had been grubbed up and replaced by the smooth grass plats for which English gardens were famous, while Evelyn abandoned the cultivation of flowers almost entirely and gave his full attention to his 'garden of trees'. 'By which I observe', his wife commented wryly, 'that there is no end of improvement and that the various fancies of men have the reward of praise, when poore women are condemned for altering their dresse, or changing the patron [pattern] of a gorget, and for this esteemed vain creatures.'[42] There was certainly a growing fashion for simpler, more symmetrical gardens which would make features of fine English grass and gravel paths. Evelyn, who was to entitle his little tract on dress after the Restoration, *Tyrannus: or The Mode*, was well aware of this kind of inexorable pressure. But there was more to his change of style than this. He was finding his own gardening manner, and it was in the cultivation of his groves that the real meaning of the garden now lay for him.

'Wood-born' as he described himself, he always had an affinity with trees. As the royal forests and avenues came under threat from the supporters of the Commonwealth, this grew into a passionate and highly politicized sympathy. It was a profoundly masculine feeling. He never tired of celebrating the mystery which he had witnessed again and again in his own nursery, by which the tiny grain, 'which lately a single Ant would easily have born to his little Cavern', with its 'insensible rudiment, or rather habituous spirit', would ascend 'by little and little . . . into an hard erect stem of comely dimensions, into a solid Tower as it were'.[43] As he surrounded his estate with trees, he

[40] BL Add. MSS 78628 A: plan of Sayes Court, 1653; 78221: JE to Sir Richard Browne, Sept. 1652, 23 Jan. 1654; 78439: ME to [Elizabeth Carey], [1657].

[41] *EB*, 139–40.

[42] BL Add. MSS 78439: ME to Sir Samuel Tuke, [late 1663]; 78628 B: plan of Sayes Court, 1685; Mark Laird, 'Parterre, Grove and Flower Garden: European Horticulture and Planting Design in John Evelyn's Time', in O'Malley and Wolschke-Bulmahn (eds.), *John Evelyn's Elysium Britannicum and European Horticulture*, 218.

[43] *Sylva* (1664), in *WJE*, 187, 190; *Sylva* (1670), 245. (There were four editions of *Sylva* in Evelyn's lifetime, all with substantial new material.)

wrote of them with a human, even a sexual warmth: the lime trees which formed the arcade leading up to his main entrance were 'the most proper and beautiful for Walks, as producing an upright Body, smooth and even Bark, ample Leaf, sweet Blossom, the delight of bees, and a goodly shade'; the elm, with which he planted out his boundaries, was 'a tree of consort, sociable and so affecting to grow in company, that the very best that I have ever seen do almost touch one another'.[44] Deeply ambivalent about human desires and appetites and the animal cycle of ingestion and excretion, he found the inexorable strength and self-sufficiency of the tree immensely appealing: 'Consider how it assimilates, separates and distributes . . . how it concocts, transmutes, augments, produces and nourishes without separation of Excrements (at least to us visible) and generates its like, without violation of Virginity.' Since the components of the material world were always more to him than just their external reality, the tree could thus readily become the embodiment of the higher nature and the spiritual aspiration of man. When he wrote that the growing tree, '(like Man whose inverted Symbol he is) being sown in corruption, rises in glory', he was again echoing the kindred spirit of Thomas Browne: 'the verdant state of things is the Symbole of the Resurrection, and to flourish in the state of Glory we must first be sown in corruption'.[45]

If singly trees were always 'sacred Shades' to him, groves were nature's temples, acknowledged in Christian and classical antiquity as numinous, predisposing to reverence, meditation, and prayer.[46] The grove at Sayes Court was not large at first, only a little larger and less formal than the parterre, with a stiff geometric design of intersecting walks, centred on a circle or small amphitheatre planted with laurel and bays. The walks were bordered with deciduous natives (oak, ash, elm, service, beech, and chestnut), the spaces between planted with thickets of birch, hazel, and hawthorn, and the whole was underplanted with evergreens and a further undergrowth of shade-loving plants and herbs. Of course it was all slow to develop, still 'a dwarf' when the parterre was established and flourishing. But Evelyn was aiming in course of time to recreate the sight he had always loved as a boy in Surrey; a 'tall wood of goodly trees whose leaves had forsaken them having in the middest of winter an under wood or Coppse of perenniall Greene, no lesse divertissant to the eye in that cold & naked season then coole & usefull in the heate of summer'.[47]

[44] *Sylva* (1664), in *WJE*, 215, 229.
[45] *Sylva* (1670), 245; Browne, *Works*, ed. Keynes, i. 177.
[46] *Sylva* (1664), in *WJE*, 190; *EB*, 150–9.
[47] BL Add. MS 78628 A: Sayes Court plan, 1653; 78346 : 'Coelum sanitatis', fos. 3–4; *EB*, 144; Upcott, 688: JE to John Aubrey, 8 Feb. 1676.

At first this was all there was of the formal garden. Its western boundary was a 500-foot promenade with a banqueting house at the end by the oval garden and at the other a small moated island set in a miniature lake and reached by a drawbridge. West of the promenade was an orchard of 300 fruit trees 'of the best sort mingled', and even this most traditional and utilitarian part of the garden had its higher significance. Indeed, according to Ralph Austen's *Treatise of Fruit-Trees*, published in the same year it was planted, it was a virtual library, even a kind of Hermetic mystery of spiritual and moral meanings; in cultivating his orchard trees man must always be attentive to their manner of teaching, 'as the Egyptians and others in former times, who were instructed by the Characters and Hyeroglyphiques'; it was by such symbols and representations that 'Dumbe Creatures speake virtually and convincingly, to the mynde and Conscience'.[48]

Yet within the decade Evelyn dispersed his fruit-bearing plants into other areas of the garden and extended his tree-planting to take in most of this orchard area, so that the promenade became the central walk of a more symmetrical pattern of groves, in which the internal paths and cabinets were allowed to become less regular.[49] From his travels in the warm lands of the Mediterranean he had brought home with him a longing for a garden which did not die or become dormant for half the year. None of the deciduous natives, however stately, were comparable for him to evergreens: the laurel, cypress, fir, yew, holly, and the more delicate alaternus, myrtle, and many more. No longer content with underplanting, he wanted to make an entire evergreen grove, a 'viridaria', adjacent to the parterre, and to remove the native trees into the new grove beyond. In due course the holly hedge extended westwards with the grove, until it was over a hundred yards long and his greatest pride: the most 'glorious and refreshing object of the kind' that could be seen, 'glitt'ring with its arm'd and vernish'd leaves'.[50] In a northern climate the cultivation of evergreens was of course one means by which art could supplement nature. They protected the house with their foliage all year round and produced an Italianate illusion of perpetually mild climate, so that those who lived amongst them 'shall seem to be placed in one of the summer islands and enjoy an eternal spring, when all the rest of the Country is bare & naked'; 'for which reguard we pronounce it a most sweete & incomparable

[48] Ralph Austen, *Treatise of Fruit-Trees* (Oxford, 1653), sig. [N]3ᵛ; JE, *Diary*, iii. 81. For the significance of hieroglyphics in Christian neoplatonism see E. H. Gombrich, *Symbolic Images* (1972), 149–50, and David Stevenson, *The Origins of Freemasonry* (Cambridge, 1988), 79–83.

[49] BL Add. MSS 78340, fo. 88: 'Husbandry for Sayes Court'; 78628 A, B: plans of Sayes Court, 1653 and 1685; Laird, 'Parterre, Grove and Flower Garden', 217–18.

[50] BL Add. MSS 78349: ME to Sir Samuel Tuke, [late 1663]; 78221: JE to Browne, 20 Jan. 1666; *Sylva* (1664), in *WJE*, 270; *Sylva* (1706), ed. John Nisbet (1908), ii. 293.

part of the Hortulane amoenitie and to our particular inclination, the most agreeable'.[51]

In this most unpromising of places he brought his vision to fruition. A passionate plantsman as well as designer, he nurtured all his trees lovingly. As the garden matured, the whole place became 'infinitly sweete & beautifull', the evergreens especially 'all so thriving and clean, that in so much variety no one could be satiated with viewing'.[52] By 1669, when Mrs Evelyn and her neighbours set out on their voyage down the river, it was one of the show-places of the metropolis, visited by the great and the curious, including the King and Queen and most of the court. In the making of it Evelyn had ceased to be merely a gentleman dilettante. As his friend Abraham Cowley wrote, 'you choose this for your Wife, though you have hundreds of other Arts for your Concubines; though you know them and beget sons upon them all'.[53] Gardens provided the best metaphors Evelyn himself had for all that was most passionate, generative, and tender, and all that was most responsible and civilizing in human relations. A gardener was a good husband, not just a good husbandman. 'He who cultivates his ground best is best capable to cultivate his wife,' he wrote to a female friend on the verge of marriage, 'and she pro-duces him fruite, and returns his affection, and they unite their diligence and enjoy naturally and innocently: For tis perpetual spring with them'; and of seeds and young plants: 'with what delight have I beheld the tender and innu-merable Off-spring . . . at the Feet of an aged Tree! from whence Suckers are drawn, transplanted and educated by humane Industry; and forgetting the ferity of their Nature, become civiliz'd to all his Employments'. For a royal-ist at the Restoration, expecting to be called away from his retreat at any moment to prepare for government, it might even represent a training for public life; 'of such they heretofore made their Captaines in warr, and their arbiters of affairs in peace, as if none were more fit to praeside in state then he that could govern his Garden well'.[54]

But for Evelyn, as for many of his contemporaries, a garden such as his was much more than all this: it was the 'place of all terrestriall enjoyments the most resembling Heaven, and the best representation of our lost felicitie'. If the tree, sown in corruption to flourish in glory, was a symbol of man, ever-greens were an even more powerful emblem: 'the most naturall Hieroglyphicks of our future Resurrection and Immortalitie' and a reminder of the perpetual spring of the garden of Eden. A garden had been God's first gift to man even

[51] *EB*, 313–15.
[52] BL Add. MS 78221: JE to Sir Richard Browne; 5 July 1658; North, *Lives of the Norths*, i. 375.
[53] *Sylva* (1679), p. cviii.
[54] BL Add. MS 78298: JE to 'Cyparissa', Sept. 1659; *Sylva* (1679), 275.

before that of human companionship, as Abraham Cowley reminded him; gardening had been man's first and prelapsarian work, and 'when Almighty God had exiled our Fore-fathers out of paradise, the memorie of that delicious place was not yet so far obliterated, but that their early attempts sufficiently discovered how unhappily they were to live without a Garden'. All horticulture was therefore an attempt to recover this lost perfection by means of art and industry. Evelyn began even his most practical manual, a monthly calendar of the gardener's never-ending round of tasks, with a reminder of this; and also that it was such a labour 'as does certainly make the nearest Approaches to that blessed State, where only they enjoy all things without pains'. To cultivate or merely to contemplate a garden was therefore to approach a state of grace.[55] In biblical teaching it was with the Fall that human desire and human thirst for knowledge became inherently corrupt; that men and women, instead of being perfect companions, became enemies to each other. A garden like Sayes Court was intended to recall that original uncorrupted reality:

a paradise; not like this of ours (with so much pains and curiosity) made with hands, but eternal in the heavens; where all the trees are Trees of Life; the flowers all aramanths; all the plants perennial, ever verdant, ever pregnant; and where those who desire knowledge, may fully satiate themselves . . . and where the most voluptuous inclinations to the allurements of the senses, may take and eat, and still be innocent; no forbidden fruit; no serpent to deceive; none to be deceived.[56]

Yet just beyond this industriously contrived Eden lay the outer world in its most intrusive form. In choosing to settle at Sayes Court Evelyn had violated Sir Henry Wotton's two cardinal principles of architecture, which he quoted approvingly to others: to build in good air and not too near a great neighbour.[57] London, 'this wretched towne', as he called it when he had to go there on occasional business, was a constant presence. With Paris and Rome fresh in his mind, it seemed to him intolerably primitive and ramshackle, 'a wooden, northern, and inartificiall congestion of Houses', with overhanging gutters and spouts which deluged the passer-by with water, 'making it a continual wet day after the storm is over'. The streets were narrow, irregular and badly paved, 'pestred with Hackney-coaches, and insolent Carre-men, Shops and Taverns'; the riversides cluttered with makeshift wharves and warehouses; and worst of all was the constant pall of sea-coal smoke, like a 'Vulcano on a foggy day', polluting, corrosive, and destructive to health; 'I have been in a

---

[55] *EB*, 29, 31, 157; *Sylva* (1679), p. clv; *Kalendarium Hortense*, in *WJE*, 353. Charles Webster, *The Great Instauration* (1975), 16–17, 465–6; John Prest, *The Garden of Eden: The Botanic Garden and the Recreation of Paradise* (New Haven, 1981); Thomas, *Man and the Natural World*, 236.

[56] *Sylva* (1706), ed. Nisbet, i. 84.

[57] BL Add. MS 78386: 'Instructions Oeconomique', 1648, fo. 20ᵛ.

spacious Church where I could not discern the Minister for the Smoak; nor hear him for the peoples barking.' In fine weather these pent-up hordes swarmed out into the neighbouring fields and gardens so that all peace was lost.[58]

Nearer at hand, two decades of naval wars against the Dutch had brought expansion to the east coast shipyards, making them the largest industrial centres in England. Between the 1630s and the 1660s the population of Deptford doubled to 5,000 and was still rising.[59] The bell in its tower rang the workers through the day, the cranes swung and creaked on the wharves, unloading raw materials, teams of horses plied to and fro, the smithy resounded with the forging of chains and anchors, the shipwrights and caulkers hammered at the skeletal hulls in the docks and slips. In the 1650s these were Cromwell's great ships, sourly watched by Evelyn as they took shape and were launched, and after the Restoration the *Loyal London*, the *Charles*, and many more. Behind the river frontage lay the storehouses, with their stockpiles of sailcloth, hemp, pitch, and rope, 'surprisingly large and in their several kinds beautiful'; the piles of timber seasoning in the open; the saw-pits and above them the rigging, sail and mould lofts where the 'lines' of the ships were laid out. A dockyard also meant large bodies of standing water: a mast-pond to season and keep flexible the fir trunks which would be shaped into masts, a wet-dock where ships could be laid up safely at anchor.[60] The nearness of these to his house produced what Evelyn could only identify as 'a continual flux of noxious Vapours', afflicting his whole family at different times with 'Agues, & other malignant distempers'.[61] This evil, not 'noxious vapours' but malarial mosquitoes, was not to be entirely removed until the Thames marshes were drained two centuries later. In the meantime, however much care Evelyn took to keep his own ditches and channels clean with tidal water, the dredging of ever larger docks and ponds remained a mortal threat.[62]

And much as he valued his privacy, he had to make his estate profitable to maintain his family. As the town expanded he and his father-in-law leased

[58] BL Add. MS 78432: JE to ME, 4 Oct. 1655; A *Character of England* (1659) and *Fumifugium* (1661), in *WJE*, 78, 82, 137–147; Hiscock II, 175.

[59] Chalklin, *Seventeenth Century Kent*, 31.

[60] JE, *Diary*, e.g. iii. 140–50, 441; BL King's MS 43, fos. 65ᵛ–87: survey of Deptford dockyard, 1688–98; Daniel Defoe, *A Tour through the Whole Island of Great Britain*, ed. Pat Rogers (Harmondsworth, 1971), 123–5; B. R. Leftwich, 'The Parish of St Nicholas, Deptford', *Ecclesiological Society Transactions*, NS, 1(1942–7), 199–224; Jonathan Coad, *The Royal Dockyards* (Aldershot, 1989), 1–2; Brian Lavery, *Building the Wooden Walls* (1991) (this describes the building of the *Valiant* at Chatham dockyard in the mid-18th century, but many of the processes would have been similar at Deptford a hundred years earlier).

[61] BL Add. MS 78614: JE to the Navy Commissioners, 22 May 1671.

[62] Mary J. Dobson, *Contours of Death and Disease in Early Modern England* (Cambridge, 1997), 320–7.

more and more of the land adjacent to Sayes Court for building, and this left his small elysium even more beleaguered. By the 1660s the trees he planted had to be constantly replaced, being dug up and stolen away sometimes as fast as he could put them in. Just upriver, on land leased from the estate, the opulent alderman and sheriff of London, Sir Denis Gauden, built his docks and victualling yards for supplying the fleet, and his cattle as they were driven down to the slaughter houses there threatened to overrun the garden.[63] 'I have no other seate to dwell in but this poore Habitation', Evelyn protested to the Navy commissioners at the end of the decade, in begging them to redress some of the damage, 'and the Expense I have been at to render it tollerable & somewhat more convenient . . . all my neighbours here know'.[64]

These neighbours were many and various. Along the southern boundary of the dockyard was a handsome row of houses with neat gardens and stables for the dockyard officials and their families:[65] the surgeon, clerk of the survey, clerk of the cheque, storekeeper, master of attendance, and master shipwright: the Turners, the Tinkers, the Uthwaits, and the family of Jonas Shish, who had been shipwrights at Deptford for a hundred years. The Evelyns' wealthy tenants the Gaudens were lavishly hospitable, and the rector Dr Robert Bretton, whose preaching style was perfectly adapted to 'our great and vulgar auditory' (as Evelyn called the Deptford population) became a close friend. A little further off he found Sir Henry Newton and his wife at Charlton and Sir Thomas Hanmer at Lewisham, all passionate gardeners with whom he could exchange seeds and cuttings and consult about his planting.[66] But more courtly than all of these were the intermittent inhabitants of the Treasurer's house.

Being so near London, Deptford dockyard was directed closely by the Navy Office and the residence of its most important official, the Treasurer of the Navy, was next to Evelyn's wall. At the time of Mary Evelyn's summer voyage in 1669 the Treasurer's post was in commission and the house stood almost empty, its state rooms stripped of their furniture and hangings. For the want of a habitable palace at Greenwich it was occasionally used for official visits and ambassadorial entries;[67] otherwise it reverted to the Duke of York

  [63] BL Add. MSS 78614: Sayes Court estate accounts; 78221: JE to Sir Richard Browne, 9 Dec. 1665.
  [64] BL Add. MS 78614: JE to the Navy Commissioners, 22 May 1671.
  [65] BL King's MS 43, fos. 65ᵛ–87; Pepys, *Diary*, ii. 13.
  [66] JE, *Diary*, iii. 191, 506–7, 603–4, 622, iv. 43, 131; BL Add. MSS 78539: ME to Ralph Bohun, 26 Mar. 1672, 27 Sept. [1674], 19 Nov. [1677]; 78435: Bohun to ME, 26 Oct. [1674]; 78221: JE to Browne, 30 June 1657; 78298: JE to Lady Newton, 12 Mar., 23 Dec. 1656.
  [67] *CSP Venetian 1668*, 273.

as Admiral and its only tenant was his housekeeper, Elizabeth Howard. Mrs Howard was a well-connected widow and courtier; her husband had been a younger son of the Earl of Berkshire and more remotely allied to the dukes of Norfolk. Her three children were often with her at Deptford: her son Craven, still a schoolboy, and his two sisters, Dorothy, a maid of honour to the Duchess of York at St James's, and Anne, at school in Putney, but with looks and confidence which destined her for the court as soon as she was old enough. To the Evelyns, and to Mary Evelyn especially, these new neighbours were a godsend; 'I still call to mind those innocent moments, and the Sweete Conversation, which fifteene-yeares since, we enjoy'd,' Evelyn wrote to Anne Howard long after, 'that our Familys being neere to one-another, gave us the hapynesse to be known to the most Obliging Neighboure in the World.'[68]

In the spring of 1669 Mrs Howard's agreeable sinecure was disturbed by the flurry of a royal visit. Surprisingly, since it would have been natural for him to pay his court, Evelyn says nothing of it in his diary. But Pepys makes up for his silence. 'And so walked to Deptford', runs his entry for March 1669, 'and there to the Treasurer's house, where the Duke of York is, and his Duchess; and there we find them at dinner in the great room, unhung.' The royal party had come down from Whitehall by barge for the day and were picnicking enjoyably in the unfurnished rooms. With them were the Duchess of Monmouth, the young wife of the King's handsome bastard son James, who was even now whispered about, to the great unease of the York household, as a possible heir to the throne; the Countesses of Falmouth and Castlemaine, both ladies of the bedchamber to the Queen and both royal mistresses of infamous glamour and beauty; Lady Peterborough, the Duchess's stately but harassed groom of the stole, and three of the maids of honour, Dorothy Howard, Anne Ogle, and Margaret Blagge, with their governess. The fourth 'maid', Arabella Churchill, now well established as the Duke's mistress, had removed herself temporarily to France, in order to give birth at a discreet distance to his child.

Having seen the Duchess served, the girls, with the half-dozen minor courtiers and officials in attendance, retired downstairs to their own meal. Pepys joined them, and it 'did me good to have the honour to dine with and look on [them]; and the Mother of the Maids, and Mrs Howard, the mother of the Maid of Honour of that name, and the Duke's housekeeper there'. He noted that they drank 'most excellent and great variety and plenty of wines', and he also observed 'how this company, both the ladies and all are of a gang,

[68] *Life*, 18–19.

and did drink a health to the union of the two brothers', that is the King and the Duke of York, 'talking of others as their enemies'. Going up to the state rooms again afterwards they found the Duke and Duchess and all the great ladies sitting on a carpet on the floor, 'there being no chairs, playing at "I love my love with an A because he is so and so" . . . and some of them, but per-ticularly the Duchess herself and my Lady Castlemaine, were very witty'.[69]

The description is typically vivid and acute, not least in its perception that male and female courtiers were allies, not to say confederates, in the face of any threat to the succession. Evelyn's reaction to this scene would have been less shrewd and certainly less appreciative than Pepys's, but he had his own opportunities to observe the court women. Margaret Blagge, who shared lodgings with Dorothy Howard at St James's, was often with the Howards at Deptford that summer. On Sundays Evelyn saw her in church, and then, as the two older women became close friends, as an occasional visitor to his house. She was strikingly pretty like all the Duchess's maids, and she had a courtier's reputation for witty repartee. Yet she seemed modest enough and her conduct at church was exemplary. Evelyn watched closely but kept his distance, morosely determined to doubt whether any woman with court breeding could be really virtuous or devout. It was his wife, talking to the girl, who discovered 'such extraordinary Charmes, marks of Vertue, & Discretion in her Conversation; that she would often Reprove the diffidence I was wont to Expresse, when they would some-times Discourse of Piety, and Religion eminent amongst the Court-Ladys'.[70]

Were these outsiders really a boon, or yet another threat to his small Eden of prelapsarian innocence? What kind of young woman was Margaret Blagge and why was Evelyn so sceptical about courtiers and so concerned to know the truth about this chance acquaintance? ∼

---

[69] Pepys, *Diary*, ix. 468–9; BL Add. MS 36916, fo. 112: newsletter, 18 Aug. 1668.
[70] *Life*, 19.

2

Man of the Shade

T H E household at Sayes Court in the summer of 1669 consisted of the Evelyns and their four children: a son, Jack, of 14 and a 'little flock of girls', all much younger: 3-year-old Mary, Betty, who was not quite 2, and the baby Sue, from whose birth her mother was still recovering when she took her river voyage with the Howards. To this nucleus was added Evelyn's father-in-law Sir Richard Browne, a bookish, courtly figure, now almost retired from public life; and for much of the time Jack's resident tutor, a young Oxford clergyman called Ralph Bohun. At Deptford Mary Evelyn and her father were in their native place. For all his transformation of Sayes Court, Evelyn was always conscious that his was elsewhere.

He had been born the second of three sons of a family of Surrey gentry, whose fortunes were founded in their rich Surrey manors and especially in a lucrative monopoly of gunpowder manufacture. George Evelyn, his grandfather, was the father by two successive wives of twenty-four children. The manor of Wotton became the portion of his youngest son Richard, John's father: another capable and thriving squire who then added to his paternal estate by marrying Eleanor Stansfield, the heiress of a Sussex merchant. Young John was sent at the age of 5 to live with his grandfather Stansfield's widow at Lewes, remaining there, happy and much indulged, until he went up to Oxford at the age of 17.[1] Thus he saw little of Wotton in his youth, and until it came into his possession in old age could be there only as a guest of his elder brother. Yet it was always to be his 'most cherished place on earth'.[2]

---

[1] Helen Evelyn, *The Evelyn Family* (1915), 19–30; she was not his grandmother, but his grandfather's second wife and later married William Newton.

[2] BL Add. MS 78431: JE to ME, 1 May 1660.

Twenty miles from London, 'and yet so securely placed, as if it were an hundred', it lay in the hilly, well-wooded, and watered landscape between Guildford and Dorking, with the long chalk spine of the downs to the north and to the south the eminence of Leith Hill, from which spread out an immense panorama of the southern counties. The Elizabethan manor house (it could never have been called a villa) was 'large and antient, suitable to those hospitable times, and so sweetly environ'd with those delicious streames and venerable Woods, as in the judgment of strangers, as well as Englishmen, it may be compared to one of the most tempting and pleasant seats in the Nation'. Evelyn spent his infancy in even deeper seclusion, in the house of his wet-nurse, the wife of one of his father's tenants, 'in a most sweete place towards the hills, flanked with wood, and refresh'd with streames, the affection to which kind of solitude, I succked in with my very milke'.[3] There the little sugar-loaf mountains, with their rocky outcrops, thick greenery, and small torrents made a miniature Salvator Rosa landscape: 'such a solitude as I have never seen any place more horridly agreeable and romantick'.[4] To Evelyn and his elder brother as young men just come into their inheritance, this topography was to cry out for the new fashion of Italianate landscape gardening. In the 1640s and 1650s Wotton duly acquired an impressive porticoed mount with a grotto, parterre, and fountain before it, of which they could boast as one of the earliest examples in England.[5] It was not all undisturbed rural idyll, however. In their youth the valley of the Tillingbourne chattered and thudded with the industries on which the wealth of the family was established. Evelyn could not remember ever to have seen 'such variety of mills and works upon so narrow a brook, and in so little a compass' as those within a few miles of Wotton: for grinding corn, fulling cloth, drawing brass wire, stamping iron, and milling gunpowder.[6]

Everywhere there seemed to be prosperity, order, and continuity. The same family, the Hyams, provided rectors for Wotton for three generations, son following father for nearly a hundred years. Richard Evelyn, as his son recalled him, was an archetype of the independent squirearchy, 'his Wisdome was greate, and judgment most acute; of solid discourse, affable, humble and in nothing affected; of a thriving, neate, silent and methodical genius;

---

³ JE, *Diary*, i. 5; ii. 4.   ⁴ Upcott, 688: JE to John Aubrey, 8 Feb. 1676.

⁵ John Dixon Hunt, *Garden and Grove: The Italian Renaissance Garden in the English Imagination* (1986), 145–8; Carola and Alastair Small, 'Evelyn and the Garden of Epicurus', *Journal of the Warburg and Courtauld Institute*, 60 (1997), 198–202. The letters of George Evelyn to JE in 1650 (BL Add. MS 78303) show that he was consulted about the making of the Wotton garden even while he was abroad.

⁶ Upcott, 689–90: JE to Aubrey, 8 Feb. 1676; P. F. Brandon, 'Land, Technology, and Water Management in the Tillingbourne Valley', *Southern History*, 6 (1984), 79–85.

discreetely severe, yet liberall upon all just occasions both to his Children, strangers, and servants; a lover of hospitality; and in briefe, of a singular & Christian moderation in all his actions'. A Justice of the Peace and High Sheriff of the county, 'he was yet a studious decliner of Honors and Titles; being already in that esteeme with his Country; that they could have added little to him, besids their burthen'. His wife was renowned amongst her neighbours for her housewifery. In looks John strikingly resembled her, having the same long prominent nose and melancholic dark eyes which gave the only touch of glamour to his features.[7] For as a reminder of the darker side of this puritan virtue and order, his mother was 'of constitution more inclyn'd to religious Melancholy, or pious sadnesse'. Her decline into mortal illness before she was 40 came quickly after the deaths of her unhappily married eldest daughter and infant granddaughter, and was to her family clearly attributable to her immoderate grief. Summoned from Lewes to attend her deathbed, John never forgot the experience. Causing all her children to be ranged by her bed, 'she express'd her selfe in a manner so heavenly, with instructions so pious, and Christian, as made us strangely sensible of the extraordinary losse then imminent; after which, embracing every one of us in particular, she gave to each a Ring with her Blessing and dismiss'd us'.[8] The step-grandmother who brought him up was also 'a Woman of extraordinary charity & piety, spending most of her time in devotion'; and so in a more lively way was his beloved elder sister Jane, 'that deare saint', who as he grew up became his touchstone of female worth, 'so deare a Friend, so true a Companion, so greate a part of my best nature & in fine the sole designe of my future felicitie in this world'.[9] It was the influence of these women which first gave him the sense that woman's piety, being subject to fewer worldly distractions, was deeper, more mysterious, and more redemptive than that of men; and like theirs, Evelyn's devoutness, though strictly Anglican in its orthodoxy, had more than a touch of puritanism.

Just as he made idealized representations of his parents, so he harked back to the 'full century of golden age' before the Civil Wars, which the 'ancient simplicity' of their way of life at Wotton exemplified:

Things of use were natural, plain, and wholesome; nothing was superfluous, nothing necessary wanting; and men of estate studied the publick good, and gave examples of true piety, loyalty, justice, sobriety, charity, and the good neighbourhood compos'd

---

[7] JE, *Diary*, ii. 2–3. Portraits of Richard and Eleanor Evelyn are reproduced in Helen Evelyn, *Evelyn Family*, opp. 30 and 34.

[8] JE, *Diary*, ii, 12–15; BL Add. MS 78298: JE to George Evelyn and his wife, 15 Dec. 1656, 9 Sept. 1662.

[9] JE, *Diary*, iii. 25; BL Add. MS 78298: JE to Richard Evelyn and William Glanville, 10 Jan. 1652.

most differences . . . and laws were reason not craft, when mens titles were secure, and they served their generation with honour, left their patrimonial estates improv'd to an hopeful heir, who, passing from the free-school to the college, and thence to the inns of court, acquainting himself with a competent tincture of the laws of his country, followed the example of his worthy ancestors, and if he travell'd abroad, it was not to count steeples, and bring home feather and ribbon, and the sins of other nations, but to gain such experience as confirm'd him in the love of both of 'em above any other.[10]

It did not, however, work so straightforwardly for Evelyn himself, or indeed for most of his generation. He was a somewhat wayward boy, in some ways a typical product of his humanist education, yet intellectually far more adventurous than his two conventional brothers; much given to entertaining grandiose fancies and with a tendency as he put it, to be constantly 'diverted with inclinations to newer trifles'. When he showed an 'extrordinary fansy to drawing and designing', his father reproved him urgently for neglecting his school-work; such things were only fit for a gentleman's recreation.[11] Yet not far from Wotton was Albury, the favourite retreat of their great neighbour, the connoisseur and grandee Thomas Howard, Earl of Arundel. It was on him, more than on his methodical squire father, that Evelyn was eventually to model himself, and long afterwards he would take comfort from Arundel's remark 'that one who could not Designe a little would never make an honest man'.[12] Still his father's words were to stay with him all his long life, the voice of his conscience and of his ultimate mission: 'Learning is an excellent ornament to a Mann, & much to be desired, for it is a meanes to bringe us to the knowledge of god & of our dutyes to menn', and 'you must not lose an hour when you have lost so much already, better to be unborn than untaught'.[13] Throughout his life he was to castigate himself for time misspent or opportunities not seized in his youth: for not preparing himself better for his Confirmation, for his unsystematic studies at school and university; for 'dancing and fooling' away his time at the Middle Temple. 'Redeeming the time that has been lost' became his constant preoccupation. When he began while still a schoolboy 'to observe matters more punctualy' and set them down in an almanac as he had seen his father do,[14] it was not just from the impulse to record, but also to account for the use of his days.

[10] JE, *Numismata* (1697), 110; Preface to *Mundus Muliebris* (1690), in Upcott, 701.
[11] JE, *Diary*, ii. 9, 22; Hiscock II, 7.
[12] JE, *Sculptura* (1662), ed. C. F. Bell (Oxford, 1906), 103.
[13] BL Add. MS 78302: Richard Evelyn to JE; 15 Dec. 1635; n.d. [1635].
[14] JE, *Diary*, ii. 9.

Leaving Lewes for Oxford at the end of the 1630s Evelyn saw the last of what he looked back on as the 'blessed Halcyon tyme in England', when the Church of England was 'in her greatest splendor, all things decent, and becoming the peace'. In London he saw Charles I ride in state to open 'that long, ungratefull, foolish and fatal Parliament, the beginning of all our sorrows for twenty yeares after, and the period of the most unhappy Monarch in the World'. When his father died a few weeks later, it was an unpropitious time to come to manhood. Evelyn was 20, and, as he described himself in retrospect with his powerful instinct for the drama of his times, 'of a raw, vaine, uncertaine and very unwary inclination . . . in a conjunction of the greatest and most prodigious hazards that ever the Youth of England saw'. All props to order and stability seemed to have fallen away. With little reliable guidance, he had to decide what to do with himself and where his allegiances lay; and 'if I did not in the midst of all this, impeach my Liberty, nor my Vertue, with the rest who made ship-wrack of both; it was more the infinite goodnesse and mercy of God, then the least providence or discretion of myne owne, who now thought of nothing, but the pursute of Vanity, and the confus'd Imaginations of young men'.[15]

Wotton of course went to his eldest brother, who soon embarked on the leisured and prodigal beautifying of the landscape which his father's industry had made possible. John aided and abetted him. 'The court of Wotton', now filled with his brother's youthful company, became for him a rich and highly sexualized source of fantasy, a scene of 'ingenious divertisment from whence some Boccacio might furnish a better Decameron':

Imagine yet how my thoughts waite on you into the grounds & about the foun-taines; now they assent in your preferring of that Tulip or this Anemonie; that I breath the same ayre, commend the same prospect, philosophize . . . upon that artificial Iris which the sunn reflects from the watry girondoles below it, or the beauties of the faire Nymphs which admire it . . . where you do nothing but feast and enjoy the creature, day and night too (I had almost sayd) for it cannot else sinke into my Comprehension how my Brother should possibly lodge so jolly a troupe, unlesse you lye like the family of Love . . . you see what it is to be dreaming of good company and good cheer.[16]

Dreaming was one thing, but his future did not lie at Wotton. His father and grandfather had left him with his own settlement in land, so that he avoided a common plight of younger sons: poverty and dependence. In fact, however unnerving it was to be unguided in such unstable times, he was also left unusually free from any kind of compulsion. Afterwards he was to stress the

---

[15] Ibid., ii. 19–20, 26.   [16] BL Add. MS 78298, JE to Gasper Needham, 14 June 1653.

importance of a gentleman's having an occupation or 'calling' of some kind, whatever his circumstances.[17] The law, 'that impolish'd study' for which his father had intended him, could now be rejected outright, and for all his piety he had no desire to take orders and 'study Divinity for bread'. He was in theory more drawn to commerce, despite the habitual gentry prejudice against it. Although 'I have not that I know one drop of bloud from the Shop, or Citty in all my Veines', he wrote disingenuously later (his grandfather had after all been a Sussex iron merchant), 'yet such is the Esteeme I have for that calling (which above all we of this Island ought to encourage) that I think a Merchant no reproch to the noblest & most illustrious families; not onely because the greatest of them had their rise from that Calling . . . but because there goes so much worthy Industry to the gaine, and that it brings us in as well as carries out so many usefull things for Life'.[18] Yet he did not go into trade either. For all that he valued his inherited standing as 'pure squire', he was drawn in spite of himself by the magnetic attraction of the courts, their glitter, potency, and cultivation. With Arundel as his patron he might have sought his fortune there in better times. But now, as Charles I prepared to take up arms against his defiant Parliament, it was not a place for any young man to think of making a career. In November 1642, he took part on the King's side, but rather half-heartedly, as a volunteer in the last stages of the battle of Brentford; but when the worsted royalist army moved off to the west, he did not go with it. Estates in Surrey and Sussex now lay in the power of Parliament and those belonging to the King's adherents would be plundered or confiscated. Evelyn was advised to go abroad to avoid declaring himself one way or the other, 'since my estate in the County, would have maintained more against his Majestie, than I could for him'.[19] It might have been good sense, but it was a judgement of the head rather than the heart.

And so in the summer of 1643 he obtained the King's leave and set out with some companions for the Continent, where he remained for the next three years. It was travel in the most educative mode: through France to Italy, Genoa, Florence, Rome, Padua (where he took his farewell of the ageing Arundel, homesick for his beloved Albury),[20] Venice, then back again to Paris, all accompanied by the strenuous sight-seeing, copious record-keeping, and study which Francis Bacon had recommended, and it more than remedied

[17] Ibid.: JE to Thomas Keightley, 1651; Michael Hunter, 'John Evelyn in the 1650s', in *Science and the Shape of Orthodoxy* (Woodbridge, 1995), 69–71.

[18] BL Add. MS 78386: 'Oeconomics to a Newly Married Friend', [1676], pp. 60–1, 71.

[19] JE, *Diary*, ii. 79; BL RP 5460: JE to Thomas Clifford, 23 Nov. 1670.

[20] Thomas Howard, Earl of Arundel, *Remembrances of Things Worth Seeing in Italy Given to John Evelyn 25 April 1646*, ed. J. M. Robinson, Roxburghe Club (1987).

the deficiencies of his earlier schooling. Like most royalists in Paris he was made welcome at the house of Sir Richard Browne in the pleasant suburb of Saint-Germain; 'the Asylum to all our persecuted and afflicted countrymen'.[21] Browne had a carefully nurtured only daughter, a fair-haired child with a fragile prettiness and a serious eager expression:

besides the pretynesse & innocence of her Youth . . . [she] had something in her me-thought that pleas'd me, a Gravity I had not observ'd in so tender a bud: for I could call her Woman for nothing but her early steadines, & that at the age of playing with Babies [dolls], she would be at her Book, her needle, Drawing of Pictures, casting Accompts & understood to Govern the House. I tooke notice that she began to discourse, not Impertinently, was Gay enough for my humor, & One I believ'd, that might one day grow-up to be the agreable Companion of an honest Man; but . . . with all this I had no more Designe to make her my Wife, than I had to dive for Pearle upon Salisbury-Plaine, or the sands of Lybia; and yet I made this Creature my Wife, & found a Pearle in a place as un-likely to produce them as the Desarts [of] The Louvre, & Whitehall.[22]

What caused him then to change his design and marry her, as he did in the summer of 1647, when she was barely 13 and he twice her age? In a sense he was marrying the whole family, not just the daughter. Between himself and Sir Richard there was a real affection and community of interest. After his long period of wandering, the Brownes fixed his allegiances, gave him the stability and security which he had lacked since the death of his father. With England in the throes of revolution, their house was 'little Britaine and a kind of sanctuary'.[23] Nevertheless the decision to marry a child of 13 requires more explanation.

Evelyn was always attracted to the company of young girls. In later life he would give the daughters of his friends such nicknames as 'Madame Would-Be' and 'Playfellow'. Yet he was sufficiently susceptible to women and was not without self-confidence or his share of vanity. His natural temper, he says at this time was 'Free and without constraint'. What degree of sexual experience he had had is not clear. He only says vaguely that he 'had tasted of the softnesses of Life, been in Conversations & upon the brinks of folly'.[24] But young women in the conscious power of their sexual maturity made him uneasy even while they attracted him. 'We oftener inslave men, than men inslave us', another of the Brownes' protégées, Margaret Cavendish, wrote, 'they seem to govern the world, but we really govern the world, in that we

[21] JE, *Diary*, iii. 77.
[22] BL Add. MS 78392: JE, 'The Legend of Philaretes and the Pearle', [*c.*1673].
[23] BL Add. MS 78298: JE to John Cosin, 28 July 1651.
[24] BL Add. MS 78392: 'The Legend of Philaretes and the Pearle', [*c.*1673].

govern men'.[25] To Evelyn this knowingness was an alarming reversal of the natural order. It was of the greatest importance to him that his own wife should be young enough to be formed by him and to accept his authority without question; 'woman converts to man, not man to her', he insisted, 'the Woman is the weaker vessell . . . whose propertie it is to be obedient unto her Husband'. Mary Browne was well educated and self-possessed beyond her years, but she was also sexually innocent and of a 'quiet & mild disposition', dutiful, biddable, and devoted to her parents; to her father especially. In marrying her Evelyn secured a congenial and unthreatening helpmeet for all the forseeable stages of his life: 'the present Mistris of my Youth, the hopeful Companion of my riper Yeares and the future Nurse of my old Age',[26] though at the expense of passion and (for the time being) maturity.

Since the marriage could not be consummated immediately, etiquette required that he absent himself for a while. He returned to England and remained there for nearly two years. By letter he observed the proper forms of courtship but they had something of the air of simulacra. He conjured his young wife to believe that his love was 'most reall, unfeyned and inviolable'. He assured her, somewhat crassly, that he was not tempted by other women even though he was of an age and vigour when it might be expected. He had a fine, self-regarding, perhaps deliberately posturing portrait painted of himself in the moping posture of a melancholic lover, 'wherunto he is (dearest, for your sake) too often reduced'.[27] Yet he did not want to let a girl think she was in control. Every word of the little handwritten manual of 'Instructions Oeconomique', which he compiled for her, was designed to reinforce his expectations of her, to make her into 'such a wife as I may truly call *Auxilium commodium*, an Help-meet for me'. Yet he warned her not to show it to anyone else, realizing that to 'irregular and loose persons' it would seem, even in an age so accustomed to manuals of conduct, too much like inappropriate pedagogic fussiness in a young husband.[28] They would mock him, which he hated.

For Evelyn, with his rigorous upbringing, sexual relations, the gratification of an importunate bodily appetite, were inevitably hedged around with precepts and prohibitions, reinforced with the punishing consequences of violation. He grimly set these out in due course for his son:

[25] Quoted by Sara Heller Mendelson, *The Mental World of Stuart Women* (Brighton, 1987), 23.
[26] BL Add. MS 78430: 'Instructions Oeconomique', 1648, fos. 6, 21, 26.
[27] BL Add. MS 78431: JE to ME, 16 Sept. 1648; for the portrait, see Hunter, 'John Evelyn in the 1650s', 67 and n.
[28] BL Add. MSS 78430: 'Instructions Oeconomique', 1648, fo. 6ᵛ; 78431: JE to ME, 16 Sept. 1648.

Be none of those who brag how frequently they can be brutes in one night, for that intemperance will exhaust you, and possibly create importunate expectations, when your inclinations are not so fierce . . . forbear when your wife is in her monthly purgations, not only for the indecency and pollution, but for that the conception (which frequently then happens) disposes of leprosy and marks the children with evident signs of the parents incontinency . . . It is likewise experimentally found that carnal caresses upon a full stomach, or in the day time, or in excessive heat or cold of weather are very pernicious, and too much frequency of embraces dulls the sight, decays the memory, induces the gout, palsies, enervates and renders effeminate the whole body and shortens life.

However he did concede that 'young married people will hardly be reasoned into that temperance, and perhaps they are to be indulged some liberties . . . especially at first'; 'Decent satisfaction' was allowable at any time; 'a man may eat . . . not only to satisfy hunger, but to cheer him, and if there were not some gratification of the inferior sense accompanying this and other natural action, the world would cease'.[29] On the whole, therefore, it was a happy reunion when he returned to Paris; 'my deare wife is a singular good girle, though I should not say so', he wrote to his sister Jane in England.[30]

He was now almost 30 and his formal education was over. Since he could not settle in England or put what he had learnt to public use, he would at least employ the time to methodize his studies. He began to build a systematic library and to compile an elaborate series of commonplace books in preparation for the works he intended to publish in the future, 'no man being able to build any thing whatever without the help of others which may stand or last longer than the Cobwebs spun out of the bowels of an Insect'.[31] He attended courses in experimental chemistry. His attitude to the older, more speculative study of alchemy remained sceptical, though never entirely dismissive. Its more pretentious practitioners, such as his flamboyant countryman Sir Kenelm Digby, could be dismissed as 'arrant mountebanks'. Yet he would seek out and transcribe recipes for the philosopher's stone or elixir of life, even while pointing out the latter amounted no more than 'well rectified spirit of wine'.[32] His own garden laboratory was to have more than a passing resemblance to an alchemist's sanctum, and in the last resort, as time was to show, he would turn to an alchemical remedy when all other hope was gone.

[29] Quoted in Hiscock II, 122–3.
[30] BL Add. MS 78296: JE to Jane Glanville, 27 Nov. 1649.
[31] Hunter, 'John Evelyn in the 1650s', 71; JE, *Memoires*, 44.
[32] BL Add. MS 78418: 'Les Choses necessaires a la composition de la pierre des sages', copy in a calligraphic hand of a text concerning the philosopher's stone, with an addition by JE; Add. MS 78346. 'Coelum sanitatis', an account of the elixir of life in JE's hand; JE, *Diary*, iii. 48 (for Digby).

In September 1651 Charles II escaped to Paris with barely his life after an attempt to regain his crown at the battle of Worcester. Republican government was established in England beyond any immediate hope of change and crown lands, including the Brownes' Deptford estate, were to be sold off. In a complicated arrangement, which laid up a train of difficulties for the future, Evelyn agreed to preserve Sayes Court in the family by purchasing the lease and making his home there, so enabling Sir Richard to redeem his debts and continue in his post abroad. In return they secured a written undertaking from Charles II to grant the estate to them in perpetuity if he should ever be restored to the throne.[33]

It was a bitter disappointment to Evelyn that back in England, 'this madd extravagant country, where every body are at their witts end', there was less prospect than ever of any kind of public career; 'I shall therefore bring over with me no ambitions at all to be a statesman, or meddle with the unlucky Interests of Kingdomes, but shall contentedly submitt to the losse of my education, by which I might have one day hoped to have bin considerable in my Country.'[34] It was not until his wife gave birth to their first child that he found a new role. The boy, named Richard after both his grandfathers, immediately became 'the jewel, the joy' of their lives. At eighteen months, as Evelyn reported to Sir Richard in Paris, he was already 'so forward, & full of prate (for he speakes very many words & goes about daintely), so naturall a lover of bookes & pictures, so serious & yet so cheerful & quiet a humor that I hope to present him one day to you as one that may possibly afford you some hopes of his presaging an honest man'. Within five years there were two more boys; 'Dick, Jack, George: I ring the bells backward you see,' Evelyn wrote delightedly to his father-in-law. He began to plan their education and even their professions, intending that the baby George should become a merchant, 'though of all the most beautifull & lovelie child'.[35] Here was an unforeseen kind of public service. His household would be a kind of microcosm, preserving the values of the Stuart polity:

for even Private Families, the Husband & Wife, being the first Politiq & Society in the World, are the seminaries both of Church and State, a Compendium of absolute monarchy and the best of Governments; and therefore (to resolve a scruple which some have troubled themselves much about) Those who have a Family needs no Publiq Calling to redeeme themselves from idlenesse; the Employment of

[33] JE, *Diary*, iii. 58–9; BL Add. MS 78615: Prettyman lawsuit papers; BL Add. MS 78299: JE to Sidney Godolphin, 23 Mar. 1682.

[34] BL Add. MS 78221: JE to Sir Richard Browne; 18 Oct. 1656; Hunter, 'John Evelyn in the 1650s', 70.

[35] BL Add. MS 78221: JE to Browne, 23 Jan. 1654, 30 June, 13 Dec. 1657.

Instituting, and regulating it well is sufficient to take-up our whole time, and to exercise our choycest Talents; especialy if there be Children who are to be Educated.[36]

The children also cemented the rather uncertain bond between himself and his wife, to whom in her first pregnancy he found himself 'affected with a kind of tendernesse, such as I never perceived in my selfe before'.[37]

There were also his intellectual projects. In such matters he was not, and never pretended to be, genuinely original. All his works were translations or compilations from commonplace collections. But he was intensely receptive to the intellectual and cultural currents of his time, and he sought not just for himself, but for all his countrymen the full realization of their potential, what he called 'that incomparable fruition of a mans selfe'.[38] Embracing the Baconian programme of useful learning, he began an ambitious project for the systematic documentation of trades and technical practices, though this proceeded no further than those he could easily observe in his own neighbourhood and the connoisseur arts he enjoyed himself.[39] He undertook the translation of a series of cultural and scientific works from the French: on architecture, on the ordering of libraries, on chemistry, on gardening.[40] He embarked on an English version, with commentary, of the *De rerum natura* of Lucretius, the Roman poet of Epicurean philosophy: a fashionable though controversial choice, since in the Epicurean universe there was no divine order and providence, only a flux of atoms.[41] It was however a philosophy which flattered his present circumstances: of retired pleasure, of ambition and passion subdued, of garden communities of friendship. Finally he planned to

---

[36] BL Add. MSS 78386: 'Oeconomics to a Newly Married Friend', [1676], p. 33; 78430: 'Instructions Oeconomique', 1648, fo. 20.

[37] BL Add. MS 78431: JE to ME, 10 May 1652.

[38] JE to George Evelyn, 15 Oct. 1658, quoted in Hunter, 'John Evelyn in the 1650s', 83.

[39] BL Add. MS 78341: 'Trades, Secrets & Receipts Mechanical', [1650s]; Hunter, 'John Evelyn in the 1650s', 74–81.

[40] The following were all begun in the 1650s: translations of Gabriel Naudé's *Advis pour dresser une bibliothèque* (1644) (Keynes, *JE*, 104); Roland Fréat's *Parallele de l'architecture antique et de la moderne* (1650) (Keynes, *JE*, 166); a course in chemistry by Nicasius Le Fèvre studied by Evelyn in Paris and later published as *Traicté de la Chymie* (F. Sherwood Taylor, 'The Chemical Studies of John Evelyn', *Annals of Science*, 8 (1952), 285–92); and Nicolas de Bonnefons, *Le Jardinier français* (1651); although only the last was published in this decade. The translations of Naudé and Fréat were published in 1661 and 1664; an English translation of Le Fèvre not by Evelyn, *A Compendious Body of Chymistry*, by 'P.D.C.' appeared in 1664.

[41] BL Add. MSS 78353–78356; see also *John Evelyn's Translation of Titus Lucretius Carus De rerum naturæ*, ed. Michael M. Repetzki, Münsteraner Monographien zur englischen Literatur, 22 (Frankfurt, 1997). The fashion for Lucretius and Epicurean philosophy, stimulated by Gassendi, was so marked amongst devotees of the new science that it provided the opening scene of Thomas Shadwell's satire, *The Virtuoso*; see the edition of M. H. Nicolson and D. S. Rodes (1966), pp. xviii–xxx.

make available the fruits of his observation and experience in a comprehensive guide to 'the intire Mysterie' of gardening: not just the practicalities
of soil, situation, and planting, but every kind of ornament, design, and
contrivance which he had observed in the great gardens of the European
Renaissance. His intention with this work, to be called the 'Elysium
Britannicum', was to make horticulture a part of liberal knowledge, one
of the arts a cultivated gentry could practice to the general benefit of their
country.[42] Soon his various projects attracted the attention of the leading
virtuosi of his day; Samuel Hartlib, John Wilkins of Wadham, and Robert
Boyle all began to correspond and visit.

   At the same time he undertook a systematic examination into the roots of
his own Anglican faith. His adherence to it was never an untroubled process.
Aspects of Roman Catholic worship, the 'Devout Humanism' of the French
court especially, always had an attraction for him, and it would have been easy
for him to follow the same path as his cousin Thomas Keightley and accept
conversion; 'you partly know what my Education hath bin, and how freely I
have lived from compulsion', he wrote to Keightley, 'though I have wrestled
with infinit temptations, enjoyed much Liberty, frequent doubts and reluct-
ances as to matters of Conscience . . . I protest before God, that I am herein
merely balanced with an Affection to the Truth (for I doe confesse it, there is
now no other temptation to be of the Church of England).'[43] The resulting
'Rationall Account of the True Religion' was intended to fortify himself not
just against the doctrines of Rome and the dissenting sects but the philosophy of Descartes and Hobbes as well. For all his labours over Lucretius,
in this context he dismissed the explanations of 'those lazy philosophers',
who 'left all to chance and atoms'. To the atheists' assertion that religion was
an invention 'to intimidate men and reduce them to obedience, for the better government of the world', he responded simply that man was a spiritual
animal: nothing would persuade people to embrace a belief in God, 'had they
not been before inclined to it already'. But the strongest support of his own
faith in a divine providence came from his observation of the natural world,
its beauty, ingenuity, and its adaptation to man. Some of his examples of this
were facile: the disposition of the continents and seas, 'fitted for navigation
and commerce of distant nations' for instance, or the provision of winds to fill
sails and 'give motion to mills and other useful engines'. The most compelling lay at his feet in the gardens of Sayes Court, Wotton, and Charlton:
'the flowery parterres of roses, lilies, tulips, anemonies, aramanths, frittillarias,

    [42] Bray, iii. 384: William Nicolson to JE, 25 Mar. 1701; Hunter, 'John Evelyn in the 1650s', 95;
EB, passim.
    [43] BL Add. MS 78298: JE to Thomas Keightley, 1651.

gentianellas, hepaticas and carnations . . . and thousands more, dressed, figured, fringed, folded, miniated and decked by the hand of Him who made the heavens; nor was Solomon, in all his glory, clad like one of these'. But the strongest argument of all was his own driven, unsatisfied nature, his 'large and immense desires' and ambitions, the sense of something lacking in spite of all the blessings he enjoyed, 'whilst all other creatures are contented with food and natural things'; 'the infinite thirst of our souls after knowledge and the love of good; its restless passion after something more perfect than what she can find here in any condition whatsoever'; these 'tell us aloud, that there is something still behind the curtain of more perfect and consummate wanting to fill our capacities and complete our happiness'.[44]

By the latter part of the 1650s, for all the frustration of his ambition, Evelyn's life appeared very enviable: an idyllic garden of his own creating, a growing intellectual reputation, a companionate marriage, and promising sons. 'Truely', he wrote to Sir Richard Browne, 'we want noe earthly felicity but the enjoyment of your society.'[45] When Jeremy Taylor touched a nerve by suggesting that he might be fixing his happiness too much on material things, Evelyn disclaimed it guiltily; 'really I take so little satisfaction in them, that the censure of singularity would no way affright me from embracing a hermitage, if I found that they did in the least distract my thoughts from better things'. But he agreed that 'my condition is too well; and I do as often wonder at it, as suspect and fear it'.[46] The blow fell in the first months of 1658 with the death, probably from a malarial infection, of the 5-year-old Richard, 'the prettiest, and dearest Child, that ever parents had . . . even at that tender age, a prodigie for Witt & understanding; for beauty of body a very Angel, & for endowments of mind, of incredible & rare hopes'; not just in his mastery of languages, his feats of memory, and his passion for mathematics, but his precocious piety: 'astonishing were his applications of Scripture upon occasion, & his sense of God . . . He declaim'd against the Vanities of the World, before he had seene any.' The impression of an over-receptive small child too zealously crammed was so strong that Evelyn felt obliged to add that most of what his son had learned was 'without constraint or the least severity, unseene, and totally imported by his own inclination'. His death could have only one meaning: 'God found me so unworthy to keepe him longer,

[44] BL Add. MS 78367: 'A Rationall Account of the True Religion . . . Collected for the Settling and Establishment of my own Choice', 1657–1704, with the quasi-imprint, 'Begun in the yeare 1657 when the Church of England was in persecution'; published as *The History of Religion* by R. M. Evanson (1850); the quoted passages are from i. 9, 14, 27–8, 30, 50, 55.

[45] BL Add. MS 78221: JE to Sir Richard Browne, 25 Feb. 1653.

[46] Bray, iii. 73: JE to Jeremy Taylor, 27 Apr. 1656.

in whom I had so greate a felicity'.[47] Within weeks little George died also. Only one son, Jack, remained, the least hardy of all the children, and he was a constant source of anxiety.

The shock transformed Evelyn's appearance utterly from the dark and soulful young husband of the marriage portrait: 'upon the suddaine I grew so severe and stoical, as it had even twisted my countenance and given me a peruq of Grey-haires before I was of an age to countenance the decays of nature'.[48] The garden at Sayes Court, now grown to be 'infinitly sweete & beautifull', reminded him piercingly of what he had lost. He told his father-in-law that 'I will as soone as I can let my house & goe & sojourne in the country . . . in some solitude where I may deplore my losse'.[49] The confusions which followed the death of Cromwell prompted ideas of alternative communities; 'why should not Monasticall Societies, decently qualified, revive amongst us in other places of the Nation; and not be confined onely to the Universities; where it is impossible to redeem them from Pedantry, for want of that addresse & refinement of a more generous Conversation'. He could recall Lord Falkland's informal 'college' of theological and political thinkers at Great Tew before the Civil War. By the autumn of 1659 he had set down a plan for a small community of half a dozen separate cells, each with a study and a garden. It was to be part religious foundation on a Carthusian model, part scientific college for the advancement of 'experimental knowledge'. To Thomas Browne, the Norwich physician whose writings he admired, he explained that its members were to be 'persons of ancient simplicity, Paradisean and Hortulan Saints . . . by whome we might hope to redeem the time that has been lost in pursuing vulgar errors and propagating them'. In his mind at least he recruited Browne himself, Robert Boyle, his royalist cousin Samuel Tuke, the visionary Herefordshire clergyman Dr John Beale who helped him so liberally with his horticultural writing, his friend Abraham Cowley, as well as Sir Richard Browne, and even Mary Evelyn, whose presence, he explained to his doubtful male colleagues, would 'be no impediment to the Society, but a considerable advantage to the oeconomic part'.[50]

Meanwhile political events were moving to a climax, and when Evelyn did leave Sayes Court in the autumn of 1659 it was not for some rural solitude

[47] JE, *Diary*, ii. 206–8; Introduction to *The Golden Book* of St John Chrysostom (1658), in *WJE*, 41–4. BL Add. MS 78219: JE to Browne, 6 Feb. 1658.

[48] BL Add. MS 78392: JE, 'The Legend of Philaretes and the Pearle', [c.1673].

[49] BL Add. MS 78221: JE to Browne, 6 Feb., 5 July 1658.

[50] BL Add. MS 78298: JE to Samuel Hartlib, 4 Feb. 1660; Bray, iii. 116–19: JE to Robert Boyle, 3 Sept. 1659; Michael Hunter, *Establishing the New Science* (Woodbridge, 1989), 181–4; Graham Parry, 'John Evelyn as Hortulan Saint', in Michael Leslie and Timothy Raylor (eds.), *Culture and Cultivation in Early Modern England* (Leicester, 1992), 132–48.

but to lodgings in Covent Garden. It was a frightening time, with 'no Government in the Nation, all in Confusion; no Magistrate either own'd or pretended, but the souldiers & they not agreed', and he found himself swept up into active royalist plotting. 'I have bin instrumental for considerable sums of mony to be sent to his Majesties Entertainment', he was able to claim afterwards, 'and concealed divers persons of quality in my house, when it had bin Treason to have but conversed with them.' Under the influence of the royalist agent John Mordaunt, who had married his wife's childhood friend, he even tried to persuade his old Lewes schoolfellow Col. Herbert Morley, who held the Tower of London, to declare for the King in advance of General Monck's arrival in London. It is an unexpected episode which reveals both his determination to break out of his years of inaction and also the extent of his ambition. In fact success was by no means as certain as he afterwards claimed and the Restoration proceeded without his intervention. The only effects of the attempt were a long bout of illness, to which the stresses of the affair probably contributed, and a residual, frustrated sense of what might have been if only Morley had been ready to seize the opportunity: he and not Monck would then have been made a duke, 'and I God knows what', by a grateful restored monarch.[51] As it was he was only just well enough to witness Charles II's ceremonial entry into London in the most glorious of May sunshine, and as his gift was on such occasions, to record it movingly in his diary:

I stood in the Strand & beheld it, and blessed God: And all this without one drop of bloud, & by that very army, which rebell'd against him: but it was the Lords doing, *et mirabile in oculis nostris*: for such a Restauration was never seene in the mention of any history, antient or modern, since the returne of the Babylonian Captivity, nor so joyfull a day, & so bright, ever seene in this nation: this hapning when to expect or effect it, was past all humane policy.[52]

Yet afterwards he was uncertain of his ground. He was more conscious than ever of abilities which might make him 'considerable'; Pepys noted his air of conscious superiority and even conceit.[53] But he was now in his fortieth year and though he might write of gardeners, 'of such they heretofore made their Captaines in warr, and their arbiters of affairs in peace, as if none were more fit to praeside in state then he that could govern his Garden well',[54] he was

[51] Esmond de Beer, 'Evelyn and Col. Herbert Morley in 1659 and 1660', *Sussex Archaelogical Collections*, 78 (1937), 176–83; A. H. Nethercot, 'John Evelyn and Colonel Herbert Morley', *Huntington Library Quarterly*, 1 (1938), 439–46; BL Add. MS 78298: JE to Sir Philip Warwick, 18 July 1662; *The Letter-book of John, Viscount Mordaunt 1658–1660*, ed. Mary Coate, Camden Society, 3rd ser., 69 (1945), 64–5.

[52] JE, *Diary*, iii. 246.   [53] Pepys, *Diary*, vi. 289–290.

[54] BL Add. MS 78298: JE to 'Cyparissa', 14 Sept. 1659.

quite unpractised in any public role. At court there were hundreds pressing forward for notice and preferment, many with conspicuous sufferings in the King's cause to qualify them. Although Evelyn made the most of his pamphlets and cyphered correspondence, his one attempt to play an active part had failed and there was little to distinguish him from many others with royalist sympathies who had been content to save their estates and live peaceably under the Cromwellian government.

He also found the new milieu dismaying. Both as a humanist intellectual and as the descendant of country squires he was predisposed to distrust courts. The decorum and magnificence of Charles I's reign at Whitehall might have subdued this instinct, but now everything he witnessed at the Restoration revived it. The new King was universally genial and performed all the necessary ceremonies gracefully: his coronation, touching for the King's Evil, feasting in the City, the state opening of Parliament; but even before his Restoration his reputation was well known. Charles I had been sober, formal, and monogamous; his sons were young men of strong and unembarrassed sexual appetites which they gratified promiscuously and without concealment. Continuing the informality of their years in exile, they surrounded themselves with like-minded cronies, who embraced the philosophy of the King's old tutor Thomas Hobbes as justification for their libertinism. Evelyn had already written of 'the want of mony, conduct, addresse & sobriety of the Cavaliers'. Now these men, their wits and appetites sharpened by their hardships, flocked to court in the newly-made fashions. The King's inner circle soon appeared to him to be nothing more than a disreputable gang of 'magnificent Fops, whose Talents reach but to the adjusting of their Peruques, courting a Miss, or at the farthest writing a smutty, or scurrilous Libel, which they would have pass for genuine Wit'.[55] Before the second year of the Restoration was out he could interpret a violent storm as 'Gods hand against this ungratefull vicious Nation, & Court'.[56]

Amongst them of course there were some men of intellect and cultivation, as Evelyn had to admit: Sir Henry Bennet, Keeper of the Privy Purse, an extremely able and cosmopolitan diplomat and courtier with his own 'pretty villa' in St James's Park, or Sir George Savile, the future Lord Halifax, whose displays of wit Evelyn primly set down as 'a little too prompt and daring'.[57] But their sophistication was in a very different style from his. 'Since the King was restored it was looked upon as a piece of pedantry to produce a Latin sentence in discours . . . to be earnest or zealous in any one thing', it was

---

[55] BL Add. MS 78221: JE to Browne, 12 June 1659; *Sylva* (1670), p. lxxxviii.
[56] JE, *Diary*, iii. 316.   [57] Ibid., iii. 337, 404.

noted, 'but all, forsooth, must be gentile and neat—no paines taken, Bantring.'[58] Although he was still in early middle age, Evelyn found his freight of ostentatious learning, his compulsive industry, his elaborate formal courtesy and sententious morality already outmoded. In company with Bennet or Savile he could feel uncomfortably like a pedant or a bumpkin.[59] He did not shine amongst the court women either. He was well aware that 'it requires a particular politnesse & great addresse to be well with the Ladies & the Misses', but he still took the assemblies of Henrietta Maria's court as his model, where men and women would meet in polite converse on 'sublime platonick notions'. When he tried his 'hard words and superfine compliments' on the girls of the Restoration court, they laughed at him, 'said that I had a forbidding countenance and were in earnest afraid of me'; 'some tooke me for a schoolmaster, & I believe thought my wife the unhappiest woman in the world'. He felt altogether ill-equipped and out of place: 'I was a man of the shade, and one who had conversed more with plants and books than the circle: I had contracted an odd reservedness, which rendered me wholly unfit to converse among the knights of the carpet and the refined things of the antechamber'. In an age so given to satire, he even feared being 'brought on the stage' to be publicly made fun of.[60]

In some moods he seemed about to withdraw altogether, protesting that he had discovered 'infinite felicitie in a retired and even life' and had no desire to forgo it. But to his confessor Jeremy Taylor he wrote more revealingly that this was not because he had no ambition, 'but because I have too many and would depress them'. To friends in office he was apologetic about his 'unactive life', and seeming to live 'unconcern'd and unprofitably'.[61] In fact he continued to seek favour not just for himself, but even for his self-effacing wife and reluctant father-in-law. Sir Richard's innocent assumption that 'Honors & Estates & Offices &c would have rain'd from heaven on him, & all his Majestie's party if once he came home again' only exasperated Evelyn. He knew nothing was to be gained without competing for it. Now that crown lands were restored the lease of Sayes Court, at the very least, had to be renegotiated; and for all his efforts the King would not grant this to them outright

---

[58] Quoted in Anna Bryson, *From Courtesy to Civility: Changing Codes of Conduct in Early Modern England* (Oxford, 1998), 181; see also John Spurr, *England in the 1670s: 'this Masquerading Age'* (Oxford, 2001), 102–10.

[59] BL Add. MS 78298: JE to Sir Henry Bennet, 7 Oct. 1661.

[60] BL Add. MS 78299: JE to his son, 7 Mar. 1681; David Roberts, *The Ladies: Female Patronage and Restoration Drama* (Oxford, 1989), 25; BL Add. MSS 78309: Anne Howard to JE, [1670s]; 78392: 'The Legend of Philaretes and the Pearle', [c.1673]; 78298: JE to James Hamilton, 27 Apr. 1671.

[61] BL Add. MS 78298: JE to Sir Philip Warwick, 2 Sept. 1660; to Taylor, 9 July 1661.

as promised, but only renew it for a term of years to set off against the debt owed to Sir Richard. Although Evelyn urged his father-in-law to press his claims to the Treasurership of the Navy, in the end that post went to Sir George Carteret. He was relieved that Sir Richard at least managed to retain his old post as Clerk of the Council.[62]

The King's match with the sister of the King of Portugal was put in hand immediately on his Restoration, and this meant a new female household with a number of posts to be filled. Although his stated preference was always to keep his wife 'worthily employed and at home',[63] he now encouraged her to seek one of them. Claiming in his diary that the King promised her the office of Keeper of the Queen's Jewels, he made it a grievance when in the end the post went to Sir Henry Bennet's witty mistress Lady Scrope; only because, he claimed, she had been willing to bribe for it. Actually he understood quite well that his wife had been only one of many candidates whom the King had amiably encouraged to think themselves suitable, while declining to commit himself until his bride actually arrived.[64] In public he liked to pretend that his wife was pursuing her worldly ambitions quite independently of him. Could not Socrates and Epicetus still be philosophers without their wives, he asked when Tuke protested that if she went to court she must be excluded from their plans for a scientific college; 'if the wise discourses of such a Master worke not the Effect let her try the Mistresse of Fooles, and serve in a Court'; he himself still preferred the quiet of Sayes Court to the mindless chatter of the Presence Chamber.[65] Yet all the while he was continuing to press his own claims to be noticed. A panegyric on the coronation was followed by a tract on smoke abatement in London, and a few months later by a *jeu d'esprit* on the prevalence of French fashion. What he sought, as he explained to Sir Henry Bennet, was to put himself at the service of the King and his ministers as a kind of official writer and adviser to the court on cultural and scientific trends. 'In this diffusive age, greedy of intelligence and publique affairs', he argued that the court needed to retain writers and intellectuals in its service, men able to read and write if need be with equal facility in Latin and French. He reminded the minister that Cardinals Richlieu and Mazarin had thought it worthwhile to 'cultivate the productions of a Bookish-Confident or two, who were wont from time to time to

---

[62] BL Add. MSS 78299: JE to Sidney Godolphin, 23 Mar. 1682; 78221: JE to Browne, 1660; JE, *Diary*, iii. 273.

[63] BL Add. MS 78430: 'Instructions Oeconomique', 1648, fo. 22; JE, *Memoires*, 71–2.

[64] JE, *Diary*, iii. 259, 275; Harvard University, Houghton Library, MS Eng. 991: JE to ME, 19 June 1661.

[65] BL Add. MS 78298: JE to Sir Samuel Tuke, 8 Apr. 1661.

informe them of all that was rare and new both in the sciences, and Bookes, on which, though their great affaires permitted them not to looke so steadily; yet were they (by their meanes) ignorant of nothing that pass'd in either'.[66]

However uncongenial the court was, Evelyn justified himself by arguing that if he did not make the effort to fit himself for it, he would leave the field to others far less suitable; too many men of learning made no attempt to accommodate themselves to 'liberal conversation', but appeared 'like so many fantosmes in black, and by declining a seasonable exerting of themselves, and their handsome talents, which Use and Conversation would cultivate and infinitely adorn; they leave occasion for so many insipid and empty fopps to usurp their rights'. But in return they should be given proper incentives to leave their 'beloved Recesses'. Their laurels could only flourish 'under showrs of Gold and the constellations of Crowns', but the court appeared reprehensibly willing to spend more on ephemeral balls and masques than rewarding a poet or historian, 'who have it in their power, to give more lustre to their Heros, than their Crowns, and Purple; and can with one dash of their pen, kill more dead, then a stab with a Stiletto'. What he had in mind was a specific post with a suitably resounding title: historiographer royal for example.[67] No such appointment was forthcoming, and certainly no showers of gold from the overstretched Treasury; but the King was interested, by the proposals for smoke abatement especially. He began to take Evelyn aside and talk to him, enlist his help with Greenwich palace, try him out with minor commissions of government propaganda.[68] But it was all at a cost. Work on his larger projects, his gardening compendium especially, was interrupted. More to the point he found that he was temperamentally unsuited to the work. Prolonged periods of time at court, trying to snatch a few minutes' attention of the great, fitting himself to their veering aims, left him exhausted and disoriented, needing days in the peace of his own house to recover. Although he was capable of prodigies of sustained work, as he told Pepys years later, 'I can't bussle'.[69] It was a disadvantage for a Restoration courtier.

A happier effect of the Restoration was that he was very quickly recruited to the 'Philosophical Society' at Gresham College, soon to be incorporated under charter as the Royal Society. This was a metropolitan and secular realization of his project for a college of experimental philosophy, and it brought

---

[66] Ibid.: JE to Sir Henry Bennet, 7 Dec. 1661; to the Duke of Ormonde, 12 May 1662.

[67] *Public and Private Life in the Seventeenth Century: The Mackenzie–Evelyn Debate*, ed. Brian Vickers (New York, 1986), 221, 227–8; *PF*, 130: JE to Pepys, 28 Apr. 1682.

[68] JE, *Diary*, iii. 299–300, 313.

[69] JE, *Diary*, iii. 300, 313; *PF*, 130: JE to Pepys, 28 Apr. 1682.

him the fellowship of more like-minded men than he found at court, most
notably its exceptional vice-president, Sir Robert Moray. Moray was a Scot
who had served in the French army for many years and had latterly been a
diplomat and a royalist agent in Scotland; but at intervals of imprisonment
and exile he had also devoted himself to his studies, which included hermetic
philosophy and experimental chemistry. He was not, any more than Evelyn,
a major scientist in his own right, but he was the Society's 'Prime Virtuoso'
and in the beginning its 'life and soul', persuading the King, whose dilettante
chemical experiments he directed, to grant its charter, and giving constant
thought to its sound funding. More than any other individual Evelyn
encountered in this new milieu, Moray seemed to embody his ideal of a
Christian hero, a disinterested intellectual and a natural philosopher, a man of
action and a courtier, but one unsullied by the corruption of public life. For
in his devotion to the memory of his wife who had died in childbirth, Moray
set himself conspicuously apart from the debauchery of the court, and being
'as free of Covetousness as a Carthusian', was almost uniquely ready to use his
royal favour to 'doe a kindnesse *gratis* upon an account of Friendship'. Even
the cynical King was impressed by Moray's sheer disinterested goodness, his
'diffused love of all mankind'. In fact he was a Christian stoic, who had made
it his lifelong project 'to understand and regulate' his passions. His highly
personal form of deism might be at variance with Evelyn's orthodox
Anglicanism (the King liked to tease the Scot with being head of his own
church), but his practice of daily meditation on 'such of the divine attributes
as appeared to him in the new occurrances of providence', his sense that 'all
our other most serious employments should be but as parentheses to con-
templations of that nature', were entirely congenial. To Evelyn he became
'my most religious friend'.[70]

It was the Royal Society which gave him the means of bringing a number
of his earlier projects to fruition. He was commissioned to expand one element in his history of trades into a full treatise: *Sculptura: or The History and
Art of Engraving in Copper and Mezzotinto*. Since England, as it was left by the
despoilers of the Commonwealth, appeared to him such a 'naked & miserably demolished Country' where no suitable models could be observed, he
also completed and published his translation of a seminal French work on
ancient and modern architecture as a source of examples for the improvement of London building.[71] He compiled a treatise and a reading list to show

[70] Alexander Robertson, *The Life of Sir Robert Moray* (1922), 168–80; David Stevenson, *The
Origins of Freemasonry* (Cambridge, 1988), 166–8, 179–80. BL Add. MS 78330: commonplace book,
fo. 12ᵛ.
[71] BL Add. MS 78298: JE to Benjamin Maddox, 21 Sept. 1656.

how a deplorably uneducated elite 'might become very knowing . . . by the onely assistance of the modern languages'. He let himself be co-opted onto a Royal Society project for refining the English language.[72] Finally, when the Commissioners of the Navy requested the Society to turn its attention to the dwindling supply of timber for shipbuilding, he found himself the natural choice to lead the project and perform the greater part of it personally. Not only was he a passionate and knowledgeable tree-lover, but he had lived cheek by jowl with the 'King's Yard' at Deptford for ten years, and his wife's family had overseen the expansion of the Tudor Navy. Of course he knew that generations of shipbuilding for defence, trade, and colonizing had devoured prodigious quantities of timber and that his own family's fortunes were built on industries which systematically depleted the Surrey woodlands. But for his present task he was again content to cast all the blame for this on the 'sacrilegious Purchasers, and disloyal Invaders, in this Iron-age', as (echoing Ovid's *Metamorphoses*) he called the supporters of the Cromwellian government:

for it has not been the late increase of Shipping alone, the multiplication of Glass-works, Iron-Furnaces, and the like, from whence this im-politick diminution of our Timber has proceeded, but from the disproportionate spreading of Tillage, caused through that prodigious havock made by such as lately professing themselves against Root and Branch . . . were tempted, not only to fell and cut down, but utterly to grub up, demolish, and raze, as it were, all those many goodly Woods and Forests, which our more prudent Ancestors left standing, for the Ornament and service of their Country.[73]

Ostensibly his task was simply to compile a manual of advice about the cultivation and uses of different varieties of trees; but having covered the principal natives, oak, elm, ash, beech, and yew, he could not resist adding the newly fashionable evergreens and ornamental exotics of which he had made Sayes Court a famous showcase,[74] or lifting his manual of a gardener's monthly tasks, the 'Kalendarium Hortense', out of his unfinished 'Elysium Britannicum' to use as an appendix. The whole work was designed to appeal to the gentry and not just to their stewards and foresters.[75] Its practical advice was drawn not just from his own experience and from expert contemporaries, but from Pliny's *Natural History* and Virgil's *Georgics*. Seductively he

[72] Keynes, *JE*, 116–18; Hunter, 'Evelyn in the 1650s', 78; Bray, iii. 159–62: JE to Sir Peter Wyche, 20 June 1665; *Gentleman's Magazine*, 67, pt 1 (1797), 218–19: JE to [Sir Joseph Williamson], 28 Jan. [1671]; *PF*, 203: JE to Pepys, 26 Aug. 1689.

[73] Keynes, *JE*, 130, 154; *Sylva* (1664) in *WJE*, 173–5; 178–80, 189, 197–8.

[74] *Sylva* (1664) in *WJE*, 265–7; cf. *EB*, 22, 139–50, 313–16.

[75] Hunter, 'John Evelyn in the 1650s', 95.

combined reminders of the profits to be made from the commercial cultivation of timber ('pretty encouragements for a small and pleasant industry')
with an infectious passion for the beauty and numinousness of trees and
forests. Every landowner was shown the way to participate in a project which
was at once elite, patriotic, and rewarding, both materially and spiritually.

Sylva: or A Discourse on Forest Trees (named in recollection of Bacon's *Sylva
Sylvarum*) appeared in 1664, with the distinction of being the first publication
officially sponsored by the Royal Society. It was a resounding success. More
than any other, Evelyn could claim, as it went from one enlarged edition to
another, it encouraged the large-scale planting of the landscape in his generation, not just as an economic resource but also as an amenity. Its author's
standing increased accordingly. For all his moralizing and schoolmasterly
manner, he began to be recognized as a useful and energetic public man. He
did not receive the dignities he conceived for himself: historiographer royal
or surveyor of forests. But he was recruited to several worthy, unglamorous
commissions: for paving the streets, maintaining the sewers, and regulating
hackney coaches;[76] and then on the outbreak of the Second Dutch War came
a much more substantial responsibility: he was made one of the commissioners for Sick and Wounded Seamen, with responsibility for all the south
coast ports from Dover to Portsmouth. 'Farewell: sweet repose, books, [and]
gardens,' he wrote posturingly to Robert Boyle. Yet the work was not only
well renumerated (the initial salary of £300 a year was shortly raised to
£500); it could be embraced as a philanthropic and Christian duty.[77] With a
strong sense of pastoral care towards his 'sick flock', he designed the official
seal of the commissioners himself, a depiction of the good Samaritan with
the motto, 'Fac Similiter' ('do likewise'). At the Buoy of Nore he thrilled
with pride at the sight of 'the most glorious fleet that ever spread sail', and on
board the *Prince* with the King and the Earl of Sandwich he was dazzled at
'the good order, decency, & plenty of all things'.[78]

Yet in the autumn of 1665 his duties overwhelmed him in a manner he
could never have foreseen. By this time the plague was raging, not only in
London but through the crowded tenements of Deptford and up to his own
gates, so that he scarcely dared enquire after his neighbours, 'for it ever
affrights me, & our bell never lies still'. Evacuating his family to Wotton, he
stood to his duty, 'trusting in the providence & goodnesse of God'. But he
was inexperienced in dealing even with the routine shifts of government

[76] JE, *Diary*, iii. 318–19, 328, 361, 364, 379.
[77] Bray, iii. 148–9: JE to Boyle, 23 Nov. 1664; J. J. S. Shaw, 'The Commission for Sick and
Wounded and Prisoners 1664–1667', *Mariner's Mirror*, 25 (1939), 306–9.
[78] JE, *Diary*, iii. 390, 407, 413.

finance, much less with such a paralysing crisis. To his charge of sick and injured seamen was added hundreds of Dutch prisoners of war and he had no means to make them safe; 'Dover Castle has not cover for above 60; The Forts will not containe 40 apiece; The County Gaoles are narrow & all infected with the Plague in every quarter; we have no money to feed them, nor can I procure officers to governe them; so as I am even at my witts end.' His officials succumbed as fast as they were appointed. Money which should have come to him was diverted to other parts of the service. With the court in the remote safety of Salisbury and Oxford, he felt abandoned, 'for there is no mony raised, nor . . . any to be hop'd for: They at Court no more minding us then if there were not a Navy in nature, or such a thing as 3,000 men to be fed & payd'. The burden of administration alone was crippling: three London hospitals, nine more headquarters in the Kent towns, and Leeds Castle, which he managed to hire for the prisoners of war. Even so he had to resort to compulsory mass billeting amongst poor householders in the already stricken Kent towns and villages, 'even to our doores at Deptford, having filld up all the County'. The providers were 'a sort of wretched people that starve if they are not daily fed', and the debts he could not avoid running up exposed him to vicious hostility. Having at last secured an assignment of £2,000, he had to go into the City to fetch it, where 'I was invironed with multitudes of poore pestiferous creatures, begging almes; the shops universaly shut up, a dreadfull prospect.' When his wife gave birth at Wotton in October, this time to the daughter she longed for, he had scarcely attention to spare for her; 'I am so used to motion now that I can hardly stand still though I desire nothing more.'[79]

Gradually the most acute crisis eased. The Dutch took responsibility for their prisoners and more assignments of money came grudgingly through. In the breathing space Evelyn applied himself characteristically to devising a model system for making up his accounts. Friendship with Samuel Pepys was the one good to come to him from these searing months, though the more seasoned official thought he agonized excessively over difficulties any government employee must resign himself to.[80] Together they put forward a proposal for a seamen's infirmary at Chatham, so that the uneconomical billeting in inns and houses could be avoided another time. Evelyn was at his most admirable, sitting up late during his short and hard-earned Christmas recess at Wotton, drawing up the plans and specifications. He and Pepys

[79] BL Add. MSS 78221: JE to Browne, Sept.–Dec. 1665; 78431: JE to ME, Oct.–Dec. 1665; Bray, iii. 164–75: JE to Lord Cornbury, 9, 12 Sept. 1665, to Sir Philip Warwick, 30 Sept. 1665, to Sir William Coventry, 2 Oct. 1665; Shaw, 'Commission', 310–16.

[80] *PF*, 33–51: correspondence between JE and Pepys, 23 Sept.–13 Dec. 1665.

paced the site. At Hampton Court he had a rapturous reception from the King; but of course there were not sufficient funds in the Treasury to meet regular expenditure, much less for such capital projects, and the seamen's hospital had to wait for another thirty years.[81] He was pressed to accept a knighthood; 'but I got most dextrously off', he told his wife, and escaped the court 'a squire as pure as ever I went'.[82]

No acknowledgements could wipe out his agonizing memories of mediating between the grinding financial machinery of government and the desperate plague-stricken poor of the seaports. Unlike his fellow commissioner, Sir Thomas Clifford, who was rapidly establishing himself as ministerial timber, Evelyn had to acknowledge that he had neither the ability nor the temperament for political life. 'I find the happy difference betwixt speculation and action', he confessed to the Treasury secretary Sir Philip Warwick, 'learning that at once, which others get by degrees; but I am sufficiently punished for the temerity, and I acknowledge the burthen insupportable.'[83] He kept his employment and matters were never so acutely bad again. But his diary entries after the destructive sea battles of the following summer were very different from those at his setting out: 'more than halfe of that gallant bulwark of the Kingdome miserably shatterd, hardly a Vessell intire, but appearing rather so many wracks & hulls, so cruely had the Dutch mangled us . . . none knowing of what reason we first ingagd in this ungratefull war . . . neere 600 men slaine, & 1,100 wounded, 2,000 prisoners, to balance which perhaps we might destroy 18 or 20 of the Enemies ships & 7 or 800 poore men'.[84] This was the end of all his Christian self-dedication and his naive enthusiasm for rebuilding the navy.

Then came the apocalytic event of the Great Fire of London: 'O the miserable and calamitous spectacle, such as happly the whole world had not seene the like since the foundation of it, nor to be outdon, 'til the universal Conflagration of it.' Was it the divine judgement he had feared 'for our prodigious ingratitude, burning Lusts, disolute Court, profane & abominable lives'?[85] If so, it was divine judgement very unfairly misdirected, since the court itself escaped both epidemic and fire largely unscathed. Of the plague deaths, Clarendon dispassionately remarked, 'the greatest number were women and children, and the lowest and poorest sort of people; so that few

[81] Ibid. 52–5, 336; BL Add. MS 78431: JE to ME, 1 Jan. 1666; Pepys, *Diary*, vii. 29; JE, *Diary*, iii. 441–2; paper by Gillian Darley, 'Evelyn, Greenwich, and the Sick and Wounded Seamen', at the conference, 'John Evelyn and his Milieu', British Library, 17–18 Sept. 2001.

[82] JE, *Diary*, iii. 428–9; Helen Evelyn, *Evelyn Family*, 73–4: JE to ME, 29 Jan. 1666.

[83] Bray, iii. 172: JE to Sir Philip Warwick, 30 Sept. 1665.

[84] JE, *Diary*, iii. 441–2.   [85] Ibid. iii. 450–4, 464.

men missed any of their acquaintance when they returned', and the memory of the panic soon faded. When Evelyn came to Whitehall in the aftermath of the fire, he found it more preoccupied with the latest fashions in cross-dressing—cavaliers' outfits for the Queen and her maids of honour, and tunics 'after the Persian mode' for the men—than with mending its ways.[86] Yet perhaps even the fire could be regarded as providential in other ways. Whole crooked, crowded, wooden-built districts which he had deplored were now swept away. Within days he had presented the King with his plan for rebuilding on a regular design of classical and Continental models, with broad paved streets, piazzas and fountains, uniform public buildings and gardens, triumphal gateways and quays, 'fitter for commerce, apter for government, sweeter for health, more glorious for beauty'.[87] But of course for the colossal and urgent task of rebuilding London the King depended on the professionalism of Wren and Robert Hooke, not on Evelyn's amateur utopianism. The city rose slowly again, its building circumscribed by the same boundaries as before, but with neat brick façades replacing the rickety wooden houses which had fed the conflagration. In conjunction with some Royal Society colleagues Evelyn was tempted to try his hand at brick-making at Sayes Court. The advantage, as Mrs Evelyn remarked dryly, was only in prospect, while the expense was certain and immediate. The clay proved unsuitable and the scheme came to nothing.[88]

The train of national disasters was still not over. With the opening of peace negotiations early the following year, it was decided not to put a battle fleet to sea. The Dutch were less backward. In June their fleet sailed into the Medway, attacked the fleet at anchor at Chatham, and went on to blockade London by riding in the mouth of the Thames. Evelyn stood on the Kent shore and watched them: 'a Dreadfull Spectacle as ever any English men saw, & a dishonour never to be wiped off'. At Deptford an accidental fire amongst the dockyard stores spread a panic rumour of a Dutch invasion; 'every body went to their armes & all my family alarm'd with the extraordinarie light & confusion'.[89] With the Newcastle colliers unable to get through, Evelyn, who had long been interested in alternative sources of fuel, was asked to report on peat and turf supplies and diligently experimented with mixtures of coal dust and loam. But when peace was made at Breda in August, this was

---

[86] Edward Hyde, Earl of Clarendon, *Life . . . in which is Included a Continuation of his History* (Oxford, 1857), ii. 241; JE, *Diary*, iii. 463, 464, 466, 477–8.

[87] *Londinium redivivum* (1666), in *WJE*, 333–5; JE, *Diary*, iii. 463.

[88] JE, *Diary*, iii. 471, 476, 495; BL Add. MSS 78539: ME to Ralph Bohun, 14 Apr. [1667?]; 78435: Ralph Bohun to ME, 17 June [1667?]; 78340: fo. 88ᵛ: 'Husbandry for Sayes Court'.

[89] JE, *Diary*, iii. 484–5.

dropped as well.[90] Well aware, as many were, that the losses and sacrifices of
the last three years had been for nothing, he unburdened himself for hours
together to Pepys about his disillusion with the King, his ageing chief ministers, the self-indulgent nobility, and negligent court clergy.[91] Neither of
the two ministers survived the crisis. The ailing Lord Treasurer Southampton
died, devolving the public finances into the hands of a younger, tougher,
more professionalized generation. The chief scapegoat, the Lord Chancellor
Clarendon, was banished before the end of the year. Evelyn had known him
well, as the tireless upholder of the royalist cause in exile: an intellectual and
a profoundly moral being as well as a man of action. Acknowledging that
the cantankerous old man now had few friends even among the royalists,
and many enemies, especially 'the boufoones & Ladys of Pleasure', Evelyn
knew that he was nevertheless 'one who kept up the forme & substance of
things in the nation with more solemnity than some would have', and was his
own 'particular kind friend on all occasions'.[92] His going signalled the end
of an era.

Even the Royal Society was no longer so great a source of inspiration.
Sir Robert Moray, sent to Scotland as the King's secret agent, stayed away
for more than a year. Without his presence, Evelyn wrote plaintively, 'not I
alone, but the whole R: Society plainly withers. Why should we suffer two
Winters at once; the absence of her worthiest Member and of the Sun?
Can any concerne be so precious to you as Philosophy? Must not Scotland
flourish without the Society dye? . . . Returne then, and quit the helme of
the giddy and Ungratefull States to guide that of a more intellectual & nobler
Commonwealth, that of Letters & Philosophy which languish for your
presence.' In reply Moray fondly recalled 'the little world that goes under the
name of Sayes Court', where 'if the two luminaries that keep up a perpetual
spring in that rich place did but shine perpetually on such an obscure guest',
he could be content and 'not covet the courted glories of our terrestrial
planet'.[93] In the midst of all his public difficulties Evelyn had never ceased
his projects for the improvement of it, refurbishing the house, clearing the
ground beyond the existing grove for his new plantation of exotics, impor-
tuning the courtiers at Oxford to procure him seeds and specimens from
the botanic garden, and petitioning the Treasury to improve the dockyard

[90] *Sylva* (1664), in *WJE*, 306–7; BL Add. MS 78393: report by JE to the King on supplies of peat
and turf adjacent to London, [1667].

[91] Pepys, *Diary*, vii. 29, 298; viii, 181, 183.   [92] JE, *Diary*, iii. 493.

[93] BL Add. MS 78298: JE to Sir Robert Moray, 13 Dec. 1667; BL Add. MS 15858, fo. 81: Moray
to JE, 17 Jan. 1668.

boundary.[94] After the ravages of the past three years, it seemed more than ever before a precious refuge; 'I returnd with a sad heart to my house,' he wrote after watching the devastation of the fire, 'blessing & adoring the distinguishing mercy of God, to me & mine, who in the midst of all this ruine, was like Lot, in my little Zoar, safe and sound.'[95]

He was more than halfway through his life. He had achieved distinction, even fame, in a limited field. Yet he felt frustrated and disillusioned, thrown back on his own resources and uncertain how to regenerate himself. Though everything he had seen confirmed his commonplace book maxim that 'a court is but a pretty misery',[96] he knew that he could not remain at Sayes Court and renounce public life altogether. A second daughter Betty was born a month after the Dutch peace, and by the following year his wife was expecting another child. Daughters were expensive to settle in the world and in spending so freely on his house and garden he had not troubled to follow his own precept by saving to provide for them.[97] His attempt to develop a commercial enterprise on his estate had failed, so his only recourse was public office. He still believed profoundly in the neoplatonic ideal of a balance between the active and contemplative lives; but how to reconcile public life, now he knew what it was, with purity and honour?

Yet men such as Clarendon and Sir Robert Moray had shown that it could be done. As he turned the problem over in his mind Moray gave him the opportunity to debate it publicly, by drawing his attention to a small work by a rising Edinburgh advocate, Sir George Mackenzie.[98] Mackenzie, already the author of a work called *The Religious Stoic*, had now published a 'moral essay' on the benefits of solitude and virtuous retirement. When Evelyn answered this with his *Public Employment and an Active Life Preferr'd to Solitude*, it was more than just an academic exercise; it was a definition of his own ideal role:

Could his happy man remain in that desirable estate, without the active lives of others to protect him from rapine, feed and supply him with Bread, Cloaths and decent necessaries? For 'tis a grand mistake to conceive, that none are employ'd, but such as are all day on horse-back, fighting battels, or sitting in Tribunals: What think you of Plow-men and Artificers? nay the labours of the Brain that excogitates new Arts?

---

[94] BL Add. MSS 78221: JE to Browne, 9 Dec. 1665, 20 Jan. 1666; 78614: petition to the Lord Treasurer, [1666].

[95] JE, *Diary*, iii. 457.   [96] BL Add. MS 78327, p. 61.

[97] BL Add. MS 78386: 'Oeconomics to a Newly Married Friend', [1676], p. 38; JE, *Memoires*, 12.

[98] Upcott, 504: JE to Mackenzie, 15 Mar. 1667, mentioning Moray's involvement.

As for the 'seraphick Mr Boyle', whom Mackenzie had mocked, 'there lives not a Person in the world whose moments are more employ'd'. Virtue was possible in public life, as Moray had shown, 'if men continue humble and govern their passions, amidst the temptations of Pride and Insolence; if they remain generous, chast and patient amongst all the assaults of avarice, dissolution and the importunity of Clients'; 'to conserve ones self in a Court, is to become an absolute Hero; and what place is more becoming Heros than the Courts of Princes?' As the creator of Sayes Court he could claim to be more experienced than anyone in the delights of rural retirement, but 'even those without action are intollerable: You will say it is not publick: If it contribute and tend to it, what wants it but the name and sound?'[99]

He had the best of the argument without too much difficulty. Mackenzie good-humouredly acknowledged himself so convinced that he had decided to keep his own public employment.[100] But for the time being Evelyn continued to demonstrate that he could be just as active and publicly useful at Sayes Court as in London. He applied himself again to 'the drudgery of translation', so as to make Fréat's *Idea of Perfection in Painting* a companion piece to his treatises on architecture and engraving and 'perfectly consummate that designe of mine, of recommending to our countrey, and especially to the nobless[e], those three illustrious and magnificent arts which are so dependent upon each other'.[101] Then he turned to the more congenial task of preparing a new edition of *Sylva*, though with a rather different emphasis from the first. It was now clear to him that the King and his government were as much iron age despoilers as Cromwell's had been, and he was also seeking a regeneration of his own spiritual resources through the natural world. To what had been largely a manual on the practical and economic uses of trees, he added a whole new section on 'the sacrednesse and use of standing groves', celebrating the primal woods of the golden age: 'Groves and Forests, such as were never Prophan'd by the Inhumanity of Edge-tools: Woods, whose Original are as unknown as the Arcadians . . . *Arbores Dei* according to the Hebrew, for something doubtlesse which they noted in the Genius of those venerable Places besides their meer bulk and Stature'. To the thinking man these should not be just a resource to be exploited, but what they had always been to him, a perennial source of wonder, 'sufficient to employ his Meditations and his Hands, as long as he had to live, though his years were as many as the most aged Oak . . . In every Hedge, and every Field they are

[99] *Public and Private Life*, ed. Vickers, esp. 149, 155–6, 176–7, 228.
[100] Upcott, 503–4: Mackenzie to JE, 5 Mar. 1667.   [101] Upcott, 559.

before him; and yet we do not admire them, because they are Common, and obvious.'[102]

This done, he turned again to his rich, unwieldy manuscript of the 'Elysium Britannicum', now crammed and fattened with marginalia and addenda. Knowing in his heart that it would be beyond his resources to bring it to completion, he felt that he had committed himself too far to retreat with honour,[103] and the subject was still an unfailing source of meaning for him. As a practical diversion he made an Epicurean landscape design for Arundel's beloved retreat at Albury, now inherited by his grandson Henry Howard.[104] Otherwise it pleased him to let the rising men at court, Arlington and Clifford, seek him out in his retirement, drawn by his ideal and the fame of his private elysium. Once again, however temporarily, he put on the persona of the reclusive 'hortulan saint': 'I minded my Books and my Planting . . . I aspir'd to no Offices, no Titles, no Favours at Court, and really was hardly known to my next Neighbours, whom I had lived almost twenty years by'.[105] Thus it was when Mrs Howard and her daughters took up residence at the Treasurer's house, bringing Margaret Blagge along with them. ❧

---

[102] *Sylva* (1670), 225–7, 247.

[103] BL Add. MS 78298: JE to Thomas Lloyd, 16 Oct. 1668.

[104] JE, *Diary*, iii. 496, 561–2; Small, 'John Evelyn and the Garden of Epicurus', 60, 202–7; Michael Charlesworth, 'A Plan by John Evelyn of Henry Howard's Garden at Albury Park, Surrey', in T. O'Malley and J. Wolschke-Bulmahn (eds.), *John Evelyn's Elysium Britannicum and European Horticulture*, (Washington, DC, 1995), 289–93.

[105] BL Add. MS 78392: 'The Legend of Philaretes and the Pearle', [*c*.1673].

3

Nuptial Love

Unlike her husband Mary Evelyn kept no diary and left no account of her own life. The narratives he encouraged her to write down of her vivid and coherent dreams, tantalizingly referred to in one of his letters,[1] have now vanished. If, like many of her female contemporaries, she kept devotional notes these have also failed to survive. We know most about her from her letters. She had been familiar from her childhood with the salon culture of Paris and for all her modest and self-effacing demeanour she was essentially a social being; conversation and correspondence came more naturally to her than solitary self-communing. She took great pains with her letters, modelling them on the most urbane French epistolary stylists; not straining for wit or effect, but taking pleasure in her recipients'—especially her male recipients'—appreciation, and copying those she was most pleased with into small paper-bound notebooks to ensure they would not be lost.[2]

She had been well educated in the humanist tradition; wrote a fine italic hand, understood Italian, was fluent in French, and confident enough of her style in English to criticize the shoddy vernacular of some male classicists.[3] She had also studied drawing and mathematics beyond the level of conventional female accomplishment. Both she and her parents were concerned that marriage so young should not prevent her continuing her education or put a stop to her life of the mind. When Evelyn made plans for them to move back to England in 1652, she was unwilling at first: 'I should have bin very glad for some time to have practised those things I now begin to understand, fearing the care of house keeping will take up the greatest part of my time.' She was also reluctant to leave her parents, especially her father, telling Evelyn that it

---

[1] *PF*, 207: JE to Pepys, 4 Oct. 1689.
[2] Frances Harris, 'The Letter-books of Mary Evelyn', *English Manuscript Studies* (1998), 204–13.
[3] BL Add. MS 78539: ME to Ralph Bohun, 22 Mar. [1668?].

was the greatest mark of affection she could give him that she should do so for his sake. But, she added sedately, 'I am most dutifully and affectionately yours to dispose of.'[4]

She loved Paris and especially the suburb of Saint-Germain where the Brownes lived, writing of it wistfully in later life 'with that affection persons in age remember the satisfaction of their youth, to which happiness was the nearest . . . and so past that there is no hopes of a return'.[5] She made the best of Deptford and the renovated Sayes Court. Although the house, as she reported to her father, was 'somthing inferior' to a Parisian palace, it had all the conveniences, and her cabinet, closet and coach were 'very fine'.[6] But she also exchanged Parisian society, where women such as Marie le Jars de Gourney, Madeleine de Scudéry, and the salonières had given women an accepted public role in intellectual life, to encounter for the first time 'that ancient and formidable legacy of misogyny' which lingered perhaps more stubbornly in England than elsewhere.[7] In this orthodoxy female learning was suspect and women were admonished to be silent and subordinate and to mind their houses. Both influences left their mark on her. Though she never again travelled out of England, she took quiet satisfaction in being seen by her countrymen as one in whom 'English Gravity' was 'moderately allayed, sweetened and spirited, by the mettlesome Aire and education of France'.[8] She conformed, but she kept her own counsel and never surrendered her independent judgement.

Evelyn was prepared to give priority at first to his wife's continuing education. The 'Closset of Collections' over the porch, 'inferior to none now in England' in his opinion,[9] was put in her charge. She continued to have a French drawing-master and under his tuition 'improved to admiration'; while her actual accomplishments, flower painting, an imitative design for the frontispiece of his *Lucretius*, and miniature copies of old masters, remained so modest that they could cause him no misgivings.[10] He was well fitted himself to continue her education in other matters, indeed most at ease in relationships in which he could take a didactic role. By marrying so young Mary

[4] BL Add. MS 78300: ME to JE, 25 Feb., 30 Mar., 13 Apr., 7 June 1652.

[5] Bray, iv. 13: ME to William Glanville, [1668–9].

[6] BL Add. MS 78221: ME to Sir Richard Browne, 28 Sept. 1652.

[7] Patricia Phillips, *The Scientific Lady: A Social History* (1990), 12.

[8] Pierre Gassendi, *The Mirrour of True Nobility & Gentility, being the Life of the Renowned Nicolaus Claudius Fabricius* (1657), introduction by William Rand, sig. A6.

[9] BL Add. MS 78298: JE to ME, 28 Apr. 1652.

[10] Frances Harris, 'Living in the Neighbourhood of Science: Mary Evelyn, Margaret Cavendish and the Greshamites', in Lynette Hunter and Sarah Hutton (eds.), *Women, Science and Medicine 1500–1700* (Thrupp, 1997), 201; for the public knowledge of her accomplishment, see *Lorenzo Magalotti at the Court of Charles II*, ed. W. E. Knowles Middleton (Waterloo, Ont., 1980), 136.

Evelyn had in effect been transferred from one form of parental custody
to another and accepted the restriction as the price of continuing security.
'Marriage to such minds as yours and mine requires plenty and quiet', she
told a friend many years later. Evelyn's care of her, she added with a significant order of words, was 'such as might become a Father, a Lover, a Friend
and Husband'. Even in extreme old age, after he was several years dead, she
would still pay tribute to her parents for placing her in such good hands.[11]

Evelyn's attitude to female attainment was ambivalent. He could reel off
conventional lists of learned women of the classical and European past, from
'Hilpylas, the mother-in-law of young Pliny' to their famous Dutch contemporary Anna Maria van Schurman.[12] Small-scale drawing and painting
such as his wife's made a safe and acceptable female hobby, which 'entertaines
the fancy usefully, and disposes it to order in other things'.[13] But in other
matters he was conventionally repressive. His wife's facility in translation
could be cautiously encouraged, but only because 'her modesty may be well
trusted with more than the ordinary erudition of her sex, whome learning
dos commonly but corrupt'. Women might safely be introduced to the
commoner classics, Virgil, Seneca, Epicetus in translation, but 'more than
this (unlesse it be very much more . . .) is apt to turne to impertinence and
vanity'.[14] Above all he insisted that housekeeping should have priority over
all other claims on her time. On the authority of the Bible and of Aristotle it
was prescribed as the natural role of women. His mother had been renowned
for her housewifery, and one of Mary Browne's best qualifications to be his
wife was that she had been trained from a child 'to govern the house'. Although
he agreed that she should have her mother's assistance at first, this was only to
be 'till you are a little entered in the misterye of that calling for which you
were ordayned by nature'.[15] Whatever decision a man might take about
his involvement in court or city affairs, 'what an Advantage is it', he told his
grandson much later, 'to have your country Oeconomy with a discreete and
faithfull Wife whom you will always find worthily Imploy'd and at home'.[16]

All the renovated domestic offices were her domain: the kitchen, buttery,
still-room, pastry, larder, dairy, wash-house, and brewhouse, and the produce
of the kitchen garden and orchard, together with that of the beehive, carp

[11] Bray, iv. 27: ME to William Glanville, 8 Oct. 1671; Helen Evelyn, *The Evelyn Family* (1915),
110: will of ME, 9 Feb. 1709.
[12] Bray, iii. 244–5: JE to Duchess of Newcastle, 15 June '1674' (the Duchess died in 1673).
[13] BL Add. MS 78386: JE, 'Oeconomics to a Newly Married Friend', [1676], p. 63.
[14] BL Add. MSS 78221: JE to Sir Richard Browne, 29 Nov. 1656; 78386: 'Oeconomics', p. 63.
[15] Margaret R. Sommerville, *Sex and Subjection: Attitudes to Women in Early Modern Society*
(1995), 13–15; JE, *Diary*, ii. 3; Hiscock II, 17; BL Add. MS 78431: JE to ME, 22 Feb. 1652.
[16] JE, *Memoires*, 72.

pond, hog-sties, dairy, and hen house; enough for a small kitchen and still-room industry. Evelyn had specified the equipment of the still-room in minute detail, from the furnace, bain-marie, and refrigeratory, down to the tongs, scissors, corks, packthread, wax, bladders, and hourglass.[17] Amongst the commonplace books which he began in the first years of his marriage was a folio recipe book, with sections for medicine, surgery, preserves, perfumes, and cookery. To begin with he had been a collector of recipes in his own right, from hog's pudding to syrup of violets and surfeit water;[18] but soon his wife was able to take over this function entirely. Having praised Evelyn's standing as a virtuoso, Samuel Hartlib noted her expertise in conserving and distilling, 'and for all manner of sweetmeates most rare'. 'Though gally potts and stone bottles are no Rarityes', her brother-in-law William Glanville wrote, 'That which I desire you herewith to accept, may serve for foyles to those excellent conserves and Wines with which Deptford is so constantly stored.'[19]

Her mother, who was to have helped her, died not long after her marriage, 'the sorrow wherof hung long upon her'. Afterwards, Evelyn thought, her soul lived more in her father and her sons than in her own person.[20] The death of Richard especially was so crippling a blow that 'without God's great mercy' she believed that she would not have survived, 'all my constancy being too weak to carry me through'. Recollections of the child's face and voice haunted her in every corner of the house. Although she did not see it self-punishingly as a sign of her own unworthiness, she felt in retrospect that it was an inevitable outcome: 'I was in too happy a condition, such blessings seldome last, to have a good husband, hopefull Children, and a contented mind'.[21] Her letters only hint at the slow and inward process by which she struggled back to stability, by the same conscious and painful regulation of the passions which a professed stoic such as Sir Robert Moray practised. A hermit in his cell, she wrote later, might be considered as heroic as Alexander if his conflicts were known, 'who fights only with himself, whose Enimies are his passions, and whose greatest care is not to make an esclat here, who reserves his triumph for another world'.[22] Seeking some release from the sad associations of Sayes Court, she entered willingly enough into Evelyn's plans for placing her in the new Queen's household; but his project for a religious community in which

[17] BL Add. MSS 78628 A: plan of Sayes Court, 1653; 78340, fo. 89: 'still house'.

[18] BL Add. MS 78296: JE to Jane Glanville, 17 Nov. 1650.

[19] University of Sheffield Library, Hartlib Papers 29/8/10B: Ephemerides, 1660; BL Add. MS 78434: Glanville to ME, 1 June 1664.

[20] BL Add. MS 78221: JE to Browne, 11 Oct. 1652, 25 Feb 1652/3; JE, *Diary*, iii. 87.

[21] BL Add. MSS 78221: JE to Browne, 11 Mar. 1657/8; 78439: ME to Susan Hungerford, [1658].

[22] BL Add. MS 78539: ME to Ralph Bohun, 12 Apr. [*c.*1670].

they would live together but 'decently asunder' appealed to her even more. 'Doe but imagine how we designed to live in our cells and you may judge of my life from the time I rise to my going to bed,' she wrote to him during one of his absences, 'as regularly and as pleasantly as I could propose it, if I might add the contentment of visiting you in your solitude which is the only want I finde, my ambition being not soe great as it is beleeved.'[23]

In fact her life at Sayes Court after the Restoration continued much as before. Her husband was away more often, but her father returned from France and joined the household. She made more of Evelyn's pleasure than her own in her resumed childbearing; 'though I am dayly indisposed, I cannot much lament my condition, because it may prove a satisfaction in the conclusion to some persons who pretend to be well pleased with the hopes of an addition to their care'. But the child, another boy called Richard, died after only a few weeks.[24] Occasionally she came up to London, paid her respects to the Queen Mother at Somerset House, visited the playhouse, and was more at home there than her husband. Just as conscious as he was of the gulf which separated the Restoration theatre from the idealizing, platonic modes of their youth, she was quite prepared to relish the sharp, cynical comedy of 'moderne humours' which he found irredeemably vicious and degenerate: 'plays now are but . . . Epitomies of the folly of life', she admitted, 'great and noble parts are layde aside, the desire of transmitting virtue to posterity dos not much torment the minds of the living', and yet even if it was an errant age they lived in, it was a discerning one. While Evelyn thought the presence of women on stage an incitement to immorality and Nell Gwyn an impudent comedian, to his wife 'ayrey Nell' was 'the life of the play' whenever she appeared.[25]

Her life at Sayes Court was not altogether secluded. The navy and dockyard folk were nearby. In imitation of the traditional hospitality of his childhood, Evelyn always entertained his tenants and neighbours over the Christmas season. In summer there were exchange visits between Sayes Court and Wotton, and a constant stream of visitors, from royalty downwards, to see the famous garden. 'Do not impute my silence to neglect', Mary Evelyn wrote to one of her correspondents, 'Had you seen me these ten days continually entertaining persons of different humour, age and sense, not only at meals, or afternoon, or the time of a civil visit, but from morning till night, you will be assured it was impossible for me to finish these lines sooner.'[26] But

[23] BL Add. MS 78300: ME to JE, 27 Apr. 1660.
[24] BL Add. MS 78439: ME to Sir Samuel Tuke, [1663]; JE, *Diary*, iii. 368, 371.
[25] BL Add. 78359: ME to Bohun, 19 Mar. [1667], 23 June 1668.
[26] Ibid.: ME to Bohun, 21 May [1668].

in winter their circle could contract to 'a philosopher, a woman and a child, heaps of books our food and entertainment, silence a law so strictly observed that neither dog nor cat dares transgress it, the crackling of the ice and whistling winds are our music which if continued long in the same quarter may possibly freeze our wits as well as our penns though Apollo were himselfe amongst us'.[27] Evelyn would sometimes refer to Sayes Court as 'this Monasterie', where they were employed 'Reading, Working, Painting, &c as well content as they who Dresse, & Droll & Play'. Whether Mary Evelyn was always as well content is less clear. Court acquaintances, he noted wryly, pitied his wife as the unhappiest woman in the world, and her cousin Sir Samuel Tuke was concerned that having 'layen soe long with a Philosopher', she was becoming too used to 'spiritual cognation'.[28]

Tuke was a former cavalier who had converted to Roman Catholicism during his exile in France. After the Restoration he joined the household of Arundel's grandson, Henry Howard, as tutor to his sons. He was an early member of the Royal Society, a successful playwright, and noted for his 'fine discourse'.[29] So when he made it clear that he relished Mary Evelyn's conversation as much as her husband's and told Evelyn himself that he loved her, 'but with soe faultless a passion that it can never offend the respect I have for her, nor my friendship to you', she was flattered and his admiration drew her out. She even felt free to make mild mockery to him of her husband's growing fame, comparing his *Sylva*, with its 'Kalendarium Hortense', to an astrologer's almanac, 'foretelling the disasters of plants if not sett just in such a face and minute of the Moone, with rules and secrets how to governe plantation from the Tallest Tree to the meanest shrub'.[30] A franker and more mischief-making admirer was Evelyn's widowed brother-in-law William Glanville, who told her that he was glad they had not come to know each other until middle life; 'for I am conscious I could not have Trusted myself with loving you twenty years agoe as well as I doe now; you in those dayes might have been safe in your Vertue but I could not then bee sure of my peace'.[31]

Meanwhile the only remaining boy, Jack, was growing up with his long-lost brother's unattainable standard always before him. He was only 2 years old when his father pronounced him 'a goodly child, but not of so ready an apprehension as the other was at his age'.[32] He grew up wayward and unstable

---

[27] BL Add. MS 78439: ME to Tuke, [late 1660s?].
[28] BL Add. MSS 78298: JE to Jael Boscawen, 1 Oct. 1689; 78392: JE, 'The Legend of Philaretes and the Pearle', [c.1673]; 78435: Tuke to ME, 22 May 1663.
[29] Pepys, *Diary*, ix. 449.
[30] BL Add. MSS 78306: Tuke to JE, 9 Dec. 1659; 78439: ME to Tuke, [late 1663].
[31] BL Add. MS 78434: Glanville to ME, 21 Aug. 1673.
[32] BL Add. MS 78221: JE to Browne, 6 Mar. 1657.

and with the added handicap of a crooked leg, which his father contracted
expensively with a surgeon to correct.[33] And so Jack had to wear 'coats' long
past the age when most boys were put into breeches to conceal the braces on
his legs. In a society which valued graceful movement in its men of fashion
he was already relegated to second class status. His mother was affectionate but
detached. When his tutor sent an unduly flattering report after he had been
a few weeks away from home, she remarked with mild incredulity that it was
next to a miracle that the boy 'should sing, paint, be civill and which is more,
cleanly in so short a time'.[34] His disability meant that he was never sent to
school. He had his first education under Tuke in the Howard household; then,
when further contact with Roman Catholicism was deemed imprudent, a
tutor of his own at home. The first, Milton's nephew Edward Philips, did not
last long, but his replacement was the young Oxford man, Ralph Bohun.[35]

Like Mary Evelyn's husband and father, Bohun was a highly educated
man. Unlike them he was not set in authority over her. In theory a tutor had
a subordinate status in the household, but Bohun was already a friend of the
Wotton Evelyns (his ancestors had once owned the estate) and in practice he
lived at Sayes Court on equal terms with the family. In asking his Oxford friends
to recommend a likely candidate, Evelyn had assured them that 'he will find
his condition with us easy, his scholar a delight, and the conversation not
to be despised; this obliges me to wish he might not be a morose or severe
person'. Bohun for his part took the post because it would enable him 'to live
in good company & see the world with lesse restraint than in a Bishop's
family'.[36] While he could not be called morose, they did find he was given
to moods, fits of spleen as he called them, which he could mock amusingly
in himself:

> When strangers come he sits alone
> And of his spleen makes hideous mone
> Come Mr Bohun why sit you so
> Come pray go in, but spleen says no
> The ladys fain would have you play
> Ladys say so, but spleen says nay . . .
> Yet for all this he never came
> Tis rudnesse though spleen bear the blame
> Define it then, spleen's a disease
> Of doing allways what we please.[37]

[33] Hiscock II, 73.   [34] BL Add. MS 78539: ME to Bohun, 19 Mar. [1667].
[35] JE, *Diary*, iii. 364–5, 401.
[36] Bray, iii. 154: JE to Christopher Wren, 4 Apr. 1665; BL Add. MS 78314: Bohun to JE, 22 Apr. 1667.
[37] BL Add. MS 78456: verses by Bohun, [*c.*1669–70].

His relations with Evelyn were never quite easy, and his pupil tried to run away after a few weeks, complaining of his tutor's severity, and reached New Cross before he was intercepted by a neighbour and sent home;[38] but he struck up a lasting friendship with Mary Evelyn. She could tease him out of his moods and bring out his sense of humour—she called him a 'droll'—and his capacity for good talk. In turn he appreciated her 'even style, & masculine notions' and her calm self-possession: 'you are almost the only Lady living that can content your selfe with doing well & not dote upon prayse: you performe that in a silent closset which whole courts & Theaters would unanimously applaud'.[39] The basic premiss of their friendship, elaborated with much enjoyable self-parody on both sides, was that Bohun brought companionship and intellectual stimulation to her secluded domesticity, while she exercised a much-needed civilizing influence over a personality warped by the pedantic and masculine collegiate life of the university. The 'wooden parlour' became not so much the common-room of a group of monastic cells as a kind of miniature Parisian salon. 'Though I never breathed the soft aire of the continent', Bohun wrote, 'yet since my admission into the good company of Says Court, I am almost grown civil by contact'; and since she was only a country housewife who would not have known of the Fire of London if she had not been taken to Southwark to see the flames, or of the Dutch invasion of the Medway if she had not heard the guns go off at Chatham, 'I hope you'l acknowledge my company though with some grains of rudenes much better then the solitude either of the Wooden Parlor & working closett.'[40]

After a trial period at Oxford which was not a success, Bohun returned with his pupil to Sayes Court and for the next two years was a full-time member of the household. Meanwhile Mary Evelyn's childbearing had fully resumed. While Evelyn took it for granted that she would bear him more sons, Tuke was more sensitive: 'I know the common preference of the genders, yet truly Cozin I would it might bee a Girle like the worthy Mother.'[41] Little Mary, or 'Mall', was a solemn doll-like baby whom her father called 'the puppet' and Bohun 'the infanta of Sayes Court' or 'the little Vertuosa'.[42] Unlike her brothers she throve, and her mother in her undemonstrative way doted on her. Two years later Mary Evelyn was able to announce to Glanville with her usual mild irony, that 'another of the trifling sex is now added to our number'.[43] Then in 1669 Susan arrived, making the 'little flock of girls' complete.

---

[38] BL Add. MSS 73431: JE to ME, 22 Sept. 1665; 78317: R. Waith to JE, 20 Aug. [1666].

[39] BL Add. MS 78435: Bohun to ME, [Feb.], [Mar.–Apr. 1667?].

[40] Ibid.: Bohun to ME, postmarked 13 Feb. [1668?].

[41] Ibid.: Tuke to ME, 23 Nov. [1664?].

[42] BL Add. MSS 78221: ME to Sir Richard Browne, 8 Nov. 1665; 78435: Bohun to ME, 17 June [1667], 10 May 1668.

[43] BL Add. MS 78438: ME to Glanville, [Sept. 1667?].

Bohun would not be won over even by little Mall's engaging first addresses to him as 'Mitte Boun'. His ideal, fostered by Oxford college life, remained a household 'where the kitchen & Nursery [are] as remote as your pigeon house'.[44] Sayes Court was not a large house and the children, the cherished survivors of so many bereavements, were allowed to be unruly. 'Your Godaughter beggs your Blessing', Mrs Evelyn wrote to her niece at Wotton, 'and is allmost able to make her party good with her sisters persecuter'— Jack—'by scratching and calling names, which he teaches her in great perfection. I wish you heere often that wee might laugh somtimes. The new Nursery proves a great affliction to Mr Bohun.'[45] His fits of spleen increased. Partly in revenge for her amusement at his discomfiture, partly in jealousy at these new claims on her attention, he began to tease her for wasting her finer abilities in domestic trivia:

is it not something odd to consider that a Lady who has been applauded in two great courts, prays'd and admir'd, and her friendship desir'd of all . . . shoud now wholly be abandon'd to the conduct of her domestic affairs, And her most important concerns either to make laws in the nursery, or pyes and tarts in the kitchen, or serve under Mrs Turner in the stilhouse. These are employments that degrade from her self, & render her mortal as other women. Thus Madam Evelyn is farr greatest in idea, & the way to maintaine her character to the best advantage is not to contemplate her in the stilhouse or nursery, but as she was heretofore in her agreeable conversation.[46]

Although Mary Evelyn had adapted herself so thoroughly to the domesticity prescribed by her husband, the frustration of her other abilities remained a sensitive subject, as Bohun had evidently discerned. While he was at Oxford she had sent him an uncharacteristically bitter account of a visit to her old acquaintance, Margaret Cavendish, at her Clerkenwell mansion. As a gauche maid of honour, Margaret Lucas had been married from the Brownes' house in Paris. Now a duchess, with an indulgent husband and no domestic responsibilities, she was flaunting her singularity by publishing, in immense and costly folios, her frank and eccentric opinions about science and philosophy (the latest in the form of a feminist utopian romance entitled *The Blazing World*), and accepting the homage of Oxford and the Royal Society as her due. Her works, however self-indulgent, were genuinely interesting and she was willing to acknowledge her long acquaintance with Mary Evelyn by addressing her as 'daughter' and escorting her down to the courtyard of the ducal town house when they parted. Yet the 'daughter' remained implacably

[44] BL Add. MSS 78314: Bohun to JE, [Mar. 1667?]; 78435: Bohun to ME, 26 Oct. [1674].
[45] BL Add. MS 78439: ME to Mary Evelyn of Wotton, [late 1669?].
[46] BL Add. MS 78435: Bohun to ME, 26 Oct. [1674].

hostile to this woman who had refused to be confined by conventional female roles and behaviours:

Her mien surpasses the imagination of poets, or the descriptions of the romance heroine's greatness; her gracious bows, seasonable nods, courteous stretching out of her hands, twinkling of her eyes, and various gestures of approbation, show what may be expected from her discourse, which is as airy, empty, whimsical, and rambling as her books, aiming at science, difficulties, high notions, terminating commonly in nonsense, oaths, and obscenity . . . then she took occasion to justify her faith, to give an account of her religion, as new and unintelligible as her philosophy, to cite her own pieces line and page in such a book, and to tell the adventures of some of her nymphs. At last I grew weary and concluded that the creature called a chimera, which I had heard speak of, was now to be seen, and that it was time to retire for fear of infection; yet I hope, as she is an original, she may never have a copy. Never did I see a woman so full of herself, so amazingly vain and ambitious.[47]

She knew very well that Bohun usually read her letters aloud to his Oxford coterie, so this was not just an outlet for her own feelings, but a rebuke to these learned men for their readiness to condone in the eccentric Duchess of Newcastle what they would not have tolerated for a moment in their own womenfolk. For even while he teased her for keeping her own abilities 'confind in the parlour cupboard, lock't up with the spirit of mint & oranges, & a new receipt for plum cake', Bohun was able to turn the screw by hinting at the ridicule which awaited her, a mere country gentlewoman, if she followed the Duchess's example and abandoned her proper sphere: 'I could make much pleasnt'ner reflexions, should you neglect your family concerns only to appear a vertuosa, should the lady be counted a wit while the children look't like little blacks & the house in disorder, whilst she was composing poems & books of Blazing worlds.' And his parting comment was very close to the bone: 'I really and in earnest condole within my self, to foresee that a Lady who might have been compared to Madam Scureman or Scudery for her refined and admirable parts must now in a few years degenerate into a good Queen Elizabeth Huswife.'[48]

Mary Evelyn did not let all this, disturbing as it was, upset their friendship. With his tendency to melancholy, Bohun needed her regard and her correspondence long after he had left her household to become a country clergyman in an isolated parish. And so while they both knew that much of her ability had been frustrated by her life at Sayes Court, he learnt that the other claims on her attention were not a threat and paid tribute to her

[47] JE, *Diary*, iii. 478–83; Harris, 'Living in the Neighbourhood of Science . . .' 198–9; Anna Battigelli, *Margaret Cavendish and the Exiles of the Mind* (Lexington, Ky., 1998), 85–113.
[48] BL Add. MS 78435: Bohun to ME, 29 Mar. [1668?], 26 Oct. [1674].

capacity for sustained, intelligent, and various friendship: 'I have sometimes wonderd, how so many of them, & of so different inclinations could consist together like the images in the phancy or memorie, which tho they are so various . . . remain all distinct without disordering or the confusion of each other'; and 'those who have observed your brother Glanvil & myself, sitting at your table amidst all our disputes . . . will conclude that Mrs Evelyn had no lesse an influence in governing the passions of others then her own'. Glanville agreed, not just about her practised stoicism but about her underlying moral worth: 'you are a great mistress of your passions, a good and a generous minded person'.[49]

Evelyn was less ready than Tuke or Glanville to praise his wife openly, but he agreed that she had more than fulfilled the promise he had seen in her as a child and become the pattern of a domestic companion: 'sweet, and (though not charming) agreeable; pious, loyal, and of so just a temper, obliging and withall discreet, as has made me very happy'.[50] There was complete confidence between them: 'You are my selfe & I trust you with all,' he wrote to her during the mortal danger of the plague; and she replied, 'what have I to value if you faile, or indeed for trust to, that can be more deare to me'. In a letter written long after, during an illness from which she did not expect to recover, she vowed that she had been faithful to his bed and interest through-out their marriage, and it was clearly true.[51]

Yet it was always a match of affection and respect, not of romance or passion. Evelyn's remark to his son that the sensual pleasures of marriage were trifling and did not come up to the imagination is revealing; so is his descrip-tion of his wife as agreeable but not charming. There were longeurs, 'satiety in the estate conjugal', as he described it, probably on both sides, and some-times absence was necessary 'to reinforce and kindle their Affections'.[52] Certainly there were failures of sensitivity and understanding on his part. Simply by following his precepts and devoting herself to housekeeping, his wife came to seem to him insufficiently spiritualized, more a Martha than a Mary; and he could claim the highest biblical warrant for valuing the latter as 'the better part'.[53] Mary Evelyn's mainstay was her Christian stoicism, and her piety was unostentatious. Her chronic ill health in the winters, perhaps

---

[49] Ibid.: Bohun to ME, 26 Jan. [167-]; 78434: Glanville to ME, 25 May 1669.
[50] BL Add. MS 78392: 'The Legend of Philaretes and the Pearle', [*c.*1673].
[51] BL Add. MSS 78431: JE to ME, 22 Sept. 1665; 78300: ME to JE, 28 Sept. 1665; 1 June 1693.
[52] BL Add. MS 78386: 'Oeconomics', [1676], p. 9.
[53] When Evelyn's granddaughter was baptized Martha Maria, he prayed she might choose the better part; JE, *Diary*, iv. 324 (the reference of course is to the biblical story of the sisters Martha and Mary, for which see Luke 10: 38–42).

aggravated by repression of feeling, became something of an exasperation to him in his own robustness and constant activity.[54] So perhaps did his sense that for all her loyalty she maintained her independent judgement. In fact, from her very prescribed function as his housekeeper, his permitted sexual partner, and the mother of his children, he had never expected a wife to satisfy his desire for romance and idealism. For this he turned to his friendships.

He had been familiar with courtly neoplatonism from his youth as the pre-vailing culture at the Parisian salon and, under the auspices of Henrietta Maria, of the Caroline court. After his return to England in the 1650s he had links through Jeremy Taylor with the indigenous 'circle of friendship' estab-lished by the poet Katherine Philips, whose members, both men and women, all had coterie names (Orinda, Silvander, Palaemon, Cassandra, and so on) drawn from platonic plays and romances. In his 'Discourse on Friendship', addressed to Katherine Philips, Jeremy Taylor defined friend-ship as 'the nearest love and the nearest society of which the persons are capa-ble', but he explicitly rejected the platonic trappings; 'they being but the images of more noble bodies, are but like tinsel dressings, which will shew bravely by candle-light, and do excellently in a mask, but are not fit for . . . the material intercourses of our life'; and he cautioned against 'dreaming of perfect and abstracted friendships', and making them 'so immaterial that they perish in the handling'. And when she asked whether men or women made the better friends, he conceded that 'in peaceful cities and times, virtuous women are the beauties of society and the prettinesses of friendship', but took it as self-evident that they could not be such effective friends as men.[55] Clarendon, whose intense friendships were the support of his turbulent public life, agreed; and so did Bacon.[56] For these men, making their careers at times of risk and subterfuge, friendship was essentially a league between trustworthy members of their own sex for mutual support and furtherance of their ends. Ultimately the last two at least were also harking back to the original platonic view that love between men was of a higher order than intercourse between the sexes.

Evelyn's early friendships with his Middle Temple companions, James Thicknesse, Thomas Henshaw, and Philip Packer, were very much in this mode.

---

[54] BL Add. MS 78431: JE to ME, 30 July 1685.

[55] *The Collected Works of Katherine Philips, the Matchless Orinda: The Poems*, ed. Patrick Thomas, (Stump Cross, 1990), 8–9; Jeremy Taylor, *The Whole Works* (1847), ix. 301–35 (quotes from 313–14, 331).

[56] 'Of Friendship', in Edward Hyde, 1st Earl of Clarendon, *A Collection of Several Tracts of the Right Honourable Edward, Earl of Clarendon* (1727), 131; Francis Bacon, *Essays*, ed. B. Vickers (Oxford, 1999), 59–65.

Like Clarendon addressing his beloved Lord Falkland as 'dear sweetheart', they called each other 'charissime', 'sweet Mr Evelyn', 'dearest amico', even my better part', and Packer would sign himself, 'stedfastly and constantly my Deare Thy most faithful servant & lover Philomax'.[57] All these male friendships stood the test of time, but after his first youth Evelyn came to feel that they were not fully satisfying. Aware in himself of a lack of tenderness, he thought the 'natural harshnesse of the Masculine temper' made men too 'morose, and rigorous to one another'.[58] They would always be potential rivals. In this respect he found women more rewarding companions. Although utterly conventional in his view of their social roles, he was never misogynistic; he did not, like some of his male contemporaries, see female piety simply as a manifestation of their weakness.[59] His formative experience of an exceptionally loving and pious mother, sister, and grandmother had been reinforced by the Devout Humanism he had encountered in France, with its appeal to women's pre-eminent religious and moral qualities.[60] When Robert Boyle wrote of the transitory and unsatisfying love of women, Evelyn responded with a sentimental but passionate tribute to its nurturing and saving grace: 'the committee chambers, and the parliament lobby, are sad, but evident testimonies of the patience, and the address, the love, and the constancy of these gentle creatures . . . they bear us out of love, and they give us such; they divert us when we are well, and tend us when we are sick; they grieve over us when we die, and some I have known, that would not be comforted and survive'.[61]

Whether male or female relationships were set higher, there was agreement, at least amongst lay commentators, that friendship was something apart from procreative love in marriage and in some respects superior to it: 'nuptial love maketh mankind', Bacon pronounced, endorsing neoplatonic orthodoxy, 'friendly love perfecteth it'.[62] Clarendon would even venture to say that it was 'more a Sacrament' than marriage.[63] For the cleric Taylor it was not safe to allow that a friend could ever be 'more than a husband or wife'; marriage ought in theory to be 'the queen of friendships', and in this he was following the prevailing view of puritan conduct books written by married

---

[57] BL Add. 78311: Henshaw to JE, 1645–6, Thicknesse to JE, 27 Apr. 1640, 16 Nov. 1644; Packer to JE, 3/13 Jan. 1650.

[58] BL Add. MS 78386: 'Oeconomics', [1676], p. 16.

[59] Anthony Fletcher, *Gender, Sex and Subordination in England 1500–1800* (New Haven, 1995), 347.

[60] Erica Veevers, *Images of Love and Religion: Queen Henrietta Maria and Court Entertainments* (Cambridge, 1989), 21–33, 77–80.

[61] Bray, iii. 123: JE to Boyle, 29 Sept. 1659.

[62] Bacon, *Essays*, 23.   [63] Clarendon, 'Of Friendship', 133.

clergy.[64] The painter Mary Beale, herself the partner in a notable companionate marriage and part of close-knit circle of clerical friends, drew on the same tradition from a female standpoint in her contribution to the literature on friendship.[65] But Taylor and his circle would also say that in practice a wife might be found 'not so proper for all the relations of Friendship',[66] and Evelyn was also divided. He told the unmarried Robert Boyle that 'if to have the fruition and the knowledge of our friends in heaven' would be a great part of the reward there, 'how great is that of the married like to prove, since there is not on earth a friendship comparable to it?' Yet from the very beginning of his married life he reserved the right to make 'vertuous friendships' with other women, confident that he could do so 'without violating my vows or the honour of the person'.[67] It was clear that he regarded it as necessary for the completeness, not just of his emotional but of his spiritual life. Friendship, not marriage, remained for him the platonic ideal, 'the very soule of the World', the means by which higher reality could be apprehended.[68]

In its heroic but impossible dedication to the spiritualizing of desire, platonic love could seem a forbidding and dehumanizing discipline. Even its advocates acknowledged that it was more suited to age than youth, whose overwhelming sensual feelings could not realistically be subdued in this way.[69] In its courtly forms it was simply liable to be mocked as an over-refined and over-philosophized plaything:

> Platonic is a pretty name
> But Cupid disavows it;
> It hath no body but in fame;
> Disguise alone allows it
>
> True love cannot divine its end,
> 'Twas by some spirit given

---

[64] Taylor, *Whole Works*, ix. 325–6. Ultimately the view of marriage as friendship could be traced to Aristotle and Thomas Aquinas; on the whole subject, see Edmund Leites, 'The Duty to Desire: Love, Friendship and Sexuality in some Puritan Theories of Marriage', *Journal of Social History*, 15 (1982), 383–408.

[65] BL Harleian MS 6828, fos. 510–23; Tabitha Barber, *Mary Beale* (1999), 30–4.

[65] Francis Finch of Rushock ('Palaemon' in Katherine Philips' circle), *Friendship* (1654), quoted in Hiscock I, 14 (and see also his article in *Review of English Studies* 15 (1939), 466–8); cf. Taylor, *Whole Works*, ix. 330–1.

[67] Bray, iii. 124–5: JE to Boyle, 29 Sept. 1659. BL Add. MS 78392: JE, 'The Legend of Philaretes and the Pearle', [c.1673].

[68] BL Add. MS 78328, p. 153: commonplace notes under 'amicitia'.

[69] Baldesar Castiglione, *The Book of the Courtier*, trans. George Bull (Harmondsworth, 1967), 333–6; Jill Kraye, 'The Transformation of Platonic Love in the Italian Renaissance', in Anna Baldwin and Sarah Hutton (eds.), *Platonism and the English Imagination* (Cambridge, 1994), 82–3; Veevers, *Images of Love and Religion*, 17–18.

That ne'er knew further than a friend
Its proper sphere is heaven.[70]

It was the contribution of the salon versions of platonic love to humanize it, by admitting an element of cheerful, creative, though still idealistic socializing between men and women.[71] This was precisely the aspect which made it appealing to Evelyn, though in an aside to his wife he made it clear that she was not to think of taking the same freedoms herself; not because he feared she would be unfaithful, but because he suspected being made fun of. He warned her against the 'kind of conversation . . . disguised under the name of Platonique love, they nourish now more than ever they did, to the dishonour of the whole sex: Every lady has her Gallant (as they call them) before whome if shee can jeere her husband and lay open his imperfections, she only goes for a witt amongst them . . . and therefore a modest Wife should be carefull to avoid these occasions'.[72]

Yet for all his own receptivity, in twenty years of his marriage he never encountered, he says, more than two or three women with whom he could go beyond the civilities of ordinary acquaintance, 'which did not match the Idea I had Conceiv'd'.[73] The first, during his visit to London after his marriage, was a young married woman of about his own age whom he called 'Platona'. She was Ann Russell, who had been brought up in the Treasurer's house in Deptford and had close family connections with Cromwell, but when Evelyn knew her she was the estranged wife of a Welsh royalist, Colonel John Bodvel, and a kinswoman of his sisters-in-law. As such he felt free to visit her and her two young daughters and bring them presents of cherries. Her version of the name in her lively, misspelled letters was 'Plattony', and in return she dubbed him 'the pilgrim Tassarantus' and hung his portrait by Nanteuil in her bedchamber, 'and doe dayly make it my s[ain]t for it is the first object I see when I am at my beads fastinge'.[74] It was this combination of wit, cheerfulness, and piety by which he was always to define his ideal female friend. When he returned to Paris there was another young woman whom he called 'Electra' to fill her place; she was Elizabeth Carey, daughter of Thomas

[70] Roger, 3rd Lord North, 'Platonic', in *The New Oxford Book of 17th Century Verse*, ed. A. Fowler (Oxford, 1991), 175–6.

[71] Veevers, *Images of Love and Religion*, 14–18.

[72] BL Add. MS 78430: 'Instructions Oeconomique', 1648, fo. 23.

[73] BL Add. MS 78392: 'The Legend of Philaretes and the Pearle', [c.1673].

[74] BL Add. MSS 78315, 78316: Ann Bodvel to JE, 3 Sept. [1649]; 13 Jan. 1651. In her letters she mentions the Offleys (the family of George Evelyn's second wife); she was also related to Anne (Mynne), wife of Sir John Lewknor and sister of Richard Evelyn jun.'s wife; see 78315: Lady Garret to JE, 5 Nov. 1649; J. Comber, *Sussex Genealogies* (1933), 156, 162; A. H. Dodd, 'The Tragedy of Col. John Bodvel', *Transactions of the Caernarvonshire Historical Society*, 6 (1945), 1–22.

Carey, one of the grooms of the bedchamber (as was Margaret Blagge's father) to the exiled King. She and Mary Evelyn were constant companions and called each other sister, but Elizabeth had all the vivacity her friend lacked. Evelyn drew a vivid picture of her as 'a fine built Creature', entertaining the gallants in the drawing room and enjoying their homage, strolling with him in the Tuileries gardens and quick-wittedly exchanging impromptu verses. Yet she was also devout and deferential. On her table one day he found 'a piece of solemn devotion' for the regulation of her life, which he read without her knowledge and afterwards observed that 'she liv'd up to it exactly'. She would often ask his advice, and he found himself 'infinitly betterd by hers'; soon this 'grew to a Confidence so innocent, so intire that if she had ben my sister, & that sister an Angel I could not have lov'd her more, nor was anything so agreable to me as the progresse of our friendship'.[75]

Back in England they continued to correspond, she addressing him as 'Dear Master' or 'Dear Governor', he responding with letters of extravagant compliment to her 'many perfections'; but 'your good humour, and Piety, do in my opinion gild all the rest, and render you infinitely deare to me'.[76] The friendship with Mary Evelyn was unaffected; she wistfully named one of the arbours of friendship in the Morin garden at Sayes Court 'Caryes cabinet' and embellished it with emblems of the more adventurous Elizabeth; 'it is a place I often visit, not without wishing you with me, and for want of so agreeable a companion I entertain my self with *Cassandra*; yet fancy your life well written would make a better romance'.[77] An heiress with many suitors, Elizabeth Carey was eventually matched with the most daring and effective of the royalist agents, John Mordaunt, a younger son of the Wotton Evelyns' neighbour, Lady Peterborough. When he was arrested in 1658 she shared his imprisonment and helped to save his life when he was tried for treason, and it was by her means that Evelyn was also swept up into the royalist plotting which preceded the Restoration. Afterwards he continued to address his exuberant epistles to her in the best salon manner as 'my muse and my mistress' and it must have been at his suggestion that the Mordaunts named their house at Parson's Green 'Villa Carey'. But by this time she had a growing family (eventually seven sons and four daughters) and her erratic husband had become a source of anxiety in quite different ways. In 1668 they had to go

[75] BL Add. MSS 78392: JE, 'The Legend of Philaretes and the Pearle', [c.1673]; 78439: ME to 'Dear sister' [Elizabeth Carey, Viscountess Mordaunt], [1657]; 78221: JE to Sir Richard Browne 30 June 1657.

[76] BL Add. MSS 78298: JE to Elizabeth Carey, 12 Sept. 1655, 3, 20 Feb., 19 May 1656; 78309: Elizabeth Carey to JE, 11 Apr. 1656.

[77] BL Add. MS 78439: ME to [Elizabeth Mordaunt], [1657].

abroad hastily when he was accused of seducing the daughter of one of his subordinates and unlawfully imprisoning her father.[78] Although she maintained her exemplary devotional life, what she wanted from her male friends, especially in widowhood and as her health began to fail, was not platonic or spiritual fellowship, but financial advice and guardianship for her children.[79] Evelyn never ceased to honour her piety, but he was inclined to feel thwarted at the petering out into practicalities of a relationship which he regarded as a necessary complement to his marriage.

A light-hearted platonic flirtation nearer at hand with Lady Newton of Charlton, 'the fayre Genius in Garden and Grove', ended when she and her husband moved to Warwickshire in 1658.[80] Then it was not until the Carterets moved into the Treasurer's house after the Restoration that Evelyn glimpsed any further possibility. Sir George Carteret was an able and genial Jersey cavalier, colonial proprietor, and man of business. Samuel Pepys, who saw much of the family during marriage negotiations between Carteret's son and his patron Lord Sandwich's daughter, found him 'the most kind father and pleased father in his children that ever I saw', and his wife 'a most noble lady and most mighty kind'. They had five daughters, of whom the two eldest, Anne (Lady Slanning) and Caroline (Lady Scot), were just married and Louise-Margaretta, Betty, and Rachel still in the nursery. Evelyn quickly became friendly with the whole family and Lady Slanning was soon singled out for his special attention. Pepys, who found her 'the best humoured woman in the world', observed that she also spent much time on her knees at her closet devotions; it was exactly the combination of beauty, liveliness, and religiosity which Evelyn always looked for.[81] At the end of a laboriously playful letter addressed to Lady Carteret as 'My deare Mother', he added, 'Be pleas'd to make my Servises acceptable to the three Graces (your Lady Daughters): my Seraphic, my Lady Scot, and Madam Would-be. I have not the honor to be knowne to the Star of the East [Jemima Montagu, Lord Sandwich's daughter] . . . but I am humble servant to all that call you Mother.'[82]

'My Seraphic': the term was also a platonic one but one with a Christian context, signifying 'the seraphic fire' or ardent angelic devotion of the

---

[78] *The Letter-book of John, Viscount Mordaunt 1658–1660*, ed. Mary Coate, Camden Society, 3rd ser., 69 (1945), pp. vii, x–xi, xv, xx–xxi, 64; BL Add. MS 78298: JE to Lady Mordaunt, 1 Jan. 1662.

[79] JE, *Diary*, iv. 80–1, 108–9, 140, 173.

[80] BL Add. MS 78298: JE to Lady Newton, 12 Mar. 1656. Lady Newton (afterwards Puckering) was a relation of Sir Robert Moray; see *The Memoirs of Anne, Lady Halkett, and Ann, Lady Fanshawe*, ed. John Loftis (Oxford, 1979), 69; also in general David McKitterick, 'Women and their Books in Seventeenth Century England: The Case of Elizabeth Puckering', *Library*, 7th ser., 1 (2000), 372–8.

[81] Pepys, *Diary*, iv. 254, vi. 182, vii. 295.

[82] BL Add. MS 78298: JE to Lady Carteret, 4 Dec. 1665.

seraphims, and the earthly love which prefigured it. Pietro Bembo's famous exposition of platonic love in the fourth book of Castiglione's *Book of the Courtier* traced the stages by which love guided the soul from individual to universal beauty, and 'so, in the last stage of perfection, it guides the soul from the particular intellect to the universal intellect. And from there, aflame with the sacred fire of true divine love, the soul flies to unite itself with the angelic nature.'[83] But the work which naturalized the concept in England was Robert Boyle's treatise, *Some Motives to the Love of God, better known as Seraphick Love*, the last but only surviving essay of a series on the nature of love and love-making. Couched in the form of a letter to a friend Lindamor (also the name of a character from Honoré d'Urfé's platonic romance *L'Astrée*), who had been slighted by the woman he loved, it urged him to convert his human passion into religious devotion; 'that unsatisfiedness with transitory fruitions that men deplore as the unhappiness of their transitory nature' being 'a sign that the only true satisfaction could come from the love of God'. The work, which ran to four editions in the first decade of the Restoration, made the term 'seraphic love' almost as familiar as its platonic variant.[84] Soon Mary Evelyn could refer to her husband's 'seraphicks', a courtier could remark on the King's utter lack of interest in the 'seraphic part' of love-making, the charismatic London clergyman Simon Patrick could engage in 'seraphic discourse' with a devoted female parishioner, and suburban congregations could hear sermons which echoed Boyle's treatise almost to the letter.[85] Inevitably the term acquired an ironic edge as well, signifying a fanatical or pretentious concern with sublimities, one too exalted for the uses of this world: a meaning well caught by George Mackenzie's mock-precious reference to 'the seraphick Mr Boyle'.[86]

If Evelyn began to envisage any such friendship with Lady Slanning, the prospect soon vanished. By 1668 Carteret had been implicated in the financial mismanagements of the Dutch war. The family had to vacate the Treasurer's house and leave Deptford for good, and within a year or two Lady

[83] E. H. Gombrich, *Symbolic Images* (1972), 153, quoting the *Heptaplus* of Pico della Mirandola; Castiglione, *Book of the Courtier*, 340.

[84] Robert Boyle, *Works*, ed. Michael Hunter and Edward B. Davis (1999), i. 51–133; Lawrence M. Principe, 'Style and Thought of the Early Boyle: Discovery of the 1648 Manuscript of *Seraphic Love*', *Isis*, 85 (1994), 247–60; J. F. Fulton, *A Bibliography of the Honourable Robert Boyle*, Oxford Bibliographical Society, 3 (1932–3), 13–16.

[85] BL Add. MS 78539: ME to Bohun, 19 Nov. [1677]; George Savile, Marquess of Halifax, *Complete Works*, ed. J. P. Kenyon (Hamondsworth, 1969), 252; Simon Patrick, *Works*, ed. A. Taylor (Oxford, 1858), ix. 605–6: Elizabeth Gauden to Patrick, 27 Dec. 1665; BL Add. MS 78364: p. 580: notes by JE of a sermon at Deptford by Dr Richard Parr of Camberwell, 20 Oct. 1672.

[86] *Public and Private Life in the Seventeenth Century: The Mackenzie–Evelyn Debate*, ed. Brian Vickers (New York, 1986), 111.

Slanning was dead in childbirth. Evelyn became more wary and resolved 'never to . . . give myself the anxiety of losing a thing I should value by what accident or misadventur soever'.[87] The Treasurer's office was put into joint administration, and since neither of two officials could lay sole claim to the residence, the state rooms were left to stand empty except for the one apartment occupied by Elizabeth Howard and her children.

This time the acquaintance was a family one. Mary Evelyn and Mrs Howard became close friends and Craven Howard paired off with Jack Evelyn, agreeably distracting him from his classical studies with his schoolboy passion for the gadgets of the new science. Bohun converted his scolding of his pupil at these times into rough and ready verse:

> Jack, you're idle all this day
> You never study, never pray
> What, do you think it just or right
> To gossip on a Sunday night
> From church you stay, you're so untoward
> Till 12 a clock with Madam Howard
> Or for that idle Craven seek
> That studys stars instead of Greek
> Plays with Will Smith and idle boys
> And fills his pocket full of toys
> Brasse ink hornes, dials, burning glasses
> and such idle trump'ry fit for asses
> Such senceless things you're always studying
> Craven's the mountebank you're the jack pudding[88]

With her beauty and conspicuous piety Dorothy Howard might have seemed another promising 'seraphick' for Evelyn—except that she lacked the essential quality of cheerfulness. There were whispers that the Duke of York, with Arabella Churchill in France, had begun to cast eyes on her, but if so she gave him no encouragement. In fact she was a cautious, rather withdrawn young woman, whose chief worry was that the escapades of the other maids of honour would damage her marriage prospects. The Evelyns kindly described her as calm and prudent; others simply called her surly.[89] Her sister Anne was utterly different: an irrepressible *prima donna* of twelve or thirteen, whom they called 'Lady Nanny' or 'ranting Nanny', a red-haired romp and

[87] BL Add. MS 78392: JE, 'The Legend of Philaretes and the Pearle', [c. 1673].

[88] BL Add. 78456: verses by Bohun, [c. 1669–70].

[89] *Lorenzo Magalotti at the Court of Charles II*, 78 ('Miss Libonard' in this context must be a mistranscription from the Italian script for 'Miss Howard'); BL Add. MS 78317: Dorothy Howard to JE, 25 Aug. [1675]; Bray, iv. 33–4: ME to JE, [Dec. 1672]; BL Hammick Papers: SG to MG, 13 Dec. [1675].

a mimic who was in awe of no one and whose presence at Sayes Court dispersed its over-serious atmosphere like a breeze. Clearly she was no seraphic, but Evelyn was still completely charmed. Well aware of being a favourite, she danced around him, teasing him with being a second Diogenes in his tub, calling him 'Morose' (after the character in Jonson's *Epicene*) and setting out to transform him from a disapproving schoolmaster into 'a very grig'. Soon they were calling each other 'playfellow' and Evelyn was lavishing on her his most ecstatic 'nursery language' (as Mrs Evelyn called it), as in this letter written while she was spending part of one summer with friends in Shropshire:

Well I wish there may be never a greene Abricot in all Shrop-shire, that the Pearce & Apples & the plums were guarded like the Hesperides for your sake, and a dreadful Dragon somewhere . . . There's now I thinke on't a Bag-pipe, the Morrice, & the Goose at the end of harvest, and your mind runs a dancing with the Bumkins. What a dismal creature will Playfellow returne . . . such another for a Gemple-woman as was poore Craven for a Squire when he came from Schoole: She must be taughte to Curtsey again, hold in her body, hold out her head, & will forget that ever she was in Putny, & was the best Mime, and the boniest Gyrle, & the frankest, sweetest, sprunkenst, prettiest, Cherr-lypt, Chirping cheerful Playfellow in the world.[90]

One of her witty, chaotic responses, written some years later and supposedly from a vantage point of greater maturity and 'soberiety', recalled her first summer at Deptford:

Most conestant and Loving playfellow, I was I confesse in deep mortification having banisht all thoughts both past and presant of the vanityes of Sayis court—abesence and the mulligrubes begining now to cure those feates of acttivity I wonce playd thare . . . yet as soon as I parceved my self growing to such maturity and wisdom I thought it might be no small favoer to give you the titell of my frind insted of playfelow and ranting Nany: thus was I becom a new cretuer: and full of soberiety when in comes the humble pietiction [petition] as I thought of John Evellin esqier: which I had no sooner parused but all thees good resoluetions vanishit and vanety wonce more took posession for which it had a large subject: together with hard wordes: and supuerfin compilements which you know ganes much upon the weaker vessill: espassally when told wone by a man of conscience: then on the other sid[e] it brought into my memory the begining of my victory over that second dioginus [w]hom with much labour I have at last brought in suj[e]ction to my will and made a very grig: . . . so that I am now as full of mischife as ever, therefor look to your self play-fellow for I shall come lick a lion broke loos from his den and play more tricks than robin goodfellow.

Then she broke into doggerel verse and in a few lines conjured up the Sayes Court household as she had first known it: 'Diogenes' Evelyn; Sir Richard

[90] BL Add. MS 78298: JE to Anne Howard, 27 July 1672.

Browne, 'that sleepy wight', with his early hours and gaping yawns; Mrs Evelyn, 'that lives so circumspect and looks so shy'; Jack, 'in frock like hermit poor'—a reference to the coats which concealed his crooked leg; and 'that quintessence of snuff and spleen', the disapproving Bohun, to whom this addition to the unruly children of the house was the last straw.[91]

Of their friend Margaret Blagge, however, Evelyn was far more wary than of either Dorothy or Anne. At 17 she was no child playfellow, nor was there much sign of innocent good humour. She had the same conscious beauty as Dorothy, but her reputation for raillery was far more intimidating; 'it was said withall that it was something singular, not to say piquant, and that it was hard to acost her without the protection of that which few do carry about with them, a great deal of spirit and a genius fitted for the court'. He now knew himself by hard experience to be 'the most un-fit person in the world for the Enterteinement of the Ante-chamber, and the nimble Spirits that dwell in Fairy-Land'. His wife might be struck by the girl's 'extraordinary Charmes, marks of Vertue, & Discretion in her Conversation', and in his debate with George Mackenzie he had been willing to concede that there were some at court who were genuinely virtuous and devout. But now, having retreated to Sayes Court to nurse his disillusion after the Dutch war, he morosely refused to be convinced that Margaret Blagge was one. He might overlook the gossip and make an exception of Dorothy Howard, 'but to believe there were many Saints in that Country I was not much Inclyn'd'.[92]

Margaret Blagge's background, as Evelyn discovered later, was not unlike his own: that of long-established county gentry. In East Anglia the usual networks of kinship and marriage at this level of society were particularly dense and intricate. The Blagges, settled at Horringer near Bury St Edmunds, were related not once, but sometimes two or three times over generations to a cluster of other county families in the area: the Herveys, the Jermyns, and the Norths. It meant that their court connections were strong; but what they lacked was the solid foundation of wealth and land which the Evelyns had derived from rural industry and trade. Thomas Blagge, Margaret's father, was an eldest son, but after the death of his mother his father had remarried, disposed of his estate, and taken up residence in Bury itself. A second marriage, followed as this was by another brood of children, was usually unwelcome to the sons and daughters of the first, since it could only reduce their patrimony. Effectively dispossessed, Thomas Blagge set out for London and the court to make his fortune.

[91] BL Add. MS 78309: Anne Howard to JE, 20 Nov. [*c.*1673–4], quoted in Hiscock 1, 18–20.
[92] *Life*, 19–20.

By the patronage of his Jermyn relations he was made groom of the bedchamber to Charles I and in 1641 married a young woman of his Suffolk kin, Mary, the daughter of Sir Roger North of Mildenhall.[93] But he clearly had more aptitude for soldiering than for court life, and when the Civil War broke out he commanded a regiment for the King and was made governor of Wallingford in the heart of royalist territory. The fragmentary records of his service give the strong impression of energy, professionalism, and courage. After the royalists' defeat he got away to France, was appointed to the household of the Prince of Wales, and continued to be in the thick of any action or plotting that was going forward, making frequent clandestine journeys to and fro between the Continent and East Anglia as the King's chief agent there.[94]

In the disturbed first decade of their marriage his wife bore him three daughters, but the dates and places of birth of all of them are unknown. Then in 1651 Blagge followed Charles II to Scotland, was captured after the battle of Worcester, and as 'a very dangerous and considerable person', brought to London under close arrest and imprisoned in the Tower.[95] Evelyn particularly remembered Margaret Blagge's birth-date, 2 August 1652, because she shared the month and the year with his son Richard. Mary Blagge was allowed access to her husband in the Tower and this birth-date for her youngest daughter must mean that Margaret was conceived there.[96] Eventually Blagge was freed or managed to make his escape and rejoined the impoverished Charles II in exile.[97] Soon his wife and daughters went abroad as well. The English community on the fringes of Henrietta Maria's court at the Palais Royal, which Evelyn had known well a few years before, offered a safer refuge than Suffolk for the family of a royalist conspirator. Mrs Blagge's kinship with the Queen Mother's Lord Chamberlain and favourite, Henry Jermyn, stood her in good stead, and she and her daughters were soon in

[93] BL Add. MS 19118, fos. 313ᵛ–14: genealogical tables for Blagge; JE, *The Life of Mrs Godolphin*, ed. Samuel Wilberforce (1848), 278; S. A. H. Hervey (ed.), *Horringer Parish Registers* (Woodbridge, 1900), 289.

[94] *Catalogue of the Collection of . . . Alfred Morrison*, ed. A. W. Thibaudeau (1883–92), i. 82–3: Thomas Blagge to Prince Rupert, 'Monday' [1643]; *The Life and Times of Anthony Wood*, ed. Andrew Clark, Oxford Historical Society, 1 (1891), 114–16; *Charles I in 1646*, ed. John Bruce, Camden Society, 59 (1856), 58–9; HMC *Portland MSS*, i, 578–80: Thomas Coke to the Council of State, 2 Apr. 1651; *Calendar of the Clarendon State Papers*, ed. W. Dunn McCray (Oxford, 1869), 41: Charles II to the gentry of East Anglia, 24 Jan. 1650.

[95] Allan Fea (ed.), *After Worcester Fight* (1904), 75–82; *CSP Domestic 1651*, 426, 450, 479, 484.

[96] *Life*, 8; *CSP Domestic 1651*, 492.

[97] BL Add. MS 34326, fo. 10ᵛ: Thomas Blagge to the Council of State, Mar. 1652; *CSP Domestic 1654*, 408; G. S. Steinmann, 'Memorials Preserved at Bruges of King Charles the Second's Residence', *Archaeologia*, 35 (1853), 337.

good standing there.[98] When the rest of the family returned to England at the Restoration, the 7-year-old Margaret was left behind for several more months in the charge of the Queen Mother's groom of the stole, Lady Guildford. A pretty and quick-witted child, she was already marked out as likely to do well in a court, and this household, which included Charles II's favourite young sister Minette, was an agreeable place for young people; though it was not without dangers as well, as she afterwards told Evelyn. Lady Guildford, a Roman Catholic convert, tried to persuade Margaret to go to mass with her:

our young Saint would not onely not be perswaded to it; but Asserted her better Faith with such readynesse and Constancy, as (according to the Argument of that keene Religion) caused her to be rudely treated, and Menac'd by the Countesse: So as she was become a Confessor, and almost a Martyr before she was Seaven-yeares old: This passage I have from herselfe, and she would Relate it, with pretty Circumstances.[99]

She returned to England in the Queen Mother's train a few months later. All should now have been well for the Blagges, but within a matter of weeks Thomas Blagge was dead, before he could begin to enjoy the rewards of his loyalty, pay his debts, or provide for his family. His widow was left with sole responsibility for their four daughters, the eldest approaching marriageable age and the youngest still only 8 years old. The King immediately promised her £2,000 to pay her husband's debts and a pension of £500 for her life,[100] but there were many royalists with pressing claims, and the resources of the Treasury were quite insufficient to satisfy them all. Soliciting for payment was a delicate matter, even for so privileged a widow as Mrs Blagge. 'As for my Pention', another female courtier lamented, 'I have yet no hopes to hear of it. I am desier'd still to have patience, and I dare not be importunate least they put me out of all hopes.'[101] But a letter from Mary Blagge to William Godolphin, the Under-Secretary of State, shows a woman well practised in the deployment of influential connections:

I cam just now from my lord fitzharding [Godolphin's cousin, Charles Berkeley] who hath moved the king in my behalf, the king hath promised to grant me a privy seale for £500. My Lord Fitzharding will consult with the secretary how it shall be done; now deare Mr Godolphin is the time you must be my frind: in getting the sec-retary [Sir Henry Bennet] to be as ready in my behalf as is my lord fitzharding. They

[98] Mary Edmond, 'Bury St Edmunds: A Seventeenth Century Art Centre', *Walpole Society*, 53 (1989), 113.
[99] *Life*, 10.
[100] BL Add. MS 36989, fo. 133: Bassingbourne to William Gawdy, 22 Nov. 1660; *CSP Domestic 1660–1661*, 554.
[101] Bodleian Library, MS Rawl. D. 78: Memoirs of Lady Elizabeth Delaval, p. 91.

were both great frinds to Mr Blagge; and you are mine, and I am your very humble servant . . . I know my Lord Fitzharding is both your kinsman and your frind: pray put him in mind of me if he forgetts me: hee hath many affayres I know.[102]

Some intermittent payments were made, though always long in arrears, until in 1668 the pension was finally made a regular charge on the receipts from the Hearth Tax.[103] No cash payment could be expected for the clearing of Thomas Blagge's debts, but Mrs Blagge was eventually granted a lease of crown lands at Spalding in Lincolnshire worth £150 a year; sufficient to make this little family of women independent of the uncertainties of court bounty.[104]

They had no settled home of their own during these years, but relied on the grace and favour of relations. At first they lodged in the Savoy, formerly a medieval palace and now 'a little town, being parted into innumerable tenements and apartments', of which another of their innumerable cousins, Dr Henry Killigrew, was Master.[105] They also seem to have spent some time with the Norths, both at Mildenhall and at the Charterhouse in Finsbury just north of the City. A former Carthusian monastery, this had been surrendered at the Reformation, and portions of it sold off, the largest for conversion into an almhouse and a charity school; Evelyn described this about the time Margaret first knew it, as 'an old neate, fresh solitarie Colledge', with a grove, bowling-green, garden, chapel, and dining hall.[106] But part of it was retained as a dwelling by the Norths, at this time 'a half-decayed family with a numerous brood and worn-out estate', but still with an ample endowment of intelligence and ability. At the head of the household was the octogenarian 3rd Lord North, who thought that 'we have much adoe to become pleased in our selves, as much in others'. Margaret can have made little of this embittered and self-absorbed old man if she ever encountered him, but his eldest son, Sir Dudley North, was a loving father and kindly disposed towards all 'little credulous Impertinents'. His own were all more or less remarkable: Francis, already a rising lawyer when Margaret first knew him and a future Lord Keeper, the merchant Dudley, and the clergyman John, later Clerk of the Closet to Charles II. Closer to Margaret in age were Roger, who would one day write the lives of all of them, and a group of sisters, the eldest foundress

[102] PRO SP 29/98, fo. 2: Mary Blagge to William Godolphin, 2 May 1664.

[103] *CTB 1660–1667*, 234, 628; Dorset RO, Ilchester MSS, Box 267: account book of Sir Stephen Fox, 1660–1, p. 8 (£500); *CSP Domestic 1663–1664*, 600; *CTB 1667–1668*, 575, 585.

[104] PRO SP 29/62, fos. 69–70: Mary Blagge to Joseph Willliamson, 6 Nov. [1662]; *CSP Domestic 1661–1662*, 548–9; *CSP Domestic 1663–1664*, 32, 119; PRO PROB 11/337/129: will of Mary Blagge, 6 July 1669.

[105] *CSP Domestic 1663–1664*, 577: Mary Blagge to William Godolphin, 2 May 1664; Sir Robert Somerville, *The Savoy Manor, Hospital, Chapel* (1960), pp. xiii, 64–5, 70.

[106] JE, *Diary*, iii. 192.

of a platonic coterie of 'wittified' young ladies in the mode of Katherine Philips.[107]

Mary Blagge saw to it that as soon as she could speak Margaret was raised in the traditional Anglicanism of her family. At 11 she was taken to be confirmed by Bishop Peter Gunning, whose services in the chapel of Exeter House in the Strand had been much frequented by royalists under Cromwell. She later numbered her early blessings as having had 'so religious a Mother, such good-breeding: Early receiving the Sacrament; The prayers of many for her, & the assistance of a Spiritual Guide, Which (she says) I am confident was the Reward of my receiving at the Charter-House'. 'From that moment forward', Evelyn says, '(Young, and Spritfull as she was) she was observ'd to live with great Circumspection, prescribing to her selfe, a constant Method of Devotion, and certain dais of Abstinence, that she might better Vacate to holy Duties, and gaine that Mastry over her Appetites.'[108]

In 1665, with the plague raging in London, there was a general exodus to the country and Mrs Blagge and her daughters retreated to Suffolk again, this time to live among Thomas Blagge's relations. Two of his sisters were still living in Horringer, the spinster Margaret who was probably her young niece's godmother, and Judith, married to Thomas Covell, the estate steward of their grander kinsfolk, the Herveys of Ickworth. Under John Hervey, who was also the Queen's treasurer, Covell had a minor court appointment as receiver of her revenues from the crown estates in Norfolk and Suffolk, but otherwise all the evidence is of long, prosperous, rural lives and settled Anglican piety.[109] In this milieu, Evelyn says, Margaret 'pass'd the Recesse with so much Devotion, Order, & Satisfaction; that with extraordinary Regret, she being taken notice of (for the Graces that then appear'd in her) and demanded by the then Dutchesse of York for a Maide of Honour: her Mother was prevail'd with to place her little Daughter at the Court'.[110]

This has a slightly fairy-tale note: the fame of a hidden rural beauty somehow reaching the court and causing her to be summoned there. But there must have been a good deal more to the transaction than this. The pension and lease which Mrs Blagge had been granted might provide subsistence for herself and her children, but the girls' long-term future would depend on

[107] Dale B. J. Randall, *Gentle Flame: The Life and Verse of Dudley, 4th Lord North* (Durham, NC, 1983), 6, 14, 22–4, 29, 54–7, 80–3; Roger North, *Lives of the Norths*, ed. A. Jessopp (1890), *passim*.

[108] *Life*, 9–10.

[109] Hervey (ed.), *Horringer Parish Registers*, 295–6; Manners W. Hervey, *Annals of a Suffolk Village* (Cambridge, 1930), 86–87; PRO PROB 11/309/114: Ambrose's Blagge's will, 2 Aug. 1662; PRO LR 5/76: order on a petition of Thomas Covell as the Queen's Receiver, 17 June 1676. A portrait by Lely of 'Judith Blagge, afterwards Mrs Thomas Covell', in court dress, was sold at Sotheby's, 3 May 1978, lot 303; there is a print in the National Portrait Gallery Heinz Library and Archive.

[110] *Life*, 10.

their having marriage portions. Again the one source Mrs Blagge could look to was the court. In fact, although Evelyn does not mention it, Margaret's eldest sister Henrietta Maria had been appointed a maid of honour when the Duchess of York's household was first set up in 1662.[111] Within a few months, with a dowry provided by her mistress, she was duly married to a prosperous Yorkshire squire, Sir Thomas Yarburgh, who carried her off to his northern estate for a life of constant childbearing and occasional visits to London. Courtiers mocked, as they always did at such country exiles:

As for the pale Lady Yarborough, who appeared so proud of her match, she is wife to be sure, of a great country bumpkin, who, the very week after their marriage, bid her take her farewell of the town forever in consequence of five or six thousand pounds a year he enjoys on the borders of [Yorkshire]. Alas! Poor Miss Blague! I saw her go away . . . in a coach with four such lean horses, that I cannot believe she is yet half way to her miserable little castle.[112]

In the unreliable court memoirs of Anthony Hamilton, brother-in-law of another of the maids of honour, Henrietta Maria Blagge is described as excessively fair in colouring, vain, and empty-headed.[113] In fact she had been trusted while she was only in her teens with sending messages to her father when he was at risk of his life as a royalist conspirator.[114] She was popular at court, and her match was a good and substantial one, giving her the kind of established security her mother and sisters always lacked. She and her husband were high church Tories and supporters of the Stuarts all their long lives,[115] and in Margaret's mind their household remained a refuge which would always be open to her.

The next two sisters, Dorothy and Mary, 'sister Doll' and 'sister Mall', were not sent to court in her place.[116] Dorothy at least would probably have

---

[111] HMC *8th Report*, pt 1, p. 278: household book of the Duke of York, 1662 and later.

[112] Anthony Hamilton, *Memoirs of the Count de Grammont*, ed. Horace Walpole (1911), 262; Hamilton, whose brother George married Frances Jenyns, another of the maids, actually says that the Yarburghs went off to Cornwall. Writing in retrospect, he evidently confused their Yorkshire connection with Margaret Blagge's marriage into a Cornish family, both being equally remote to a courtier.

[113] Hamilton, *Grammont*, 144–5, 248–9.

[114] *Calendar of the Clarendon State Papers 1657–1660*, ed. F. J. Routledge (Oxford, 1932), 291: Blagge to Hyde, 21/31 July 1659.

[115] C. B. Robinson, *History of the Priory and Peculiar of Snaith* (1861), 68–73; Denis Granville, *Remains*, ed. G. Ormsby, Surtees Society, 47 (1865), 253–4; Robert Walmesley, 'John Wesley's Parents', *Proceedings of the Wesley Historical Society*, 29 (1953–4), 51–4.

[116] It is sometimes said (e.g. Hamilton, *Grammont*, 144) that Mary Blagge was also a maid of honour. The confusion arises from pension payments to a Mary Blagge in *CTB 1669–1672*, 237, 336, 578, which actually refer to her mother (see the reference to her death in 1670, p. 445) and from the inclusion of a Mary Blagge amongst the Duchess's maids in the Edward Chamberlayne, *Angliae notitia* (1669), 321, though this is clearly an error for Margaret, who certainly was a maid at this time and whose name is not listed; see also Pepys, *Diary*, ix. 468.

been too old, and perhaps they both lacked the necessary looks and confidence. Without this help they stayed in their mother's household with little prospect of ever being married. But by the time the court reconvened in London after the plague Margaret was rising 14, pretty, self-confident, and exactly the right age for a maid of honour. Far from parting with her reluctantly, Mrs Blagge must have worked hard to secure a place for her in succession to her sister, as the one chance of her being settled independently. Evelyn was always to write of the court as a corrupt environment profoundly alien to Margaret. The solitariness of the Charterhouse, the remoter rural lives of the Covells in Suffolk certainly lingered in her mind, but the court was at this time her natural place. She had been trained in its ways from a child and many of its most prominent members were her relations. For the next seven years her world was the female household to which Evelyn had once wanted his wife to belong: first that of the Duchess of York and then that of the Queen. ⮞

4

Courtly Love

THE court to which Margaret Blagge had been called consisted of two royal households subsisting side by side, the one headed by the King and the other by his brother, James, Duke of York. At the time of his Restoration Charles II was 30 but still single, his marriage having been delayed by his years of penurious exile. Until it should take place and produce issue, his heir remained his brother and his brother's children, though they would be displaced in the line of succession whenever the King should have legitimate children of his own. It was a situation of insecurity and tension for them and their households.

An observant foreign visitor described the brothers vividly in the first decade after their return from exile: the King, tall, with the manners of a fine gentleman, 'free and attractive in his person and in all his motions'; swarthy and saturnine in features, with deeply creased cheeks, but with 'a certain smiling look coming from the width of his mouth'. He had abundant charm and wit and a universal affability. The Duke of York was fairer in colouring and utterly different in features; 'all the outlines of his face are prominent: a square forehead, the eyes large, swollen and deep blue, the nose curved and rather large'. With none of his brother's grace and air of fine breeding, he went about 'hurriedly, bent and without dignity', his dress 'always careless and matter-of-fact'. Abrasive, obstinate, and inarticulate, 'in no way has he the style and character of a prince'.[1] But he was active and brave, with a presence of mind in danger which he lacked elsewhere, and the obedience and loyalty he gave his brother survived all the stresses and rivalries of their situation.

---

[1] *Lorenzo Magalotti at the Court of Charles II*, ed. W. E. Knowles Middleton (Waterloo, Ont., 1980), 27–8, 35–7.

Unlike the King, James was married at the time of the Restoration, though rather dubiously so. While the court was at Breda in the last weeks before their return to England, he had secretly and without his brother's consent contracted to marry Anne Hyde, daughter of the principal royalist minister and maid of honour to the King's sister, Mary, Princess of Orange. Half resentfully and half respectfully, James remembered that she had both the wit and the virtue to refuse to give into his advances without the certainty of marriage. By the time of the Restoration she was already expecting his child. Although the King reluctantly gave his retrospective consent, James's family remained disgusted at the misalliance. One of the purposes of the Queen Mother's visit to England in October, with young Margaret Blagge in her train, was to try to put a stop to it. There followed a discreditable interlude in which James's servants fabricated a pretext for him to break the marriage by swearing that Anne Hyde had been notoriously promiscuous and therefore no one could be sure of the paternity of the child she was carrying. But in the course of her labour she continued to swear that she had been both legally contracted and faithful to him. The King refused to withdraw his support and with James in 'all the pain and confusion imaginable', his servants recanted their tales. In February 1661 Anne Hyde was recognized formally as Duchess of York.[2] Although her father was now created Earl of Clarendon and the highest secular officer of state, her parents marked her new status by standing in her presence.[3]

She adapted quickly and thoroughly to her new role. She not only had to establish her own contested position, but with the encouragement of the Queen Mother, whose favourite James was, uphold that of her husband as heir to the throne, and she did not disappoint them; 'it must be confessed, that what she wanted in birth, was so well made up by other endowments, that her cariage afterwards did not misbecome her acquired dignity'.[4] She was not conventionally beautiful; her complexion was spoilt by smallpox scarring and her mouth was too wide—'oyster-lipped', according to one satirist. But she had abundant chestnut hair, a sumptuous figure, and all the physical confidence of a woman sure of her hold over her husband. Three years after their marriage the couple would still be seen petting in public.[5] The Duke, abrasive and domineering as he was in other matters, 'lived towards her with an affection so remarkable and notorious, that it grew to be the public discourse and commendation . . .', Clarendon wrote; 'It was very

    [2] John Miller, *James II* (1989), 44–5; Edward Gregg, *Queen Anne* (1980), 2–3.
    [3] Pepys, *Diary*, viii. 33.   [4] J. S. Clarke (ed.), *The Life of James the Second* (1816), i. 388.
    [5] *Lorenzo Magalotti at the Court of Charles II*, 38; Andrew Marvell, *Complete Poetry*, ed. George deF. Lord (1984), 154; Pepys, *Diary*, iv. 4.

visible that he liked her company and conversation very well, and was believed to communicate all his counsels, and all he knew or thought, without reserve to her.'[6] Her position as the mother of heirs to the throne also fortified her. The son whose paternity and legitimacy had been called in question died to no one's real regret at a few months old, but between 1662 and 1666, two daughters, Mary and Anne, and two more sons, James, Duke of Cambridge, and Charles, Duke of Kendal, were born to her. The importance of the first little boy was made plain when he was invested Knight of the Garter in the King's private apartments at the age of 3.[7]

For her poise, intelligence, and style and not just her newly acquired rank, Anne Hyde stood out amongst the women at court. Her household was soon seen to be better organized and its personnel more 'select' than those of the King and Queen. Foreign envoys and visitors were impressed; but inevitably she was less popular with her own countrymen, who felt that she 'took state on her rather too much'.[8] Her manner was mimicked, as was the Duke's submission to her superior intelligence, and as her father noted uneasily, there was no lack of troublemakers to foment rivalry between the two royal households; 'the Duchess was reflected on, and the whole household', which was said to be grander than the king's, 'lived in much more plenty' and was more highly regarded abroad.[9]

In addition to his numerous casual liaisons, the King had a *maîtresse en titre* at the Restoration: Barbara Villiers, Lady Castlemaine, the most glamorous and rapacious of a long succession. His marriage to Catherine of Braganza, announced shortly after his coronation, was a matter of state. Scrutinized uncharitably by her new subjects, the new Portuguese Queen was found to be small, almost dwarfed by a 'monstrous fardingal', with abundant glossy hair, the 'foretop long & turned aside very strangely', large dark eyes, and an unfashionably olive skin, which she used cosmetics to lighten. Her face tapered to a narrow jaw and pointed chin, which meant that her teeth were crowded together and her mouth misshapen, a failing which she unwittingly emphasized by constantly smiling and 'thrusting her face forward'. But 'for the rest', Evelyn conceded, she was 'sweet and lovely enough', and there was

---

[6] Edward Hyde, Earl of Clarendon, *Life . . . in which is included a Continuation of his History* (Oxford, 1857), ii. 266.

[7] BL Add. MS 10117, fo. 184ᵛ: newsletter, 3 Dec. 1666.

[8] Pepys, *Diary*, i. 245; ii. 142, 210, 462, iii. 64, 143; Gilbert Burnet, *History of his own Time*, ed. M. J. R[outh] (Oxford, 1833), i. 307–8, 566; Bodleian Library, MS Carte 36, fo. 125: Sir Alan Broderick to Duke of Ormonde, 28 Jan. 1668; Anthony Hamilton, *Memoirs of the Count de Grammont*, ed. Horace Walpole (1911), 249; J. J. Jusserand, *A French Ambassador at the Court of Charles II* (1892), 107.

[9] Clarendon, *Life*, ii. 265.

even some hope that her modest demeanour would encourage some of the 'wild ladies' of the court to reform. She soon learnt to speak 'very pretty English' and with her costume and hairstyle naturalized was attractive enough to please the King.[10] But she committed two cardinal faults: she made scene after scene before being forced to accept his mistress into her household as lady of the bedchamber, and she failed to bear him children.

The question was soon raised whether she was capable of conceiving at all. Clarendon's enemies claimed that he had known or suspected all along that she was not, and had promoted the match so that his own grandchildren would not be displaced from the succession. Her condition was watched from month to month and gossiped about unsparingly by her women servants, and even by her doctors. Frequent intercourse with the King was said to cause her 'extraordinary and ill-timed purges'.[11] These in turn gave rise to repeated rumours of pregnancy and miscarriage, while leaving it still uncertain whether she really was capable of conceiving. Her own consequence and that of her household rose or declined accordingly. Soberer courtiers told themselves that if a child resulted from one of her rumoured pregnancies the King would have an incentive to put away his mistresses and devote himself to the responsibilities of government. Doctors declared the Queen's miscarriage at Oxford in 1665 to have been genuine, but the King, Clarendon resentfully claimed, let himself be persuaded otherwise by some of the bedchamberwomen.[12] As one such disappointment followed another, he veered between Lady Castlemaine and his new *inamorata*, Frances Stewart, the most beautiful of the Queen's maids of honour, said to have been initiated by Barbara herself in a mock wedding ceremony with lesbian byplay.[13]

The Queen drew consolation from her own identity—'she has the highest opinion of herself, her family and her country', it was noted; from the few Portuguese servants she was allowed to retain (although the Countess of Penalva, 'madame nurse' to the English, soon had to retire from encroaching blindness); from her pets and their costly accessories; and above all from her religion.[14] Her marriage contract, like her mother-in-law's, permitted her and her household free exercise of the Roman Catholic ritual, and this

[10] Pepys, *Diary*, iii. 97, 100, iv. 229, 230, v. 4; JE, *Diary*, iii. 320–1; *Lorenzo Magalotti at the Court of Charles II*, 29; Margaret M. Verney, *Memoirs of the Verney Family from the Restoration to the Revolution* (1899), 13.

[11] *Lorenzo Magalotti at the Court of Charles II*, 30–1   [12] Clarendon, *Life*, ii. 260.

[13] J. H. Wilson (ed.), *Court Satires of the Restoration* (Columbus, Oh., 1976), 7.

[14] *Lorenzo Magalotti at the Court of Charles II*, 31–4; Agnes Strickland, *Lives of the Queens of England* (1840–8), viii. 389; Lincolnshire RO, Worsley MSS: Privy Purse accounts of Catherine of Braganza, Dec. 1664, 12 July 1670, 26 Oct. 1671, 22 Apr. 1672; Sonya Wynne, 'The Mistresses of Charles II and Restoration Court Politics', Ph.D. thesis (Cambridge, 1997), 22–3.

provided the structure of her day-to-day life. Her role was not negligible; her withdrawing room, hung with blue damask and lit with chandeliers, was the normal place of evening resort of the court for both men and women, the centre of news, talk, and sociability;[15] but she had no confidence or inclination to take a lead in cultural matters. Evelyn was outraged, when he brought a carving of the crucifixion by the young Grinling Gibbons to show to her, that she deferred to the judgement of one of her dressers, a former 'French pedling woman', who found fault with it, though she understood it 'no more than an Asse or Monky'.[16] Although she learnt not to anger the King with scenes about his mistresses, the Castlemaine episode left its mark on her whole household. Catherine became prone to take her stresses out on her servants in fits of irrational irritation and dislike and they found it hard to know where their loyalties lay. When her turn came, Margaret Blagge quickly became aware of the constant risk in this household that by trying to please some she would displease others. It was all in marked contrast, in the early years at least, to the harmony which prevailed in the York household.[17]

As long as the Queen failed to bear children the King's favourite bastard son James could not fail to be a significant presence at court. Margaret Blagge must have known him in Paris and when he came to England in the Queen Mother's train at the age of 11: a tall, graceful boy with dark, spoilt good looks and a precocious sexual awareness. The King made much of him. He was created Duke of Monmouth, his education was belatedly put in hand (though at first writing 'made the poor young Duke sigh and sweat'), and a match was made for him with a 12-year-old Scottish heiress, Lady Anne Scott, whose surname rescued him from his own nameless condition.[18] His mother tried to maintain that the King had contracted a marriage with her while he was in exile. He always repudiated the claim, but his fondness for James beyond all his other illegitimate children and the continuing failure of the Queen to produce issue made Monmouth a further intermittent source of tension between the two households.

The headquarters of this extended family was Whitehall, the rambling Tudor palace of Henry VIII on the Thames. As foreign visitors never failed to note, it was not really a palace at all, but rather a heterogeneous group of

[15] Lorenzo Magalotti, *Travels of Cosmo III, Grand Duke of Tuscany through England during the Reign of King Charles II* (1821), 177–8; Thomas Bruce, 2nd Earl of Ailesbury, *Memoirs*, [ed. W. E. Buckley], Roxburghe Club (1890), i. 82.

[15] JE, *Diary*, iii. 572; David Esterly, *Grinling Gibbons and the Art of Carving* (1998), 29–31.

[17] Wynne, 'The Mistresses of Charles II', 23; Pepys, *Diary*, v. 153; *Lorenzo Magalotti at the Court of Charles II*, 3; *Life*, 15; Clarendon, *Life*, ii. 145–6.

[18] Elizabeth D'Oyley, *James, Duke of Monmouth* (1938), 34–42; *Lorenzo Magalotti at the Court of Charles II*, 40; Clarendon, *Life*, ii. 18.

buildings of different ages and functions straddling the road, King Street, which ran from Charing Cross down to Westminster and the Houses of Parliament. The only ceremonial components were the Chapel, the Banqueting House, whose Palladian symmetries stood out amongst the surrounding confusion of architectural styles, and the Great Hall, converted to a permanent theatre for masques and balls shortly after the Restoration. Surrounding these was an agglomeration of lodgings and offices, from the royal apartments to those of the humblest servants, linked by a network of courtyards and galleries. East to west at first floor level ran the Privy Gallery, from the King's covered landing stage on the river called the Privy Stairs, over King Street at the Holbein Gate and descending by an open staircase to the parade ground and radiating paths of St James's Park. Out of this, 'the original corridor of power', opened not just the Treasury and Council Chambers and the offices of the Secretary of State, but the private apartments of the King and Queen, and those of Barbara Villiers and the King's closet-keeper and reputed pimp and spymaster, William Chiffinch.[19]

Across the park St James's Palace was refurbished for the Duke of York's household and set off with newly made gardens. Although they retained a range of waterside apartments at Whitehall for winter use, it did not go unnoticed that in their own house they were better lodged than the King and Queen in theirs.[20] In the Duchess's bedchamber, with its walls painted to look like white marble, there were lavish gilded mouldings and wreathed pillars, and—most eloquent of her status—a bed, alcoved and railed off in the French royal style, decorated with festoons and trophies.[21] The Park itself was spruced up. Gangs of soldiers were set to relay the paths and dig a long canal. Thanks to Evelyn's passionate appeal to the Council of State, the tall elms had been saved from felling and still stood, 'nor do I ever pass under that Majestical shade but methinks I hear it salute me'. Rooks nested in them, which the King thought a good omen.[22] The Office of Works put in hand shelters and nesting-places (including 'withy-potts' carefully mounted at water level which delighted Evelyn) for his menagerie of exotic animals and birds, the symbols of his trade and plantation in the four corners of the globe. Evelyn's suggestion for a register of the 'names and portraitures' of all these

[19] Survey of London, XIII, XIV, *The Parish of St Margaret, Westminster (Neighbourhood of Whitehall)*, i and ii (1930–31), *passim*; Howard Colvin, *The History of the King's Works*, v (1976), 263–76; 'Introduction', in David Starkey et al. (eds.), *The English Court from the Wars of the Roses to the Civil War* (1987), 17–18; Simon Thurley, *The Whitehall Palace Plan of 1670*, London Topographical Society Publication, 153 (1998).

[20] Balthasar Monconys, *Les Voyages de M. de Monconys en Angleterre* (Paris, 1695), iii. 38.

[21] Colvin, *King's Works*, v. 234.

[22] *Sylva* (1664) in *WJE*, 188; BL Egerton MS 2539, fo. 178ᵛ: newsletter, 23 Mar. 1668.

creatures was not taken up, but the King was painted sauntering amongst the beasts in his 'paradise'.[23] For courtiers the Park was a place of assignation by day and night. The thickets of the Spring Garden at the east end especially, seemed to be 'contrived to all the advantages of gallantry'. Young women of the court might spend much of the night walking there with their lovers.[24] To the north beyond Pall Mall fashionable streets and squares were rising, and beyond those, at the most western end of Piccadilly, two great mansions: Clarendon House for the Lord Chancellor, and next to it Berkeley House for the Duke's steward and the Duchess's groom of the stole. Evelyn, now the foremost gardening consultant in the metropolis, advised about the grounds for both of them.

A little downriver, Somerset House was renovated as the Queen Mother's dower house, with the addition of a handsome arcaded river frontage based on a earlier plan of Inigo Jones. Just as hers had been the most enjoyable of the female courts in Paris, so now it quickly registered that there was more company, laughter, and enjoyment in her circle than in the new Queen's.[25] The Villiers cousins, the Duchess of Richmond and Lady Guildford, still presided. Mary Evelyn came to make her court there with small presents and the recommendation of a gardener.[26] So probably did Mary Blagge and her daughters when they were lodged close by at the Savoy. The chapel, staffed by its neighbouring small convent of Capuchin friars, was a showpiece; the chief place of resort for metropolitan Catholics, as well as for curious Protestants.[27] Upriver the other great Tudor palace at Hampton Court had been refurbished for the King's honeymoon but was seldom used afterwards, while the despoiled fragments of Richmond, where he had spent his childhood, were granted to Lady Castlemaine's uncle Edward Villiers, and for the sake of its healthy situation kept up as the royal nursery, with his wife presiding as governess to the Duke of York's children.[28] Windsor Castle, the only royal house at any distance from London, awaited dramatic rebuilding later in the reign.

The royal household was again set up under its traditional establishments: the stables under the Master of the Horse in the Royal Mews at Charing

---

[23] JE, *Diary*, iii. 398–400; Peter Mundy, *Travels*, ed. R. C. Temple and L. M. Anstey, Hakluyt Society, 2nd ser., 5 (1936), 155–8; Colvin, *King's Works*, v. 273; Bray, iii. 136: JE to Thomas Chiffinch, [1662]. Hendrik Danckerts' picture of Charles II and his courtiers shows a range of exotic beasts grazing in St James's Park (see Plate 4).

[24] Norman Brett-James, *The Growth of Stuart London* (1935), 467; JE, *Diary*, iii. 96–7; Bodleian Library, MS. Rawl. D.78: Memoirs of Lady Elizabeth Delaval, p. 230.

[25] Colvin, *King's Works*, v. 255–6; Pepys, *Diary*, iii. 299.

[26] BL Add. MS 78439: ME to Lady Guildford, [1663].

[27] A. S. Barnes, 'The Catholic Chapels under the Stuarts', *Downside Review*, 20 (1901), 160–3.

[28] John Cloake, *Palaces and Parks of Richmond and Kew* (Chichester, 1995–1996), i. 1–2.

Cross; the Lord Steward's department, 'a vast catering establishment' in Scotland Yard just north of Whitehall; the Lord Chamberlain's province, which extended over the state apartments above stairs; and 'the Bedchamber' under the groom of the stole.[29] The courts of the Queen and the Queen Mother had their own parallel structures and staff, and so, more controversially, did that of the Duke of York. His steward Lord Berkeley, Clarendon complained, 'had formed a family without rule or precedent, and made the servants in a much better condition than the master by assigning liberal pensions and allowances to them who had paid him dear for their places'. But when he protested to his daughter, she brushed his misgivings aside, saying she did not think him a competent judge 'what expenses princes should make'.[30]

The age, inclinations, and habits of the monarch did much to determine the tone of the court at any period. Charles II's household might have been set up on the old model, but it was very different from that of his father. Where Charles I had been 'temperate, chaste, and serious', his son was the reverse in every particular: pleasure-loving, sociable, informal, and valuing novelty more highly than tradition.[31] For all his intelligence, affability, and charm he was also deeply marked by his years of exile, taking it for granted that all human behaviour, even the most idealistic, was deeply self-deceiving and self-interested, and that there was no such thing as sincerity or chastity in the world 'out of principle, but that some had either the one or the other out of humour or vanity'. To some he could seem the very embodiment of the dangerous scepticism of his old tutor Thomas Hobbes, on which they blamed the moral degeneration of the age.[32]

The King enjoyed watching the creatures in St James's Park copulate. His own unembarrassed sexual appetites, his very techniques of love-making, were freely gossiped about. Lord Halifax commented dryly that his intimacies with women 'were the effects of health and a good constitution, with as little mixture of the seraphic part as ever man had'.[33] His brother, for all his

---

[29] Robert Bucholz, *The Augustan Court* (Stanford, Calif., 1993), 37–42; J. M. Beattie, *The English Court in the Reign of George I* (Cambridge, 1967), 23–105; Thurley, *Whitehall Palace Plan of 1670*, 16–26.

[30] Clarendon, *Life*, i. 367.

[31] Lucy Hutchinson, *Memoirs of Col. Hutchinson*, ed. C. H. Firth (1906), 69; Kevin Sharpe, 'The Image of Virtue: The Court and Household of Charles I', in Starkey et al. (eds.), *English Court*, 226–48; Miller, *James II*, 37–41.

[32] Burnet, *History*, i. 170; Samuel Mintz, *The Hunting of Leviathan* (Cambridge, 1962), 23–4, 134–7.

[33] Pepys, *Diary*, viii. 68; George Savile, Marquess of Halifax, *Complete Works*, ed. J. P. Kenyon (Harmondsworth, 1969), 252.

uxoriousness, indulged with even less finesse in what Evelyn distastefully called 'bitchering'.[34] Watchful husbands removed their wives into the country as soon as he showed the slightest interest in them. The foreign ambassadors all had mistresses; so did most of the ministers. Arlington's was the 'great wit' Lady Scrope, whom Evelyn resented for usurping the post he wanted for his wife.[35] The young men who frequented the court hoping for preferment followed suit, and women were expected to accommodate themselves to this state of affairs. When one of them broke off an advantageous match after discovering that her suitor had a mistress, a court newsmonger commented ironically that it was 'so odd an exception in our age that her Ladyship has almost lost her credit by it, & look'd upon as somewhat unreasonable, not to say worse, for expecting or desiring to have a whole man to herself'.[36]

After the years of royalist hardship there was a general sense of release and conspicuous display, with everyone competing to make a show with clothes and coaches; 'even the poor Cavaliers will be as fine as the best, tho' they never live to pay their Taylors'.[37] The Queen at her first arrival was said to have been concerned that English ladies spent so much time in dressing themselves, 'she feares they bestow but little on God almighty and in houswivry'.[38] But within a few years she had entered into the obsession with dress. In the beginning she tried to set a fashion for Portuguese costume, but the Englishwomen insisted on Parisian modes, sending their dressmakers there for the latest styles. The 'French pedling woman' who supplied small items of fashion to Catherine's household was eventually appointed one of her dressers and to Evelyn's disgust general arbiter of artistic taste.[39] He did not blame the French, 'that Protean nation', for their constantly changing fashions, 'it is plainly their Interest and they thrive by it; besides the pleasure of

---

[34] Pepys, *Diary*, viii. 297.

[35] HMC *Portland MSS*, iii. 294: Denis de Repas to Sir Robert Harley, 24 Nov. 1665; JE, *Diary*, iii. 275, iv. 345.

[36] Harry Ransom Humanities Research Center, University of Texas, Pforzheimer Library: newsletter to Sir Richard Bulstrode, 7 Aug. 1676.

[37] Roger Coke, *Detection of the Court and State of England*, 4th edn. (1719), ii. 102; Cornwall RO, RP 1/35: John Penneck to John Rogers, 28 Feb. 1671.

[38] HMC *Beaufort MSS*, 53: Cornbury to Marchioness of Worcester, 10 June 1662.

[39] Strickland, *Lives of the Queens of England*, viii. 311. Lincolnshire RO, Worsley MSS: Privy Purse accounts of Catherine of Braganza, 11 June, 18 Oct. 1666, 6 Jan 1667, 4 Nov. 1668, record repeated payments to Mlle Bardou (also mentioned in Hamilton, *Grammont*, 239) for small items of French fashion. It is not clear if the former 'French pedling woman' of the Queen's household, Henriette des Bordes, mentioned by Evelyn in 1671 (JE, *Diary*, iii. 572; cf. *CTB 1669–1672*, 743, 837), was the same person under a married name; she appears to have come from an English family called Carter (information supplied by Sonya Wynne).

seeing all the World follow them, and be fond of it'. But 'what have we to do with these Forreign Butterflies? . . . why should I dance after a Monsieur's Flagolet only, that have a set of English Viols for my Consort?'[40] The most dazzling displays were reserved for the court balls and masques. At the beginning there was a ball or a theatrical performance every other day, and full-scale masques were danced by the leading courtiers 'in rich and antique dresses' in the Hall theatre at regular intervals, especially at Candlemas. The costumes were designed to show most dazzlingly in the massed lights of winter evenings. On Catherine's birthday in November 1666 it was reported that no one would ever 'be smiled on again by the Queene that doth not come that day very richly clad'. With this encouragement the ball was 'the richest assembly since the coronation', the *belle*, Frances Stewart, in black with silver lace and diamonds, and the men in cloth of silver which shimmered in the candlelight. Evelyn himself was ready to suspend his disapproval at the spectacle of 'a magnificent Ball or Masque in the Theater at Court, where their Majesties & all the great Lords & Ladies daunced infinitely gallant: the Men in their richly imbrodred, most becoming Vests'.[41]

On summer evenings there were concerts on the river. The musicians might play from barges on the river while the courtiers listened from the leads of Whitehall, or they might take to the water themselves, the King and the Duke's families in the royal barges, the court and city beauties in open boats, with music, collations, and fireworks as the finale.[42] Gambling was the daily recreation at all seasons, with 'deep play' at the groom porter's and the mistresses' lodgings, where 'the greate Courtiers', men and women, sat at basset with a bank in gold in front of them. Thousands might be won, but were usually lost at a sitting, since the odds were heavily weighted in favour of the bank. Evelyn observed, as in a different species, 'the wiccked folly, vanity & monstrous excesse of Passion amongst some loosers, & sorry I am that such a wretched Custome as play to that excesse should be countenanced in a Court, which ought to be an example of Virtue to the rest of the kingdome'.[43] Basset was always regarded as a court game, since only those who could afford to stake and lose huge sums were eligible to play, but cardplaying for money in some form or other was almost universal. Even

[40] *Tyrannus, or the Mode* (1661), in *WJE*, 164, 168.

[41] Jusserand, *French Ambassador*, 91; HMC *Beaufort MSS*, 54: Duke to Duchess of Beaufort, 14 Nov. 1666; JE, *Diary*, iii. 476; Peter Holman, *Four and Twenty Fiddlers: The Violin at the English Court* (Oxford, 1993), 359–62.

[42] Survey of London, XIII, *Parish of St Margaret Westminster (Neighbourhood of Whitehall)*, i. 58, 69; Harry Ransom Humanities Research Center, University of Texas: newsletter to Bulstrode, 15 June 1676.

[43] David Parlett, *A History of Card Games* (Oxford, 1990), 77; JE, *Diary*, iii. 308, 504, iv. 413.

Margaret Blagge, who disapproved of it in principle, found that she often had to do it 'to comply with others and unavoidabley'. Even when she lost and her funds for charity were depleted, she would only resolve to confine herself to threepenny ombre, knowing that she would never be able to keep a solemn vow to renounce cards altogether.[44] The tennis courts at Whitehall were yet another gambling venue. 'Everybody wagers at these games,' a foreign visitor noted, fascinated; the galleries were full of tradesmen, everyone down to lackeys laid bets, and the King and courtiers mingled with the crowd without distinction of rank.[45]

For the handsome, adventurous, quick-witted, and sexually adept of both sexes the court therefore seemed to offer a constant round of pleasure:

There is no othere plague here but the infection of love; no other discourse but of ballets, dance and fine clouse; no other other emulation but who shall look the handsomere, and whose vermilion and spanish white is the best; none other fight then for 'I am yours'. In a word there is nothing here but mirth, and there is a talk that there shall be a proclamacon made that any melancholy man or woman coming in this towne shall be tourned out and put to the pillory.[46]

Could there be any religious dimension to such an environment? The Duchess of Newcastle thought courtiers too much concerned with their bodies to pay much regard to their souls.[47] Yet the fact was there was much better formal provision for religion at court than in most parish churches. When it came to singing the psalms, it was too often 'sad to hear what whining, toting, yelling, or skreeking there is in many country congregations'; the liturgy might be reduced to a 'confused murmur'; preaching was likely to be unsophisticated, and communion infrequent.[48] At the Chapel Royal ordinances issued in the King's name decreed that public prayers were to be held there morning and evening all year round, 'with solemn Musick like a Collegiate Church'. A new organ loft was built and a choir of men and boys in robes and surplices accompanied each service. Communion was held monthly and the preaching by the most eminent churchmen of the Anglican hierarchy, especially at the major festivals and during Lent, was of legendary quality. Strict orders were laid down about precedence and seating. To the left and right of the King's closet, divided from it by hangings, were the forms reserved for the court women: on the one side the Queen's ladies of the

[44] *Life*, p. 107.

[45] François Brunet, 'A French Traveller in Charles II's England', *Cornhill Magazine*, new ser., 20 (Jan.–June 1906), 664.

[46] HMC *Portland MSS*, iii. 293: Denis de Repas to Sir Robert Harley, 19 Oct. 1665.

[47] Margaret Cavendish, 'The Presence', in *Plays never before Printed* (1668), 4.

[48] John Spurr, *The Restoration Church of England* (New Haven, 1991), 350–1, 355–6.

bedchamber, on the other her subordinate servants and those of the Duchess of York.[49]

Yet for all this, Hobbes's notorious definition of religion as 'Fear of power invisible, feign'd by the mind, or imagined from tales publicly allowed', added to the prevailing weariness with gravity and moralizing, did not make for the uncomplicated practice of piety.[50] The King would be seen to come to Chapel directly from his mistresses' lodgings in 'a company of sad idle people', sit with studied inattention when the sermons were indifferent, and snigger if the anthem was badly sung. The Duke of York and Lady Castlemaine might be observed talking 'very wantonly' through the hangings which separated the royal closet from the ladies' seating. When one of the bishops delivered a reproof against plays and gaming or the chaplain in waiting read a lesson from St Paul about marriage and constancy, there might be outright laughter.[51] Margaret Blagge was not the only young woman at court who had to vow not to let fashionable scoffing deter her from the pious practices in which she had been brought up.[52]

When clergy complained of conduct in Chapel no more devout than at a playhouse, it was an apt enough comparison in more ways than one. The almost equal status of the Chapel Royal and the Hall theatre in the calendar of court performance was neatly caught by the country visitor who could not tell whether his wife had caught cold at a court masque or the Lent sermons.[53] The royal closet was very much like a box at the theatre. The singers and musicians were professionals who performed alternately at the chapel and the playhouse, and Evelyn for one thought the innovation of violin music between each verse of the anthems too much 'after the French fantastical light way, better suiting a Tavern or a Play-house than a Church'.[54] Not just the Chapel Royal, but all the fashionable London churches were as much places of public resort as of worship. Young women dressed to attend service with as much care as for the playhouse or the opera. The royal chaplains complained of 'sighing and ogling' which distracted attention from their eloquence, of congregations grown 'sermon proof', and discourses attended

[49] BL Stowe MS 562, fos. 5–9: ordinances for the conduct of the Chapel Royal [*c.*1679] (for the date, see Brian Weiser, 'A Call to Order: Charles II's Ordinances of the Household (BL Stowe 562)', *Court Historian*, 6 (2001), 151–6); Edward Rimbault (ed.), *The Old Cheque Book . . . of the Chapel Royal 1561–1744*, Camden Society, new ser., 3 (1872), 82; J. B. Harley, *Music in Purcell's London* (1968), 78–81; Holman, *Four and Twenty Fiddlers*, 391–2; BL Egerton MS 2539, fo. 90: newsletter, 20 Mar. 1667; JE, *Diary*, iv. 6.

[50] Mintz, *Hunting of Leviathan*, 142.

[51] Pepys, *Diary*, i. 265–6, iii. 293, v. 155; Burnet, *History*, i. 168, 316; Ailesbury, *Memoirs*, ii. 93.

[52] *Life*, 16; Bodleian Library, MS Rawl. D.78, Memoirs of Lady Elizabeth Delaval, p. 45.

[53] HMC *Buccleuch (Montagu House) MSS*, i. 321: William to Lord Mountagu, 4 Mar. 1675.

[54] Harley, *Music in Purcell's London*, 125; JE, *Diary*, iii. 347.

to, not for their improving content but in order to be criticized afterwards like the latest new play.[55] They might, however, have been reminded that their own carefully cultivated repertoire of performative techniques encouraged this. Evelyn, a connoisseur of sermons, would assess each performance carefully and relish the different preaching styles: the Bishop of Rochester making 'a most passionate & pathetic discourse according to his usual way'; the Bishop of Exeter being 'a little too critical about words at first, but the rest very well'; or the Bishop of Gloucester preaching 'very allegorically according to his manner, but very gravely & wittily'. But the growing fashion, as he noted, was for 'plain and practical' discourses, 'of which sort, this Nation nor any other ever had greater plenty, & more profitable (I am confident) since Apostles time: so much has it to answer for thriving no better on it'. Robert Creighton of Bath and Wells, 'the most famous, loquacious, ready-tongued preacher of the court', could electrify even a Chapel Royal congregation with 'a strange bold sermon' against its sins, 'and particularly against adultery, over and over instancing how for that single sin in David the nation was undone'. Peter Gunning, Bishop of Chichester, whom Evelyn thought, 'could do nothing but well', was criticized by his fellow cleric Gilbert Burnet for being 'a dark perplexed preacher', whose sermons were 'full of Greek and Hebrew, and of the opinions of the fathers'. Yet he admitted that 'many of the ladies of a high form loved to hear him preach; which the king used to say, was because they did not understand him'. Burnet himself burst on the court scene somewhat later, but with 'such a flood of eloquence and full-nesse of matter' as immediately marked him out as 'a person of extraordinary parts'.[56]

Yet the Duchess of Newcastle still thought that the most significant form of religion at court was the worship of female beauty.[57] The Restoration court might have little overt truck, except by way of knowing travesty, with the platonic ideal which had made service to them a source of moral refinement and virtue, but the conventions lingered,[58] and the conspicuous display of the early years certainly put women at the forefront from the

[55] Harley, *Music in Purcell's London*, 79; Spurr, *Restoration Church*, 237, 249–50, 266; C. F. Richardson, *English Preachers and Preaching 1640–1670* (1928), 48–57; Bodleian Library, MS Rawl. D.78, Memoirs of Lady Elizabeth Delaval, p. 76.

[56] JE, *Diary*, iii. 624, iv. 35, 47–8, 84, 130; Richardson, *English Preachers*, 40, 57, 82–3.

[57] *Sociable Letters* (1664), 15–16, quoted in Anna Battigelli, *Margaret Cavendish and the Exiles of the Mind* (Lexington, Ky., 1998), 135.

[58] J. Douglas Stuart, *Pin-ups or Virtues: The Concept of the 'Beauties' in Late Stuart Portraiture*, William Andrews Clark Memorial Library Seminar (Los Angeles, 1974), 5–14; Catharine MacLeod and Julia Marciari Alexander (eds.), *Painted Ladies: Women of the Court of Charles II* (2001), 53–5 (on the 'Beauties Gallery' of court portraits).

beginning. Their beauty and richness of costume were recognized as a large part of the public spectacle. In setting out the advantages of London for educating youth, Sir William Petty remarked that in no other European capital was there such liberty, 'at the Court, in St James & Hide parks, in Churches, at Theaters & elsewhere, to see beautiful Women with & without impunity'.[59] And it was not just a matter of show. Men of influence, whose support the crown needed, expected that their wives should be received suitably at court and the women expected to have their own milieu there. The female households had the same hierarchy of offices as the male, with the difference that the bedchamber posts would always be held by women. These appointments, with their possibilities of patronage and influence, gave women access to public life and their opportunities once there were enhanced by the informality and overt sexuality of Charles II's court. The French ambassador noted that women were soon involved in everything.[60] When Sir Charles Sedley asked a new arrival amongst the female courtiers whether she intended to set up as 'a Beauty, a Miss [mistress], a Wit, or a Politician', he was acknowledging in his unregenerate way that these posts offered a wide scope for a woman.[61] Whitehall was a community of men and women, who shared the same environment, performed the same services, and needed each other's support. They were 'of a gang', as Pepys shrewdly noted, watching Margaret Blagge and her companions dining at the Treasurer's house in Deptford.[62]

Within the female household the highest-ranking women were the groom of the stole and the ladies of the bedchamber, always peeresses and usually the wives of leading male courtiers or ministers. Their official function was to play a part in formal dressing and dining rituals and to provide their mistress with an entourage and suitable companionship in public and private. Below them were the bedchamber women, also called chamberers or dressers, the equivalent of grooms of the bedchamber in a male court. Waiting in a weekly rota, they performed the same functions as chambermaids in a private household, sleeping on a truckle bed in the royal bedchamber, caring for their mistress's clothes, dressing her, making up her hair and tending her in illness and childbirth. They had to have the status of gentlewomen, and were often

[59] David Roberts, *The Ladies: Female Patronage and Restoration Drama* (Oxford, 1989), 81; Pepys, *Diary*, iv. 229–30; 'Beautiful Ladies of London' in *Lorenzo Magalotti at the Court of Charles II*, 154–5; *The Petty Papers*, ed. 6th Marquess of Lansdowne (1927), i. 42.

[60] Jusserand, *French Ambassador*, 224.

[61] Quoted in Antonia Fraser, *The Weaker Vessel: Woman's Lot in Seventeenth Century England* (1984), 454.

[62] Pepys, *Diary*, ix. 469.

the fixtures of the court, having come into the household as nurses to the royal children and remaining there for life.[63]

For those who simply attended the court it might seem to be a constant round of pleasures, but for those who held office there the reality was very different. Disillusioned office-holders, male and female, would call themselves 'voluntary slaves', 'fawning, creeping, and serving in offices troublesome and servile enough in themselves, however gilded by the fancies of men'.[64] Lady Tuke confided to the Evelyns that 'there is nothing has troubld me more since I had the honour to serve the Queene than that restraint of my liberty that I cannot enjoy the companie of my friends as I did heretofore, it makes life lesse pleasing to me, and really makes one value the world very little, nor that grinning honour which many esteeme'.[65] Evelyn had his own experience of the reality of this at supper one night with the Queen's groom of the stole; when a message came that Catherine chose on a whim to walk in the Park at eleven at night, she had to rise in a fluster, abandon her guests, and hurry away to attend her mistress; 'by which one may take an estimate of the extreame slavery & subjection that Courtiers live in, who have not time to eat & drinke at their pleasure'.[66] They were assumed to have compromised their integrity, and women their chastity, along with their dignity and independence;[67] Evelyn's first published work, a translation from the French entitled *Liberty and Servitude*, dwelt on the enslavement of the courtier, body and mind, to the will of princes.

For the Restoration courtier it was not even well-paid servitude. Within months of being set up, the Queen's household was short of money.[68] Periodic retrenchments by the Treasury meant that all salaries and pensions could be halved or suspended for months at a time. Within three years of the Restoration public diets, one of the chief attractions of the court, were curtailed as a permanent economy. Fees, bribes, and perquisites became the universal currency: 'no progress can be made and nothing obtained without presents and without money'.[69] Lady Tuke, who had sought her bedchamber post in widowhood out of financial necessity, was soon complaining that it

---

[53] Bucholz, *Augustan Court*, 118–19, 123–4; Sonya Wynne, '"The Brightest Glories of the British Sphere": Women at the Court of Charles II', in MacLeod and Alexander (eds.), *Painted Ladies*, 37–42.

[64] Pepys, *Diary*, iv. 197; Bodleian Library, MS Rawl. D.78: Memoirs of Lady Elizabeth Delaval, p. 24; *Savile Correspondence*, ed. W. D. Cooper, Camden Society, 71 (1858), 37.

[65] BL Add. MS 78435: Lady Tuke to ME, 20 Mar. 1682.   [66] JE, *Diary*, iv. 318.

[67] Perez Zagorin, *Ways of Lying: Dissimulation, Persecution and Conformity in Early Modern Europe* (Cambridge, Mass., 1990), 6–8; Steven Shapin, *A Social History of Truth* (Chicago, 1994), 100.

[68] *Letters of Philip [2nd] Earl of Chesterfield* (London, 1829), 127–8: to Cornbury, May 1663.

[69] Bucholz, *Augustan Court*, 13, 19–20; Miller, *James II*, 40.

was 'much like that of the soldier, more toyle and trouble then content, and at last die a beger and leave nothing to ons children for whome we have taken all the paines. This is my sence and what is wors my condition.'[70] Evelyn warned his son when he considered a career there that 'attendance at court is most exceedingly tedious . . . You will be paid at great leisure after you are perhaps exceedingly out of purse. For a mere courtier there is not so much as eating . . . the young gallant must play deep and pay dear for his experience.'[71]

The youngest members of the household, the pages and maids of honour, for whom the court was a kind of finishing school, apparently fared the best. For generations some poorer gentry families had sought to place their promising adolescent children into aristocratic households, to complete their education and advance their marriage and career prospects. Placing a child in a royal household was simply taking this custom one step higher. In a great household or at court, it was hoped that they would 'learn handsome Fashions, Graceful Behaviour, Noble Entertainments', while their good looks would be 'set out in general View, their Wits to the general Observation, their Worth and Merits to the general knowledg of the Chief of the Kingdom'.[72] In return bonds would be formed between the crown and all ranks of gentry society.

Unlike the other ranks of court women, the maids of honour were not bedchamber servants. Strictly speaking they were not supposed to enter the royal bedroom at all, but 'the King having given one or another permission to do so', a foreign visitor noted meaningfully, 'the thing has been taken advantage of'.[73] Officially the girls' function was simply to 'adorn the court': to 'wait' in the Presence and Privy Chambers or the withdrawing room and help entertain the ladies who came to visit their mistress, to accompany her, suitably costumed and decked out, when she walked or rode out, and to dance at balls and masques, where they might be called on to give the principal couples a respite.[74] Though purely decorative, the function was not negligible: the looks, style, and accomplishments of these girls did much to set the tone of the court. They had to be in their teens, pretty, and of marriageable age. Ideally they would then attract husbands within a year or two, retire, and give place to younger candidates, so that there would be a constantly renewed circle of young attendants. The maxim of Frances Jenyns, one of the Duchess of York's most successful maids, was that 'a lady ought to be

[70] BL Add. MS 78435: Lady Tuke to ME, 20 Mar. 1682.   [71] Quoted in Hiscock II, 127.
[72] Cavendish, 'The Presence', in *Plays never before Printed*, 124.
[73] *Lorenzo Magalotti at the Court of Charles II*, 33.
[74] C. H. Hartmann, *La Belle Stuart* (1924), 11; *Life*, 14; Pepys, *Diary*, iv. 229–30.

young to enter the court with advantage, and not old to leave with a good grace'.[75] Appointments made more as a reward for family loyalty than because of the girls' personal qualifications might be less successful. Pepys thought only a very few of the Queen's first establishment of maids from deserving royalist families outstandingly pretty, and three of them, Henrietta Maria Price, Simona Carew, and Catherine Boynton, certainly lingered in post for longer than the acceptable time, though all eventually married.[76]

The girls were given lodging at court, sharing bedchambers in pairs, with a closet for writing and private devotion and a common reception room where they could entertain visitors.[77] Each had a waiting woman, who might act as go-between with her suitors and with whom she would often develop a close bond; Margaret Blagge was to tolerate her Beck's 'want of good service' for years afterwards because they had grown up at court together, while Sarah Jenyns hotly contested her mother's criticism of Betty Moody, 'which I can't but take to myself', and Dorothy Howard's 'Mrs Mandy' 'loved her mistresse infinitly and was loved againe of her'.[78] Even after the general curtailment of court catering, a 'table' was provided for the maids of honour on the Lord Steward's establishment. Some expenses, lodgings at Bath or boxes at the theatre, were met for them, and an allowance was paid by way of pocket money, though this was very small in the first years of the Restoration: £20 a year for the Duchess's maids, only £10 for the Queen's. Annual Valentine gifts were also traditionally part of their fees, although these were soon discontinued. But the great drawback was that they had to 'find their own clothes', a huge expense given the constant display required of them, and one which could easily cancel out other benefits.[79] Sarah Jenyns complained of receiving a 'ridiculous sum' as her allowance, at the same time as she was obliged to spend £500 a year on these expenses.[80] Occasional payments

[75] Hamilton, *Grammont*, 257.

[76] They married respectively Alexander Stanhope (1673), Bevil Skelton (1670), and Richard Talbot (1669); see Wynne, 'Mistresses of Charles II', 263.

[77] BL Add. MS 78539: ME to Ralph Bohun, 6 Nov. 1676; Cavendish, 'The Presence', in *Plays never before Printed*, 17; Mary Catherine, Baronne d'Aulnoy, *Memoirs of the Court of England in 1675*, ed. G. D. Gilbert (1912), 100, 131.

[78] *Life*, 80; BL Add. MS 61453, fo. 12: Sarah Churchill to Mrs Jenyns, 10 Apr. [1680?]; W. S. Churchill, *Marlborough: His Life and Times* (1947), i. 124; BL Add. 78539: ME to Bohun, 6 Nov. 1676.

[79] Lincolnshire RO, Worsley MSS: Privy Purse accounts of Catherine of Braganza, 21 Sept. 1663; Roberts, *The Ladies*, 107; Strickland, *Lives of the Queens of England*, viii. 388; Edward Chamberlayne, *Angliae notitia* (1669), 321; Bucholz, *Augustan Court*, 19–20, 135; Julia Longe, *Martha Lady Giffard: Her Life and Correspondence* (1911), 111; *Lorenzo Magalotti at the Court of Charles II*, 33.

[80] Frances Harris, *A Passion for Government: The Life of Sarah, Duchess of Marlborough* (Oxford, 1991), 14.

might be made for costume for special events: a masque or a birthday ball, and the *belle*, Frances Stewart, was given a special allowance from the King's Privy Purse for her clothes and jewels. But for most of the girls, lacking her privileged position, these *ex gratia* payments were nothing like enough. Families could quickly find daughters a far greater expense to them at court than at home, and it was not sufficiently clear to all of them that they were being favoured by the arrangement. The father of one of the Queen's maids told the King 'He had been at great charge to maintaine her there, and he would not be able to do it any longer, unless his Majestie would give her some allowance; the King said he might take her away when he pleas'd, for he would give no allowance.'[81]

Within a year or two he did have to agree that the girls should each have £100 a year from the Exchequer, but this was still inadequate. As time went on the needy situation of 'the young beggarly bitches' (as a male courtier called them) became more and more notorious. In attempting to outshine the other maids and catch the Queen's attention, Betty Livingston ran heavily into debt at first, and then had to live in fear that this would embitter relations with her husband, when she did find one, from the outset.[82] The allowance was eventually raised to £200 a year and in the following reigns to £300. But even with the most careful management, the likelihood of their ending seriously in debt remained. As late as Queen Anne's reign, a mother was warned 'how great the charge is (were it obtain'd) in setting out a maid of honour & how seldome (if ever) tis they don't run out'.[83] If families were still willing to run these risks it was because, at best, the posts offered the chance of glittering marriage prizes. The maids were seen as a source from which 'young unthinking men of quality and estates' might choose themselves 'wives of fancy'.[84] The Duchess of York herself had started as a maid of honour; so had the Duchess of Newcastle, both of them from quite modest backgrounds; and occasionally this could still happen. Mary Bagot, one of the Duchess's maids, married the King's ambitious favourite Lord Falmouth in 1664, after she had been only a few months in post. Although he was killed at sea not long afterwards, she and her daughter were maintained at court for several years, and when the Duchess died the Duke of York himself talked of marrying her. It was only when this was vetoed by the King (who said that

[81] Bodleian MS Rawl. D.78, Memoirs of Lady Elizabeth Delaval, pp. 99–100.

[82] John Wilmot, Earl of Rochester, *The Rochester–Savile Letters*, ed. J. H. Wilson (Columbus, Oh., 1941), 49; *Meditations of Lady Elizabeth Delaval*, ed. D. G. Greene, Surtees Society, 190 (1978), 68, 123–4.

[83] Frances Harris, '"The Honourable Sisterhood": Queen Anne's Maids of Honour', *British Library Journal*, 19 (1993), 183.

[84] Delariviere Manley, *The New Atalantis*, ed. Ros Ballaster (1991), 17.

his brother should not play the fool twice), that she agreed to a further, highly advantageous match with the Earl of Dorset.[85] Like Frances Stewart, she was evidently one of the 'blazing stars' of the court:[86] sufficient in herself to be a trophy wife for a man of the highest rank.

But for most maids of honour their looks alone would not be enough to bring this about. After the Restoration the King himself remarked, 'I find the passion Love very much out of fashion in this country, and that a handsome face without money has but few gallants upon the score of marriage.'[87] The main compensation for the smallness of the maids' allowance was that those who resigned their posts in order to marry acceptably were by custom entitled to have their dowry paid by the court, albeit only after persistent solicitation and in intermittent instalments rather than a lump sum. For families without reserves of their own, 'the portion at last is the inducement', as one them put it, and worth all the risk of running into debt.[88] Parents with access to court patronage might even agree a marriage in advance of their daughter's appointment in order to have the dowry paid by this means. This was probably the case with Henrietta Maria Blagge, whose suitor had been acquainted with her family in Paris before the Restoration, and the Evelyns were advised to use the same tactic with their eldest daughter when the time came.[89] It followed that the maids' posts were chiefly sought after by those who did not have large enough estates to provide for their daughters themselves: minor royalist gentry such as the Blagges and the Evelyns, or professional courtiers such as Sir Herbert Price, whose daughters were included in the first establishments of both the Queen and the Duchess. Well-established families would normally consider it beneath them to tout their daughters in this way. Catherine Sedley, as a substantial heiress, lost caste when she agreed to take a post as maid of honour to the Duchess of York, even though she had her own ends in view: 'I admire she ever lookt so low as to think of itt,' one observer commented.[90] Lady Suffolk could accept the post of groom of the stole to the Queen and both her daughters, Lady Betty and Lady Essex Howard, frequented the court, but there was no question of their doing so as maids of honour. Yet their cousins Dorothy and Anne Howard, daughters of a younger son of the family, were glad to find places there.

[85] C. H. Hartmann, *The King's Friend* (1951), 130, 239–41.

[86] HMC *Various Collections*, viii. 65: Elizabeth Frazier to Mrs Warmestry, 10 Feb. 1662.

[87] C. H. Hartmann, *The King my Brother* (1954), 87: Charles II to his sister, 18 Jan. 1664.

[88] Harris, 'Honourable Sisterhood', 184–5.

[89] Sir John Reresby, *Memoirs*, ed. A. Browning (Glasgow, 1936), 27–9; BL Add. 78435: Lady Tuke to ME, 10, 13 June [1683].

[90] HMC *Rutland MSS*, ii. 42: Lady Chaworth to Lord Roos, 2 Nov. [1676], 4 Dec. [1677].

Of course not all suitors, country gentlemen especially, might favour a court-bred wife, however beautiful and well dowered. When two of the Duchess's maids disguised themselves as orange-sellers for a prank Pepys remarked censoriously that few would venture on them for wives; and this was just what staider girls such as Dorothy Howard were afraid of.[91] As the Duchess of Newcastle succinctly put it, 'Men are afraid to Marry Maids of Honour, because they are so used to Courtships, that they will give leave to be Courted when they are married; besides Men think them vain and expensive.'[92] At the first sight of Carey Frazier's costume of ermine, velvet, and cloth of gold at a birthday ball, her suitor backed off in alarm, protesting that his whole estate would not be sufficient to keep her in clothes.[93] A court-bred girl would also have few of the necessary skills to be a country housewife, might soon become discontented with rural retirement, and expect to spend part of each year consuming her husband's rents in London. Anthony Hamilton, whose brother married Frances Jenyns, imagined one maid asking another on the eve of marriage whether she really wanted to spend the rest of her life in the country, casting up the weekly bills of housekeeping and darning old napkins.[94] In remote Northumberland after her marriage Betty Livingston quickly found out that what was applauded as witty conversation at court, 'in this part off the world is look'd upon to be a gidynesse unbecominge a wife, and want of a prudent sober temper'.[95]

If country gentlemen were frightened away, there would be all the more risk of male courtiers coming to regard the maids of honour as 'amusements, placed expressly at court for their entertainment', and never seeking to marry them.[96] A 'Mother of the Maids' or governess was employed in each household to chaperone the girls, but the Queen's, Lady Sanderson, was known to be elderly and ineffectual, and in any case could do little to protect them from the King, his brother, or his son. Some girls, Carey Frazier and Catherine Sedley amongst them, had no intention of letting themselves be protected. A royal liaison could seem a far more exciting means of making their fortunes than marriage, while not necessarily being a bar to it in the long term. Winifred Wells, one of the Queen's first maids, became the King's mistress for a time, as Goditha Price was to the Duke of York. The latter, a constant butt of Rochester's lampoons, eventually had to leave the Duchess's service for

[91] Pepys, *Diary*, vi. 41; BL Add. 78317: Dorothy Howard to JE, 25 Aug. [1675].

[92] Cavendish, 'The Presence', in *Plays never before Printed*, 58–9.

[93] HMC *Rutland MSS*, ii. 31: Lady Chaworth to Lord Roos, 11 [Dec. 1677].

[94] Hamilton, *Grammont*, 265.

[95] 'Notes from a Delaval Diary', *Proceedings of the Society of Antiquaries of Newcastle upon Tyne*, 3rd ser. 1 (1903–4), 153.

[96] Hamilton, *Grammont*, 262.

the more liberal household of Lady Castlemaine, but Winifred Wells was eventually married off, well dowered, to a minor courtier who was willing to overlook her past, and her colleague Ellen Warmestry, who became pregnant by another of the courtiers, also found a country gentleman to whom proof that she could bear children was more important than an unblemished record of pre-marital chastity.[97] Frances Stewart was adroit and self-possessed enough to exploit the King's passion for her while taking care not to let it interfere with her chance of an eminent (though crashingly dull) match with his cousin, 'the booby Duke' of Richmond.[98]

But in general the needy situation of many of the girls made them, or at least their reputations, vulnerable. The Duchess of Newcastle complained of court gallants for singling one woman out for extravagant praise while reviling women in general.[99] Few new arrivals escaped the crudest lampoons, satire, and casual denigration, from Henry Savile's 'young beggarly bitches' to these verses of 1663 'on the court ladies':

> Steward's looke is very pale
> If you would know what she doth aile
> I'le tell you for a farthing
> It was her hap to get a clap
> By the new made Lord Fitzharding
>
> Carew's face is not the best
> Yet she's as useful as the rest
> Though not so much a luring
> Yet she's as good as Madam Wood
> For pimping and for whoring . . .
>
> Boynton, Price and all the rest
> Take heed of leapfroge though in jest
> Obey your reverend Mother
> Who warnes you all with non to fall
> But Caesar and his brother . . .

And so on for eighteen more crude verses, in which all the maids of honour and dressers were singled out for individual mention.[100] It was even hinted that male courtiers were not the only risk. The most mature of the Duchess of York's maids, Frances Hobart, was transferred to another post in her household amid gossip that she had made sexual overtures to two of the

[97] Ibid. 242–6; *CTB 1669–1672*, 1312.   [98] Hartmann, *La Belle Stuart*, 100–30.
[99] Quoted by Sara Heller Mendelson, *The Mental World of Stuart Women* (Brighton, 1987), 17.
[100] Versions in *English Language Notes*, 10 (1972–3), 201–6, and (exhaustively annotated) in Wilson (ed.), *Court Satires of the Restoration*, 3–9.

younger girls.[101] In fact the Queen was the only woman at court whose chastity was never called in question. A foreign visitor was assured that none of the maids of honour was 'so stupid that they cannot get maintenance and extras; and the governesses . . . are tactful enough to let them enjoy the fruits of their industry'; and this was not just the opinion of outsiders; of all the girls at court when she first arrived Betty Livingston thought only her cousin Lady Essex Howard virtuous enough for her to be intimate with.[102]

Although some girls did have parents at or near the court, their role was not necessarily protective. Carey Frazier's mother was seen to aid and abet her ambitions to become a royal mistress. Sarah Jenyns, the future Duchess of Marlborough, never forgot the sight of Mary Trevor leaving the maids' lodgings at St James's 'with infamy', wringing her hands and wailing that her mother had undone her by her advice; Thomas Thynne of Longleat had said that he would not marry any woman unless he was certain she could bear children, and rather than lose the chance of such a wealthy match, her mother advised her to comply, only to find her abandoned once she became pregnant. Sarah Jenyns herself won a noisy battle to remain at court against the wishes of her mother, who declared that 'two of the maids had had great bellies at court, and she would not leave her child there to have the third'.[103] It all recalled Clarendon's lament about the breakdown of parent–child relations after the disruption of the Civil War years: the young no longer asked the blessing of their parents, 'nor did they concern themselves in the education of their children; but were well content that they should take any course to maintain themselves that they might be free from that expense'.[104] In practice a good many of the girls seem to have been left to their own devices or to have been quite willing to take responsibility for themselves. Certainly it suited the court wits to regard them as free spirits from an early age; 'Courage', says Hippolyta to herself, in Wycherley's *Gentleman Dancing Master*, '. . . thou art full fourteen years old, shift for thyself.'[105]

Margaret Blagge was just Hippolyta's age when she joined the Duchess's household, and she did so under reasonably good auspices. Her two predecessors of most dubious reputation, Frances Hobart and Goditha Price, had already been transferred elsewhere, and the others, Anne Temple and her cousin Frances Jenyns, had just married quickly and well: the first to a widowed soldier, Sir Charles Lyttelton, with whom she settled down to a long, happy, and fruitful married life; the second (who had laid it down as

---

[101] Hamilton, *Grammont*, 259–79.

[102] *Lorenzo Magalotti at the Court of Charles II*, 33; *Meditations of Lady Elizabeth Delaval*, 123.

[103] Harris, *Passion for Government*, 21, 24–5,

[104] Clarendon, *Life*, i. 305.   [105] Act II, sc. 2.

her maxim that a young woman 'in so dangerous a situation . . . ought to use her utmost endeavours not to dispose of her heart until she gave her hand') to Sir George Hamilton, nephew of the Duke of Ormonde and the King's favourite page.[106] The four new recruits who came in their place were Arabella Churchill, Anne Ogle, Dorothy Howard, and Margaret herself. It was soon clear enough that the first would take Goditha Price's place with the Duke, but the families of the other three girls were already closely linked; the Ogles were based at Pinchbeck near Spalding, where Mrs Blagge had her estate and the Howards acquired Revesby Abbey nearby. They were able to band together and make their own small society.[107]

'This was indeede a Surprizing Change of Aer', Evelyn wrote afterwards of Margaret's first coming to court,

and a perilous Climate for one so very Young to breathe in, as had Scarsely yet attain'd to the Twelfth year of her Age: But by how much more the Danger, so much greater the Vertue and discretion; which not only preserv'd her Steady in that slipery & giddy station; but so Improv'd; That the example of this little Saint, Influenc'd not her honorable Companions alone, but some who were Advanc'd in yeares before her, and of the most Illustrious Quality; What shall I Say? She, like a young Apost'lesse, begun to Plant Religion in that Barren Soile, and (like the River Arethusa) past thro' those turbulent waters, without so much as the least staine or tincture to her Chrystal.—With her Piety, grew up her Wit; which was so Sparkling, accompany'd with Judgement, a Natural Eloquence, and so Extraordinary a Beauty, & Aire so charming and lovely. In a word, an Addresse so universally taking; that after few yeares, the Court had never seen such a Constellation of Perfections, among all their Splendid Circles . . .[108]

In fact, as he admitted himself, he had not known Margaret at all at this time, and his fantasy of a pious infant beauty bringing religion to a corrupt court is questionable on every count. In the first place Margaret was not 12 but rising 14, a much more usual age, at her first appointment. Far from being recognized as exceptional, she was not mentioned in any contemporary record until she had been at court for three years, and then only as a name in the lists of household officials. While Arabella Churchill and Dorothy Howard figured in an Italian visitor's inventory of striking court beauties, Margaret did not.[109] Except perhaps for a more punctilious religious observance than most (and this was not unique amongst the court woman), she does not seem to have stood out from the crowd of young women or made any such striking impression there at first as Evelyn assumed.

[106] Hamilton, *Grammont*, 257.
[107] Craven Howard eventually married Anne Ogle; see JE, *Diary*, iv. 70–1.
[108] *Life*, 10–11.   [109] *Lorenzo Magalotti at the Court of Charles II*, 154.

Initially, whatever the calculations and misgivings of their families, the girls usually arrived in a state of great excitement and anticipation. The pleasures of the court were those most likely to appeal to the young: dressing, dancing, attending and acting in plays, hunting, music, and 'all sorts of devertions', with the additional delights of 'new caught lovers'.[110] Margaret was no different from the rest. Knowing how closely new maids were scrutinized, her first anxiety, she told Evelyn afterwards, was not to be found wanting: she came young 'into the World; (that is about fourteene years of Age) where no sooner was I entr'd; but various Opinions were deliverd concerning Me . . . The first thing which Tempts Young Women, is Vanity, and I made that my greate Designe.' Her later self-castigation for indulging in thoughtless pleasures and 'childish and foolish frindships', for dashing about the stairs and galleries of Whitehall and St James's when she should have walked, as well as the reputation for wit and raillery which made Evelyn keep his distance from her at first, all suggest that she was a typical young courtier.[111] When her mother, who was now feeling her age, went off to spend the last summer of the decade with her ailing brother at Mildenhall, Margaret found it far more enjoyable to remain behind with her court friends at Deptford.

But all the Blagge sisters were aware of their mother's straitened circumstances and Margaret had no doubt of the main purpose of her being at court. A year or two later she was to advise the Howard sisters to pay due attention to their appearance, not to attract lovers, who might include rakes and married men, but 'purely for the honest designe of disengaging yourselves as soon as you can from the place you are in, in an honourable way'; but on no account were they to run into debt in the process, 'for no duty to the Queene in making a shew behind her can excuse one from justice to our Neighbour, before that God in whose Presence we walke'. Her mother gave her £100 of her legacy in advance to help with the expenses of her clothes and she became adept at dress-making contrivances to make it go as far as possible. She was aware of the dangers of her situation but not alarmed by them, reassuring the Howards sensibly that 'in this Age you know, Women are not so wonderfully solicited that have the Vertue, & Modesty of you Two; That good service, the Ladys of other Principles have don you; that men sooner find their Error: & without much difficulty, suspected Conversation may be avoided'.[112]

After a year or two her first pleasure probably began to give way to disillusion. Sarah Jenyns thought that anyone with sense and honesty must tire of a

---

[110] *Meditations of Lady Elizabeth Delaval*, 6, 123.

[111] *Life*, 15, 30; BL Add. MS 78392: prayer 'for Tuesday' by MB, [1673], copied by JE.

[112] *Life*, 100, 102.

court very quickly, and having arrived eagerly at the age of 13, after a year said that she wished herself out of it 'as much as I had desired to come into it before I knew what it was'.[113] For all the surface gaiety and glamour, fundamental sleaziness and aimlessness were inescapable. Whitehall, made 'nasty and stinking' by its crowds of human and animal inhabitants, was no place for the fastidious. Delicacy or weakness were mocked; Pepys was disgusted by the 'silly sport' amongst the royal party when two of the Queen's women became seasick during a barge trip, 'in very common terms methought . . . and below what people think these great people say and do'.[114] The King particularly enjoyed discomforting women with bawdy remarks; Margaret had to resolve not to respond to him and his cronies 'when they speake filthily, tho' I be Laugh'd at'.[115] The court had also changed a good deal since the first cheerful years. After the public disasters of the plague, the Great Fire, and the humiliation of the Dutch naval invasion, complaints of mercenariness and corruption increased. As if to emphasize the contamination at all levels, a newswriter made a point of recording the arrest of the Lord Chamberlain's footman for an act of bestiality committed on one of the Queen's pet cows who grazed in St James's Park. The King had to listen to lengthy harangues about his wayward life from the pulpit, and when he disembarked at the Privy Stairs on his birthday he found scrawled on the whitewashed wall of the gallery the couplet:

> Hobbes his Religion, Hyde his Moralls gave
> And this day birth to an ungratefull knave.[116]

The York household in particular suffered by association with the scapegoat Clarendon and the Duchess was blamed for putting her father for so long above the reach of his opponents. To prevent the Duke's being able to form a party to reinstate him, his opponents worked to undermine confidence between the brothers. For over a year afterwards relations between the two households were very strained.[117] Lady Berkeley, dismissed as groom of the stole by the Duchess for 'something relating to my Lord Ch[ancellor's] business', was immediately taken into the Queen's household.[118] At Whitehall the King had his lodgings reconstructed and plans for a complete and uniform rebuilding of the palace were resurrected;[119] no longer would it be said that he was more meanly housed than his brother. At times it even

---

[113] Harris, *Passion for Government*, 16.   [114] Miller, *James II*, 38; Pepys, *Diary*, v. 306.

[115] Halifax [George Savile], *Complete Works*, 257; *Life*, 16.

[116] BL Add. MS 36916, fos. 100, 103: newsletters, 16 May, 6 June 1668.

[117] Pepys, *Diary*, viii. 286; Miller, *James II*, 55–6.

[118] BL Add. MS 36916, fo. 27: newsletter, 26 Nov. 1667.

[119] Simon Thurley, *The Lost Palace of Whitehall* (1998), 33–9.

seemed that the Duke's place in the succession might be under threat. The Duke of Monmouth appeared at the Queen's birthday dressed regally in cloth of gold and ermine, and there was the renewed possibility that the King might at last have a legitimate child. When the Queen miscarried in the spring of 1668, the event actually increased her standing because for the first time everyone, including the King, was convinced the pregnancy had been genuine. Under the supervision of Peter Chamberlen, the leading 'man midwife' of the day, she adopted a regime of outdoor exercise designed to improve her health and increase the likelihood of future pregnancies.[120] The worst tension between the two households was dispelled when the King declared publicly in December 1668 that he had no intention of disinheriting his brother, but the 'gang' of male and female servants whom Pepys observed at Deptford drinking to the union of the two brothers, had some reason for their anxiety.[121]

Originally the Duchess's court might have been livelier and more select than the Queen's, but by the time Margaret arrived it was beginning to be past its prime. No longer satisfied with casual liaisons, the Duke installed Arabella Churchill as his official mistress with her own financial settlement. When she left the court in the summer of 1668, it was common knowledge that she had gone away to bear his child.[122] 'One of the highest feeders in England', the Duchess became hugely overweight and began to decline in health, retaining little of her former good looks but her magnificent chestnut hair. The Dukes of Cambridge and Kendal died within weeks of each other in 1667 and a further little boy born shortly afterwards was never considered likely to live. When she began to appear less and less in public, supposedly to conceal ulcers on her face and legs, it was hinted that she and her younger children had been infected with venereal disease by her errant husband.[123] A foreign visitor, who evidently had his information from Clarendon's opponents, set her down as 'a woman obstinate, proud, vindictive, hot-tempered, deceitful, cruel, scornful, worshipping gluttony and amusements . . . the universal hatred and abhorrence of all her closest servants (to whom she is insupportable because of her scorn, her ingratitude, and her arrogance), the court, the household, and all three kingdoms'. Certainly her household

---

[120] BL Add. MS 36916, fo. 119: newsletter, 18 Nov. 1668; Hartmann, *King my Brother*, 216; BL Egerton MS 2539, fo. 193: newsletter, 12 [May] 1668; Add. MS 10117, fo. 232: newsletter, 5 Sept. 1669.

[121] BL Add. 36916, fo. 121: newsletter 12 Dec. 1668; Miller, *James II*, 52–3.

[122] BL Add. MS 36916, fo. 112: newsletter, 18 Aug. 1668; *CTB 1702 and addenda*, 690, secret service payment to her (then) husband Charles Godfrey on a settlement of 18 Feb. 1669.

[123] Hamilton, *Grammont*, 311; HMC *Rutland MSS*, ii. 10: Lady Chaworth to Lord Roos, 4 [May 1668?]; George deF Lord (ed.), *Poems on Affairs of State*, 1 (New Haven, 1963), 216.

by this time was unhappy, unpopular, and in financial disarray, and for the last her own extravagance was blamed.[124] Having dismissed Lady Berkeley, she had difficulty in keeping another groom of the stole, until the post finally devolved on Lady Peterborough, whose husband held the equivalent office in the Duke's household, and she sought it chiefly as a refuge from her own desperately unhappy marriage. Complaining that her husband had forsaken her bed and was taking his pleasure elsewhere, and that he encouraged the children and servants against her, she declared that she would be his housekeeper no longer, 'which was all he used her for'.[125] At the lower levels there was secrecy and divided allegiances. One of the dressers, Katherine Elliott, was an intriguer with long and intimate connections in the King's household (her mother had been his nurse and had supposedly undertaken his sexual initiation as well), and she used these to spread intimate details about the reality or otherwise of the Queen's pregnancies.[126] Another, Lelis Cranmer, was entrusted with a more momentous secret. However careless the general behaviour in the Chapel Royal, Anglican observance in the Duchess's household had always been punctilious. She was a regular communicant, making her confession beforehand to her father's long-time friend Bishop Morley and afterwards giving him £20 in gold to distribute as charity. Now she began to make repeated excuses to avoid prayers and communion according to the Anglican rites. Her ill health was the ostensible excuse, but Lelis Cranmer knew and others soon began to suspect that the Duchess, like her husband, had begun to take instruction in the Roman Catholic faith.[127]

Margaret could take comfort from the fact that she would not need to remain in the household for much longer. In the three years she had been at court she had grown from a child into a young woman. 'I had not then indeed the honour to know her', Evelyn wrote, 'but I have heard from Others that her Beauty & her Wit was so extraordinarily Improvd; as there had nothing ben seene more surprizing, & full of Charmes.'[128] A portrait of her in the style of Lely at about this time shows her still in the slenderness of adolescence, with a delicate oval face, a long shapely nose, and arresting dark eyes. The graceful, indolent pose was a standard one, used in full-length or three-quarter versions for a number of more famous court beauties, including

---

[124] *Lorenzo Magalotti at the Court of Charles II*, 37; Pepys, *Diary*, viii. 286–7.

[125] HMC *13th Report, App. VI*, 267: Lord Anglesey's diary, Sept. 1671.

[126] BL M.636/23 (Verney MSS): Margaret Elmes to Sir Ralph Verney, 9 June 1669; for her mother Christabel Wyndham, see Antonia Fraser, *King Charles II* (Mandarin, 1993), 14, 37.

[127] Joyce Henslowe, *Anne Hyde, Duchess of York* [1915], 240–1; Clarke (ed.), *The Life of James the Second*, ii, 452; Burnet, *History*, i. 417.

[128] *Life*, 29.

Lady Falmouth, Lady Henrietta Hyde, the Duchess of Portsmouth, and Lady Oxford.[129] The last had been painted with one breast bared. Modesty is preserved in Margaret's case, though her costume is disordered and precariously clasped at the bosom. With her hair elaborately ringleted, she gazes out, if not with the languid full-blown voluptuousness of Lely's mature beauties, yet still with something of their air of provocative sensuality; though at the same time, if one can read so much into so standardized an image, there is a suggestion of chaste self-possession, a slightly withdrawn and challenging air. 'Every body was in Love with, & some almost dying for her,' Evelyn wrote of her at this time, 'whilst (with all the Modesty, & Circumspection imaginable) she . . . would often checq the Vivacity which was Natural . . . for feare of giving Occasion to those who Lay in waite to Deceive. But it was not possible *here* to make the Least Approch, but such as was full of honour; And the distance she observ'd, the Caution, & Judgement she was Mistris of, protected her from all Impertinent Addresses, 'til she had made a Choice without Exception, and worthy her Esteeme.'[130] In the painting one elbow rests on a plinth containing a relief sculpture of a cupid; her other hand holds what may be a sprig of laurel, a symbol of love and virtue. It is 'an elegant image of an official beauty, carefully caught and defined by the conventions of courtly portraiture', with vestigial traces of the neoplatonic mode in which virtuous love is the fruition of beauty and redeemer of men.[131]

The 'Choice without Exception' which Margaret had made from amongst her admirers was Sidney Godolphin, a young courtier in his early twenties belonging to the King's household. When she first came to court, as she told Evelyn, 'various opinions' were delivered about her, 'and the Person whome you know, was more favourable to me than the rest, and did after some time, declare it to me'. For a while she was flattered by the many attentions, 'but Love soone taught me another lesson; And I found the Trouble of being tied to the hearing of any save him, which made me Resolve, that either He, or None should have the Possession of your Friend . . . This,

---

[129] Richard Wendorf, *The Elements of Life: Biography and Portrait-Painting in Stuart and Georgian England* (Oxford, 1990), 65–8 and plate 11; MacLeod and Alexander (eds.), *Painted Ladies*, 30–2, 56–7. There is a version of this portrait with an Evelyn family provenance at West Lodge Park, Hadley Wood (Plate 5) and another, presumably made for Lady Berkeley, at Berkeley Castle. They differ in some details of costume and appear not to be by the same painter. The usual attribution of the first to Mary Beale is a tempting one because she had close links both with Margaret's Suffolk relations (her associate Matthew Snelling was Thomas Blagge's step-brother) and with the Anglican community in London, but it is unlikely on stylistic grounds. I am grateful to Tabitha Barber, curator at the Tate Gallery and of the 1999 exhibition on Mary Beale at the Geffrye Museum, for discussion of this point.

[130] *Life*, 29.   [131] Wendorf, *Elements of Life*, 66; Stuart, *Pin-ups or Virtues*, 5–14.

under Gods Providence, has ben the meanes of preserving me from many of those Mis-fortunes, Young Creatures meete with in the World, and in Court especialy.'[132]

Sidney Godolphin held the same rank in the King's household as Margaret in the Duchess's: that of page of honour. His duties were to accompany the King on his journeys and to perfect his courtly skills, and in due course if he made himself agreeable and useful he could expect to be promoted to some higher post by the King's favour. Their backgrounds amongst the royalist and Anglican gentry were also virtually identical. In fact both had places in the intricate network of kinship which linked the Killigrews, the Berkeleys, and the Jermyns. A cousin of Sidney's in the Secretary of State's office had helped Mary Blagge in her difficulties over her pension. Another, Charles Berkeley, Lord Falmouth, had been one of her mediators with the King, while Godolphin's chief mentor at court was the Covells' patron and cousin, John Hervey of Ickworth. 'You knew each other before you knew each other,' as Evelyn put it later to Margaret.[133]

Sidney Godolphin was the third son of twelve children of Sir Francis Godolphin and Dorothy Berkeley, of the leading branch of the much ramified Cornish clan which was based at Godolphin in the extreme west of the county. In closer touch by sea with Spain and France than with London and the rest of England, the gentry society of the long peninsular was of an almost claustrophobic neighbourliness: a cultivated society, but one which felt its physical and moral remoteness from the metropolis. The Godolphins' steward on a reluctant visit to the capital could wish his friends the opportunity of seeing *Macbeth* on the London stage, but not that they should have to come to 'this wicked town' to do so.[134] Yet the family always had close connections with the court. The high point of their fortunes had been reached in the last years of Elizabeth under Sidney's great-grandfather, Sir Francis Godolphin I. Governor of the Scilly Isles and Lord Burghley's leading man in the county while it was in the front line of defence against Spain, his tin mines employed 300 men and provided a revenue to the crown 'not to be matched again by any of his sort and condition in the whole realm'. He duly improved his remote and mine-scarred estate to match his status, laying out a deer park and modelling his gardens on those of Burghley at Theobalds. His grandson Sir Francis III, Sidney's father, went on to renovate the old Tudor house in a

---

[132] *Life*, 30.

[133] PRO SP 29/98, fo. 2: Mary Blagge to William Godolphin, 2 May 1664; BL Add. MS 78386: JE, 'Oeconomics to a Newly Married Friend', [1676], p. 6.

[134] Richard Carew, *The Survey of Cornwall*, ed. F. E. Halliday (1953), 136; Cornwall RO, RP 1/35: John Penneck to John Rogers, 28 Feb. 1671.

fashionable Palladian style.[135] Although the Civil War curtailed his activities, the produce of the tin mines remained one of the supports of the royalist cause, and the house sheltered the Prince of Wales on his flight from England in 1646.[136] At the Restoration he devoted himself energetically to establishing his large family of able, intelligent sons and daughters as well as his overstretched resources would allow, relying on the great advantage that no family in England had 'more near kindred and friends at court'.[137]

Then in 1667, just as Sidney Godolphin and Margaret Blagge were forming their first attachment, Sir Francis died, followed a year later by his wife. Their eldest son Sir William became head of the family, but it was already clear that he would never marry or succeed fully to his father's position. He had completed his education by travelling in Italy; his father had bought a baronetcy for him at the Restoration and sought an advantageous local match on his behalf, only to be defeated at every turn by his 'modesty'. Although he did not lack the abilities for a public career he preferred retirement, sometimes in Cornwall, but for longer periods at his house in Suffolk Street just north of Whitehall. There he could observe the world from a distance and without involvement. Cultivated and studious, with a particular fondness for abstruse theological matters, he later became a friend of Evelyn, who found him 'a most learned Gent: & excellent Divine'.[138] His unmarried sisters provided his company. The two eldest had been married in the lifetime of their father into prominent west country families, Elizabeth to the Devonshire squire Sir Henry Northcote and Jael to the Cornish merchant Edward Boscawen. But the four who were unmarried at his death remained so, partly perhaps for the want of ready resources to dower them, but chiefly because none of them seemed to have had much desire to leave the close-knit, pious family circle.

The younger brothers had to be more active. The family estate could provide only small annuities for their bare maintenance, so if they wished to marry and form their own households they must first make their fortunes.[139] The second, Francis, was launched by his father on a career in the Secretary of State's office and soon developed something of a reputation as a virtuoso,

---

[135] Peter Herring, *Godolphin, Breage: An Archaeological and Historical Survey* (Truro, 1998), 63–71, 209.

[136] Cornwall RO, RP 1/23 and 24: Francis Godolphin to John Rogers, [Feb. 1644?]; Mary Coate, *Cornwall in the Great Civil War* (Oxford, 1933), 184; S. Elliott Hoskins, *Charles II in the Channel Islands* (1854), 342–51.

[137] Hugh Elliot, *The Life of Sidney, Earl of Godolphin* (1888), 39–40.

[138] Ibid.; Burnet, *History*, vi. 143; JE, *Diary*, iv. 159.

[139] PRO PROB 11/325, fo. 132: will of Sir Francis Godolphin; Cornwall RO, Godolphin Papers 858: calculations of the value of the estate and family settlements, [c.1667].

amassing a fine library in his chambers in the Temple; but his advancement was hindered by failings of temperament quite different from those of his elder brother. He had inherited his father's ill-governed temper (his mother was still apologizing in her widowhood to offended family members for this one failing of 'the worthiest husband and the tenderest father'); any sense that he was being outdistanced in preferment produced corroding resentment and fits of violent anger, so that he soon began to be known amongst those who had crossed his path as 'that envious and malicious little gentleman'.[140] His relations with Sidney in particular were never easy, and eventually their rivalry was even to encompass Margaret Blagge.

Sidney Godolphin remarked of himself in later life that his 'countenance was none of the best at any time'.[141] He was small like all his family, and dark-complexioned at a time when this was unfashionable. But he was also straight and well made, an expert horseman and tennis player. Although he could lapse into gravity and silence and seem forbiddingly grim and withdrawn, his face was 'enliven'd with a quick piercing Eye' and now and then 'sweetened with a Smile',[142] and he could be engagingly light-hearted amongst his friends. He took readily to the court, his shrewdness of judgement, quiet self-assurance and equable temperament contrasting with the handicaps of his two elder brothers. Without casting off the Anglican piety of his family or involving himself closely in the libertinism of the King's circle, he made himself quite at home amongst the wits, developed a facility for scribbling light verse, and became an adept gambler. Yet he never neglected an opportunity to make himself unobtrusively useful to his patrons and would stage-manage Sir William's occasional obligatory public appearances, and excuse his much more frequent absences, with adroitness and tact. The King neatly described him as 'never in the way, never out of the way'.[143] His powerful cousins, Charles Berkeley and Lord Sunderland, liked and trusted him, and Arlington made a special protégé of him. Godolphin's letters to him were more like those of a favoured godson or nephew than a junior courtier addressing a chief minister.

---

[140] HMC *4th Report*, 279: Sir Francis Godolphin to Charles Berkeley, 22 Oct. 1662; Roger North, *Lives of the Norths*, ed. A Jessopp (1890), ii. 283–9 (where Sidney Godolphin is named by mistake as the owner of the library); BL Add. MS 28052, fo. 4: Lady Godolphin to Lady Fitzhardinge, 12 Apr. 1667; *CSP Domestic 1672*, 547: Francis Godolphin to Arlington, 31 Oct. 1672; ibid. *1673–1675*, 55–6: Roger Jones to Viscount Conway, 11 Dec. 1673.

[141] BL Add. MS 57861, fo. 83: SG to Coningsby, 1 Dec [1706].

[142] Abel Boyer, *The History of Queen Anne* (1735), 17.

[143] A. W. Thibaudeau (ed.), *Catalogue of the Collection of . . . Alfred Morrison* (1883–92), ii. 185, and National Library of Scotland, MS 3420, fo. 44: SG to Sir William Godolphin, 26 July [1669], 9 Oct. [1675]; Elliott, *Godolphin*, 48; Burnet, *History*, i. 183.

It was soon clear that his ambitions went far beyond those of a mere courtier. In 1667 he volunteered for service in a newly raised cavalry troop against the Dutch, reassuring the doubtful Sir William that his keenness would be noticed and enhance his prospects. Above all his aim as soon as he was of age was to get himself elected, 'for love or money', to one of numerous Cornish boroughs, well aware that a vote in Parliament at the service of the court would be the greatest boost he could possibly have to his advancement there. When his brother Frank resentfully claimed prior right, he pointed out that a seat in the House would 'bee of ten times more advantage to me than it could possibly have been to him', and politely declined to step aside. In the aftermath of the Dutch war it was not an advantage for a parliamentary candidate to be a courtier; his friend Bab May had just been told by his constituency that they did not want a court pimp for their burgess. But Godolphin was determined not to be handicapped with these tin-mining boroughs in a matter of such 'infinite concern' to him; 'is there no kind of thing wherein the towne of Helston may be the better for a courtier as you call me?' he prompted the electors persuasively: 'think a little seriously'. He was duly elected their MP.[144] By Arlington's favour he then went on to a temporary diplomatic posting in Paris, mastered the language, and returned in the summer of 1669 with a glowing report from the ambassador Ralph Montagu of having 'succeeded so well here with everybody, that the longer he stayed it had been the better for him'. He was no sooner back at court than he was promoted into the adult post of groom of the bedchamber.[145]

At the time of her first encounter with the Evelyns at Deptford Margaret's future therefore seemed settled. Her suitor might only be a younger son without the country estate of a Sir Thomas Yarburgh, but he was already established as one of the more promising young men at court. It might be some years before they could afford to marry and set up their own household, but they had no doubt that their future together was assured; 'we thought of nothing, but living allways together', Margaret told Evelyn, 'and that we should be happy'.[146]

---

[144] Elliott, *Godolphin*, 45–58; Thibaudeau (ed.), *Catalogue of the Collection of . . . Alfred Morrison*, ii. 185: SG to Sir William Godolphin, [Aug. 1668]; Sir Tresham Lever, *Godolphin* (1952), 12–15.
[145] Lever, *Godolphin*, 16; Roy Sundstrom, *Sidney Godolphin: Servant of the State* (Newark, NJ, 1992), 17.
[146] *Life*, 30.

5

Conversion

WHEN Evelyn first encountered Margaret at Deptford she belonged to his wife's circle rather than his own. More than two years passed before their distant acquaintance became friendship and in the course of this time, unknown to him, all the apparent securities of her position, the family, the court post, the promising engagement to marry, one by one came under threat or were lost.

Her mother had been ailing for some time. One of the petitions concerning the arrears of her pension mentioned an illness which was increased by this long-drawn-out anxiety.[1] But the end when it came in the spring of 1670 was unexpected; she was 'at first Surpriz'd and very un-willing', wrote Margaret, '[but] she was afterwards Resign'd, Receiv'd [communion] often, Pray'd much, had holy things read to her: Delighted in heavenly Discourses; Desir'd to be dessolv'd & to be with Christ; Ended her life cherefully, & without Paine; left her Family in Order and was much lamented'. It was an exemplary end, but it left Margaret very aware that she was now an orphan.[2] Her mother's will, made the preceding summer at Mildenhall, was a simple, sensible, and scrupulously fair document. In it she bequeathed the unmarried girls, Dorothy, Mary, and Margaret, equal shares in the Spalding lease, worth £50 a year each. The remainder of her fortune consisted of £200 in cash and a further sum of £500, probably an interest-bearing loan, in the hands of her nephew Henry North. This was left to Mary and Margaret in equal shares; Dorothy's portion had already been used to purchase an annuity of £40 from her brother-in-law Sir Thomas Yarburgh. Since Margaret had anticipated £100 of her legacy to meet her expenses at court, this was deducted from her

---

[1] PRO SP 29/240: Mary Blagge to Joseph Williamson, 13 May [1668].
[2] *Life*, 12: BL Add. MS 78308: MG to JE, [Jan. 1676] (postscript to a letter of Lady Berkeley to JE).

share, but she was bequeathed the arrears of her mother's pension, a highly uncertain benefit but one which only she would have any chance of securing. The executors, Francis North, Henry North, and Thomas Covell were asked to assist in the management and improvement of the estate.[3]

Of these, Francis North, the future Lord Keeper, was by far the most useful and influential, but he was also a busy lawyer intent on his career. He could not be expected to interest himself in the affairs of his female cousins beyond the formal duties of his executorship and appears not to have done so. Covell had connections with the Queen's revenue, but he lived mostly in the depths of the country and could be of little personal support to a young woman at court. More obviously dependable were Mrs Blagge's brother Sir Henry North and his son, who held £500 of the daughters' inheritance, but by this time they had desperate troubles of their own. In his middle years Sir Henry had been an active and able Member of Parliament. He was also an idealistic, bookish man, the author of a full-blown platonic romance called 'Eroclea or the Maid of Honour' and a good deal of occasional verse which circulated in manuscript amongst his acquaintance. But he had been painfully declining in health for some years; his paraphrase of the 38th Psalm was headed poignantly, 'made . . . in time of his extreame pain, 12 March 1667/8'. When his wife of nearly forty years died a few months after Mary Blagge, it severed the root of his being. 'Oh thou art blest, but what I wretch am I,' ran the epitaph he composed for her, 'Thou mayst not live, I'm not allowed to die.' One morning a year later he was found dead in his bed, the pistol by him with which he had shot himself in the head. As was usual in such cases, the coroner pronounced him of unsound mind, so that his estate would not be subject to forfeiture, 'nor his body to the scorn and contempt that attends such deaths'. But his son's life was already blighted. Believing that the woman he loved was the daughter of his own illegitimate half-brother, he had never married, and in the year of Mrs Blagge's death she too died of smallpox. Whether their kinship had been a reality, a cruel uncertainty, or simply a neurotic delusion, it seems to have ended Henry North's hopes of happiness. Little else is recorded of the remainder of his life, except that he died unmarried and childless, the property at Mildenhall eventually passing to his sister Peregrina and her son Sir Thomas Hanmer, the grandson of Evelyn's 'prince of florists'.[4]

---

[3] PRO PROB 11/337/129.

[4] History of Parliament, *The House of Commons 1660–1690*, ed. B. D. Henning (1983), ii 152–4; BL Add. MSS 18220, fos. 9, 43–44ᵛ: verse by Sir Henry North; 19095, fos. 203ᵛ, 205ᵛ: notes concerning the North family; 36755: 'Eroclea'; Harold Love, *Scribal Publication in Seventeenth Century England* (Oxford, 1993), 28–9; *Correspondence of Sir Thomas Hanmer*, ed. Sir H. Bunbury (1838), 320–33; Roger North, *Lives of the Norths*, ed. A. Jessopp (1890), i. 407.

Within a year of Mrs Blagge's death the Duchess of York gave birth to one last sickly daughter and began to decline into mortal illness herself, suffering apparently from breast cancer. The suspicion that she had converted to Roman Catholicism contributed to her isolation and unpopularity, as she knew it would. Her deathbed was bleak and harrowing, and its aftermath still more so. Hostile newsmongers reported that in her last hours she had cried out in terror at the ghost of Lady Denham, one of her husband's mistresses, whom she was accused of poisoning. On the morning of her death she asked the Duke to tell the Anglican bishops of her conversion, and that if they still insisted on seeing her, they were not to disturb her by talking of it. The Bishop of Oxford, Dean of the Chapel Royal, was in attendance and the Duke accordingly gave him his instructions. 'Modest and humble, even to a fault', he replied humanely that 'he made no doubt but that she would do well . . . since she was fully convinced and did it not out of any worldly end'. He went in to her, and seeing the Queen already there, only said that he hoped she still continued in the truth; 'upon which she asked, what is truth'. As she sank into unconsciousness, the Duke, who had long since ceased to love her, 'called "Dame doe ye know me", twice or thrice, then with much strivings she said "Aye", after a little respite she took a little courage & with what vehemency & tenderness she could she said, "Duke, Duke, death is very terrible", which were her last words'. No Roman Catholic priest was allowed to be alone with her, so that in the end she was denied the last rites of her new faith. Those she was given after her death were brutally short: 'The Dutchesse of York died on Friday, opened on Satterday, embalmed on Sunday & buried last night', the newswriters reported baldly. More shocking details were told privately. The court physician Richard Lower, who conducted the post mortem, reportedly 'found her heart consumed to nothing, her Vitalls all rotted and her head instead of brains was full of water, [so that] she lived as long as it was possible for one in her condition to do'. As the body was prepared for burial, one of the breasts burst, 'being a mass of corruption'.[5] The woman who had outlived her usefulness and endangered the court by changing her faith was huddled privately into the vault at Westminster Abbey with neither the King nor the Duke present. Mourning was curtailed by the King's order, so that it would not interfere with his birthday celebrations on 29 May, and for so short a period it was not considered worth draping his apartments in black or putting his servants into mourning clothes. This was a great relief amongst others to Frances Hobart, who had been concerned at

[5] BL Add. MS 36916, fos. 217–18: newsletters, 4, 11 Apr. 1671; Gilbert Burnet, *History of his own Time*, ed. M. J. R[outh] (1833), i. 417; J. S. Clarke (ed.), *Life of James the Second* (1816), ii. 451–3; HMC *7th Report (Verney MSS)*, 464.

her mistress's death, 'not so much for the losse', as because she would have had to borrow to meet the expense of mourning.[6]

Margaret Blagge, who had attended the Duchess constantly in her illness, observed all this and drew her own hard lessons:

The D[uch]esse died, a Princesse honoured, in power: had much Wit, much mony, much esteeme: She was full of un-speakable torture, & died (poore Creature!) in Doubt of her Religion, without any Sacrament, or Divine by her, like a poor Wretch: None Remembred her after one Weeke: None sorry for her: She smelt extremely; was tost, and flung about, & every one did what they would with that stately Carcasse:—What is this World! What is Greatenesse! What to be esteem'd & thought a Wit! We shall all be strip't, without Sense or Remembrance: But God, if we serve him in our Health, will give us Patience in our Sicknesse.[7]

The last little Duke of Cambridge gave up his weak hold on life a few weeks later, followed by the baby sister whose birth had precipitated their mother's last illness. Of all her children only the 9-year-old Mary and her sister Anne remained, and they were kept chiefly in the seclusion of Richmond until the time should come for their public emergence at court. It only remained to provide for the Duchess's household in one way or another. It was dynastically inevitable that the Duke would shortly remarry. The older and more permanent female servants, the bedchamber women especially, could expect to be found places in the new household, since it would be cheaper than pensioning them off. Lelis Cranmer, having borne the state secret of the Duchess's conversion, was transferred to the Queen's household at once. Of the maids of honour, more ephemeral creatures, Arabella Churchill already had independent provision; Anne Ogle, now too old to continue as a maid, was found a more suitable place as Lady of the Queen's Privy Chamber; and Margaret Blagge and Dorothy Howard were moved across the park to fill vacancies in the maids' lodgings at Whitehall.[8] Even so their situation was rather precarious. There was no record of an allowance to them from the Treasury and it was not clear who, when the time came, would take responsibility for paying their marriage portions.

It was a different, but no more lively household in which Margaret found herself. The Queen, one of the court secretaries wrote, was not by this time 'a lady of great delights'. Her dress was plain, 'more like that of a widow than

---

[6] Christopher Lindenov, *The First Triple Alliance*, ed. W. Westergaard (New Haven, 1947), 396. BL M.636/24 (Verney MSS): Frances Hobart to Sir Ralph Verney, 5 Apr. [1671].

[7] *Life*, 12.

[8] National Library of Scotland, Adv. MS 31.1.22: warrant for Mrs Ogle, 21 Mar. 1672/3; *Life*, 28–9; Catherine of Braganza, 'Establishment of her Majesty Queen Catherine', 1671–2, *Catholic Record Society*, 38 (1941), pp. xxix–xxxii.

of a young princess', and her apartments less luxurious than those of the King's mistresses.[9] The brief period when she had been considered likely to produce an heir to the throne was over. After one final disputed miscarriage, it was now universally taken for granted, presumably because the King had ceased to have sexual relations with her, that she would never bear a child. There was occasional talk of a divorce, to which he showed himself willing to listen, 'if any of the Bishops could but satisfy him of the lawfulness of doing it'; but to little purpose, since there was no question of her misconduct and he himself had accepted that she was capable of conceiving. Her loss of weight, debility, and crippling headaches provided the excuse for his personal physician to examine her and pronounce her 'in a consumption' and unlikely to live more than a few months. 'The doctors all talk thus to ingratiate themselves with the king', the French ambassador commented.[10] In fact there was little reason to suppose she would not have a normal lifespan, during which her only dynastic significance would be as an impediment to the direct line of succession. The term 'our puppet queen' caught something of the emptiness of her role and the mechanical nature of her functioning from now on.[11]

Of the English women of her household she had most in common with the Duchess of Buckingham, the slighted wife of the King's boon companion from childhood, George Villiers. Barbara Castlemaine's influence over the King was declining, but she had borne him several children. Her aunt, Lady Suffolk, remained as groom of the stole; Barbara herself was still a lady of the bedchamber and so was her cousin Lady Marshall.[12] Lady Bath and Lady Arlington served because their husbands' positions required it; Lady Falmouth and the Duchess of Richmond because the King or his brother had once cast eyes on them. Two of the maids of honour, Winifred Wells and Henrietta Maria Price, were original appointees, both now well past the normal age for marriage. The delicate and pious Catherine Boynton, the only one of the Queen's maids with whom Margaret had anything in common, had just been unaccountably married, though 'a zealous Protestant', to the militant Irish Catholic Richard Talbot. In her place, setting the seal on the

[9] Harry Ransom Humanities Research Center, University of Texas: newsletter to Sir Richard Bulstrode, 14 Dec. 1676; *Lorenzo Magalotti at the Court of Charles II*, ed. W. E. Knowles Middleton (Waterloo, Ont., 1980), 30.

[10] Mark Knights, *Politics and Opinion in Crisis 1678–1681* (Cambridge, 1994), 35; BL M.636/24: Frances Hobart to Sir Ralph Verney, 21 Dec. 1671; Henri Forneron, *Louise de Kéroualle, Duchesse de Portsmouth* (Paris, 1886), 60.

[11] George deF Lord (ed.), *Poems on Affairs of State* (New Haven, 1963–75), i. 422.

[12] Sonya Wynne, 'The Mistresses of Charles II and Restoration Court Politics', Ph.D. thesis (Cambridge, 1997), 21.

Queen's humiliation, came the King's new *maîtresse en titre*, the Breton Louise de Kéroualle, whom he had first seen and coveted at Dover, when she came over in 1670 in the train of his sister for the signing of the new treaty of alliance with France. Soon she was assigned separate lodgings at the end of the Stone Gallery, opulently furnished at his expense. Shortly afterwards another controversial beauty, Sophia Stewart, younger sister of the Duchess of Richmond, came to join the maids.[13]

The female household was not without its small round of recreations; in summer the ninepins, fishing, and archery which had originally been recommended to improve the Queen's health and so her hopes of conception.[14] But even her few 'frolics' were apt to turn sour. Her fondness for dancing was criticized and an expedition in disguise to Bury fair with some of her household ended when they were recognized and pursued by a disorderly and rather menacing crowd back to the gates of Audley End.[15] Religion continued to be her chief solace. In addition to her private chapel at Whitehall she had a little closet oratory, furnished with 'pretty pious pictures and books of devotion and holy water'. At religious festivals she would attend her public chapel, first at St James's, and then after the Queen Mother died in 1669, at Somerset House. During Margaret's first summer in her household, the arms of France were replaced by the arms of Portugal in the state bedchamber there. The chapel and the Queen's closet within it were refurbished. The Capuchins who had done duty for the Queen Mother returned to France, and Catherine's Portuguese friars from St James's took their places. Trunks of goods were moved in, and on festival days throughout the summer and autumn the Queen's barges plied to and fro between Windsor and Somerset House. They also took her to visit Frances Bedingfield's convent school at Hammersmith. There were even rumours that she might be intending to retire from the humiliations of Whitehall altogether and take up a conventual life herself.[16] Margaret could go no further than the door of the Queen's chapels, but she observed and took note of these refuges. But if her mistress should retire, how would her household fare?

[13] BL Add. MS 78299, JE to Lady Sylvius, 4 May 1679 (marginal note); Catherine of Braganza, *Catholic Record Society*, 38, p. xxx; JE, *Diary*, iv. 74.

[14] Lincolnshire RO, Worsley MSS : Privy Purse accounts of Catherine of Braganza, Sept.–Oct. 1669; July–Aug. 1670.

[15] Lord (ed.), *Poems on Affairs of State*, i. 421–2; [A. W. Thibaudeau] (ed.), *The Bulstrode Papers* (n. p., 1897), 202.

[16] *Survey of London*, XIII, *St Margaret's Westminster (Neighbourhood of Whitehall)*, i (1930), 69; Howard Colvin, *The History of the King's Works*, v (1976), 257, 267; *Bulstrode Papers*, 121, 188; Lincolnshire RO, Worsley MSS: Privy Purse accounts of Catherine of Braganza, Aug.–Sept. 1671, May 1672, Aug. 1672; John Miller, *Popery and Politics in England 1660–1688* (Cambridge, 1973), 128.

Margaret and Sidney Godolphin still considered themselves bound to each other and had done so now for five years. Neither of them, she told Evelyn later, had ever given the other any cause for jealousy; 'nor will I presume to dive into the Circumstances, which made them so long resolving,' he added, 'she being then very young and both of a Temper so very discreete'.[17] Margaret had certainly been very young at first, but she was now fully of marriageable age, and at her own disposal. Where was her lover as one by one her other supports fell away?

He was no longer just an impoverished junior courtier. Since his return from France in 1669 he had continued to receive his page's allowance along with his new salary as groom of the bedchamber and to this was added the grant of some tin mines in Cornwall. Twice in the following year he was given the kind of diplomatic missions of compliment which were intended to give ambitious young courtiers experience of foreign courts, as well as the chance to receive handsome presents on their departure. With uncharacteristic promptness which was a measure of the favour with which he was regarded the Treasury paid him £500 for his expenses.[18] But all this meant that he was often away. He had been in France when Margaret's mother died. During her first summer in the Queen's household he was in the west country, organizing relays of coaches for the King's journey of inspection to Portsmouth. 'If I were ever in my life time the least serviceable it was in those kind of journeys', the dutiful courtier wrote, adding that his greatest pleasure was the hope of one day being able to do his master more substantial service.[19] He began to take colour from his surroundings, keeping such late hours and living so undomesticated a life that he could not share lodgings with his brother and sisters without disturbing them.[20] In the eyes of his countrymen at least he was becoming something of a 'monsieur', and used his increased income to gamble heavily, not just at the groom porter's but at the tennis courts. The family steward, up in the capital on business, wrote disapprovingly back to his friends in Cornwall of 'the vanities of London, everybody in Coach and Cloaths endeavouring to surpass one the other', and of 'Mr Sidd', and his gambling cronies; 'its a wonder if they do not lighten his pockett and make his heart heavy'.[21]

Opportunities for this increased when the King began to spend two or three weeks of each spring and autumn at Newmarket. Audley End, the huge and decaying folly house built by James I's Lord Treasurer, was taken

[17] *Life*, 29.   [18] *CTB 1669–1672*, 600. 726, 801, 818, 828, 832, 934.
[19] Sir Tresham Lever, *Godolphin* (1952), 16.
[20] National Library of Scotland, MS 3420. fo. 42: SG to Sir William Godolphin, 8 Dec. [1672].
[21] Cornwall RO: RP 1/35: John Penneck to John Rogers, 28 Feb. 1671.

over from the Earl of Suffolk to house the court at these times, its former council room even being fitted up as a chapel for the Queen.[22] But to be at the centre of things the King also bought an old house in Newmarket itself, demolished it, and much to Evelyn's disgust, built a new one on the foundations, 'meane enough & hardly capable for a hunting house', set 'in a dirty street without any court or avenue, like a common Burgers . . . the most improper [site] imaginable for a house of sport and pleasure'. The King loved it. He set up his racing stables nearby and in plain country clothes would show visitors around himself, knocking at the gate and waiting patiently until the groom chose to open it.[23] All his courtiers who could afford to do so followed suit. Above the irregular star-shape of the town, with its muddy streets, huddle of undistinguished buildings and flanking windmills, rose the broad expanse of the heath, where the four-mile racecourse was marked out between white posts. In the intervals between horse matches there were cockfights, bowling, tennis matches, hare-coursing with Monmouth's greyhounds, and of course the groom porter's gaming tables, so that the whole business of the place, except for the knockabout comedies played in the barn theatre, was sport and gambling. Sidney Godolphin could not yet afford to keep his own racehorses, but otherwise he took to it all with a passion. 'Newmarket's a rare place, there a Man's never idle,' a character in a play of Shadwell enthuses, 'We make Visits to Horses, and talk with Grooms, Riders, and Cock-keepers, and saunter in the Heath all the Forenoon: then we dine and never talk a Word but Dogs, Cocks and Horses again, then we saunter into the Heath again; then to the Cock-Match; then to a Play in a Barn; then to Supper . . . then to the Groom-Porters, where you may play all night. Oh, 'tis a heavenly Life! We are never idle.' 'For ought I see, you are never otherwise,' comments his companion Lady Cheatly.[24]

Margaret would no doubt have agreed with Lady Cheatly. In the autumn after she joined the Queen's household, the whole court made an East Anglian progress and she was able to see for herself. From Norwich, where the Queen took pleasure in her unexpected popularity and 'let allmost all sorts of people (of what degree soever)' kiss her hand, they moved on to the Hobarts at Blickling, the Pastons at Oxnead, the Townshends at Rainham, and so back to Audley End and Newmarket. There the great match of the season was run, the King's Woodcock against Flatfoot, owned by his groom of the bedchamber Tom Elliot. Then for light relief another of the grooms, James

[22] Colvin, *King's Works*, v. 131–2.
[23] Ibid. 214–15; JE, *Diary*, iii. 555; François Brunet, 'A French Traveller in Charles II's England', *Cornhill Magazine*, new ser., 20 (Jan.–June 1906), 664.
[24] Peter May, *The Changing Face of Newmarket 1660–1760* (Newmarket, 1984), 27.

Hamilton, offered to walk the course backwards and forwards in two hours for a wager of £100.[25] But the real headquarters of the court during this visit was not Newmarket or Audley End, but Arlington's Euston. In 1665 Bennet had put aside his witty mistress, bought an estate near Thetford, and married a Dutch woman of the royal house, Isabella de Nassau, who bore him one adored daughter and joined with him in making his houses centres of princely hospitality. Around the core of a much older country house Euston was transformed into a virtual palace, 'very magnificent and commodious', with four great pavilions in the French style. Every day or two the King would come over from his cramped quarters at Newmarket to dine and sometimes to stay the night. It was on one of these occasions that he was first formally bedded with Louise de Kéroualle. Arlington welcomed her because it was clear that the King must always have mistresses and she was not only an essential link in the alliance with France, but more decorous and amenable than Barbara Villiers or Nell Gwyn.[26] The county gentry gathered, ambassadors were in attendance, and diplomatic appointments were announced. Godolphin could counter any disapproval of Margaret's at the idleness of the place by showing that an ambitious young man could make it his business as well as his pleasure to be there. Between the hare-coursing and cock-matches he found himself appointed to accompany Sunderland on an urgent mission to Spain, to try to forestall its alliance with Holland, when war should again be declared by England and France against the Dutch Republic.[27]

It was a very different matter from a jaunt to Portsmouth or Paris. In November the two young men and their entourage set out on a strenuous overland journey through France, followed by a winter crossing of the Pyrenees which left several members of their party as casualties by the way, and weeks more strung out between the meagre staging posts of northern Spain, until they reached Madrid with relief at the very end of the year. There they were welcomed by the resident ambassador, Sidney's cousin, Sir William Godolphin. But with the mission established as fruitless almost from the first, this, his first serious exercise in diplomacy, was chiefly useful as an introduction to its *longeurs* and frustrations. The creaking ceremonies of the Spanish court, the ponderous rituals of hierarchy and precedence with which their hosts parried all attempts at negotiation were an intolerable irritation after the informality he had been used to. 'They talk here of other business', he

[25] R. W. Ketton-Cremer, *Norfolk Portraits* (1944), 10–21; HMC *LeFleming MSS*, 81: newsletter, 18 Oct. 1671; *Bulstrode Papers*, 205–6.

[26] JE, *Diary*, iii. 588–92; Forneron, *Louise de Kéroualle*, 49–54.

[27] J. P. Kenyon, *Robert Spencer, Earl of Sunderland* (1958), 11–12; Ronald Hutton, *Charles II* (Oxford, 1989), 283.

complained, 'but they have none but how to get the hand of one another.' With heavy irony he wrote of being 'so transported with the great variety of Delights which this place affords that my friends had need take more than ordinary pains to make me remember them'. He set off home with dispatches as soon as he could, but left his cousin, who had not seen him since he was an adolescent, impressed with his growing mastery of the complexities of their European business.[28]

No sooner was he back in London early in March than he was preparing to be dispatched again, this time to the court of France on his first independent appointment. War had now been declared against the Dutch and his role was to accompany Louis XIV on campaign, part of a concerted Anglo-French operation by land and sea. His preparations took up what little time he had in England. Margaret, anxious about her financial affairs, was hurt to find that he was too preoccupied to attend to them; and so they parted again for the whole of the summer with misunderstanding and distance between them.[29] As she entered on her second year at Whitehall, Godolphin set out across France with Monmouth's Anglo-Scottish brigade, one small component of the immense French army which rolled on from Verdun to Metz and so across the Rhine and into the Netherlands, with a juggernaut invincibility which was alarming even to an ally. So was 'the pitifull defence' put up by the Dutch, now shown to be as timid and vulnerable by land as they were bold and formidable at sea. Fortress after fortress surrendered at sight and within days the provinces of Gelderland and Overijssel were at the mercy of the French. With the army constantly on the move Godolphin had barely time to record each conquest for his dispatches and add the warning that 'if it goes on at this rate all Holland will be overrun in this one campaign'. In fact he had difficulty keeping up at all. Weakened by his months of strenuous journeying, he had succumbed to dysentery and fever before the army crossed the Rhine, but he struggled on with it, knowing that if he were once left behind he could never hope to catch up. By the time the Dutch sued for peace he was so weak that he could not cross a room without help. Yet his dispatches continued to be detailed and acute and his advice sound. He urged the King to send plenipotentiaries at once to ensure that his own peace terms were pressed. He was glad the fleet was putting to sea with a great show of might, not just 'with relation to the Dutch but to the King of France whom

---

[28] PRO SP 94/59, fos. 90–162: dispatches from Spain, Dec. 1671–Feb. 1672, *passim*; *Hispania Illustrata . . . in letters from . . . the Earl of Sandwich, the Earl of Sunderland and Sir William Godolphin* (1703), 136–42; *The Right Honourable the Earl of Arlington's Letters* (1701), ii. 358; BL Add. MS 75376: SG to Henry Savile, [Jan. 1672].

[29] *Life*, 22.

it will certainly make the more ready to accommodate the King in what he pretends to'. 'We are in league with France', he concluded,' . . . but I confesse I have no opinion of their sincerity to us from the moment our interests begin to be separate.'[30] Buckingham and Arlington were hastened over, and with their arrival Godolphin could lay down his responsibilities with relief. By this time, against all the odds, the French progress had been stopped. With the Dutch government in disarray, power passed into the hands of Charles II's nephew, the young and untried William of Orange. As an extreme emergency measure the sluices were opened and the countryside between Amsterdam and the invading army flooded. The Prince then stiffened his demoralized people, sought European allies, and prepared to continue the war.[31] Louis XIV returned to Paris early in August, leaving his marshalls and plenipotentiaries in charge, and Godolphin trailed after him to await his formal recall.

In his dispatches he reported laconically that he was 'pretty well' again,[32] but Sunderland, newly arrived as ambassador in Paris, was shocked at the change in him and and reported him 'so extreamly weake that he is in danger without greate care and some rest'. In the comfort of the ambassadorial house he had both, but weeks went by without producing any real improvement. Early in October, with the effort of trying to make ready to return, he suffered a relapse; 'Mr Godolphin has so great a mind to be at Newmarket that if it would onely have ventur'd his Life he would certainly have gone from hence a fortnight agoe,' Sunderland reported dryly. He was persuaded to stay, drink the spa waters, and try again to recover sufficient strength for the journey.[33] But in such a chronically low state and with winter approaching it was possible that he might never do so; that he might die without ever seeing England again. In August Margaret's twentieth birthday came and went. She was no longer of an age to remain about the court unmarried, yet she had to realize that now her marriage might never take place.

The circle of friends who sustained her at Whitehall seemed to be deserting her as well. With the appointment of Sir Thomas Osborne as sole Treasurer of the Navy, the Deptford house had an official resident again. No longer able to use it as a summer retreat, Mrs Howard took her daughters away to Lincolnshire in August, depriving Margaret not just of her chamber-fellow Dorothy, but of what had become since her mother's death effectively

---

[30] Lever, *Godolphin*, 19–22; PRO SP 78/134, fos. 6–107: SG's dispatches, 11 May–28 June 1672.

[31] There is an excellent account of this campaign in John Childs's introduction to 'Captain Henry Herbert's Narrative of his Journey through France with his Regiment 1671–3', *Camden Miscellany*, Camden Society, 4th ser., 39 (1990), 284–9.

[32] PRO SP 78/34, fo. 102: SG to Lord [?], 28 June [1672].   [33] Lever, *Godolphin*, 23.

her surrogate family. Then Lady Sunderland, who had taken Margaret under her wing while Godolphin was with her husband in Paris, left to join them herself.[34] Margaret turned to the only supports she seemed to have left: the religion in which she had been brought up and John Evelyn, who in visiting the Howards at court that summer had reluctantly renewed his acquaintance with her.

Exemplary female piety was well attested throughout Christian history, and never more so than in Evelyn's time. His own mother and grandmother, as he never tired of recalling, had been notable examples of it. Contemporaries asked themselves, as historians have asked since, whether women were naturally more inclined to religion than men or whether it was mainly a response to their circumstances: a means of filling their greater vacant time; a compensation for subordinate roles in society; a source of meaning and even pre-eminence and power in a sphere beyond the mundane whose importance was universally acknowledged. The desire to gain honour was common to all, Bishop Ken wrote; 'men have more advantages of aspiring to honour in all public stations of the church, the camp, the Bar, and the city than women have, and the only way for a woman to gain honour is by an exemplary holiness'.[35] These devout women were as notable a feature of the court as of the domestic sphere. This was what the Howards tried to make clear when they talked to the sceptical Evelyn of the 'Piety and religion eminent among Court-Ladys'. The heads of all the female households, including the Duchess of Monmouth, set conspicuous examples, and John North, Margaret's cousin and the King's clerk of the closet, was chiefly thinking of the women when he testified that even in 'a place reputed a centre of all vice and irreligion', he had found 'as many truly pious and strictly religious as could be found in any other resort whatsoever.'[36]

Even if she had sought praise as a child for adopting the conventional piety of her elders, Margaret Blagge did not turn back to it now just as a means of 'gaining honour'. Religion is also a response to the human condition. It seeks to explain who we are and why we are here and why insecurity and suffering are so much a part of our experience. Margaret was asking herself

[34] Bray, iv. 28, 33: ME to JE jun., 9 Oct. 1671, to Lady Anne Car. 26 Mar. 1672; JE, *Diary*, iii. 626.

[35] Patricia Crawford, *Women and Religion in England 1500–1720* (1993), 73–97; Anthony Fletcher, *Gender, Sex and Subordination in England 1500–1800* (New Haven, 1995), 347–8; Jacqueline Eales, *Women in Early Modern England 1500–1700* (1998), 94–5; Margaret R. Sommerville, *Sex and Subjection: Attitudes to Women in Early Modern England* (1995), 43 (for the quotation from Ken).

[36] *Life*, 19; Roger North, *General Preface and Life of Dr John North*, ed. Peter Millard (Toronto, 1984), 124.

all these questions. When she first came to court her pious upbringing had not prevented her taking her share in its pleasures. Her aim had simply been to perform her devotional duties without appearing singular or conspicuous, something which the regularity of Anglican observance in the Duchess of York's household made easy enough. What happened to her now was quite different. She forswore the pleasures of the court altogether and rededicated herself entirely to religion:

> Ah Lord! 'Tis true I have committed sinn
> And follow'd after vanitie;
> But to Repent I now begin
> Nor will I cease untill I die . . .
>
> The sinns & folly of my Youth
> I will each day I live lament
> With teares implore the God of truth
> To pardon all my time misspent . . .
>
> Love Youth & pleasur I forsake
> And past Imployments do despise
> They fade away & wings do take
> Whilst Lord thy love is all I prize

'I know full well this is but stuff', Margaret wrote to Evelyn later, 'how ever I like it because when I writ it, I thought what I said.'[37]

Deprived of her usual supports and companionship, she pared her life down to two aims only: to 'perform my Constant Duty to God, and the Queene'. Whatever time was not given up to the duties of her post, she devoted to some form of religious observance, making these her refuge from the uncertainties which beset her. There were four main components of Anglican worship: public and private prayer, the sermon, and the sacrament of communion, and Margaret practised all of them zealously. She would rise early and go straight from her bed to her oratory for a period of private devotion. At hand, according to the recommendations of popular manuals such as Wetenhall's *Enter into thy Closet*, would be a bible, a prayer book, blank paper notebooks, pen and ink for making excerpts from her reading and setting down her own meditations. Evelyn afterwards found that 'the innumerable Papers & Fragments' which she compiled at these times, if put together, 'would make a Considerable Folio'.[38] While she went through the elaborate ritual of formal dressing to attend her mistress, she had a servant read a

---

[37] BL Add. MS 78391: 'Devotions of Mrs Blaggs', copied by JE.

[38] *Life*, 91–3; BL Add. 78391: 'Devotions of Mrs Blaggs'; cf. John Spurr, *The Restoration Church of England* (1991), 341–4.

devotional work to her. Then she went up to the drawing room, reminding herself all the while, 'what my Calling is: To Enterteine the Ladys; not to Talke foolishly to Men: More especially the King'. Her reputation for witty repartee was now something to be renounced: 'without pretending to Wit, how quiet & pleasant a thing it is, to be silent, or, if I do speake; that it be to the Glory of God'. To discourage casual talkers she carried a book in her pocket with suitable readings already marked, 'anything which may decently keep you from Conversing with Men'. A footman would bring her word when morning prayers began in the Chapel Royal, to which of course the Queen did not go. In fact she was discovering the unlikely truth that the regular round of observance at court made it more feasible to lead an unob-trusive life of devotion there than in most other places, for those who really wished to do so. In addition to the public service, those in waiting could attend the King's 'closet prayers' before dinner, as Margaret did whenever she could slip away from the company in the Queen's drawing room without being missed. Having served her mistress at dinner, she then went down to the maids' quarters for her own meal, reminding herself to eat sparingly of one or two dishes at most. Then she would spend the rest of the afternoon reading, sewing, or visiting, breaking off again to go to public prayers at four o'clock. Later there would be supper with the maids, 'which must not be much if I have Din'd well'; then back to the Queen for the evening; then a further session of private prayer with her servants before going to bed.[39]

On Sundays she devoted the entire day to religious observance; 'how late soever her attendance on the Queene and her own extraordinary preparation kept her up', Evelyn recorded, 'she would be dress't, and at her privat Devotions some houres before the Publiq office began'. It amused him that to avoid oversleeping she would tie a string around her wrist and pass it through her keyhole for the sentry to tug and waken her in case her maid failed to do so. Then, 'were it never so Dark, Wet or Uncomfortable Weather, she rarely omitted being at Chapell by Seaven a Clock Prayers'. At the main service of the day the focal point was the sermon. In the Chapel Royal Margaret might hear William Sancroft ('when I wake up I am present with thee') or the Bishop of Salisbury ('in whom are hid all the treasures of wisdom and knowledge'). Or she might go further afield to hear Simon Patrick in her sisters' parish of Covent Garden ('how much more shall your heavenly father give his holy spirit to them that aske it'), or John Tillotson at one of Whitehall's parish churches, St Martin in the Fields ('remember thy Creator in the daies of thy Youth'). Under the Protectorate, taking notes in

[39] *Life*, 14–16; cf. *The Meditations of Lady Elizabeth Delaval*, ed. D. G. Greene, Surtees Society, 190 (1978), 89.

shorthand from the preacher's own lips had been a much paraded and admired female accomplishment. Now it was considered too ostentatious. Instead Margaret would train herself to commit the substance to memory as she listened, and between church and dinner go straight to her closet to write down her notes.[40]

The culmination of this devotional regime was the communion service, now restored to its central place in the Anglican cycle. In country parishes this might take place no more than twice a year, but in the Chapel Royal it was held once a month. Even this was not enough for some; Evelyn's researches satisfied him that weekly communion had been the norm in early Christianity, '& I would to God, that holy Custome were as frequent now.'[41] In fact devout courtiers were amongst the few who could quite easily take communion once a week if they wished, by combining the Chapel Royal services with those of neighbouring parishes on intervening Sundays. The Duchess of Monmouth made a conspicuous point of doing so, and now so did Margaret.[42] This in turn determined how she spent the rest of the week. For on biblical authority it was a worse fault to take communion unprepared or in an unworthy state than not to take it at all. Being properly prepared meant not just leading a devout life in all respects, but following a prescribed regime of prayer and meditation which occupied at least the two preceding days, and ideally the whole week beforehand. There were numerous published works to assist in this process and one of the most popular reinforced the longer regime with its title: *A Week's Preparation towards a Worthy Receiving of the Lords Supper*.[43] For those who took weekly communion, preparation would thus become a constant state. Lay people, especially men, who were engaged in business or had many calls on their time, would of course find this impossible to keep up, but for Margaret it provided exactly the sanction she needed for her regime of continuous observance. The culmination of the week's preparation was confession to a spiritual adviser. Rather curiously, since this was one of the most controversial of Roman Catholic practices, it had become fashionable for devout Anglican women at the Restoration to choose a personal confessor from amongst the court clergy, someone who might resolve their doubts and moral dilemmas as well as hearing this formal act of contrition. As a child Margaret's had been Bishop Gunning. Now it

---

[40] *Life*, 85–8; C. F. Richardson, *English Preachers and Preaching 1640–1670* (1928), 76; BL Add. 78391: 'Devotions of Mrs Blaggs'.

[41] *A Devotionarie Book of John Evelyn*, ed. Walter Frere (1936), 7.

[42] Denis Granville, *Remains*, ed. G. Ormsby, Surtees Society, 47 (1865), 85–6; J. Wickham Legg, *English Church Life from the Restoration to the Tractarian Movement* (1914), 23–4.

[43] Spurr, *Restoration Church*, 345–53.

was one of the royal chaplains, Dean Benson of Hereford, who was often at court and willing to correspond with her when he was away from London.[44] The long 'prayer before communion' in her book of personal devotions showed that from her absent and unsatisfactory earthly lover she was turning to a more predictable spiritual union, that each weekly communion had become her 'marriage supper'.[45]

Shortly after his first acquaintance with Margaret in 1669 Evelyn's life changed a good deal also. Looking back he could see that it marked the beginning of a decade in which he seemed to be 'in perpetual motion', hardly able to spend two months of the year with his family.[46] Much of this time was spent at court, in not one but several different capacities.

Having retreated to Sayes Court after his first period of trial in public life, he might claim that his dearest wish from now on was to cultivate his garden and finish his 'Elysium Britannicum'; but in some moods these occupations could still seem no more than 'planting cabbages and blotting paper'. More to the point, a third daughter had now joined the other two. Even though they were all very young, he realized that unless he could provide for them by increasing his income there would be no dowries when the time came.[47] If his ordeal as Commissioner of Sick and Wounded had brought him little else, it had at least given him a powerful new patron in Sir Thomas Clifford. From Sayes Court Evelyn wrote to draw the minister's attention to two accounts of the war, both written from the Dutch side and both highly critical of England, and suggested that someone should be appointed to compose 'a solid and useful History' to answer them. It looked as if he were soliciting for the post of Historiographer Royal again. In fact his candidate for the task was a cousin of his wife's who held a minor post in the Secretary of State's office. What he aimed at for himself was much more substantial: the Clerkship of the Council, which the King, at Arlington's prompting, had once vaguely promised him in reversion when his father-in-law should retire: a post which would put him close to the heart of government.[48]

These priorities were an irrelevance to his patrons. The King, who was being urged by his sister to make a treaty with France for a new Dutch war,

---

[44] Roger North, *General Preface and Life of Dr John North*, 124; *Life*, 95–6.

[45] BL Add. MS 78391: 'Devotions of Mrs Blaggs'.

[46] Bray, ii. 393: JE to John Beale, 11 July 1679.

[47] BL RP 5460: JE to Clifford, 23 Nov. 1670. This letter, which casts much light on Evelyn's relations with the government in the 1670s, is given only in a much shortened and altered version in his letter-book copy (BL Add. MS 78298), and misdated there, '28 Jan. 1672'.

[48] Bray, iii. 213–16: JE to Clifford, 1 Feb. 1669; JE, *Diary*, iii. 526; BL RP 5460: JE to Clifford, 23 Nov. 1670.

quite agreed that a public answer to criticisms of the last one and a fresh rehearsal of the causes of conflict would be highly desirable. Having raised the subject, Evelyn was soon under pressure to undertake the work himself. While he demurred, the secret treaty of Dover committed England to the war and Arlington settled the matter briskly by saying that the King would be displeased if he did not comply. At the same time he swept aside Evelyn's other pretensions by making it clear that when Sir Richard should retire, the Clerkship of the Council must go to his own indispensable Under-Secretary and intelligence officer, Joseph Williamson. Evelyn could only swallow his grievance, accept the promise of some compensating post when it arose with as much grace as he could, and shoulder the burden which he had brought on himself.[49] In the summer of 1670 the King took him aside on to the balcony over the terrace at Windsor and urged him to press on with the history vigorously, and make it 'a little keene'.[50]

On New Year's Day 1671 he fortified himself by taking communion, 'with extraordinary resolutions', as if he were preparing himself for a long period of difficulty and danger.[51] In the few years of his absence from Whitehall, the youthful exuberance of the court seemed to have settled into a middle age of hardened debauchery and violence. During the shrovetide festivities of this winter it 'fell into much extravagance in masquerading'. In earlier years these had been formal rituals at the Hall theatre or harmless showcases for the royal children. Now they spilled out into the streets and became more frenetic and sinister. Not just the courtiers but the King and Queen as well 'came into houses unknown and danced there with a great deal of wild frolic . . . so disguised that without being on the secret none could distinguish them'. When the Queen became separated from the crowd on one occasion, and had to make her way back to Whitehall alone and frightened in a hackney coach, it prompted Buckingham to whisper to the King that she might be made to vanish altogether by such means. There was duelling and brawling and finally there was homicide. On 26 February a gang of drunken young peers, led by the Duke of Monmouth, murdered a watchman, he 'praying for his life upon his knees'. The King did nothing to punish his son, but he did issue a proclamation forbidding masquerades. Henceforth there was only to be 'common dancing'.[52]

Evelyn set down his forebodings grimly in his diary: 'We have had a plague, a Warr, & such a fire, as never was the like in any nation since the

---

[49] BL RP 5460: JE to Clifford, 23 Nov. 1670; JE, *Diary*, iii. 523.
[50] JE, *Diary*, iii. 559.   [51] Ibid. 566.
[52] Burnet, *History*, i. 482–3; HMC *Kenyon MSS*, 88: G. Ayloffe to Lord Kenyon, 24 Jan. 1671; HMC *Portland MSS*, iii. 320: Sir Edward to Lady Harley, 7 Feb. 1671; *Poems on Affairs of State*, i. 173; John Spurr, *England in the 1670s: 'This Masquerading Age'* (Oxford, 2001), 110–16.

overthrow of Sodome', and now 'the leudnesse of our greatest ones, & universal luxurie, seemed to menace some yet more dreadfull vengeance'.[53] It was not just that Clarendon's fall had deprived the Anglicans of their bulwark at court, or that the Church was under threat from atheism and immorality. There was the sense of something more radical afoot. When Evelyn chose a confidant for his worst fears it was an apparently unlikely one: James Hamilton, the same courtier who had amused the King at Newmarket by offering to walk the course backwards for a bet. Another of the Duke of Ormonde's cohort of likeable nephews (his brother George had married Frances Jenyns), Hamilton was outwardly the pattern of a Restoration gallant in wit and fashion. While the rest of his family remained Catholic, he had converted to Protestantism at an early stage. Although his mother claimed bitterly that this was only because he found the older faith too strict to accommodate the life he chose to lead at court, he must have been able to convince Evelyn otherwise—no easy matter given his distrust of courtiers—and Margaret Blagge as well, since she always had a special affection for him.[54] So it was to Hamilton that Evelyn now lamented that 'a sincere & well grounded faith will come to be a precious and a rare thing, I see it to my griefe; and especially that the Church of England finds no more reverence amongst the Wits and Gallants'; although it was a faith 'as well adapted to the courtier as for the most resign'd Christian', there was 'a buisy spirit' at work at court 'that maligns her . . . she is still to be militant here on earth'.[55] He could not of course know that the Secret Treaty negotiated under Madame's auspices at Dover had bound the King to declare his conversion to Roman Catholicism at some unspecified time, but he dined frequently at Clifford's as his history progressed and from the talk and the company there it gradually dawned on him that Clifford and even Arlington were 'warping to Rome'.[56] With the death of the Duchess of York amid rumours that she too had forsaken the staunch Anglicanism of her family, the court appeared more and more to be taking on a crypto-Catholic complexion. One evening across Clifford's table Evelyn encountered the most busy and ubiquitous of all the court Catholics, the Queen's sub-almoner Father Patrick McGinn, and allowed himself to be drawn out to display his learning in a public debate over what exactly Anglicans did believe about the divine presence in the sacrament of communion; although this was a mystery which even clerical theologians preferred to leave unexpounded. He did it partly no doubt out

[53] JE, *Diary*, iii. 569.
[54] Ruth Clark, *Anthony Hamilton* (1921), 12–17; BL Add. MS 78307, fo. 15: MB to JE, [2 June 1673].
[55] BL Add. MS 78298: JE to Hamilton, 27 Apr. 1671.   [56] JE, *Diary*, iii. 577.

of vanity, relishing the chance to show himself equal to a debate with professional clerics; but partly also out of the same militant Anglicanism he had expressed to Hamilton: a sense that when he found his faith publicly challenged he must be ready to defend it, especially as the 'modern carpet priests', as he called them, were showing themselves so unequal to the task.[57]

Meanwhile the laborious task of history-writing was turning sour on him. After toiling through 'multitudes of books, remonstrances, treatises, journals, libels, pamphlets, letters, papers, and transactions of state', which 'for the more part did rather oppresse and confound than inlighten', he had no more to show Clifford after several months than a synopsis and a warning that the whole work would 'require more time to finish than at first setting out could well have been imagined'. He was galled and discouraged in equal measure by the appearance of a further Dutch work on the subject, running to over 1,000 pages, which he had to peruse in the knowledge that he had scarcely begun to draft the preface of his own. Just as the Dutch with their industry and boldness had had the better of the war, now they were effortlessly outdistancing him in the propaganda contest. Evelyn tried to tell himself and his patrons that this was because the Dutch author had been better supported. In fact he had been given all the access he needed to state papers. But in taking on the immense and unremunerated commission he had expected to receive 'some (at least) honorary title that might have animated my progress'. To his rival Williamson he grumbled obliquely: 'I have my beads to say, and a family to consider . . . I lay by all my *Amoena studiorum* and refreshments to emerge a statesman (what not?) at 50, and be laughed at, if I do not succeed'; yet, he added, 'I can write sharply and make the world feel the nib of my pen an hundred years to come . . . Therefore treat your Historiographer kindly.' More frankly he complained to Clifford, that 'after near 40 years service' of his family, 'and some royall promises both to my Wife and myselfe', he was still 'planting Cabbages, or blotting Paper', and begged him to be a 'good Angell; not only to stir the poole, but to put me into it, who have layne so long in the portico'.[58]

It was clear that the court really did owe him something and the compensation when it came seemed unexpectedly handsome. When the Council for Foreign Plantations was enlarged in February 1671 he found himself appointed one of its salaried members. It seemed the ideal post for him. Its

[57] Miller, *Popery and Politics*, 21; BL Add. MS 78317: JE to Patrick McGinn, [Mar. 1671?] (in Bray, iii. 231–8, as 27 Sept. 1671); Spurr, *Restoration Church*, 344–5; BL Add. MS 78298: JE to MG, 18 July 1676 (for 'carpet priests').

[58] BL RP 5460: JE to Clifford, 23 Nov. 1670; Bray, iii. 221–3: JE to Clifford, 20 Jan [1671]; *CSP Domestic 1671*, 55: JE to Williamson, 28 Jan. 1671; *PF*, 123: JE to Pepys, 6 Dec. 1681.

president Lord Sandwich was another of his court patrons; its secretary Henry Slingsby a long-time friend who had just consulted him about the rebuilding of his country house; and several other members were his Royal Society colleagues. It was also, as Evelyn proudly noted, 'a considerable honour', and in theory a lucrative one, carrying a salary of £500 a year out of the Treasury. Although the Council met in rented accommodation near Lincoln's Inn Fields rather than in Whitehall, it was effectively a council of state with a very wide commission: to investigate, report, and advise on the condition of 'all the King's Plantations, Colonies and Dominions', but chiefly those in America and the West Indies. Its first business after Evelyn joined it was to assess the strength of New England, which seemed to be 'on the very brink of renouncing any dependence on the Crown'. The members met with due style and consequence, around a formal board of green cloth, with maps and globes to hand, and clerks, messengers, and a porter in attendance. When the evenings drew in the entrance was lit with flambeaux and the windows blazed with candlelight. Great officers of state attended, coaches stood at the door, and there was 'great passing in and out'. The members took an oath 'very little differing from what is given the Privy Council', as Evelyn noted with pride, and when they reported their findings, 'the King in Council ordered as of Course'. Unlike most of his fellow counsellors, he was not a colonial proprietor and had no major interest in the great trading companies. But he had kept his idealistic passion for the overseas trade for which the world seemed so providentially disposed, nursing hopes of what might be achieved 'if princes and people did Unanimously, and with true publique Spirit, and as our natural advantages prompt us; apply them selves honestly and industriously about it'. When the Council came to discuss such matters as the trade in North American log-wood for masts, for example, or the improvement of the American plantations by the cultivation of senna, nutmeg, silk, and flax, he could feel that his 'cabbage-planting' expertise was at last being turned to the highest ends of the state.[59]

But as before, the experience soon opened his eyes to more brutal realities. The Council was shortly called upon to remonstrate with the Royal African Company on behalf of the planters of the Leeward Islands about the escalating price (from £16 or 8 lb weight in sugar to £25 or 30 lb of sugar per head)

---

[59] JE, *Diary*, iii. 571, 574, 577–80; Library of Congress: Phillipps MS 8539: Journal of the Council of Trade and Plantations, 1671–2, *passim*; Roger North, *Examen* (1740), 461; Charles M. Andrews, *British Committees, Commissions and Councils of Trade and Plantations 1622–1675* (Baltimore, 1908), 96–106; R. P. Bieber, 'The Plantation Councils of 1670–4', *English Historical Review*, 40 (1925), 93–106; BL Add. MS 78386: JE, 'Oeconomics to a Newly Married Friend', [1676], p. 60; *PF*, 140: JE to Pepys, 19 Sept. 1682.

of the 3,000 or 4,000 black African slaves a year without which the colony could not function, the native Indians being 'unfitt to the like Labour'. It was also asked to persuade the King to order convicted criminals to be transported to St Christopher's 'for the better Peopling of that Plantation'.[60] The lavish style of the Council was also causing difficulties, with the Treasury falling far behind in payments for both running expenses and salaries. They all agreed that what they needed was a purpose-built apartment in or near Whitehall, both to save house-rent and to allow the King to attend whenever he chose. Wren duly submitted plans, but it was disconcerting to learn that these would not be executed unless the members could raise the money from their own resources.[61]

Still, the recognition did give a much-needed boost to Evelyn's labours on his history. At the end of August he presented Clifford with the completed preface in the form of a discourse on 'the origin and progress of navigation and commerce': Arlington's suggestion, since 'all our contests and differences with the Hollanders derive only from that source'.[62] Parts of this must have given the minister pause however. Evelyn had recycled from his unfinished 'Rational Discourse on True Religion' a rhapsodic description of a world, in all its 'rugged and dissever'd parts, rocks, seas and remoter islands' and all its 'ample baies, creeks, trending shores, inviting harbours and stations', so conveniently disposed by divine providence for trade and commerce. There followed arcane speculations on whether 'the first authors of traffick were the Tyrians, Trojans, Lydians, those of Carthage, or (as Josephus will) the mercurial spirits soon after the flood, to repair and supply the ruines of that universal overthrow'. There was an improving homily on the loadstone: 'that by virtue of this dull pebble such a continent of land, such myriads of people, such inexhaustible treasures, and so many wonders should be brought to light . . . may instruct the proudest of us all not to contemn small things'.[63] This characteristic mix of the scholarly, the moral, and the spiritual which had served the discourse on forest trees so well was much less suitable for the kind of hard-hitting polemic the government had commissioned, and Evelyn's concluding survey of all the great trading nations included far more praise of the Dutch for their liberal customs, religious tolerance, frugality, and industry than Clifford would have thought at all to the purpose. But he was at least

[60] Library of Congress: Phillipps MS 8539: Journal of the Council of Trade and Plantations, 16 Sept., 18 Oct., 13 Nov. 1671.
[61] Ibid., 26 June, 12 Aug. 1671; JE, *Diary*, iii. 582–4.
[62] Bray, iii. 230: JE to Clifford, 31 Aug. 1671.
[63] *Navigation and Commerce* (1674), in Upcott, 628–36; cf. JE, *The History of Religion*, ed. R. M. Evanson (1850), i. 27–28.

able to add that two of the three main sections of the history were effectively finished and awaited only official guidance on a few controversial points before they could be fair copied and presented to the King.[64]

As a matter of course, now that he was a virtual member of the government, Evelyn accompanied the court on the same East Anglian progress which had launched Godolphin on his missions to Spain and France. At Norwich a visit to the newly knighted Sir Thomas Browne recalled him from his time-serving preoccupations to a higher purpose. His house and garden, 'a Paradise & cabinet of rarities', were a much needed refreshment of spirit in themselves and he was the most congenial of guides to the antiquities of the city, with its walls, cathedral, churches, and merchants' houses, all so mingled with flower gardens and trees, that it seemed either 'a city in an orchard or an orchard in a city'; and the 'verdant state of things', Browne could remind him, was not just a civic amenity, but a symbol of the redemption; just so could man, being sown in corruption, flourish in glory.[65] Back at Newmarket Evelyn sourly watched 'the jolly blades Racing, Dauncing, feasting & revelling, more resembling a luxurious & abandon'd rout than a Christian Court',[66] and wondered how redemption could come to them, but at Euston 'the leudnesse of our greatest ones, & universal luxurie' which he had so deplored appeared in their most suave and seductive form.

Arlington, at this efflorescence of his power, was the most generous and civilized of hosts. The sheer style, discreet opulence, and accommodating hospitality of his great houses could render even the sleaziness of Charles's court dignified and uncontaminating. While Evelyn was there, 'the whole house fill'd from one end to the other, with Lords, Ladys & Gallants, and such a furnish'd Table had I seldome seene . . . so as for 15 days there was entertain'd at the Least 200 people, & halfe as many horses, besids Servants, Guards, at Infinite expense'; yet everywhere was taste, order, comfort, and ingenuity, from the gallery, with its alcoved billiard table, the state rooms, the library, and the chapel, to the guest apartments, 'furnish'd with all manner of convenience and privacy', the bathing rooms and laboratory; even the offices in two large quadrangles, where 'never servants lived with more ease and convenience'. Inevitably there were cards and dice until the small hours of the morning, but 'without noise, swearing, quarell or Confusion of any sort'. Evelyn could chat with the French ambassador, walk in the gardens with their exquisite fountains and canal, admire Sir Samuel Morland's ingenious

---

[64] Bray, iii, 228–31: JE to Clifford, 31 Aug. 1671.

[65] JE, *Diary*, iii. 594–5; 'The Garden of Cyrus', in Sir Thomas Browne, *Works*, ed. Sir G. Keynes (1964), i. 177.

[66] JE, *Diary*, iii. 596.

screw bridge and waterwheel which ground corn for the household and raised water for the fountains and offices. He could go out with Arlington into the distant park, 'the best for riding and meeting the game that ever I saw', and show him how it could be gracefully united with the gardens by the planting of lime and ash avenues. Or he could retire to his 'prety apartment', 'quite out of all this hurry', to read or devise a scheme for Arlington's library, taking care to precede the section on statecraft with one on ethics, because, he reminded the minister, it was especially necessary 'to drink deep of pious and moral knowledge before we taste of politics'. There he could see to it that only rumours reached him of the mock marriage ceremony at which Louise de Kéroualle finally yielded to the diplomatic pandering of Arlington and the French ambassador and was bedded with the King. 'I acknowledge she was for the most part in her undresse all day, and that there was fondnesse, & toying, with that young wanton,' he recorded stiffly in his diary, but as for the suggestion that he had witnessed and condoned the ceremony himself, 'tis utterly false, I neither saw, nor heard of any such thing whilst I was there, though I had ben in her Chamber & all over that apartment late enough'.[67]

Yet despite all these favours and intimacies he was more thoroughly disillusioned with the court, both personally and politically, than he had ever been. War, declared against the Dutch in March on the overt grounds of trading rivalry, made a final mockery of his idealistic view of commerce. The immediate excuse of the failure to strike the flag to a small English vessel seemed to him what it was: contrived and paltry; 'surely this was a quarel slenderly grounded, & not becoming Christian neighbours, & of a Religion: and we are like to thrive accordingly'. Worse was the Stop of the Exchequer on Clifford's advice: the temporary diversion of the 'sacred stock', earmarked for the payment of the government's creditors, to finance the war, 'which not onely lost the hearts of his subjects, & ruined many Widdows & Orphans whose stocks were lent him, but the reputation of his Exchequer forever'. Then came the Declaration of Indulgence, suspending penal laws against both Roman Catholics and Nonconformists, confirmation that not only Clifford but Arlington as well sought 'to gratifie that partie . . . to the extreame weakning of the Church of England & its Episcopal Government'. Soon Evelyn was able to visit the French ambassador's full-size waxwork tableau of the *Last Supper* on public view at York House, 'such liberty had the Roman Catholicks at this time obtained'.[68]

---

[67] Ibid., iii. 590–2, iv. 116–18; Douglas D. C. Chambers, *The Planters and the English Landscape Garden* (New Haven, 1993), 35–6; BL Add. MS 78317: JE to Arlington, 16 Oct. 1671 (draft).

[68] JE, *Diary*, iii. 606–8, 612.

As he turned reluctantly again to the task of organizing billets for the sick and wounded at Gravesend, he could see rising from the marshes on the opposite shore the sinister star-shaped profile of the new Tilbury Fort, its outworks imitating the angular symmetries of Louis XIV's barrier fortresses. Ostensibly it was to protect London from further Dutch incursion, but with the City merchants and the court at loggerheads it could easily seem 'a royal Work indeede, & such as will one day bridle a greate City to the purpose before they are aware'. Amongst the 'divers wounded and languishing poore men' in Evelyn's quarters was a sailor with a shattered and gangrened leg. He steeled himself to witness the amputation, but in spite of the man's stoic courage he could not be saved; 'Lord, what miseries are mortal men obnoxious to', he wrote in anguish in his diary, '& what confusion & mischeife dos the avarice, anger, and ambition of Princes cause in the world, who might be happier with halfe they possesse: This stout man was but a common sailer.' From the Dover cliffs he again witnessed the 'goodly, yet tirrible' sight of the English fleet under full sail in the sunshine to meet the Dutch; 'such a gallant & formidable Navy never I think spread saile upon the seas'. But soon the day-long thud of cannon off the Suffolk coast filled his hospital quarters with more shattered beings. The dead floated amongst the wreckage of the ships and amongst them, recognizable only by his garter ribbon, was the body of the Admiral, Lord Sandwich. He had been an impressive figure of wide interests, 'learned in Mathematics, In Musique, in Sea affaires, in Political'. As ambassador at Madrid he had taken the trouble to send Evelyn detailed accounts in his own hand of Spanish gardens for his gardening encyclopedia and they had sat together week after week in Council. The loss of one whom he counted his 'particular friend' and the pattern of a nobleman, and whom he knew to have been 'utterly against the War', struck Evelyn more deeply than anything else with the waste and unreason of the court's policy. Like Godolphin, watching Louis XIV's army overrunning the Low Countries at this very time, Evelyn now had far more distrust of the French than of the Dutch, and they were both right. But Clifford would not let him give any expression to this in his history, 'though in justice to truth (evident as the day), I neither would, nor honestly could, conceile (what all the world might see) how subdolusly they dealt with, and made us their property all along'.[69]

Evelyn now found himself with too much business in London to come and go from Deptford every day, and so for the nights he had to stay in town he took over his retired father-in-law's lodgings in a remote part of Whitehall

[69] Ibid., iii. 609–10, 614, 620; Sandwich's long letter about Spanish gardens, 12 June 1668, is in BL Add. MS 78343, fos. 99–114; *PF*, 123; JE to Pepys, 6 Dec. 1681 (where it is noted that 'subdolusly' means 'cunningly'); cf. Hutton, *Charles II*, 286.

near the Ewry.[70] Although the proposed new council chamber was never built, the Council did move from Queen Street to the neighbourhood of the palace, finally fixing in a rented house on King Street.[71] Evelyn could now count himself a regular denizen of the court, lodging there, consulting with ministers, attending the Treasury, deliberating in Council. He was living in the very midst of a place reputed to be the 'centre of all vice and irreligion', where his Anglican faith was under threat and all appearances were deceptive. He had sometimes thought of the court as a desert, barren and infertile in comparison with the garden or the countryside. But he now saw that it could be a paradise as well, and that temptations lurked in both: 'what violence must be apply'd to be humble in the midst of so much flattery; chast amongst such licence, where there is so much fire and so much tinder, and not to look towards the fruit which in that Paradise is so glorious to the eye, and so delicious to the taste?' 'To conserve ones self in a Court, is to become an absolute Hero', he had told Mackenzie; a heroism not of military might but of militant virtue, which could 'conflict with the regnant Vices, and overcome our selves'.[72] So he kept himself armed and vigilant and attended strictly to his duties; not frequenting the drawing room, but confining himself to the Council chamber, the Treasury, and the Royal Society, and at intervals retreating to his remote apartment to labour on with his history.

And so he went on until Anne Howard on her occasional visits began to tease and hector him for failing to keep up his acquaintance with her sister, now that he also lodged at Whitehall and had so much opportunity to do so. Reluctantly, as 'oblig'd in good manners', he agreed to call at 'the Queen's side' and pay his respects.[73] ❧

---

[70] JE, *Diary*, iii. 571–2.   [71] Bieber, 'The Plantation Councils of 1670–4', 99–100.
[72] *Public and Private Life in the Seventeenth Century: The Mackenzie-Evelyn Debate*, ed. Brian Vickers (New York, 1986), 176–7.
[73] *Life*, 20.

6

Seraphick Love

I<small>F</small> Evelyn continued to be wary of female company at court, it was not so much for fear of sexual temptation as because he remembered his former mockery at the hands of the 'misses'. To Anne Howard he protested that it was not her sister he was avoiding but her companion; 'there was a Wit with her, whom I fear'd'. Anne assured him that on the contrary he would find their friend Margaret as 'humble, Religious, and Serious' as he could wish. Sceptical, sure that he was still being teased, he nerved himself to make a courtesy visit to the two young women.[1]

Knowing nothing of Margaret's renewed devotional life and her resolution that 'no Raillery almost can be innocent', he was surprised to find her withdrawn and silent, and so obviously unprepared for a formal visit that he felt awkward and would have gone away; but Dorothy pressed him to stay and share their supper. Except to explain that it was 'a Day of solemn Devotion' for her, Margaret scarcely said a word during the meal either, and sat with downcast eyes. Yet Evelyn, instead of being put off, was reassured; this was certainly not the 'pert Lady' he had expected. When they next met by chance in the galleries of Whitehall, she gave him the encouragement to return by apologizing and saying that she hoped she had not frightened him away. As the visits were repeated Evelyn noted approvingly that she 'had all the Arts and Innocent stratagems imaginable, of interposing serious things, & of seasoning diversions with profitable notices', and that 'however Wide or Indifferent the Subject of the Discourse was amongst the Rest of the Table', she 'would allways divert it to some Religious Conclusion'. Although she was cheerful and good-humoured on occasion, unlike the other court women she could also 'indure to be serious', and instead of teasing would

---

[1] *Life*, 20.

only 'gently reprove' him when he became too morose, 'which put me out of all feare of her Raillery'. In a favourite scientific metaphor for the miraculous and the moral, he thought of her as like the magnetic needle of a compass, 'set to whatsoever Aspect; she stil pointed to the divine Attractive, God'. He also noticed that some older women of much higher rank, Lady Sunderland, the Duchess of Monmouth, and even the wayward Lady Falmouth, appeared to defer to her piety. At 19 Margaret was in the full flower of her beauty. More and more he wondered 'that so young; so Elegant; so Charming a Wit & beauty, should preserve so much Vertue in a place, where it neither naturaly grew, or much was Cultivated'.[2]

By the summer he had become an established visitor, sometimes alone, sometimes with his wife. In July he escorted them all to a play, Dryden's safe, popular, good-hearted farce, *Sir Martin Mar-all*. A fortnight later Mrs Evelyn invited the young women to Sayes Court.[3] To observers it seemed a harmless, rather amusing court acquaintance: two of the more serious-minded maids of honour had captured one of the court's most unbending intellectuals as their squire of dames. But the friendship was rapidly becoming much more in Evelyn's mind. He began to think that here at last he had found the ideal platonic friend, the 'seraphick' he had so long sought. In fact it was Margaret Blagge who now defined this type of friendship for him. All his platonic friendships until now had been light-hearted flirtations, an elaborate parade of outward conventions, not taken very seriously by either side. Margaret for the first time gave them a reality and began to show him how they might be a means of salvation. In his own mind, in subversion of all his former categories, her court lodgings with the little oratory she had set up there began to transform themselves into 'a holy Cell'.[4] Mary Evelyn saw his undisguised interest, but with her long and intimate knowledge of him and what she could perceive of the girl, she was undisturbed by it. She continued to have her own emotionally charged but carefully managed friendships, with Ralph Bohun and with her brother-in-law Glanville (while Evelyn was at Euston the latter had written to her, 'should I discover I am in love with my friend, it cannot justly offend her, or any other person, provided my passion be Platonique').[5] She evidently realized that her husband, in his disillusion with all his former ambitions, needed something of the same kind. Later he reminded her that she had encouraged the friendship, '& often told me I should thank you for her, . . . [saying] there were never two more alike in our way & inclination'.[6] But remembering his past disappointments he was

---

[2] Ibid. 20–2, 100–01.   [3] JE, *Diary*, iii. 623.   [4] *Life*, 21.
[5] BL Add. MS 78434: Glanville to ME, 23 Oct. 1671.
[6] BL Add. MS 78431: JE to ME, 7 July 1675.

in no hurry; 'I was resolv'd to turne her to every Light, & to examine all those perfections . . . before I pronounc'd concerning her; & took her to my heart'.[7]

There was more than exemplary piety to Margaret's conduct at this time. Once the Howards had left for the country she began to sink into a state of anxiety and depression in which even the rituals of religion did not sustain her adequately; 'reason is apter to put fears into the mind wherby it disturbs the man then hop[e]s wherby he may [be] comforted,' she once wrote to Evelyn.[8] For her own reasons she was also considering him as a friend, and in the event it was she who made the first move. She cannot have failed to notice his growing personal interest in her ('what a new thing is this'), but all her acquaintance with him before this had been dependent on the Howards. Fearing that he would now desert her as well, she asked him out of charity to continue his visits in spite of Dorothy's absence.[9] On one occasion in October Evelyn found her acutely miserable. When he asked her what was the matter, she would only say drearily that 'she had never a Friend in the World'. Knowing, presumably from the Howards, of her long understanding with Sidney Godolphin, he enquired archly 'What she Esteem'd a Certaine Gentleman beyond the Seas to be'. Margaret told him of Godolphin's illness and that he was still abroad and apparently in danger of his life; and she added more surprisingly that in any case he was not the kind of friend she meant: 'I would have realy a Friend . . . A Faithfull Friend, whom I might trust with all I have, and God knows, that's but little: For him whom you meane, cares not to meddle with my Concernes; nor Would I give him the trouble.' Evelyn asked her if she wanted him to be her friend. 'I Believe you the Person in the World', she replied, 'who would make such a Friend, had I merit enough to deserve it.'[10]

Evelyn had received such requests too often to mistake Margaret's main meaning: that she needed someone she could trust 'to govern & manage her competent stock', as he put it in his diary.[11] Her mother had taken care of such matters in her lifetime by bringing in the aid of experienced male relations. Now Margaret, no longer certain of her marriage, had to find her own substitute, and preferably someone who would take a reliable personal interest in her, a brother or a father figure. Evelyn's competence as a man of affairs was well known; so was his rectitude and his standing as a lay Anglican. Lady Mordaunt, Lady Tuke, and Mrs Howard all used him as a trustee in this way

---

[7] BL Add. MS 78392: 'The Legend of Philaretes and the Pearle', [c.1673].

[8] BL Add. MS 78307, fo. 59: MB to JE, [1675].   [9] Life, 21–2.

[10] Ibid. 22–3; in the earlier version Evelyn added, 'This, to my remembrance, were her very expressions to me' (p. 131).

[11] JE, *Diary*, iii. 628.

at different times, and in itself a further request cannot have been particularly welcome. These affairs often exploited him shamelessly, draining his time and involving him in 'tiresome mortifications' which were never sufficiently acknowledged or recompensed.[12] But Margaret's growing significance for him made this quite a different case. He was certainly old enough to be her father and when he discovered in due course that she had been born in the same month and year as his son Richard, it was to give the relationship an additional providential significance to him.[13] But it was the prospect of Margaret as a friend and not surrogate child which chiefly interested him:

Madam said I, Consider Well what you say, and what you do: For it is such a Trust, and so great an Obligation that you lay upon me, (were I indeede worthy of it) as I ought to Embrace with all imaginable Respect and Acknowledgement, for the greatest mark of your favour, and honour you could do me: Madame To be call'd your Friend, (as I now know and value you) were a Title I would endeavor to acquire, with all the Instances & Trials of that Sacred Compellation.

It was this kind of thing, 'long words and superfine compliments', as Anne Howard called them, the language of full-blown platonic romance, for which Evelyn had so often been laughed at by the court 'misses'. But what mattered to Margaret was that the verbiage contained an unequivocal yes to her request for help. So she only smiled and replied, still invoking the safer relationship, 'Pray leave your Definitions, Complements, and distinctions . . . and be my Friend then in Earnest; And look upon me hence-forth, as your Child . . . and Calle me so.'[14]

Evelyn was not satisfied with a verbal pledge. In his delight at what had come about he wanted to revive all the rather faded adolescent paraphernalia, what Jeremy Taylor had called the 'tinsel' of platonic friendships: the emblems and symbols, suns, stars, flaming hearts, and Greek mottoes, which had inaugurated the circles of Katherine Philips and the 'wittified' young women of the North family. There was pen and ink on the table, he goes on to say, 'in which I had been drawing something upon a paper like an Alter'; at his prompting Margaret took up the pen, inscribed the drawing, 'Be this the symbol of Inviolable Friendship', signed and dated it, wrote underneath, 'for my brother Evelyn', and gave it back to him with a smile. The drawing survives, treasured by him and now interleaved in his diary, but it suggests a good deal more forethought than this account allows for. It shows an altar with a bowed front and diamond-shaped lozenges on either side, the right-hand one incorporating the griffin of the Evelyn coat of arms; all carefully

---

12 Ibid. iv. 67, 70, 108–9, 173; Bray, iii. 293: JE to Lady Sunderland, 22 Dec. 1688.
13 *Life*, 8.   14 Ibid. 23.

executed in pen and ink, with lines ruled, perspective properly observed, and the curved surfaces shadowed in a grey wash which has clearly been applied before the inscriptions were added. The date, 16 October 1672, has been inscribed on the bow of altar, not by Margaret but by Evelyn in careful roman numerals. It is certainly not a rough pen and ink sketch executed on the spur of the moment with materials to hand in Margaret's lodgings. But underneath, as he describes, is her signature and her rather misspelled inscription: 'be this the symbal of our Inuiolable friendshipe in I.H.S'. Below the altar she has added, 'for my Brouther Euelyn' and he has written a variant of his usual biblical motto, followed by a pentacle or five-pointed star. Perhaps his account conflates two meetings or perhaps he was making use of an emblem taken from one of his earlier devotional manuscripts; but if the drawing he preserved is the one signed by Margaret on the day they made their pact, he must in some way have anticipated her.[15]

The bow-fronted altar with the Evelyn griffin appears in two of his earlier devotional manuscripts: the frontispiece of a daily 'office' which he compiled for his own use in France, in which it was accompanied by a kneeling figure in pseudo-clerical costume who is presumably intended to represent Evelyn himself; and the title-page of a communion office variously titled 'The Wedding Garment' or 'Trimming the Lamp', dating from the Restoration and with the altar this time surmounted in Protestant fashion by a book and cross. Evelyn later gave both volumes to Margaret.[16] When he described the making of their pact later he said that the symbols of the book and cross also appeared on their altar of friendship. In fact they did not. In their place what he actually drew was a large heart, its point uppermost and surrounded by an aura of stars, its lower curves lavishly delineated in half-tones. No doubt it was influenced by the symbols of divine love in Catholic devotional works he would have known in France; but no one seeing the sensually swelling curves of his version of the heart for the first time could have failed to find them at least as suggestive of secular as of sacred love.[17]

The motto he added below the altar was one he had used before; so, more infrequently, was the five-pointed star, an ancient talismanic symbol occurring in both Egyptian and classical sources and later invested by

---

[15] *Life*, 23–4, 131; see also Plate 9. For Evelyn's motto, 'Omnia explorate, Meliora retinete' ('explore all things, hold fast to the best'), see Keynes, *JE*, 10–12.

[16] BL Add. MSS 78371: 'Officium Sanctae et Individuae Trinitatis ad Quotidianum Johannis Evelynni vsum concinnatum', [*c*.1650], and 78374: 'An Eucharistical Office', 1660. For the Evelyn griffin see Keynes, *JE*, 26–7.

[17] *Life*, 23; cf. for example the plate from Nicolas Caussin's *The Holy Court*, reproduced in Erica Veevers, *Images of Love and Religion* (Cambridge, 1989), 81.

hermetic philosophy with a complex of meanings relating to divine order and providence.[18] More than any other, this pentacle was to become Evelyn's symbol for Margaret, regularly used as a substitute for her name in his diary, meditations, and prayers. Although he had occasionally used it in other contexts, in this one it had a quite specific source: his Royal Society mentor and the man who more than any other embodied for him the possibility of the virtuous courtier, Sir Robert Moray. Moray was not only the life and soul of the Royal Society, he was also a freemason and fond of expounding to receptive friends such as Evelyn the significance of his mark of masonic initiation, the five-pointed star which he always added to his signature. Lifting the basic star device from his family's coat of arms, he had combined it with an ingenious acrostic based on five Greek characters '*agapa*' to form a complex symbol containing 'the summe of Christian Religion, as well as stoick philosophy', so that it became a tiny icon of reciprocal human and divine love. Since the most elaborate form of the pentacle which Evelyn now began to associate with Margaret Blagge included the same Greek characters between the points, there can be no doubt that Moray's version of the ancient symbol was his model. Another of Moray's personal emblems was engraved on his seal: a rudimentary altar surmounted by a heart, accompanied by the figure of Eros and the motto 'une seulle'. This might have been taken to commemorate his devotion to his wife, dead years before in childbirth, but Moray had also had a recent and difficult experience of intense friendship with a young woman. On his return from Scotland he had brought with him his niece Lady Sophia Lindsay, only to be forced to send her back within the year because his preoccupation with her aroused knowing gossip. Moray visited Sayes Court with Sidney Godolphin and Margaret Blagge the following summer. At some point Evelyn must have made him his confidant in this new friendship of his own.[19]

Although Margaret invoked Evelyn's help as a surrogate father or brother, he was much more concerned to define their pact according to platonic norms, as the 'Nerest Relation in Nature', 'beyond all Relations of Flesh & Blood: Because it is lesse Material', and for this reason even more significant than 'the Conjugal-state it selfe', either his own marriage or her longstanding engagement. In fact the altar symbol defined it as a kind of spiritual

---

[18] Keynes, *JE*, 10–13; *Life*, 210–17; Ronald Hutton, *The Triumph of the Moon: The History of Modern Pagan Witchcraft* (Oxford, 1999), 67–8. In his paper, 'Evelyn and Arundel in Italy', at the British Library conference, 'John Evelyn and his Milieu', 17 Sept. 2001, Edward Chaney referred to Evelyn's adding the pentacle to his signature in the register of the University of Padua in 1645.

[19] David Stevenson, 'Freemasonry, Symbolism and Ethics in the Life of Sir Robert Moray', *Proceedings of the Society of Antiquaries of Scotland*, 114 (1984), 417–19, and *The Origins of Freemasonry* (Cambridge, 1988), 63, 80–3, 166–79, 183–4; JE, *Diary*, iv. 11.

betrothal; 'the Title that has Consecrated this Altar', he told her, 'is the marriage of Soules,—and the golden Thread that binds the Hearts of all the World'.[20] It was also clear that he envisaged it, not in the strict seraphic sense as a mere step in his ascent to higher love, but in the manner of salon neoplatonism, as a kind of 'lingering on the stair', a continuing form of spiritual friendship.[21] In practical terms he explained that this meant he should be allowed to visit, speak, and write to her regularly; that she was also to write, to remember him in her prayers, 'To admonish me of all my failings: To Visite me in Sicknesse, To take care of me when I am in distresse, and never to forsake me; Change, or lessen your particular Esteeme, 'til I proove inconstant or Perfidious, and no more a Friend'. In return she could freely command his help on all occasions 'without any reserve whatsoever'. 'In short', he concluded, 'there is . . . in Friendship, something of all Relations, & practical Dutys, and something above them all: These Madame are the Laws, and they are Reciprocal and Eternal.' All this was typical of Evelyn's stock of arcane lore and didactic manner, and Margaret did not take any of it very seriously at this stage. Although she was ready enough to humour him by entering into the pact, it was the promise of practical help which still mattered most to her. As they parted she smiled and told him that when they next met, 'I will tell you what I have for you to do in good Earnest.'[22]

Platonic friendships had often meant coterie names. Katherine Philips as Orinda surrounded herself with Lucasia, Silvander, Philaster, Palaemon, and half a dozen more; Robert Boyle's sister Lady Warwick and Lord Berkeley of Durdans addressed each other as Harmonia and Constans; Boyle called himself Philaretus and the addressee of *Seraphick Love* Lindamor.[23] Evelyn and his wife had once been Calianthe and Meliora to each other; his other female friends were dubbed Cyparissa or Platona; and now Margaret became Electra, the name he had once given to Elizabeth Carey.[24] Then it had been suggested to him by an English translation of the *Electra* of Sophocles dedicated to Charles I's short-lived daughter Elizabeth, a royalist icon of youthful female piety who was invoked in it as 'sweet Electra' and 'bright Saint'.[25]

---

[20] *Life*, 23–4.   [21] Veevers, *Images of Love*, 18.   [22] *Life*, 24–5.

[23] *The Collected Works of Katherine Philips, the Matchless Orinda: The Poems*, ed. Patrick Thomas, (Stump Cross, 1990), 8–9; Charlotte Fell Smith, *Mary Rich, Countess of Warwick* (1901), 178; *Robert Boyle by Himself and his Friends*, ed. Michael Hunter (1994), pp. xv–xxi.

[24] BL Add. MSS 78431: JE to ME, 27 June 1648; 78298: JE to Edmund Waller, 20 Dec. 1649; to 'Platona' [Ann Bodvel], 20 Dec. 1649; to 'Electra' [Elizabeth Carey], 19 May 1656 ('Electra' has been crossed through here and 'Penthea' substituted, probably after 1672; see also Add. MS 78392: 'The Legend of Philaretes and the Pearle', [*c*.1673], in which Electra is Margaret Blagge and Penthea clearly refers to Elizabeth Carey).

[25] The translation, by his wife's cousin Christopher Wase, was published at The Hague in 1649.

Now it was the name which best seemed to suit the ardent, seraphic devotion he saw in Margaret, He himself became Philaretes, 'lover of virtue', a version of the well-worn pseudonym of Robert Boyle. When the Howard sisters returned from the country they were added to the circle as Alcidonia and Ornithia and Mrs Evelyn in due course included herself somewhat wryly, no longer as Meliora (retained as the best by her husband), but as the countrified Hortensia.[26]

But probably the strongest influence on the friendship was one which Evelyn did not explicitly acknowledge. In the climate of 1670s England Francis de Sales's *Introduction to the Devout Life* and his *Treatise of the Love of God* were not works for Evelyn to retain in his library, but he had once been very familiar with them and with others of the same school.[27] In his encourage-ment of passionate, spiritualized friendships, in which the participants should learn to 'love on earth as they love in heaven' and become 'one spirit in diverse bodies', de Sales cited many examples between men and women from the time of the 'primitive Saints' or Church Fathers: 'St Augustine tells us that St Ambrose had an incomparable love for St Monica, because of the rare virtues he saw in her; while on her part she loved him as an angel of God . . . St Jerome, St Augustine, St Gregory, St Bernard and all the greatest servants of God have had very particular friendships.' The most notable of his own was with Jean de Chantal.[28] The motto Evelyn soon adopted for his own friend-ship, 'Un Dieu Un Amy', carried the same message, a more Christian one than Moray's 'une seulle'. In fact there was no lack of further examples amongst his Protestant contemporaries. Jeremy Taylor had paid tribute to the friendship of Lady Carbery, in whose house he had written his best work; the wife of Sir Denis Gauden, who leased his victualling yards at Deptford from the Sayes Court estate, kept up an intense 'seraphic correspondence' with Simon Patrick, the Rector of St Paul's Covent Garden; Evelyn found and marked a passage in the Presbyterian Richard Baxter's *Saints Everlasting Rest* about 'the delight which a pair of friends do find in loving and engaging one

[26] Hiscock I, 16–17, 38–9.

[27] De Sales's works are not in the post-1687 catalogue of Evelyn's library (BL Add. MS 78632), but he quoted at length from the *Introduction* in his 'Instructions Oeconomique' to his wife in 1648 (Add. MS 78430, fo. 28ᵛ).

[28] Francis de Sales, *Introduction to the Devout Life*, trans. Michael Day (1961), 140–2; Veevers, *Images of Love*, 21–4; Terence A. McGoldrick, *The Sweet and Gentle Struggle: Francis de Sales on the Necessity of Spiritual Friendship* (Lanham, Md., 1996), esp. 26–7, 101–4, 139–41, 343–4. For the influence of de Sales on Anglicans of Evelyn's generation, see John Spurr, *The Restoration Church of England* (New Haven, 1991), 372–3. In her paper, 'Mary Evelyn and Devotional Practice', at the British Library conference, 'John Evelyn and his Milieu', 18 Sept. 2001, Gillian Wright cited Evelyn's daughter's use of the 1644 Paris edition of *La Vie dévote*, which had probably come from her parents.

another'.[29] What these friendships had in common was that each participant, male and female, would acknowledge being able to reach higher levels of spiritual experience together than were accessible to them alone.[30]

In allowing himself to form an intense friendship with a beautiful and needy young woman Evelyn knew very well that he was taking a risk, not just with her reputation but with himself. Friendships between men in religious settings had sometimes been controversial, and friendships between the sexes were still more so. If the ambivalent image of the heart on the altar did not make him reflect, Moray's experience would have been a sufficient reminder. But perfection, de Sales wrote, was not in the absence of these passions but in their ordering.[31] Even Jeremy Taylor had been quite ready to encourage loving friendships between men and women provided they were prudently conducted. The theory of platonic love had evolved to take account of a spirituality which developed with age, when the soul should grow more able to rule the body. Evelyn accordingly told Margaret, or at least allowed them both to believe, that at 52 he was 'past that mighty Love to the Creature', and reassured her that her virtuous reputation, his own age, 'the Conscience of my Duty', and 'both our discretions' would be sufficient to 'Preserve our Friendship, honourable, Pious & usefull'.[32] The long tradition of 'holy friendships' reinforced his confidence that by dedicating his love to religious ends, he could transform and subsume it into the divine: 'I implore thy Goodness in particular for [her] with whose soule my life is bound up in holy Friendship and mutual vows of serving thee in purity,' he wrote in his prayer for the initiation of the friendship, 'O thou who art the lover of men, that hast commanded us to love one another and out of the fountaine of divine Charity sanctify, & improve this Celestial Virtue which shone forth in the primitive Saints and center'd only in thee.' In the halting verses with which he celebrated their spiritual marriage, the image of the heart was combined with the safer book and cross to give the same message:

> By Friendships sacred Tie combin'd,
> Devoted, and by Symbol sign'd;
> With Hand and Seale, & solemn Oath,
> To Jesu, we ourselves betroth:

---

[29] C. J. Stranks, *Anglican Devotion* (1961), 70–1; Simon Patrick, *Works*, ed. A. Taylor (Oxford, 1858), ix. 603–15; Hiscock I, 28. In his commonplace book (BL Add. MS 78330, p. 86), JE cites further early examples of 'holy friendships with women'.

[30] For a survey of such friendships throughout Christian history, see Patrick Collinson, '"Not Sexual in the Ordinary Sense": Men, Women and Religious Transactions', in *Elizabethan Essays* (1994), 119–50.

[31] McGoldrick, *Sweet and Gentle Struggle*, 338–43.

[32] *Life*, 42: MB to JE, [summer 1673]; ibid., 47.

Witness the Day, Moneth, Yeare, Ring, Vow
This Book, Crosse, Altar, Heart, & Thou
(Lover of Men) who dost impart
Such love, and shed it in our Heart.[33]

In fact it was the spiritual duty of men, he argued, to harness and transform all their 'intractable Affections' in this way; not only love, but 'desires, Emulation, Hatred, and all other emotions which us'd to transport and bring his Earthly and sensual part under their domination'; so that once they were 'Curb'd, subdu'd and plac'd on proper objects', 'Man becomes fit for Culture and for God's Husbandry'.[34]

To begin with all seemed auspicious. Over the next weeks Margaret confided her financial affairs to him and he gave her his practical help, managing to secure a part of her fortune which had been at some risk and making investments on her behalf.[35] In return he found his own spiritual life transformed. He had always been a loyal Anglican in the most difficult of times, but with the Restoration he had let himself become embattled and morose, and his religious observance had become arid. No one had taken the place of Jeremy Taylor as his spiritual adviser. The rector of Deptford, Dr Bretton, was a good friend, but he had to suit his ministry to the shipyard workers, and week after week his simple preaching warranted no more than a jotting in Evelyn's diary or commonplace book. Now almost everything he heard seemed to carry some special message which the friendship illuminated for him. Four days after the pact he found himself sitting in Deptford church listening to a visiting clergyman, Dr Richard Parr of Camberwell, as he expounded the affinity between divine and human love; 'how that virtue (or Affection rather) was naturally implanted in the hearts of men, and destined for the noblest and worthiest object', how it was to be understood as 'a divine & supernatural, not a carnal love'; how unworthy was 'the vanity of romantiq love, & the pretended, not genuine Platonic love . . . the true object of love being a divine virtue, applied to a divine object, to which we should endeavour to direct our Affections and passions'.[36] In November in the Chapel Royal he heard Margaret's confessor, Dean Benson, castigate the 'sensual and unholy living' of the court and lament, as he had often lamented

[33] BL Add. MS 78391, 'Devotions of Mrs Blaggs', copied by JE; Hiscock I, 28–9.
[34] BL Add. MS 78379: 'Tuesdays Meditation', [1674]. [35] *Life*, 26.
[36] BL Add. MS 78364: p. 580: sermon notes, 20 Oct. 1672. The notes of sermons between 1660 and 1671, all by Bretton, occupy only three pages of the whole volume. From 1672 the entries become much more detailed, and on the end-paper Evelyn notes, 'In those sermons which I have marked with an X some considerable note may occur'; all the sermons for 1672–4, the most intense period of the friendship, are so marked.

himself, that 'never was any age more barren of shining & exemplary lives'.[37]
Now the friendship let him see how this could be remedied.

Margaret had been unduly solemn and self-denying when he first knew
her. One of his first acts was to compose a long letter, almost an essay, for her,
arguing that this need not be so: 'I can't tell how Religion is come of late, to
have so ill a report attending it, as if no body could realy be good, so as to
owne & embrace it in any eminent degree, without entering into a state of
Melancholy, quitting their good humor, and absolutely resolving to take no
more pleasure of their Lives'; he himself had once been guilty of assuming
this, 'God forgive me', and he could see how it would deter the pleasure-
loving young women of the court. He now reiterated with much more conviction what he had once said to James Hamilton: that their religion was
'consistent with the secular state of life, with honours & dignitie, in Courts
& princes palaces, as well as in Cells & Cottages'. Sayes Court might be more
congenial to him than the court, but this seemed to him now just a matter of
personal choice and not because it was intrinsically preferable. Echoing de
Sales's contemporary, Nicolas Caussin, in his *Holy Court*, he urged that it was
quite possible for young courtiers to maintain 'the most cherefull and agreable Conversation in the World', and yet to live a life 'exactly religious'. With
a rather disturbing voyeurism, he followed such devout young women into
their closets and oratories:

if the pious soule now and then retires for the Exercising its Graces, & to entertaine
her God; such are the unexpressable delights springing from her heavenly intercourse, that even the most pungent sorrow and mealtings of heart, returne upon her
in the most ravishing Effects of spiritual Comfort, filling the soule with love and
admiration, and a succession of infinite pleasures, as nothing can describe.

If only, he appealed to Margaret, there were such a group of Anglican women
at Whitehall, 'and that they were of the most beautifull and eminent of it;
how would such a Conversation adorne our Religion, and bring it into
Reputation'. Her own influence amongst the more pious court women
already showed that this could be so. He told her that he would write the
story of their friendship under their coterie names, 'but in Veritable
Instances'; 'I know not realy, how one could do the Age we live in more
Justice, nor leave that to Come, a nobler Monument of Gratitude, for the
Improvement your Vertue & Conversation has taught it.'[38] If ever the
Whitehall of Charles II was 'a *Holy Court*' he wrote explicitly afterwards, it
was when Margaret Blagge was 'the life of it'; 'I prevoke Causine in all his

---

[37] BL Add. MS 78364, p. 580.
[38] BL Add. MS 78307, fos. 1–2: JE to MB, [late 1672?]; *Life*, 84.

Holy-Court, & all the Theresa's & Devotas of that Romantiq-Church, to produce me a Parallel.'[39] The more he saw of her, the more convinced he became that she had exceptional spiritual gifts. She and her like, encouraged and supported, could redeem the court, and by joining with her he would also make his own 'Calling and Election sure'.[40] In spite of all his public commitments, he made the first step by following her practice and expanding his customary two or three days of preparation for communion into a week-long course to keep himself 'in a Continual Preparation'.[41] Margaret became not just the platonic Electra, but 'the Pearle', recalling the 'pearl of great price' which was Christ's metaphor in St Matthew's Gospel for the Kingdom of Heaven.[42]

When this new friendship, combined with his public duties, began to keep him away from home for weeks rather than days at a time his wife was moved to write him one of her most finely judged letters, making delicate mockery of his courtly, high-minded coterie and reminding him of her own claims:

Dear Philaretes, I hope you do not imagine, though I live in the Countrie and converse with sea nimphs, now and then with a Tar-pauline Hero, that I do not aprehend the difference between this kind of felicity, and that which you possesse in a glorious Court amongst great beauties and wits, and those so refined that the charm of that splendor has no influence on their spirits; persons whose Ideas are of a higher nature, whose minds are pure and actions innocent; these, if I could be capable of envie, I should make the subject; but I am so farr from failing in that kind, that I rejoice in your happinesse, I acknowledge you a better judge of such perfections, and to merit the honour of being an admirer of the Calme Beautiful and prudent Alcidonia, the friendship of the sprightly Saint, and to be allowed the liberty off a playfellow to Ornithia . . . If knowledge and discernment in curious and choice speculations, joyned with virtues not common though desirable in your sex, may obtaine returnes of friendship from persons who cannot be unjust and therefore must allow you a share of their esteeme, you may pretend; but should I hope for a part, it must be upon no other account, but as I have a little interest in you and possibly am kindly thought of by you, which happinesse produces many advantages to, Hortensia.[43]

She was perhaps not the only one who realized something was afoot. Although Sunderland thought him still scarcely well enough to travel and

---

[39] *Life*, 100, 115; for Caussin, see Veevers, *Images of Love*, 77–81.

[40] BL Add. MS 78386: JE 'Oeconomics to a Newly Married Friend', [1676], p. 71.

[41] JE's MS notes on the fly-leaves of his copy of Simon Patrick's *The Christian Sacrifice*, 2nd edn. (1672), BL Eve.A.23.

[42] BL Add. MS 78392: 'The Legend of Philaretes and the Pearle', [c.1673]; George Ferguson, *Signs and Symbols in Christian Art* (New York, 1961), 43.

[43] Hiscock I, 38–9.

would have persuaded him to stay on in Paris, Godolphin declared that he could not justify 'Idling here as he cals it', any longer. A fortnight after Margaret's pact with Evelyn he set out from Paris and within a week had landed at Dover and was back in London.[44]

He had been absent for so long that he no longer had lodgings in Whitehall. He was still convalescent and not really fit to shift for himself, and so Arlington, for whom he had been book-buying during his last weeks in Paris, offered him temporary accommodation in the comfort of his great house at the end of St James's Park.[45] Except for the few weeks between his return from Spain and his departure for France he and Margaret had been separated for nearly a year. Either in her letters or on his return she told him of the conversion experience which she had undergone while he was away and that their relationship was changed as a result. It was the experience of seraphic love just as Robert Boyle had described it, in which an earthly love served as a precursor of the divine, far more serene and fulfilling. She still loved Godolphin, but this had brought her more anxiety, doubt, and isolation than security and happiness. Now she could say 'I am not where I was, My place is fill'd up with Him, who is All in All.—I find in him none of that tormenting Passion to which I need sacrifice myself.'[46]

Her first task was to share her new sources of consolation with him; 'being Thus Chang'd my-selfe, and liking it so well; I earnestly beged of God, that he would impart the same satisfaction to him I lov'd'. His life-threatening illness and recovery was to be the occasion for his spiritual rebirth: 'in a strang country wholy unacquainted with the pleasures of piety: far from the means of grace . . . that god almighty in his infinit mersy shold se fit to bring you from the grave: from death to life not only so but from sin to grace' was a sure sign that he was being called to change his life.[47] Godolphin, for all his consorting with the court wits, had been bred in the same tradition of high church piety as Margaret. In the aftermath of his illness it took little to persuade him that he had strayed too far from it and must renew his commitment to religion. He agreed guiltily that his life at court was too worldly and protested that he was 'much more troubled & griev'd for it' than pleased with it. He admitted that he did not spend as much time in religious duties as he ought to, 'nor as I hope I shall doe through his grace to me'. More strongly even than Evelyn, he was soon ready to see Margaret as his means of salvation. 'I have been today a good while considering & reflecting upon my owne

[44] PRO SP 78/135, fos. 82–96: Sunderland and Chudleigh to Arlington, 5, 8, 9 Nov. 1672.

[45] A. W. Thibaudeau (ed.), *Catalogue of the Collection of . . . Alfted Morrison* (1883–92), ii. 185: SG to Sir William Godolphin, 8 Dec. 1672.

[46] *Life*, 31.　　　[47] *Life*, 30; BL Hammick Papers: MB to SG, 'Monday night' [20 Oct. 1673].

wretchednesse & unworthynesse', he wrote to her, '& at the same time of the infinite long suffering & mercies of God to me, I have been very sensible of & sorry for the one & and very thankfull for acknowledging of the other, but I never think I doe it well to God almighty if I leave it undone to you the instrument he has made use of in shewing me good . . . all the obligations that people fancy they have to one another in this world are not to be compar'd nor to bee nam'd with those I have to you.'[48] With this understanding between them, she composed an emotional prayer on his behalf:

oh thou who hast begun a good work in him, perfect and accomplish it unto the day of christ, I can now discern nothing in him but love to thee, true sorrow for having gri[e]fed thy tender spirit and neglected his bleeding saviour, thy law is his delight and thy precepts dearer than thousands of gold and silver . . . but yet oh christ looke not on him with indignation and wrath but with pity and compassion—doe away with his iniquity and remember his sins no more.[49]

All this was in keeping with Evelyn's vision of a court redeemed by its beautiful, devout women. But Margaret had no more intention of staying there to fulfil the role he had devised for her than of allowing Godolphin to determine her future. She had already made up her own mind to leave Whitehall as soon as she could; 'seaven-yeares was long enough, and too much to Trifle any longer there'.[50] Once she had thought of marriage as the only occasion to resign her post, but with her inheritance from her mother and what she could expect from the court, improved with Evelyn's help, she was no longer dependent on it for her future security. She decided that she did not want to pass straight from one form of servitude to another, but to feel herself her own mistress 'before she determin'd concerning another change'. This meant time and peace to read, study, and reflect, to improve herself and test her new-found vocation. 'The more I know my self, the les I like my self,' she told Evelyn shortly after this, 'and yet for the treasuers of the world, I would not but know my self: and I pray I may doe so still more and more, till I com to know even as I am known.'[51] Marriage, if she did agree to it, must be such as not to interfere with this process. First and foremost this meant a total disengagement from the court and settling in some place as remote from it as possible. It was not Evelyn who brought about this change of heart. In fact he knew nothing of it for some time. But his friendship and support had strengthened her sense that she was now free to choose her own future.

[48] BL Hammick Papers: SG to MB, 'friday in the evening', 'friday 2 a clock' [1672–3].
[49] BL Add. MS 78392: prayer by MB, [1673].   [50] *Life*, 32.
[51] *Life*, 32, 35; BL Add. MS 78307, fo. 13ᵛ: MB to JE, [?11 May 1673].

There were realities to confront, however. Margaret might resign from court, but whether she married or not, she still had to secure the payment of her court dowry for her future maintenance. In the present crisis of public finances this was likely to need a good deal of time and solicitation, especially as it was not clear whether the funds should come from the Duke of York or from the Treasury, which now paid the Queen's maids. Nor was it really clear that Godolphin would be able or willing to disengage himself from the court in the foreseeable future. He was prepared to wish in an unspecific way for 'that quiet which must needs be the best preparation for the world to come',[52] but he depended on the court for most of his income. The long-postponed parliamentary session was also about to open. The war was going badly and money was needed, but the House was in a ferment of suspicion against Popery and far more hostile towards the court's French allies than to the Dutch.[53] The government had to muster all its supporters in the House of Commons. Godolphin was now recognized as a 'courtier at large', conspicuously in Arlington's favour and being groomed for government office. At the end of the year, just as Margaret took her decision to leave the court, he moved back into Whitehall lodgings: an apartment formerly belonging to the yeoman of the woodyard in the sprawling service area called Scotland Yard, to the north of the state apartments. It might be remote, but it was still within the precincts of the palace and it cost him nothing: 'two very principall considerations', as he remarked to his brother.[54]

The most he would promise Margaret was to try to keep more aloof from the King's circle than in the past, to lead a more regular life, and make his recreations at least, 'as harmlesse as I can imagine any'. In particular he undertook to restrain himself from 'some things to which I have been much accustom'd'.[55] By this he meant the gambling which was chiefly responsible for his anxieties about money. It not only continually put off the day when he could afford to support a household of his own, but there was no evading the fact that this, his chief pastime till now, was incompatible in every way with the devout life she proposed for them. Evelyn was expressing the orthodox view when he wrote implacably that 'the Time, the Money, & the patience we loose at play, will be Reckon'd amongst the severest Accompts at the Day of Judgement'.[56] Yet Godolphin was not prepared to commit himself further at

---

[52] BL Hammick Papers: SG to MB, 'friday morning' [winter 1673–4].
[53] Ronald Hutton, *Charles II* (Oxford, 1989), 290.
[54] PRO LC 5/140/153; BL Add. MS 28052, fo. 98: SG to Sir William Godolphin, 4 Jan. 1673.
[55] BL Hammick Papers: SG to MB, 'friday 2 a clock' [1673]; cf. National Library of Scotland MS 3420, fo. 42: SG to Sir William Godolphin, 8 Dec. [1672].
[56] JE, *A Devotionarie Book*, ed. Walter Frere (1936), 58.

first than restraint; hoping, as he put it to Margaret, that 'as long as wee resist all evill & struggle as much as wee can with the frailty & infirmitys of our nature . . . God will blesse the sincerity of our endeavours & suffer & helpe us to worke out our salvation with feare & trembling'.[57] It was clear that he expected this to be the work of some time.

Nevertheless he managed to deal with her determination to resign by means of a deft compromise which still kept her within his family circle. She would leave Whitehall, but only to go so far as Berkeley House in Piccadilly, where his cousins had offered her a refuge in their household. To the outside world this would seem a natural prelude to marriage and Margaret would be spared the gossip which would otherwise follow her resigning a maid's post still single. But she allowed herself to see it in a much more conventual light; 'she believed that at Berkeley-House, she should be more at her owne Disposal', she told Evelyn, 'That she should have no body to Observe, but God; Be Mistress of her Houres, and Govern her Affaires suitably to her devout Inclynations.' A year seems to have been the time settled on, while the couple waited to 'see how things would go'.[58] In the meantime she curtailed Godolphin's visits and letters so that they would not disturb her devotional regime, and he in turn acknowledged, rather too readily perhaps, that he was on probation, being 'willing (I hope) more than able to resist the temptations, the vanity's & the follies of the world':

indeed my deare I doe never think of any thing with soe much pleasure as when I fancy what a comfort & encouragement wee shall find reading & talking & praying together, if it pleases God to make us once so happy, & I wish extreamly both that you did soe too & that you had the same reason for itt, but it scarce goes further than a wish & I am not unreasonable enough to hope it.[59]

For Margaret was prepared, if need be, to take a very long view, far longer than the year settled on; she hoped that Godolphin would eventually become a fit partner in a godly marriage, but if he did not they would do without marriage. Later she summed up the understanding between them, or what she believed it to be, for Evelyn's benefit. If they should both be able to disengage themselves completely from 'the world', they would marry 'under such Restraints as were fit; and by the agreablenesse of our humour, make each other happy'; but at present Godolphin 'must perpetualy be Engag'd in Businesse, & follow the Court, and live allways in the World, and so have lesse time for the Service of God, which is a sensible Affliction to him', and so they had decided 'to Expect a while, and see how things will go; having a greate

---

[57] BL Hammick Papers: SG to MB, 'friday 2 a clock' [1673].   [58] *Life*, 31, 35.
[59] BL Hammick Papers: SG to MB, 'Saturday morning' [1672–3].

mind to be together, which cannot with decency be don, without Marriage; nor That, to either of our Satisfactions, without being free from the World'. Their aim was to serve God, she repeated, 'and if we cannot do that quietly together, we will asunder . . . if we can but passe our Younger-Yeares, 'tis not likely, we shall be much concern'd for Mariage when Old'.[60] 'Let our desiers be holy, our pastions mortifyd,' she had written in her conversion prayer for Godolphin. This and the reference to 'such restraints as are fit', suggest she might even have envisaged a kind of spiritual companionship without consummation. Godolphin, she said, had assured her that although he did not want to live without her, he was willing to live celibate. This allowed her to believe that even if they did not marry or consummate he would not be 'in danger of Sin'.[61] She began to think that a single life would be the highest state of grace for them both.

On New Year's Day 1673, knowing nothing of all this, Evelyn heard public prayers at Whitehall, distributed the customary gifts amongst the servants, and then made Margaret a visit in the maids' quarters. But she was not well and they could not pray together as usual.[62] He returned home to perform his duties there, but all the while he was distracted with anxiety for her:

My dear Friend O Lord lies under thy afflicting, yet gentle hand. Remove, I beseech Thee, the Cause, and restore [her] to her former health that we may both celebrate thy Goodnes: Lord, if this be don to the Green-tree, what will become of the Dry! [She] is thy servant, early dedicated to thee, and eminently adorn'd with thy Grace. O Regard [her] tendernes; and patient submission nor reject the humble suite of me thy poor Creature . . . [She] is dearer to me than my Life, and therefore I aske this mercy from the God of Life and Health and Mercy.[63]

He had a New Year's present for her as well: a locket containing the pentacle symbol set with turquoise and diamonds, an extravagance which was his largest single expense of the month.[64] Until now the friendship had been conducted 'between jest and earnest'. Margaret would often smile at his more extravagant flights and his wife could treat the whole affair with dry wit. But both the prayer and the present suggest that for Evelyn it was no longer a light-hearted matter; he was floundering every day deeper into uncontrolled feeling.

On the following Sunday he returned to find Margaret recovered. In fact she came to seek him out in his own lodging, to tell him that she intended to

---

[60] *Life*, 31.   [61] BL Add. MS 78392: prayer by MB; *Life*, p. 40: MB to JE, [summer 1673].
[62] JE, *Diary*, iv. 1–2.
[63] BL Add. MS 78392: prayer by JE, [Jan. 1673]; the pentacle appears in place of the pronoun.
[64] Hiscock I, 41.

leave the court as soon as possible.[65] It was not just a rude awakening from his dream of a 'holy court' of devout women, but a threat to the continuance of the friendship just as it had become central to his life. He was well acquainted with the Berkeleys. He had dined with them and they had sought his advice in the design of their gardens. But in a private house, even one which was open to him as a visitor, Margaret would be less accessible to him than before. It also brought her marriage and the end of her independent life a step closer. But she still needed the Queen's formal permission to resign. Catherine was often exacting and irritable with her servants, even in cases of temporary absence through illness; Margaret had already tried once to raise the matter without success. On this Sunday Evelyn went with her to the drawing room. There, having waited apprehensively until the rest of the company were dispersing, she approached the King and Queen and made her formal petition to be allowed to retire, this time within a matter of days. 'Tho' they look'd as if they would have a little reproch't her, for making so much hast', no obstacle was put in her way; Godolphin was a favourite with the King and seven years after all was more than enough service for a maid of honour. Evelyn went back with Margaret to the maids' quarters, 'which she was no sooner entr'd; but falling on her knees, she Bless'd God, as for a Signal Deliverance: She was come out of Aegypt, & now in her Way to the Land of Promise.'[66]

At some point between this Sunday and Margaret's departure for Berkeley House four days later he scrawled a long letter, which may have been written simply to adjust himself to her new situation and never sent. In it he compared himself to St Jerome, the fourth-century 'Doctor of the Church' and Margaret to his devout followers, Paula and Eustochium; 'I can parallel no Friendship (that ever I yet read of) so neere to that of Paula & her Hierom, as is that which is between my Electra, & her Philaretes.'[67] This episode from patristic literature had had a profound significance for Evelyn ever since he had acquired the Paris edition of Jerome's letters shortly after his marriage. Although the saint had fallen out of favour amongst Protestant theologians as 'an immoderate extoller of virginity' in his female followers, Evelyn could find nothing in the letters to take exception to: 'they breath nothing but Piety; have a force and passion in them . . . highly incentive of Virtue'. As Francis de Sales had pointed out, they also contained some of the earliest examples of spiritual friendship between men and women. Anna Maria van Schurman and the Calvinist Jean de Labadie, a famous contemporary pair of spiritual friends, were likened to Jerome and Paula, and this early Christian

---

[65] *Life*, 32.   [66] Ibid. 32–3.
[67] BL Add. MS 78307, fo. 5: JE to MB (draft), [Jan. 1673].

community had provided one of the precedents for Evelyn's Interregnum proposal for a revival of 'Monasticall Societies, decently qualified'.[68] It also provided a link between Margaret and his long-lost son. In his introduction to the *Golden Book of St John Chrysostom*, translated as a memorial to Richard in 1658, he had written rather curiously that Paula and Eustochium had not been dearer to St Jerome than the boy had been to him.[69] When he discovered that Margaret had been born in the same month and year as Richard, the circle was complete.

Evelyn might compare the war-torn latter days of the Roman Empire with the present state of Europe, but he could scarcely claim any other parallel with his personal situation. St Jerome had persuaded his female followers to leave Rome, 'that impious city', and join him in the deserts of Judaea, whereas Margaret's decision to leave Whitehall was entirely her own and it was he who was left behind. His 'Electra' was leaving the balls, the theatre, and the music of the court; she was giving up 'the gay dress, the Raillery & the Wit, which made her the life of the Conversation & the pretty Miracle of Court, that she may adorn her brighter soule & converse with Angels'. At Berkeley House she would live 'in a purer air . . . with a pious & noble friend, in liberty, without formes, frugaly, without contempt, splendidly without pomp, wher you may be arbiter of your time & serve god regularly, dispose of your person, & choose your Conversation'. When she altered her condition 'it shall be for the better, & God will conduct you'. But he would remain behind 'in bondage', and without even the consolation of regular meetings in the Chapel Royal or her 'holy Cell'. He envied her and begged for her prayers, that 'the Circumstances of my life being composed, I may imitate your Example & devote my selfe wholy to Eternity'. In the meantime, with a slightly menacing emphasis, he insisted that the friendship was still binding on her: 'the rights [*sic*] are past between us, & it is a sacrament, & you alone are the person in the world whose esteem in it I most value & care to cultivate, & I will perish ere I abandon you'.[70] The following Wednesday he hovered about her while she made ready to leave. With her bed already moved to Berkeley House, 'all her Household stuff, besids a Bible, and a Bundle of Prayer-Books, were pack't-up in a very little Compass'. She took her leave of the Mother of the Maids and then of the tearful Dorothy

---

[68] *A History of Women in the West: Renaissance and Enlightenment Paradoxes*, ed. Natalie Zemon Davis and Arlette Farge (Cambridge, Mass., 1993), 164; BL Add. MS 78298: JE to Samuel Hartlib, 4 Feb. 1660; Bray, iii. 120: JE to Boyle, 3 Sept. 1659.

[69] Dedication to *The Golden Book of St John Chrysostom* (1658), in *WJE*, 45.

[70] BL Add. MS 78307, fo. 5: JE to MB (draft), [Jan. 1673]. He later adapted the draft for inclusion in the *Life*, 35–6.

Howard. Then, still with Evelyn in attendance, she made the short journey by coach to Berkeley House.[71]

The last substantial house at the western end of Piccadilly, beyond the ill-fated pile of Clarendon House, it had been built less than ten years before and looked down over the grass of the deer park to St James's Palace. Evelyn regarded it with a characteristic mixture of qualified approval and a connoisseur's opinionated carping. The forecourt, often a failing in town houses, he admitted was 'noble', and the portico was unexceptionably modelled on Palladio, 'but it happens to be the very worst in his booke, how ever my good friend Mr. Hugh May his Lordships Architect affected it'. The central *corps de logis* was linked awkwardly to the wings on either side by single-storey corridors. Although the rooms were fine, their layout was inconvenient: all apartments of state with no closets for privacy, and the kitchen and stables badly placed. The gardens to the north, however, were 'incomparable', with their variations of level, 'prity Piscina', and terraces flanked with holly hedges according to his advice.[72]

As Margaret alighted in the courtyard Evelyn continued to take in her every mood and change of expression:

I never beheld her more Orient, than she appear'd at this time, and the moment she set foote in the Coach, her Eyes sparkl'd with joy, and a marvelous Lustur: The Roses of her Cheeks were so fresh, and her Countenance so gay . . . But ah! had you seen, with what Effusion & Open armes she entr'd Berkely house, and Sprung into the Caresses of my Lady!

Still with him in attendance, she was shown to her new apartment to unpack her belongings, and 'when she had consecrated her new Oratory with a devout Aspiration, and the incense of an humble Soule, for the Blessing of this Sweete Retirement; She sate-downe, and Admir'd her felicity'.[73]

Lord Berkeley was a first cousin of Godolphin's mother. A veteran royalist, he had held Exeter for Charles I, had been appointed the Duke of York's governor in exile and his steward at the Restoration, and later served a stormy period as Lord Lieutenant of Ireland, from which he had returned less than a year before. Now in his late sixties, he was looking and feeling his age, but his public ambitions were not yet satisfied and both he and his wife kept close links with the court. With a mass of black curls and fine dark eyes, Christian Lady Berkeley was only half her husband's age; attractive, sociable, and fashionably pious. The daughter of the immensely wealthy president of the Levant Company, at the time of her match with Berkeley she was already the widow of two short-lived marriages which witnessed to her status as an

---

[71] *Life*, 33–4. [72] JE, *Diary*, iii. 625. [73] *Life*, 34.

heiress, and this prospect had finally been realized with the death of her father a few months before. In twelve years of marriage she had borne five children, four of them sons ('Gods Bobs, Jack hath got another boy', Charles II exclaimed when numbers began to mount up).[74] She already knew Margaret well, having been groom of the stole to the Duchess when she was first appointed maid of honour. Although she welcomed the prospect of a pious and court-bred companion in her household, neither of the Berkeleys had any notion of its being a religious retreat.

Evelyn, who had scarcely left Margaret's side since her decision to leave the court, returned the following day to dine with them.[75] Although she had made clear her longing for uninterrupted time and had even curtailed Godolphin's visits and letters, he was not prepared to forgo any of the conditions he had laid down for the friendship. Tuesday, a usual meeting-day for the Council for Plantations, was fixed for his regular visits. In the intervals they would correspond in the manner of St Jerome and his female followers. With his first letter came a motto for their friendship ('Un Dieu Un Amy') and a passionate, sublimating prayer for their first Tuesday: 'we seeke no other satisfaction, then that this Love of ours, may be totally immersed in the fruition, and Love of thee: Ah, let that flaming Charity of Thine, which mooved Thee to do such great things for us . . . burne likewise in our Hearts, to consume all that is Earthy, and Sensual, and repugnant to thy Spirit of Holynesse.'[76] With the same rather oppressive didacticism which had led Elizabeth Mordaunt to call him governor and the Restoration women to compare him to a schoolmaster, he also enclosed a grammar and offered to tutor her in languages. Margaret briefly pronounced the prayer 'excellent', the motto 'good and pretty', and acquiesced in the programme of 'improvements', but with a slight note of resignation: 'if you will propos any way to improve that afternoon you giv me, put but your method into blake and whit and I will obey you, after prayers are don we may go upe'.[77]

With this encouragement he went on to compile a programme not just for their Tuesday meetings but for her whole week, in a manner more suitable for a child than a grown woman. Perhaps recalling his first encounter with her at Whitehall, he began by advising her not to display her otherworldliness too openly in the mixed company of Berkeley House; 'at meales I would have you very cherefull, and like other people: There is nothing so worthy reproofe, as to be nice and solemn, reserv'd and singular, when all the

---

[74] Barnard Falk, *The Berkeleys of Berkeley Square* (1944), 34–81; B. H. Johnson, *Berkeley Square to Bond Street* (1952), 38–64.

[75] JE, *Diary*, iv. 2.   [76] Hiscock I, 43–4.

[77] BL Add. MS 78307, fo. 6: MB to JE, [early 1673?].

World are free.' After dinner she must not apply herself to any serious work for an hour: 'it disturbs Concoction, & is very unwholesome'. But after that, if she had no visits to make, she should read history, '(not romance, which perverts it . . .)', which would give her 'a Scheme, & Prospect how God has govern'd the World'. She could also set herself to acquire some knowledge of herbs and plants, so that in the future if she lived in the country she would be able to make remedies for the poor. Beyond this there were 'Sublimer Subjects; as the Fabrick of the Vniverse, & the motions of the Planets, and many Mathematical Truths & Speculations, which would not onely exceedingly divert you, but aduance your Admiration of the All-wise disposer'. But for a woman especially, there was 'indeede but one thing Necessary, namely, the saving knowledge of Christ', and the story of Martha and Mary was a reminder that sacred was always to be preferred to secular knowledge. Mondays, Tuesdays, and Thursdays might therefore be assigned to general reading, and Wednesdays, Fridays, and Saturdays for devotional works; but not works of controversy which tended 'more to passion, than conviction, & sometimes to the disturbance of well-settled thoughts'. To prevent this he undertook to supply all her devotional reading himself and show her how to compile commonplace notes on his own model. For recreation he allowed her to read 'some chast poeme' or occasionally go to a play, provided she was assured in advance that it would not offend modesty.[78]

Then he returned to Sayes Court for ten days and when he did not hear from her after a day or two, reminded her of their agreement to correspond. She thanked him for his instructions and promised to try to follow them, and assured him 'upon the word of a Christian' that she stood by their pact of friendship;[79] but she might well have wondered where in all this she was to have the time to come to 'know herself' as she wished. She was already finding Berkeley House far less of a retreat than she had hoped. Evelyn had talked of silence, of 'liberty, without formes', of a regular devotional regime and chosen company. But none of these in such a large, sociable household was easy to come by, especially for a woman. Although Lady Berkeley was quite aware of Margaret's aspirations, she did not hesitate to override them when it suited her; Margaret soon found herself almost as much in demand to help 'entertain the ladies' as she had been while at court.[80] Although Berkeley House on its rising ground was supposed to be a healthier situation than the riverside Whitehall, she was still ailing in health. When Evelyn cautioned her solicitously against observing the Lenten fasts too rigorously, she agreed: 'the

[78] *Life*, 218–23.
[79] BL Add. MS 78386: JE, 'Oeconomics', [1676], pp. 3, 17, quoting from an early letter to him.
[80] *Life*, 38–9.

will being a great mater in holy things I am glad to find by you, it is well reseived when we can doe no more'; and she ended by begging him a little drearily not to be 'weary of improving me so little capable of it as I am'.[81] A few days later Evelyn came up to London again, this time for a continuous period of nearly three weeks. On Tuesday afternoons, as agreed, he called at Berkeley House. The first visit passed according to plan in prayer and 'improvements'. But the second on 25 February, went awry almost at once.

Evelyn complained that when he arrived Margaret looked 'contracted', that is gloomy and unwelcoming. She protested afterwards that she had actually been nearer 'disolving', that is breaking down in tears, 'therefore you se[e] you are not skild in my face though you are in my soul'.[82] Perhaps she had just had a difficult encounter with Godolphin, or perhaps Evelyn's visit was just one more interruption and his increasingly obsessive focus on her beginning to seem intrusive. Instead of shortening it or concentrating on its devotional purpose, he made matters worse by questioning her about her marriage plans, the most sensitive subject he could have chosen.

It was assumed by all her acquaintance that Margaret would marry very shortly; 'you went from Court to consummate', as Evelyn put it. Although he was aware that she wanted an interval to devote to her spiritual life, he did not yet know of the understanding with Godolphin which put her marriage off indefinitely. To him this marriage was the next obstacle to the future of their friendship. His own wife might be tolerant, but it was quite possible that Godolphin, with whom he was scarcely acquainted, would exercise a husband's authority and not allow it to continue. In his anxiety he chose this bad moment to press Margaret to tell him when it would be. Hinting first that he was prying, she told him that she was not certain that it would take place at all. In a flurry of contradictory reasons, she said that she did not think they were secure enough financially to set up their own household, that they might have a larger family than they could provide for, that in any case she dreaded childbearing; that after all St Paul had recommended celibacy as a higher state than marriage, and finally that she would be happier and more able to pursue her vocation unmarried. Their talk went on long and inconclusively, until Margaret made a pointed remark about long visits and how they interrupted her devotions.[83] Evelyn took his leave; but unable to let the matter rest, he continued the debate by letter.

The dilemma Margaret posed was an ancient one and still very much unresolved. Since the Reformation a married woman's spiritual and social

[81] BL Add. MS 78307, fo. 7: MB to JE, 'Tuesday', endorsed by him 'Feb. 1672/3'.
[82] Ibid., fo. 6: MB to JE, [early 1673?].
[83] The substance of their talk is clear from Evelyn's letter of 27 Feb. 1673, ibid., fos. 8–9.

functions within her family and amongst her neighbours were valued more highly than those of a solitary devotional regime. If the early Christians had embraced celibacy so readily, the argument went, it was just so that in time of persecution they might have fewer worldly encumbrances. In less hazardous times such renunciations were no longer necessary.[84] Yet the argument for virginity as the nobler state for both men and women was never entirely disposed of. The long tradition of platonic philosophy, which valued the spiritual over the corporeal, supported the early Christian view. A Caroline clergyman such as George Herbert could take it for granted that celibacy was the clerical ideal and that only the practicalities of ministering to a country parish could decree otherwise.[85] Jeremy Taylor, though himself twice married, was still willing to acknowledge virginity as the more holy state, not intrinsically, but because it freed an individual from worldly cares and enabled a single-minded pursuit of religion. He only cautioned that those who remained unmarried from choice, 'since they are in some measure in a condition like that of angels', must spend much of their time in suitably 'angelical employment' in order to justify it.[86] The *Seraphick Love* of Robert Boyle, a devout layman who never married, had a notable influence in the decade after the Restoration, and William Cave's influential *Primitive Christianity*, published just as Evelyn and Margaret began their own debate, noted that 'very many of us, though we do not boast on't, do inviolably preserve a perpetual Virginity'.[87] Even a generation later, supporting the annulment of an unconsummated child marriage at the court of Queen Anne, an Anglican bishop could still argue that young people should not be hastened into marriage, since some might prove to have 'the gift of Continency, and so have dedicated themselves by a perpetual virginity to the Angelical life, a state which our blessed saviour & St Paul preferr'd before Matrimony'; while it was 'no sin' to marry, 'yet no Protestant can deny that not to marry in order to attend without distraction on the Lord is better'.[88]

As a happily married man delighting in his young family, Evelyn had pointed out to Boyle that all this evaded the complex issue of married love

[84] Marina Warner, *Alone of all her Sex: The Myth and Cult of the Virgin Mary* (1976), 74; Margaret R. Sommerville, *Sex and Subjection: Attitudes to Women in Early Modern England* (1995), 251; Margo Todd, *Christian Humanism and the Puritan Social Order* (Cambridge, 1987), 97–115; Anthony Fletcher, 'The Protestant Idea of Marriage in Early Modern England', in A. Fletcher and P. Roberts (eds.), *Religion, Culture and Society in Early Modern Britain* (Cambridge, 1994), 162–3.

[85] George Herbert, *Works*, ed. F. E. Hutchinson (Oxford, 1953), 236–7.

[86] Jeremy Taylor, *The Whole Works* (1847), iii. 55–7, 61.

[87] William Cave, *Primitive Christianity: or The Religion of the Ancient Christians in the First Ages of the Gospel* (1673), 85.

[88] BL Add. MS 47131, fo. 15ᵛ: speech of the Bishop of Chichester on a petition to annul the marriage of Mary Forester, 1714 (I am grateful to Paula Backscheider for this reference).

and the simple practicalities of human reproduction; there might be 'nothing more worthy eulogies than virginity', but take away reciprocal and fruitful love between men and women, and the whole world and heaven too, would be a desert, since 'those that shall people paradise, and fill heaven with saints, are such as have been subject to this passion, and were the products of it'. St Paul had given 'the best advice in a time of persecution . . . for an itinerant apostle', but God after all had placed Eve as well as Adam in the Garden of Eden, and whatever the consequences of this, 'he that said it was not good for man to be alone, placed the celibate amongst the inferior states of perfection, whatsoever some affirm'. In paradise and the ark 'there were none but couples', he added charmingly, and 'every creature was in love'. In sum, human love should not be seen as a distraction from the divine, but as a pathway to it; marriage was not just for the perpetuation of the species or for companionship, it was itself a 'figure' for mystic union with God.[89]

Yet these were never stark choices for him. Just as he was never prepared to relinquish the claims of the contemplative life completely, so seraphic love, focused on a divine object and without the 'disorder' of human passion, never ceased to appeal to him. His quest for platonic friendship alongside his marriage, his creation of the private haven of Sayes Court on the very edge of London, were in their different ways reconciliations, or at least containments, of these unresolvable oppositions. He might have used his sympathy with both sides to help Margaret in her dilemma. Instead he adopted the hectoring masculine style of his debate with George Mackenzie about public and private virtue. Claiming that she could only have chosen to argue against marriage in order to exercise her 'faculty of maintaining paradoxes', he began with a robust summary of its social utility: 'Do you esteem it no honour to have given saints to the Church, and use-full members to the state in which you live? That you can be hospitable to strangers, institute your children, give instruction to your servants, example to your neighbours, and be parent of a thousand other blessings?' Unaware of Godolphin's gambling debts, he dismissed her financial anxieties out of hand; since a degree of uncertainty was inseparable from all human affairs, it was quite unreasonable for her to resolve not to marry an honourable suitor after so long an understanding between them, ''til you can set your Nest on high, and be out of the reach of accidents'; 'if she who had bore you had been of your mind there had been one lesse saint for heaven and I had wanted the best friend in the world, and so would many others, who now blesse God for the charities you do them.

---

[89] Bray, iii. 122–5: JE to Boyle, 29 Sept. 1659; cf. William and Malleville Haller, 'The Puritan Art of Love', *Huntington Library Quarterly*, 5 (1941–2), 239.

Where is then my Electra's humility, her Faith and her Love?' As for her fear of childbirth: 'Queenes have gon into the world before you in it, and tis to serve your Generation in the most necessary instance, indeares you to your off-spring, to your husband, your relations and the Commonwealth.' 'Marry in Gods name, Electra, Marry,' he exhorted her finally, 'and be not over solicitous for the future.' As for St Paul, 'the circumstances wholy differ and the decencies of the age permit it not'.[90]

This was the crux. Margaret might talk of living single, but there was no longer any institutional provision in England for women to dedicate themselves to a religious life apart from family ties. Anyone who tried to do so would put herself at risk, and be regarded as an anomaly, even a threat to the social order.[91] For all Evelyn's occasional hankering after a collegiate life, he was as ready on occasion as any of his Protestant contemporaries to condemn Catholic foundations; their inmates 'filled with pride, vain-glory, and singularity', subjecting themselves to 'temptations and secret lusts' and owning no allegiance to 'those princes under whose jurisdiction they were born'.[92] In Germany some Lutheran orders were formed after the Reformation, and in England there were occasional proposals for a Protestant 'College of Maids'; but it was assumed that none of the women would have chosen this way of life as a spiritual calling; they would be widows spending their last years in 'a single retired life', or 'old, decayed, deformed, or discontented maids', and they would make themselves useful by educating young girls or nursing the sick. Evelyn himself was one of the few prepared to acknowledge that some might have a spiritual motive, when he regretted that there was no place where 'single persons devoutly inclined' might live without 'ensnaring vows', but this was not until much later and in any case none of the proposals was put into practice.[93] A man so inclined might seek a form of collegiate life in the universities, but for a Protestant woman of marriageable age there was no equivalent. As Evelyn summed it up, 'the Decencys of her Sex, and Custome of the Natione . . . and the want of Monast'rys & pious Recesses' all obliged Margaret to marry. To deny it and set herself apart would be to make herself 'singular and fantastic'.[94]

---

[90] BL Add. MS 78307, fos. 8–9: JE to MB, 27 Feb. 1673 (copy); cf *Life*, 43–6, where he paraphrases the contents of this letter.

[91] Bridget Hill, 'A Refuge from Men: The Idea of a Protestant Nunnery', *Past and Present*, 117 (1987), 119.

[92] JE, *History of Religion*, ed. R. M. Evanson (1850), ii. 287–8.

[93] Hill, 'Refuge from Men', 113–15; Evelyn marked the passage in his copy of Cave's *Primitive Christianity*, 86, concerning the early Christian practice of living celibate without vows (BL Eve. a.86).

[94] *Life*, 46; BL Add. MS 78386: JE, 'Oeconomics', [1676], p. 66.

Since there was a surplus of women in the population and the levels of dowry were rising, it was likely to be true that many women who remained unmarried would not have done so from choice.[95] Virginity in these circumstances, Jeremy Taylor pointed out, was not a virtue, but 'a misery and a trouble, or else a mere privation'. In a society which privileged marriage and provided them with so few alternatives, 'old maids' were assumed to be bitter at their lack of fulfilment: 'Affected, Morose, Covetous, Obnoxious to Temptation & Reproch', in Evelyn's bugbear words to Margaret; 'the most calamitous creature[s] in Nature', in Richard Allestree's. Yet Allestree, an immensely popular devotional writer, also acknowledged the important point that for a woman to remain single *from choice* was a very different matter.[96] In classical mythology and in early Christianity as well, virginity, if chosen and maintained, was acknowledged to confer autonomy and power on a woman.[97] Evelyn freely admitted that he had his own motives for recommending it in Margaret's case; her marriage might well put an end to the friendship and all he had invested in it, whereas 'being single you are Mistris of your self'. Having exhorted 'Electra' to marry, he therefore went on disturbingly: 'if I would betray you (as perhaps I might) I could turne the Argument upon myself and shew you another face of things'; there was nothing to be said in favour of marriage, 'but what I could unravell with the glory of Virginity, the ease of a Single-life, the opportunities of doing more good, of serving God better, of prolonging life'. With 'examples and precepts from Scripture and Fathers, from Legends and Histories', he could present her with 'such a lovely picture of that state, which (approaching next the nature of Angels who neither marry or are given in marriage) would bring you to suspence indeede and make you cry out with the Apostle . . . I am in a straight betwixt two, and what I shall choose I know not—'. Then he paused rhetorically: 'but I spare my Electra; nor needes she arguments to render her more unkind to Hymen, and to the repose of One whom she knows, & I pitty'; and he concluded by reminding her, with reference to their last unsatisfactory meeting, that he also led a busy life and yet did not begrudge time for their friendship.[98]

Margaret might well feel that she was being browbeaten, manipulated, and confused. It was not unknown for young women to be subject to sinister pressures in matters of this kind. There was the case of the wife of her sisters'

[95] Hill, 'Refuge from Men', 115–16.

[96] Taylor, *Whole Works*, iii. 61; *Life*, 45; Allestree, *The Ladies Calling* (1673), in N. H. Keeble (ed.), *The Cultural Identity of Seventeenth Century Woman: A Reader* (1994), 145,

[97] Warner, *Alone of all her Sex*, 48.

[98] BL Add. MS 78307, fos. 8ᵛ–9: JE to MB, 27 Feb. 1673 (copy).

parish clergyman, who had once been persuaded by the 'grave divine' who strictly controlled her religious life to give him an undertaking never to marry anyone but himself, though he already had a wife and family.[99] Whether or not she really feared any such thing for herself, the oppressive and demanding nature of Evelyn's interest in her and her concerns, his intellectual dominance and his insensitivity, were unwelcome. A friendship begun as a means of support seemed only to be presenting her with new difficulties. She made it clear that she wanted to be left alone to work these matters out for herself. Evelyn made one more visit on 4 March, then no more for over a month.[100]

But he did write one more long letter, reminding her of her obligations to him and complaining that she was avoiding him even when all he wanted was to discuss her financial affairs. Although he was perhaps only trying to coax her to smile again at his intensities and for his own sake to recover the light-heartedness of his earlier platonic friendships, his tone this time was ill-considered in quite a different way: half piqued, half teasing; veering in a disturbing way between a secular flirtatiousness and spiritual solemnity:

I find you continuing your late reservednes, your breathings after solitude, and perpetual complaints of the multitudes of your acquaintance which makes me feare you repent of having added one to their number since October last, so much is Electra chang'd since she came into a better Ayre—The time will come when she will say, such a person was my sincere friend, faithfull, industrious and without reproch; he was one I might with confidence have relyd on, for he certainly lov'd me, I am sorry I made him no more sensible of my esteem; since I am sure it was all he sought and that such a friend so unconcern'd, so intire, is not every bodys lot to find—This will make my ashes some amends, when I am fall'n into them: Well, there is a difference in good-natures, and greate Witts and great Beautys are seldom guilty of much of that; Yet, there may be a Phoenix for any thing I know; but they say she is in Arabia and amongst the Spices, and it is a great way thither. Why was I so un-happy or so foolish to imagine that because I thought Electra the Creature in the World, whom I would wish and choose to be my friend, and the repository of my heart? . . . But stay, is there no punishment due to little Thieves, who steale away our hearts, give me that back againe if you can.

Then he changed tack: 'Now would this looke like a love-letter as any thing in the World, to any body living, who should light upon it, but you & I?' Yet it was, he explained, only so in St Jerome's manner, and 'I can shew you some more passionate betweene him and his Devota Eustochium; You would thinke the old Heremite realy in Love, and so he was, but it was divine, and doubtless very holy.' Only the conclusion was more straightforward and

[99] Patrick, *Works*, ix. 460–2.   [100] JE, *Diary*, iv. 4–8.

reassuring, reverting to the 'brotherly love' Margaret had invoked in her inscription on the altar of friendship and reaffirming their common Christian aims:

God Almighty knows my heart: I do love you; but it is because you love him; Whilst we both determine our Affections here: we shall love each other in the most perfect fruition . . . Go on, blessed Saint, make more of your sex like your selfe: The Lord is with you, and will reward your labour of love, and I will joyne my prayers and uttmost efforts . . . My longing is, that this may be the sole Object and End of our Love and Friendship: The dayes approach in which we must do something Extraordinary (I meane the passion weeke), Let us provoke one another, God allows the Emulation, and such a zeale as yours, not only pulls downe his Blessings, but suspends his judgments, and sinfull Nations I am confident subsist because your hands are lifted up: remember me in your prayers and let Brotherly Love Continue.[101]

Easter week followed, bitterly cold, with continual rain and snow. Evelyn came up to London again, but with much other business to occupy him. He continued to labour grimly over his history of the Dutch War. He had to attend the Council of Plantations, over which Shaftesbury now presided in place of Sandwich, and he intended to keep Lent and Easter at the Chapel Royal. He must have seen Margaret if only at the Chapel, but there were no visits to Berkeley House. In fact his main attention at this time was not on her but on his son, who was preparing, at the rather late age of 18, to take his first communion on Easter Day.[102]

Jack had parted with his tutor Bohun two years before and it was now becoming a matter of pressing concern what he should do with himself Evelyn either could not afford a prolonged period of travel for him or was not convinced that he would profit by it. Complaining that 'I could never yet divine to what your genius would more particularly lead you', he overwhelmed the boy with programmes of reading and study, while Jack turned from one thing to another in what looked increasingly like desperation: his father's virtuoso pursuits, translation, book-collecting, gardening, and occasional verse; his tutor's rigorous classicism; Craven Howard's star-gazing and ingenious instruments. As his moods swung between elation and sullenness, passionate enthusiasm and boredom, his father taxed him querulously with 'that Inconstancy which is thought to be the general ingredient of your temper, & that whilst you your selfe love nothing long, you blame me for filling you with too many things at once'. Having been admitted to the Middle Temple to complete his education, he was now adding to his father's

---

[101] BL Add. MS 78307, fo. 10: JE to MB, 'Tuesday morning' [18?] Mar. 1673.

[102] JE, *Diary*, iv. 6; BL Add. MS 78393: 'Catalogue of Books & papers in order to the Hist: of the Dutch Warr brought with me up to London', 16 Feb. 1673.

exasperation by talking of taking up the law as a profession, though Evelyn had always thought it the most 'venal & sordid' of any open to a gentleman. He encouraged him instead to begin cultivating patrons for public office by dedicating his translation of the *Hortorum Libri IV* of Nicolas Rapin to Lord Arlington.[103] It was a creditable performance for an 18-year-old, but whatever his abilities, until Jack should outgrow his schoolboy slovenliness it was quite unrealistic to think of his making his way in a court.

At present Evelyn's overriding concern was his son's 'better part'. In his anxiety 'to instill into him the feare & love of God, & discharge the Duty of a Father', he had set the boy a programme of 'extraordinary preparation' at Deptford before summoning him to London for the whole of the Easter week to attend the public services and hear the preaching, 'which you know we have not in the Country so solemn'. The sermons, by Bohun's uncle Ralph Bathurst, Bishop Peter Gunning, the Provost of Eton, and the Dean of Chichester, met all expectations, culminating on Good Friday in 'a most incomparable sermon' from the Bishop of Chester, 'the most learned Divine of our Nation'. The next day Evelyn took Jack for his final instruction by Bishop Gunning, and on Easter day they took communion together in the Chapel Royal.[104] The sermon by the Bishop of Exeter was disappointingly inaudible, but afterwards they stayed to see what the whole nation was waiting for. The House of Commons had just made an Act requiring all officeholders to take the sacraments according to the rites of the Church of England, a measure designed to identify and disqualify all Roman Catholic office-holders. The King had been obliged to agree to it though his own brother and chief minister were likely to be its most conspicuous casualties. The Duke of York had long been suspected of being a secret convert. Would he take the Anglican communion together with the King in the Chapel Royal on this Easter Sunday? He did not. Evelyn noted grimly in his diary:

This being the second yeare he had forborn & put it off, & this being within a day of the Parliaments sitting, who had Lately made so severe an Act against the increase of Poperie, gave exceeding griefe & scandal to the whole Nation: That the heyre of it, & the sonn of a Martyr for the Protestant Religion, should apostatize: What the Consequence of this will be God onely knows, & Wise men dread . . . I went home.[105]

There is a blank in the diary for the next week, as Evelyn took stock of both public and private matters. There were some further exchanges by

[103] BL Add. MSS 78298: JE to his son, 31 Jan. 1676; 78386: 'Oeconomics', [1676], p. 60; JE, *Diary*, iv. 1.
[104] BL Add. MS 78442: JE to his son, 16 Mar. 1673; JE, *Diary*, iv. 7.   [105] JE, *Diary*, iv. 7.

letter with Margaret, who now explained more clearly and calmly what she and Sidney Godolphin had agreed about their future. She added that if she did choose to live single, it would not be from a desire to challenge the social order or because she had been disappointed in love, but for a specific religious purpose which would make its own contribution to society: 'I should be as little Idle, as if I were a Wife: I should attend to Prayer, and to all other Christian Dutyes, and make those my Pleasures; seing I choose not the Condition out of Constraint or Caprice, & singularity; but, to Serve God the better.'[106]

For all the ignominy supposedly attached to being an old maid, it was not uncommon for women to resolve against marriage in this way. The reasons varied: fear of childbirth, dissatisfaction with available suitors, or simply a pleasure in independence and 'single retired content'.[107] But what most of these women had in common was that they had not fully experienced or had been disappointed in some way by human love. What made Margaret's situation unusual was that she had such a powerful sense of spiritual calling and yet was also deeply in love, with no insurmountable obstacle to her marriage. For her a single life might still be a choice, but it could never be an untroubled one. Evelyn continued to sympathize with her vocation and be anxious for the future of their friendship but he understood now why her health was suffering and she was so often preoccupied and distressed. He also doubted whether she could ever be happy alone in these circumstances: 'where among all the masse of mankind could my Friend have repos'd herselfe . . . but that allways something of those early and deepe, tho tender Impressions, would have disquieted her rest?' All he could do was to urge her not to resolve firmly against marriage, but to wait, as she had agreed with Godolphin, some time longer to see 'how things would go'.[108]

With this clear between them their estrangement cleared up. An undated scrawl from her, 'you are my frind all is well I se you are my frind . . . com in peace', probably dates from this time.[109] On 7 April Evelyn travelled up to London expressly to see her and the following week he brought his wife on one of her rare jaunts to the capital. She visited Margaret, renewing their acquaintance of previous summers, and accepted the friendship at its

[106] *Life*, 30–1: MB to JE, [1673].

[107] See for example Alice Thornton, *Autobiography*, ed. C. Jackson, Surtees Society, 62 (1875), 75–7; JE, *Diary*, iv. 426; C. Kirchberger, 'Elizabeth Burnet', *Church Quarterly Review*, 148 (1949), 37; Antonia Fraser, *The Weaker Vessel* (1984), 162; Sara Mendelson and Patricia Crawford, *Women in Early Modern England* (Oxford, 1998), 167–8.

[108] BL Add. MSS 78386: JE, 'Oeconomics', [1676], p. 18; 78307, fo. 12: MB to JE (copy by JE), [spring 1673]. See Appendix B for the interpretation of this letter and the reason for the copy.

[109] BL Add. MS 78307, fo. 11: MB to JE, [Apr. 1673?].

face value, making her feel that she had nothing to be uneasy about. They remained some time in London, supporting Lady Tuke who was seeking a place in the Queen's household, and visiting Lady Mordaunt, Evelyn's first Electra, now beset with family cares and failing health. As well as praying with Margaret at Berkeley House, Evelyn dined with Godolphin and the Queen's Treasurer, John Hervey, presumably in connection with the securing of her marriage portion. Later in the same month the Berkeleys, Godolphin, and Margaret all came to Sayes Court to see the garden in its spring glory.[110] Margaret made a particular pet of the Evelyns' second daughter Betty, now 6 years old, and it was agreed that whenever she was settled in a home of her own she would take her 'little favourite' to live with her for some time, as her brother Jack had once lived with the Howards. It was clear that all parties had accepted the friendship and that Evelyn was doing what he could to forward the marriage. But he now knew that it would not take place immediately, and on his Tuesday visits he was freer to concentrate on the professed purpose of the friendship, their shared spiritual life.

It was soon clear to him that the rituals of private prayer and asceticism which Margaret had devised to sustain herself during her time of isolation had evolved into something 'monstrously unlimited and even superstitiously perplexing', made up of 'abundance of lip service and forms with end'. She surrounded herself obsessively with admonitions; in every corner of her room were pinned up slips of paper, 'with some character on it, or halfe-word, that signify'd her some particular duty or caution'. She would deprive herself of sleep and food, 'not seldom even to Fainting in her Retirements'. She dwelt constantly on her sins and failings, and when Dean Benson tried to persuade her otherwise, complained that he was too gentle with her and begged Evelyn to be more severe.[111] Instead, realizing as well as Benson that these excesses were becoming neurotic, he began to introduce her to a tradition of meditation which had begun with the *Spiritual Exercises* of Ignatius Loyola. This had originally been designed to guide English Protestants away from abstruse theological study and controversy about doctrine, and encourage them to cultivate an inner devotional life drawing on the imagination and the emotions. The garden rather than the closet was the recommended place for these meditations and they might take its everyday sights as their starting point.[112] 'Upon looking in a barn', 'upon observing a snail', 'upon the weeders' sweeping in autumn of the walks', 'upon the phyllerea hedge that grew

---

[110] JE, *Diary*, iv. 8, 10.

[111] BL Add. MS 78386: JE, 'Oeconomics', [1676], p. 74; *Life*, 16, 28, 90, 95.

[112] Louis B. Martz, *The Poetry of Meditation* (New Haven, 1954), 4–19; Stanley Stewart, *The Enclosed Garden: The Tradition and Image in 17th Century Poetry* (Madison, 1966), 44–5, 116.

before the great parlour door' were some examples of Robert Boyle's sister, Lady Warwick, who was especially fond of this devotional mode.[113] Evelyn encouraged Margaret to give the early evening over to this kind of exercise, in the garden of Berkeley House whenever she could. At the same time he showed her how to address herself to a God whose relationship with humanity was not governed by implacable severity and exactions of service, but by love: the divine love which he had invoked for his own sake from the beginning as the proper focus of their friendship.[114] He had found the ideal means of drawing the friendship and her devotional needs together.

This divine love was not just an abstraction. Drawing on the powerful erotic imagery of the 'Songs of Solomon', where a woman 'sick of love' seeks mystical union with her lover in an enclosed and fruitful garden, this devotional mode encouraged the seeking of extremes of spiritual love-sickness and longing for union with Christ. 'My soul was as it were ravished with desire to converse with him in solitude', wrote Lady Warwick after one of her garden meditations, 'and I did with great plenty of tears beg for a soul sick of love for my lovely Lord Jesus'.[115] Margaret soon found her meditations softened and intensified in the same way, and began to experience these same fits of spontaneous weeping and 'tenderness', which were regarded as a particular sign of spiritual grace and 'refreshment'.[116] When Evelyn told her of being kept from church by illness one Sunday, she replied that she had prayed for him heartily,

for you were the instrument of my being bathed in tears: and from my soul I beg you may never want the refreshment I by you have received from heaven twice yesterday: first at the holy table and after that in the evening in the garden: wher being alone and with your booke, the beauty of the ground, the face of heaven did I thank god convey pleasuers indeed.[117]

She acknowledged that he 'had let her see, and tast more of the love of God, and the *Delices* of Religion, than ever she had before'.[118] Communion, always central to her devotional life, became the most ecstatic experience of all. 'I have seene her receive the holy Symbols with Such an humble & mealting Joy in her Countenance, as seem'd to be something of Transport (not to say Angelick) some thing I cannot describe', Evelyn recalled, 'and [she] has herselfe confessed to me, to have felt in her Soule, Such Influxes of heavenly joy,

---

[113]   Smith, *Countess of Warwick*, 323, 325.

[114]   *Life*, 28, 96, 220. For the similar strain of Puritan devotion, see Haller and Haller, 'The Puritan Art of Love', 264.

[115]   Stewart, *Enclosed Garden*, 37–8; Smith, *Countess of Warwick*, 163.

[116]   Martz, *Poetry of Meditation*, 199.

[117]   BL Add. MS 78307, fo. 13: MB to JE, [?11 May 1673].   [118]   *Life*, 28.

as has almost caryed her into another World'. In her own words, she was 'even disolved with love to God', and sought the experience again and again, not just out of duty, but to feel again 'the wonderfull pleasure which I feel there and no-where else'.[119]

So that she would not have to depend only on public services, he went on to introduce her to the practice of 'mental communion', a private and spiritual enactment of the sacrament which went back to the *Imitation of Christ* of Thomas à Kempis.[120] He had practised this himself during the Interregnum when Anglican services were under threat, and as soon as he mentioned it to Margaret she begged him to share it with her, 'from whom you know it was impossible to keep anything of this nature so insatiable was her devout and pious spirit, of devout & pious exercises'.[121] One of his prayers gives an unmistakable sense of the swooning intensity it encouraged. Whatever else this rite was, it was quite inescapably a form of love-making:

O pleasures, o Sweetnesses, o worldly delights, how despicable, how little things ye are! whilst my lovely Jesu shows me one glimpse of his reconciled face, one beame of the Joy of the Lord—o Ecstasie! o unexpressible Favour! o everflowing goodnesse, to me unworthy, altogether unworthy—Refraine, o Inlarge my heart, I am sick with Love! It can hold no more—yet, o sweete Jesu! delicious name! give o give me more, & more of thy Love, none but thee, none but thee—Then onely shall I be satisfied, when thy Glory appeares, Come Lord Jesus! Come quickly.[122]

It was this which transformed the friendship for Margaret. Overwhelmed by the intensity of these rites, she began to look on Evelyn, in her own words, as 'another creature' and passionately acknowledged her sense of obligation to him: 'May God of his infinite bounty reward you and may every tear I have shed be an addition to your crown of glory . . . the lord grant that at the last day I may be found to have made such use of you as that we both may be the hapyer for it . . . For you Mr Evelyn ther is nothing that I know of my selfe I would not doe . . . to my death I will love you.' Now it was she who was seeking his visits, which with the coming of the spring were longer: 'I would have you if possible be here by 11 a clocke that we may walke together, I fansy I could talk to you for ever; and endeed what else can we speake of but our god'; 'you have not known me long tis true, but I protest for all the treasures of the world I would not but have known you: not as other people who wish it to hear you talk of trees and plants and secrets of natur . . . I love to hear you because often 'tis of God, to see you because it puts me in mind of the joy the

---

[119] Ibid. 86–7. [120] Martz, *Poetry of Meditation*, 90–1.
[121] *Devotionarie Book*, 15; BL Add. MS 78389: devotional volume by JE, including mental communion, with a memorial passage to MB, 1674–aft. 1678.
[122] *Devotionarie Book*, 43.

primitive christians took in seeing one another'. The emphasis on divine love permeated the friendship until she did not know where the one ended and the other began: 'I love you for God and some times I thinke I love God for you'. Longingly she dwelt on their union in the afterlife: 'we must wait gods time but I wish it were come with all my heart and soule for never was any creature tyd to another in such bonds of frindship as is my heart to you, I am sure if I do you some good, you are the instrument of all mine . . . may you be my companion in those bless'd aboads, wher we shall without any imperfection serve our perfect lord'. His management of her affairs, formerly the most important function of the friendship for her, dwindled to insignificance. To some suggestion of his that she might want to take other advice about her money, she replied dismissively, 'for the buisness, for goodness sake my dear friend do just as you will find, who would you have me aske, whose advice would you have me take but yours'.[123]

Yet the friendship sometimes bewildered and disturbed her. She was accustomed to the attentions of men and if necessary to defending herself against them; but their purpose was usually very clear. She had not encountered so intense, and yet so spiritualized a response from a man before. She knew that she was nothing like his intellectual equal; 'alas what am I able to pleys you in? I can't find fault with you nor inform you nor edefy you: and but that you condesend understand what you say.' She had only a vague, disturbing awareness of the significance she held for him, of the ideals he was projecting on her, of the feats he had to perform to accommodate and sublimate these intense feelings: 'first you hope I am beter then I seem, and you beleev me wiser then in apearance I am; and next if I were non of all this: why, becaus of that you would if posable make me somthing'.[124] But Mrs Evelyn's acceptance of the friendship still made her feel safe, even as it grew more intense:

what mean you to make me weepe and break my heart by your love to me? take me and all I have, give me but your love, my deare frind, tusday is longed for by me and nights and days moove a tedious pace till I am near you and what is all one with you your wife, truly her kindnes gives an addition of joy which I must tell you is the greatest thing I can say for whenever I read your letters, say your prayers, or look upon any of the infallible profe of your love I can hardly have an increas of satisfaction, and yet indeed she rejoices me.[125]

It was Margaret herself, in her overwhelming sense of obligation, who disturbed this delicate balance. 'I can't live at this rate,' she announced suddenly

---

[123] *Life*, 28; BL Add. MS 78307, fos. 12, 15, 21, 30–1: MB to JE, [spring 1673], [2 June 1673], 12 Aug. [1673], [16] Oct. [1673].

[124] Ibid., fo. 13: MB to JE, [?11 May 1673].   [125] Ibid., fo. 12: MB to JE, [spring 1673].

1. John Evelyn in later life, by Sir Godfrey Kneller. He holds a copy of *Sylva*, his most famous work. In the background are the exotic trees he described in it and reared at Sayes Court.

7. Sidney Godolphin as a rising courtier and minister. The portrait illustrates Evelyn's remark about the 'gravity and singular temper' of Margaret's suitor.

8. Lord and Lady Berkeley and their eldest son by Gaspar Netscher, showing the family as it was when Margaret shared their household.

9. The Altar of Friendship. The pen and ink and wash drawing, probably executed by Evelyn himself, is inscribed by him and by Margaret Blagge. Note the rather ambivalent image of the heart and the pentacle symbol at the foot.

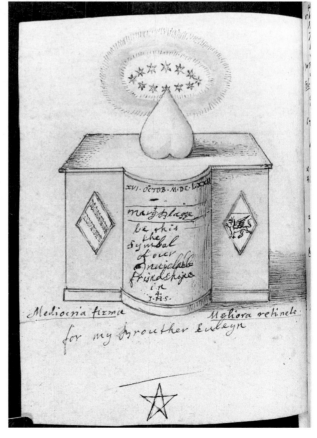

10. Margaret Blagge, painted for John Evelyn by Matthew Dixon, 1673. The image employs the conventions of the court portrait, but was painted expressly to commemorate the friendship and its spiritual basis. The pentacle symbol is shown on the urn.

in the summer, 'to be always oblidged and never able to pay you but by loving you, and even for that I must be oblidged to you for your beleev for I can only say it, never doe any thing but talke'.[126] Evelyn had already asked her to sit for her portrait, both as a reminder of their 'holy friendship' and as a devotional aid. He was, he explained, 'content to allow of images, and historical representations, especially if resembling the persons, and when meditation can be abstracted and without superstition'.[127] The exchange of portraits was a common enough rite of secular friendship, but Margaret had demurred until now, probably from the sense that in their circumstances it was not quite suitable. Now she offered of her own accord to sit for her portrait and to present it to him; 'a most ridiculous present but tis at your servis when you pleys'. So that it would be just the image he wanted, she asked him to go with her to the first sitting, to tell the painter how he would like it 'drest'. Whatever its purpose, this was a provocative invitation, as both must have been aware. With its excuse for dwelling on the female face and body, escorting a young woman to have her portrait painted was a well-understood means of conducting secular gallantry. But 'pray let me se you', Margaret urged him, 'for I long for the day'.[128]

Together they went to the studio of the painter with whom she had made the appointment: Matthew Dixon, a pupil of Lely, whom she had perhaps chosen for his Suffolk connections or perhaps simply because he was inexpensive.[129] Evelyn did not in the end have much say in how the painting was 'drest'. Whenever he urged Margaret to adopt a cheerful religious mode, she replied that she preferred to be grave and subdued; ''tis as you say plesent to my self, though not to others'.[130] Now she chose to be painted in an unadorned dress, her hair drawn plainly back, and her eyes downcast as if in the act of meditation; a marked difference from the direct gaze of most female court portraits. The setting reinforced the devotional mode; she was painted at three-quarter length, seated on a tombstone with one arm resting on a sepulchral urn; 'nor was this at all my Fancy', Evelyn declared, 'but her expresse Desire and Injunction to the Artist'. Afterwards he remembered that she always said she loved the company of mourners, since it 'reminded her of her end'.[131] 'How delightful is this love dart', Francis de Sales had written,

---

[126] Ibid., fo. 16: MB to JE [*c*.14 June 1673].

[127] Richard Wendorf, *The Elements of Life: Biography and Portrait-Painting in Stuart and Georgian England* (Oxford, 1990), 63.

[128] BL Add. MS 78307, fo. 16: MB to JE, [*c*.14 June 1673].

[129] JE, *Diary*, iv. 13. For the little that is known about Dixon, see Mary Edmond, 'Nicholas Dixon, Limner, and Matthew Dixon, Painter', *Burlington Magazine*, 125 (1983), 611–12.

[130] BL Add. MS 78307, fo. 13ᵛ: MB to JE, [?11 May 1673].   [131] *Life*, 71.

referring to the 'love as strong as death' of the Canticles, 'which wounding us with the incurable wound of heavenly love makes us forever pining and sicke . . . that at length we must yield to death.'[132] Although the pentacle on the base of the urn was Evelyn's only overt addition to the painting, in its way it was another variant on the meditations on divine love to which he had introduced her.

Yet for all this the image Dixon produced made discreet use of the conventions of the 'court beauty' portrait and was full of sensuality. Margaret's plain dress took the form of a shift and over it the 'loose dressing' which court painters since Van Dyke had favoured instead of the stiffer, more elaborate, and precisely datable costume which their sitters would have worn out of doors. Its negligent drapery also lent itself more readily to the conspicuous display of the young female body.[133] In Margaret's case the shift was arranged well off her shoulders, so the focus of the portrait was on her fine neck and bosom and the curved right arm which rested on her lap, as if she were cradling an invisible child. The downcast gaze which preserved her modesty also cast the viewer in the role of voyeur. The portrait was acknowledged to be a good likeness; but was it a religious icon and an image of the beauty which called forth virtuous love and prefigured the divine; or was it the knowing representation of an elaborate pretence: a striking example of what the Duchess of Newcastle cynically called the court practice of 'sainting' women for their beauty, but only in its outward form and not as a sign of inward grace?

The participants showed no misgivings. 'Beauty is a blessing, & a great jewell, and you may glorify God by it,' Evelyn assured Margaret, 'when she that possesses it is humble and chast, & a reproach to those who misuse it.'[134] She asked his permission to have a copy made for Dean Benson: a revealing and perhaps not very welcome reminder that whatever the uniqueness of the friendship to him, she regarded these two spiritual mentorships, one lay and one clerical, in a similar light. But it was also a sign that she was confident the image would not be misunderstood. By this time Evelyn was struggling with himself to maintain the professed basis of their friendship. 'Do what you will with me then deare friend, so you love me still,' he replied, 'and abate nothing of your prayers to God for me, which is yet a far greater obligation; for that is Substance, this Shadow, and it, and all the World must passe, God onely

---

[132] Quoted in Stewart, *Enclosed Garden*, 146.

[133] Wendorf, *Elements of Life*, 62–8; Sir Oliver Millar, *Sir Peter Lely* (National Portrait Gallery, 1978), 18.

[134] BL Add. MS 78307, fo. 4ᵛ: JE's paper, headed 'For my Electra. If you desire to be a perfect Christian and to abound in spiritual Comforts, Practise these things', [late 1672–early 1673].

remaines for ever.' He took delivery of the portrait, had it framed, and hung it in his bedchamber. Just as 'Platona' had once light-heartedly told him she had hung his own by her bed and prayed by it when she rose in the mornings, so he promised Margaret never to look on her image without 'a pure ejaculation in your behalfe'.[135] But this time Mary Evelyn felt, or was prompted to feel that he had overstepped the bounds. 'Because there is no such thing upon Earth as Seraphick Love,' William Glanville wrote meaningfully, 'I dare not wish our friendship had begun when wee first saw one another, for I am conscious I could not have Trusted myself with loving you twenty years agoe as well as I doe now',

. . . But sister why may not you doate upon a diamond, as well as the philosopher doth upon a Pearle, Tis opinion only that makes and gives price to jewells, my picture drawn by Dixon might hang as well in the closett, as the Ladyes doth in the bedchamber, my Motto should bee humble too, Domina non sum dignus, but I would presume however to fixe myne eyes where I had bestowed my heart, and not be drawn with deiected looks.[136]

Margaret began to notice that Mary Evelyn, whose cordiality had reassured her till now, was becoming more formal and distant; 'I shal till death be a real frind to all yours', she wrote to Evelyn after another visit to Sayes Court, 'though I could wish ther were more disposition in some, than ther is to this last article: ceremony you know is my avowd aversion, and they always use me with so much that I go away discontentd.'[137]

In August she accompanied Lady Berkeley to Tunbridge Wells to take the waters, and even there begged Evelyn to continue his visits: 'I fear I shall leav this place on Saterday therefore pray come before that tim[e] to your frind, the best title I have next to that of a christain [*sic*] and for all I have I would not loos you.'[138] In September their Tuesday meetings resumed at Berkeley House, with Evelyn, as his feelings grew stronger, insisting more strenuously than ever on their spirituality. He presented her with a formal meditation for Michaelmas day, celebrating 'the flaming love of the seraphims': 'they are not generated nor do they multiplie, yet are innumerable and so shall the saints in heaven which neither marry or are given in marriage but are as the Angels in heaven'.[139] On 16 October, the first anniversary of their pact of friendship, he inscribed an instruction on the fly-leaf of his folio bible, interleaved with the notes of twenty years of study, that it was to be delivered to Margaret if

[135] Ibid., fos. 19, 17: MB to JE, 11 July [1673]; JE to MB, 18 June 1673 (copy).
[136] BL Add. MS 78434: Glanville to ME, 21 Aug. 1673.
[137] BL Add. MS 78307, fo. 30ᵛ: MB to JE, [16] Oct. [1673].
[138] Ibid., fo. 21: MB to JE, 12 Aug. [1673].
[139] BL Add. MS 78376: 'A Meditation for Michaelmas Day', 29 Sept. 1673.

she survived him.[140] He now began to use Moray's pentacle interchangeably with an emblem of his own: the alchemical symbol of sublimation, signifying the soul rising toward heaven, which was also the sign of the zodiac, Libra, prevailing at the time of their pact of friendship.[141] In his anniversary prayer he put words of thanks into her mouth for 'the example, counsel, prayers, spiritual and peculiar Assistance of my deare Friend, whom (as from heaven it selfe) thou hast given & dispos'd to be so sincerely mine'; but this was no more than she had said again and again in her letters. Her anniversary letter, dated 'October the hapy month', traced the stages of this first year of the friendship. At first, 'when the symbol was made', she admitted that she did not 'thinke of the great tye that was to be between us upon that account'. It was the prayers and meditations which had won her over: 'so soon as ever you did inrich me with treasures which next to the holy scriptures I value; I lookt upon you as another creature, and did resolve if I could to indear you to me . . . I still love you more and more I se you love me, I still love you more and more I se you love God, this looks as if I were mad, but I write to a friend, ah that word how pleasant.'[142]

After an uncertain start the unlikely friendship seemed to have become all, and more than all, Evelyn had dreamt of when he inaugurated it:

so transcendently Sincere, noble & Ingenuous; as taught me all its dimensions, beyond anything I had conceived of its highest Ideas; and she her-selfe was heard to say, what she once thought to be a Name onely, and little else, she found a real existence . . . In a word, I may say, as David did of Jonathan, Her Friendship was to me pasing the love of Women: nor verily was it without an intire Sympathy on my part; and there was providence in it, as well as Inclynation; for the Exceeding and most eminent Piety, and Goodnesse that ever Consecrated a worthy Friendship, shoone so bright in this blessed Saint; as Intitl'd her to all the Service, Respect and Veneration I was capable of giving her.[143] ❧

---

[140] BL Add. MS 78360.
[141] *Diary*, iv. 27–31. For the symbol, see BL Add. MS 78345, fo. 19: JE, treatise on natural philosophy and chemistry; and Gareth Roberts, *The Mirror of Alchemy* (1994), 113.
[142] BL Add. MSS 78392: prayer by JE, Oct. 1673; 78307, fos. 30–1: MB to JE, [16] Oct. [1673].
[143] *Life*, 26–7.

7

The Serpent in the Garden

'O H that I did love nothing but God and you', Margaret wrote in her anniversary letter. For all her rapturous celebration of the friendship Evelyn was always aware that Godolphin remained central in her life. In her prayers, she told him, he was 'often the first: always the second, that is after one: and som tims both together'.[1] Though the slight suggestion that he should feel himself a rival was probably unconscious, it was clear that they both struggled to reconcile a conflict between human and divine love in which Evelyn's focus was on Margaret and hers was elsewhere. As the first year of the friendship came to an end, the problems of the older relationship were still unresolved. His attempts to debate the marriage issue with her only added to her conflicts:

I know not what to determine . . . One day I fancy No life so pure, as the Un-Married: Another day, I think it lesse Exemplary; and that the Maried-state has more Opportunitys of Exercising Works of Charity . . . Oh Lord & Governor of my Life! Leave me not to my selfe; to the Cou[n]sels of my own heart . . . I Renounce all Judgement, all Knowledge, & Discretion of my-Owne . . . I am in a streit, and know not what to Choose: Determine Thou for me, Blessed Lord! Remember, that for neere, these One & Twenty Yeares, I have ben Thy Care . . . O leave me not under this difficulty now . . .

It was not just a practical issue of which path in life would best suit her religious ends. She still loved Godolphin, more in adulthood than ever, but her experience of divine love now made this a source of self-castigation:

with what Fervor have I protested, against all Affection to the Things of this World! Resign'd them all without Exception; when the first moment I am Tried, I shrink away, and am Passionatly Fond of the Creature, and Forgetfull of the Creator . . .

---

[1] BL Add. MS 78307, fos. 19ᵛ, 31: MB to JE, 11 July [1673], [16] Oct. [1673].

Most bitterly have I wept, to think how much of my Heart he has, how little, my B:
Saviour, who has Loved, and suff'erd for me so much more . . . thus I make my
humble Confession to God, & to you, Bewayling my Loving any thing but himself,
& Imploring him to Translate my Affections, and to place them upon him-selfe
alone.

She told Evelyn that she was willing to die and 'leave him, whom here I love,
to go to my Jesus forever'. It was the constant temporary meetings and part-
ings with Godolphin and the conflicts they caused her that she could not
bear: 'I Confesse, 'tis hard for me to leave him now so often as I do, and This
breaks my Heart; And that after so many Professions to God, what I do, and
Suffer for him, I should with such Reluctancy part from This Person, to Pray,
& to Reade, and to go to holy Dutys.' Yet whenever she resolved to renounce
him altogether, 'pitty for him, that could not Live in her Absence, divided her
a fresh, and pierc't her to the Soule'. She tried to reason him into indifference,
'when (of all things in the world)', Evelyn noted shrewdly, 'it was not
Indiffrent to her that he should have Lovd her lesse'. She told Evelyn that she
envied him for being 'past that mighty Love to the Creature'. Yet renunci-
ation of it attracted her precisely because in her situation it was the greatest
sacrifice she could make to her faith:

when I call to mind the Grace of Selfe-denyal, the Honour of Suff'ring for my
Saviour, The Reward propos'd for those who Conquer: the satisfaction I shall
receive, & enjoy in the Divine Love and fruition of Jesus, I (that am thus fearfull, thus
feeble) Call, and Cry out for the Exercise of that Grace, wh[ich] is made perfect in
Weaknesse: Yea, for Tribulation, for Persecution, for Contradiction to my owne
desires, and for every thing agreable to the Spirit, and displeasing to the flesh.

'Now (D. Friend)', she asked Evelyn, 'should I Marry, & Refuse to go to my
Lord; Part unwillingly with him, when another so graciously Calls . . . No,
No, I will Remaine my B. Saviors. Hee shall be my Love, my Husband, my
All: I will keepe my Virgin, Present it unto Christ, and not put my-selfe into
the Temptation of Loving any Thing in Competition with my God.' Evelyn
was reminded, as he was meant to be, of 'the Passion of some of those tender,
and noble Vergins, whose Resolutions, and Couragious Suff'rings we find
In-roll'd in the Primitive Martyrologes'.[2]

    The conflict was real and painful, so much so that Margaret would
sometimes tell Evelyn that she longed 'to be dissolv'd, that she might be
with Christ, and freed from this Solicitude'. Yet it still owed something to
Godolphin's attitude. After his first sense of conversion he was showing no

---

[2] *Life*, 39–43: MB to JE, [summer 1673].

great haste in transforming himself into a fit partner for a godly marriage. With Margaret in seclusion in Berkeley House and strictly limiting his letters and visits, he resumed his way of life at court much as before. He assured her that he loved her better than his own life, and that 'I never pray soe earnestly for myself as when your concerns are joyn'd in mine', but his resolutions against gambling lapsed as soon as they were made, leaving it doubtful that he would ever be able to support a household securely even if they should agree to marry. He resisted her attempts to influence his public devotions. She urged him to take communion weekly, seeking it out at St Martin in the Fields or Covent Garden on those Sundays it was not held at the Chapel Royal. She assured him that even if he did not have time to prepare himself properly, 'when we do what we are able we are accepted', and he need not feel self-conscious at making such a public and un-courtier-like display of piety because he would probably not be noticed, 'or if you be, the body of christ is worth that and ten thousand times more'. But Godolphin was evasive: he was 'not fond of it'; not, he insisted, because he was afraid of making himself conspicuous, but because 'I know myselfe, if I once have done a good thing I am troubled afterwards if I omit it whatsoever be the occasion, and this I am afraid will bring me into inconveniences hereafter because I am not always master of my time'.[3] This was a common excuse and one which Evelyn had set down as particularly specious and dangerous.[4] Margaret did not reproach him overtly, but he was well aware of her disapproval; 'the most sensible trouble I have is to perceive plainly that you are more unsatisfy'd with me than you will speake . . . my deare forgive me, love me & pray for me'.[5]

What did change was the face of public affairs, as the events of Easter had shown they would. In June the Duke of York surrendered the Admiralty and Clifford the Treasury, rather than comply with the provisions of the Test Act. Monmouth's stock rose accordingly, and into Clifford's place came Sir Thomas Osborne, now Earl of Danby. With the arrival of this formidable new rival as first minister, Arlington began to talk of semi-retirement to the Lord Chamberlain's department. Godolphin was also considering his place in the new political world. Rumours reached Margaret that he was amongst those volunteering to go to sea with Monmouth, and even that he was being considered as Secretary of State in succession to Arlington.[6] This

[3] BL Hammick Papers: MB to SG, 'friday 6 a cloke', SG to MB, 'saturday morning', [*c.* May 1674].

[4] JE, *A Devotionarie Book*, ed. Walter Frere (1936), 10.

[5] BL Hammick Papers: SG to MB, 'thursday' [Sept.–Oct. 1673].

[6] W. D. Christie (ed.), *Letters . . . addressed to Sir Joseph Williamson*, Camden Society, new ser., 8 (1874), ii. 4; E. M. Thompson (ed.), *Correspondence of the Family of Hatton*, Camden Society, new ser., 22 (1878), i. 110–11.

last speculation, though still very premature, was yet another indication of the growing public stature of a young man whom she was used to seeing chiefly as an unsatisfactory suitor. At last he nerved himself to tell her outright what she must have known at heart by now: that he could not make any such retreat from 'the world' as she envisaged in the foreseeable future. In terms he evidently thought would appeal to her (and which Evelyn had also used to George Mackenzie), he argued that it was more heroic to remain at court to face its temptations and set a good example than to retreat into private life. He also set out two overriding objections to a country retreat at his time of life: that it was too solitary and 'too unfruitful of good opportunitys', in a religious as well as a secular sense. The Chapel Royal with its constant round of ritual and its succession of the distinguished preachers, was, he could point out, a far more inspiring place to worship God than a country parish. And of course he was quite right. This was why Evelyn had brought his son up from Deptford to keep Lent and why even at Wotton he could find uninspiring preaching and poor observance of Easter. Godolphin's youth in a poor and remote tin-mining parish must have given him ample experience of this kind. He still professed himself discontented by his life at court, but did not want to leave it altogether. He only wanted a better and more lucrative office; not, he told Margaret, one of such constant business and stress as Arlington's, but perhaps that of Cofferer of the Household. It was virtually a sinecure, but a highly profitable one, and it would give him standing at court while freeing him from the constraint, boredom, and ill company of the King's bedchamber.[7]

Margaret received this, as at least some of it deserved, rather sardonically. In reply she repeated her hope that as God 'has begun a good worke in you so he will perfect and accomplish it', but went on to expose the inconsistencies and evasions of his attitude: he talked of resisting the temptations of the court but also claimed that the opportunities for leading a devout life there outweighed them, so he could scarcely claim much heroic virtue in remaining. He seemed to be equally apprehensive of idleness and of business, so was he not better off in the place he had, in which he could combine both? In any case, if he really wished to avoid idleness and ill company he should set himself a course of study, for which he had plenty of spare time. This could include not just devotional works, but translation and natural philosophy, at least to a point where he could concoct herbal remedies if ever he should live among the poor in the country. These were of course much the same recommendations as Evelyn had made to her when she first moved to

---

[7] BL Hammick Papers: MB to SG, 'friday night' [Sept.–Oct. 1673].

Berkeley House. Her friendship with a man who filled every moment with such things had left her little patience with the aimlessness of courtiers. Bad company, she pointed out, would be a danger only if he sought it out. He had plenty of blameless friends to visit; and she named Lady Sunderland, Lady Harriet Hyde (the wife of his friend Laurence Hyde and niece of Robert Boyle and Lady Warwick), the Duchess of Monmouth, his court mentor John Hervey, 'when he is not drunk', and of course his own devout brother and sisters. And she ended, with a resentful dig at the selfishness of his attitude, that she did not think he could be better off than he was, 'being free from incombrance and secured from solitud'; the incumbrances from which he wished to be free presumably including herself and any family they might have.[8]

Since they now constantly wrangled, she asked him not to write and to let her know beforehand whenever he came to pay his duty to his cousins at Berkeley House, so that she could arrange to be elsewhere.[9] She was having to face the fact that if she still wanted to insist on a life of retirement devoted to religion, she must seek it unmarried. But how and where this should be was not clear. Berkeley House was clearly unsuitable as a long-term refuge, and she was counting the time till she could leave it. She wanted a genuine religious retreat somewhere remote from London. In Paris she had seen that 'their monesterys are very holy Institutions [and] if they be abusd, that is not ther fault'.[10] Only a few years before a whole family of her numerous Suffolk kin—Sir John Warner of Parham, his wife, sister-in-law, and two daughters—had converted to Catholicism and gone to settle in religious communities in the Low Countries, while the King, when petitioned to intervene, only shrugged and said there was nothing to be done with those who were determined to be 'God Almighty's holy fools'.[11] Margaret's Anglicanism was too deep-rooted for her to follow this example, but as Evelyn acknowledged much later, 'wherever her body was abroad her soule was in the Cloister'.[12] There might be no Protestant foundations in England, but she knew that women had occasionally formed themselves into small informal family-based communities to lead a life of religious observance and charity. Those of Lady Falkland and the Ferrar family at Little Gidding were well known, and

---

[8] Ibid., MB to SG, 'thursday night', 'friday night' [Sept.–Oct. 1673].   [9] Ibid.

[10] BL Add. MS 78307, fo. 75ᵛ: MB to JE, 13 Dec. [1675].

[11] BL. Add. MS 19154, fos. 212ᵛ–13, 218: pedigree and notes concerning the Warner family; Henry Foley, *Records of the English Province of the Society of Jesus* (1875), ii. 459–74. Sir John's uncle, Dr Edward Warner, who tried to invoke the King's authority, was one of the royal physicians and married to Margaret's cousin Sarah. She was well acquainted with them (in fact shared their household for some weeks after her marriage) and must have known of the episode.

[12] BL Add. MS 78328, pp. 153–4: commonplace notes concerning friendship and MG.

there was still the occasional example under the direction of a sympathetic local clergyman.[13] In the course of the long engagement Godolphin's sisters had taken her into their circle. Listening to their reminiscences of their Cornish home she came to believe that this would be the ideal place, 'Remote of Cittys, Courts (& the Subjections attending them)', in which to pursue her ideal.[14] She might well have envisaged a godly family community there, made up of Sir William and the unmarried sisters who shared his household. But of course she could have no claim to be included unless she married into it.

She cast about amongst her own relations. Her Suffolk cousins could no longer offer a refuge; certainly not Sir Henry North, unmarried and sunk in inertia at Mildenhall. Her unmarried sisters and her cousins the Warners lived in lodgings in Covent Garden; but there remained Lady Yarburgh in Yorkshire. This was certainly not an ideal solution. Lady Yarburgh, though as devout in her way as her youngest sister, seems to have been awkward in personal relations, lamenting in her book of devotions that 'my best actions and endeavours have had no other effect than to make me ill thought of, even by those I most designed to oblige'. Her house was already crowded with children and she had not yet ceased her long succession of pregnancies.[15] It was probably this example more than any other which prompted Margaret's misgivings about marrying without ample financial provision. Yet it seemed to be the best prospect she had at present of the way of life she sought. She wrote to Godolphin as if it was settled that she should leave Berkeley House at the end of the year to live with the Yarburghs, using her maid's pension for her maintenance. Someone, perhaps Berkeley, had been indiscreet in talking of their relationship:

tis not for my trouble I am vext but what people that are by will thinke when he pub-likly talks so . . . tis not long I have to enduer it my year being near expired; and then I shall go to my sister Yarboroughs: I desier to know if you thinke my lord Arlington would joyn with the duke in geting me a thousand pound for my pention: I beleive he will for then he will conclud ther will be an end of me and that you are not like to importun him for the maintenance of a family.[16]

But this, irrevocable as it sounded, was no more than an episode in the long negotiation of their relationship. Evelyn was right in realizing that she could never bring herself to renounce Godolphin completely. A few days later,

[13] Bridget Hill, 'A Refuge from Men: The Idea of a Protestant Nunnery', *Past and Present*, 117 (1987), 110–12; Anne Laurence, *Women in England 1500–1760* (1994), 191.
[14] *Life*, 82, 111.
[15] C. B. Robinson, *History of the Priory and Peculiar of Snaith* (1861), 68–73.
[16] BL Hammick Papers: MB to SG, 'thursday night' [Sept.–Oct. 1673].

having forbidden him to write, she sat down to begin a long reclaiming letter to him of her own accord, prompted by what seemed a very unlikely subject: the fate of the ex-Lord Treasurer Clifford. When Evelyn had waited on the fallen minister after his resignation he found him in utter despair at the wreck of his schemes; his Catholicizing policy had only served to frustrate his own ambitions; 'besides he saw the Dutch-Warr, which was made much by his advise, as well as the shutting up of the Exchequer, very unprosperous: These things his high spirit could not support.'[17] From Tunbridge Wells, where he tried to distract himself with music and diversions, he was forced to retreat to his country house in Devonshire under threat of impeachment; and from there at the end of October the news reached London that he had died wretchedly and in mysterious circumstances; 'he broke his heart', accordingly to the commonest version, 'to see himself disappointed in his great design of fixing Popery here'. But as Evelyn recorded it, Clifford had been found by a servant hanging from the tester of his bed, cut down before he was quite dead and 'vomiting out a great deale of bloud, was heard to utter these words; Well, let men say what they will, there is a God, a just God above'.[18]

If there was any truth in this, Clifford had only hastened an end which was coming fast on him by other means. Suffering chronically from stone in the kidneys, he already knew himself to be in mortal danger when he made his will a few days before.[19] As Margaret heard the news there was no suggestion of suicide, only what to her was almost as deplorable: a sudden, violent, and unattended end. That evening when she sat down as she always did as part of her devotions, 'to consider of the day past', she turned Clifford's fate over in her mind; first for its conventional moral lessons: 'his greatnes, his sudden change: and other circomstances naturall to such a subject'; then the manner of his death, 'how litle tim sicke, in how great pain, how he had spent his time a little before at tunbridg, I fear his being unsetled in his religion: and not as he would, had he bin to chuse, wish to be found I believe'. Then she decided to write to Godolphin. If she thought it salutary for him to contemplate public ambition ending in disaster, she did not say so directly. She did not want to engage in yet more arguments and reproaches, she assured him, or even to make conventional condolences, since there had been no intimate friendship between him and Clifford which called for them. She only wanted to remind him of his own recovery from a life-threatening illness and the religious use he had made of it: 'truly I could not forbear though it be very lat writing this before I went to bed and doe hope it will not be unacceptable

---

[17] JE, *Diary*, iii. 16.   [18] Ibid., iii. 21.
[19] C. H. Hartmann, *Clifford of the Cabal* (1937), 302.

to you sens it is only an efect of the love I bear to god almighty and your soul'.[20] It was enough to clear up their estrangement and renew the bond between them. As the end of the year approached Margaret made no attempt to put her Yorkshire plan into action. Instead she joined everyone else in or near the court in the ceremonies which welcomed the new Duchess of York to England.

There had been sneers that in choosing the 15-year-old Mary of Modena as his second wife, James would be bringing 'the Pope's eldest daughter' into England, and that she would prove stunted, crooked, ugly, and red-haired. Instead the courtiers, saw a tall, pretty girl, with dark hair and eyes and a fine pale skin. Her only obvious fault, apart from her religion, was that she had 'greater youth than is necessary', being only two or three years older than the Duke's elder daughter. Although she was convent-bred and clearly unpractised in court ways, adolescent gawkiness in her situation was reassuring. Lady Tuke was not the only one to be surprised that 'Italien breeding could have aforded such a romp as she proves'. Everyone liked her better than they expected: 'all say she will be a fine woman when she is somewhat more spread; and in the meantime praise her witt'.[21] Nor did the unpopularity of a Roman Catholic match diminish competition for posts in the new household. At last, 'after virgins have allmost scratched out one an other's eyes to be maides of honor', a fresh group of young girls made their appearance at court, two of them, Isabella Boynton and Sarah Jenyns, the younger sisters of Margaret's former colleagues, Catherine and Frances.[22] Not to be outshone, the Queen remodelled her own maids' establishment, taking in Anne Howard, now grown into somewhat more 'soberiety', and Lady Tuke's young sister Frances Sheldon. Evelyn brought his wife and eldest daughter up to London to witness the celebrations and congratulate the newcomers. Margaret was there as well, though mentally keeping her distance. When the Howards, acknowledging her authority on such matters, appealed to her for advice about reconciling their court and religious duties, she admonished them in Evelyn's most rigorous style to be 'Wise-Virgins, having Oyle in your Lamps, readly Prepar'd to meete the Bridegroom . . . Burning & Shining Lights, in the midst of a Crooked & perverse Generation'.[23]

Even so there followed a mood of self-castigation, when she considered herself punished even for such limited 'liberties in discourse', by experiencing

---

[20] BL Hammick Papers: MB to SG, 'monday night' [20 Oct. 1673].
[21] BL Add. MS 78435: Lady Tuke to ME, 12 Aug. [1675]; Christie (ed.), *Letters . . . to Sir Joseph Williamson*, ii. 86; Lord John Russell (ed.), *Letters of Rachel, Lady Russell*, (1853), i. 12–13.
[22] Christie (ed.), *Letters . . . to Sir Joseph Williamson*, ii. 27.		[23] *Life*, 101–5.

'unusuall coldnesses & backwardnesse' in her devotions.[24] It was a reminder that her rapturous devotional moods of the past year would not always be easily accessible. Godolphin hastened to comfort her. Obliged to be in constant waiting on the King, he was more discontented with his own situation than ever, dependent on the good will of his colleagues for even a few hours in her company, and 'soe weary of feasting . . . that I don't know what to doe with my selfe'. He knew that she would immediately ask why he persisted in a way of life he so disliked; 'why while I am here in this place & in this course of life I don't see how to helpe it, I wish I did, I wish with all my heart you would shew me'. He expected that as usual she would laugh at him for calling his situation unavoidable, and say he was being affected:

perhaps I am of an humour not to bee pleas'd with any condition in the world, I am sure I could not without you, I grow soe ill humour'd & soe spleenatick that I can hardly endure my selfe, how should I expect then that you should care for me & yett when I am soe . . . I desire your kindnesse as much as ever & to bee with you as long as I am to bee in this world in that quiet & peace which I imagine must needs bee the best preparative for that which is to come.[25]

This time his real unhappiness with his situation was clear enough and Margaret, less self-righteous now after her own experience, did not mock or reject him. Instead she sympathized with him, as he had with her, for his 'want of spiritual refreshments' and for his sense that he was not so affected with the contemplation of his sins as at the beginning; but she reassured him that as he was still content to keep up his devotional rituals without the rewarding sense of spiritual grace; 'in that act the spiret of god is more asuredly working in you then if you were drownd in tears'.[26] In fact both were coming to realize that a phase of their long courtship was coming to an end. They must put aside youthful fantasies of easy happiness and fulfilment and find some practical way of working out their future together.

Margaret knew that it was no longer enough for her to cultivate her private devotional life. It was a condition of salvation that she should practise the 'primitive exercises' of the early Christians, the seven corporal works of mercy: feed the hungry, give drink to the thirsty, clothe the naked, visit the sick, relieve prisoners, house the stranger, and bury the dead'.[27] Quietly she set out to practise these so that they would become a constant occupation and training for the life she envisaged for herself, a fulfilment of her assurance to

[24] BL Hammick Papers: SG to MB, 'friday 3 a clock', [Nov. 1673].
[25] Ibid., 'friday morning' [winter 1673–4].
[26] Ibid., MB to SG, Saturday 2[8?] Feb. [1674].
[27] Eamon Duffy, *The Stripping of the Altars: Traditional Religion in England* (New Haven, 1992), 358.

Evelyn that even if she did not marry she would be as little idle as if she were a wife. South of the fashionable court parishes, joined to Whitehall by the 'long, dark, dirty, very inconvenient passage' of King Street which ran under the Holbein Gate, lay the old settlement of Westminster: the huddle of parliament buildings by the waterside, the bulk of the Abbey and Westminster Hall, and spreading out from them a maze of crowded courts and alleyways, petering out into isolated cottages and then into marshy and unkempt fields. From Tudor times this had been notorious as a poor and unregulated district, 'without trade or mystery', unrelieved by the systematic guild organization of the City, although it did have its isolated almshouses and small endowments, one of them founded by a former maid of honour to Queen Elizabeth.[28]

This, the crowded tenements further in and the 'remote Hospitals, humble Cells & Cotages . . . the very Skirts and obscure places of the Towne', was Margaret's working territory, a more unfamiliar and frightening one than a rural parish, where she would have no established position to make her known. She had begun to explore it while she was a maid of honour, going out when she could by herself and on foot, 'to Visite some poor Creatures she had found out'.[29] Now as she ventured further she acquired a guide and 'almoner', a widow by the name of Vesey, who lived in the Bell Yard, off King Street. What set her apart from her neighbours was the experience, as she lingered in church one day after service, of hearing a disembodied voice, 'not like a mans nor quit[e] so little as a child', say, 'I am god, walk thou in my ways and be perfect'; and when she came out of church afterwards, her companions told her she looked frightened. Without the means of much charity-giving herself, she visited and prayed with her fellow parishioners when they were in need and made herself an agent for the distribution of others' funds. Margaret used her local knowledge and standing to extend and methodize her charity.[30] 'Nor were these sudain fits of devotion', Evelyn wrote, 'but her continual practise & which tooke a considerable portion of her life as well as monies'. Having visited the poor and sick in their homes and in hospitals and almshouses, she would find out their particular needs and then return with clothes, money, or medicine as necessary; 'yea, and administer Remedys her-selfe, & do the meanest Offices', he added. The clothes she made herself

---

[28] Daniel Defoe, *A Tour through the Whole Island of Great Britain*, ed. Pat Rogers (Harmondsworth, 1971), 326; M. Dorothy George, *London Life in the Eighteenth Century* (1966), 73–4; W. K. Jordan, *The Charities of London 1480–1660* (1960), 143–5, 163.

[29] *Life*, 105, 107.

[30] Ibid., 106; BL Add. MS 78307, fo. 14: MB to JE, [?11 May 1673]; 'Mrs Phesey', as Margaret calls her, is not further identifiable, but the parish registers of St Margaret's Westminster for the period, transcribed for the Harleian Society, contain a number of entries for a family named Ve(a)sey.

as one of her Lenten tasks. The money was distributed in the form of pensions, house rent, schooling, and apprentice costs for orphan children, or the redemption of debts. In due course she developed a substantial 'roll' of regular payments, as Evelyn found when she devolved the work on him during a temporary absence. He would even become alarmed at the sums she laid out in this way; 'I have sometimes call'd it Profusion; at which she would smile, and bid me take no Care.' In fact not all the money was her own. Some of it probably came from court friends such as the Howards, who were favourably disposed but would normally have relied on the clergy to distribute their alms, and some from Godolphin.[31]

She would take small devotional works with her to distribute and compiled her own collection of Bible readings, and with these 'she would Sit, and Reade, Instruct and Pray whole Afternoones'. When communion was to be administered privately to a sick person she could join in. 'This day has bin endeed a day of joy and gladnes for has the lord endeed bin very gracious', she wrote to Evelyn of one such occasion, 'I was very desierus to reseive the blesed sacrament: and to that end did inquier in many places but no wher was it administerd: which was great trouble to me: but when I least expected it coms an invitation to me: the blesed feast was kept in a poor sicke womans chamber and to day about ten a cloke was a frind of yours in an other world very near.'[32] Satisfying herself that she could live as useful a life in the court environs as anywhere else helped to reconcile her to remaining where she was until her future should be clearer.

Her seriousness of purpose, the fact that she had moved beyond an introspective devotional world conceded to young women, must have concentrated Godolphin's mind as well. Early in April the court was to move to Newmarket as usual, and this brought the cycle of broken resolutions about his gambling to a climax. On the Thursday evening before the King was due to leave Margaret did not receive her expected visit from Godolphin. Instead there came a letter the following morning:

My deare I was engaged at play last night & did not com to see you as I intended to doe, which are faults both, and great ones but I have griefs God knows & I will confesse to you & I hope to find some ease by it for they trouble & afflict me very much & some pitty & comfort from you I desire & want it extreamly, for that reason I wish I might bee able to speak with you tonight because I am afraid I shall not make you understand in a letter what I have a mind to say, though because the other is so uncertain I will endeavour to doe it.

<hr/>

[31] *Life*, 90, 105–7; BL Hammick Papers, SG to MB, 'thursday 6 a clock' [16 Apr. 1674].
[32] *Life*, 105–6; BL Add. MS 78307, fo. 39: MB to JE, 'Saterday past 2 a clok' [1674].

Then came the involved and sorry tale of postponed resolutions:

I play soe much & I am soe convinc'd that I doe very ill in it & provoke God Almighty's anger against me by itt that I loath the thought of continuing to use it in the excesse I have done all this winter & yett I have soe many engagments in it & many debts & tis soe very hard for me to avoid it till after this journey to Newmarket bee over that I am afraid if I should resolve against it till then I should bee too much tempted to do something contrary to that resolution.

He would be travelling to Newmarket with the Privy Purse Bab May, who had intended to leave on the Saturday. He wanted to ask him to put their journey off till Sunday morning, so that he could take communion before he left, 'which I earnestly desire to doe but am not satisfy'd whether it would not be more advisable for me to forbeare considering how ill a preparation for it soe much time mispent must needs bee, & when I certainly know I am going to expose myselfe to the same temptations which I ought utterly to renounce before I come thither'.[33] For as usual the whole business of Newmarket would be gambling and all his companions would be in the thick of it. One of three scheduled races was between Bab May's horse and another owned by Tom Elliott. May thought nothing of wagering £1,000 on a horse, when even the King would only venture a few hundreds.[34] Both Elliot and May's jockey, Thomas Felton, were Godolphin's fellow grooms of the bedchamber, but both were also well-to-do courtiers with their own establishments, while he was still occupying makeshift lodgings in Whitehall with no household of his own, no provision for the future, and the dissipation of what stock he did have in gambling. He begged Margaret for understanding and support: 'I am weary of this course of life & it lies heavy upon me . . . my deare how can I hope you should ever endure soe wicked a creature as I must appeare to you after this that I have said, but I know you soe well that though you may have lesse love for me than you had before, you will have more pitty and charity.'[35]

At Newmarket he could not lose himself in the pastimes of the place as before, and on his return, looking over his accounts before Easter, he took stock,

& find my selfe a horrid wicked creature god knowes guilty of a great many grievous faults, particularly of wasting idely & miserably almost all of my whole time at play & having been sensible of this for some time I have made several resolutions against the excesse of it, & yett hitherto having still broken these resolutions, the

[33] BL Hammick Papers: SG to MB, 'friday one a clock' [27 Mar. 1674].
[34] BL Add. MS 36916, fo. 170: newsletter, 19 Apr. 1670; Bodleian Library, MS Film 293: newsletter, 9 Apr. 1674; [A. W. Thibaudeau] (ed.), *The Bulstrode Papers* (1897), 265; Peter May, *The Changing Face of Newmarket 1660–1760* (Newmarket, 1984), 24–5.
[35] BL Hammick Papers: SG to MB, 'friday one a clock' [27 Mar. 1674].

Consideration of these grievous faults & provocations against the holy spiritt of God has fill'd my heart with infinite sorrow & repentance with shame & confusion & I loath & detest my owne ingratitude & forgetfulnesse of God's numberlesse mercy's to me, I have confessed these my sins to God most humbly and bewail'd them with abundance of teares . . . I beg my deare that you would ask forgiveness of God for me in this particular & and that you would helpe me besides to give thanks to his holy name for inspiring my heart with this last resolution against play (wch I have this day confirmed), & for the inward comfort & satisfaction wch I have already found from itt.[36]

This time, with Margaret's support, the resolution held, and with it came the prospect that they would be able to set up their own household in the foreseeable future. They renewed their joint commitment to their religious aims and to each other. Godolphin begged for regular letters to sustain his faith, telling Margaret that he longed to return to 'the humble and christian fram[e] of mind' which came with his first sense of conversion. She replied, no longer with sardonic reproofs but with generous encouragement:

ther is nothing so plain to me as that you have it now my dear, do you not ask counsill of me, crave my assistance, doe you not acknowledge to the glory of god that evil habit you are able to corect . . . and notwithstanding all these marks of love to god and sorow for your sins you think yourself barren and unfruitfull, though the great work of your repentance is finished and you sinsearly hate every evil way yet you thinke a day and a night, nay your wholl life to litle to spend in praising and praying to god. As Abraham rejoyced to se the day of our saviour so doe I to se your day . . . you hate your sins and love your saviour; have no consarns which you will not trust to him nor no pleasuer which you will not willingly quit for his sake; ther is nothing in this world that you violently long for but his grace; nor nothing you are ambitious of but eternal glory; religion is your chief design and recreation but in order to it as a refreshment not an imployment; the hops of heaven and thoughts of being forever with jesus make you freely quit all filthy injoyments and lewd pleasuers; solitude and prayer is to you more truly delightfull than a crowd and the greatest honour; you will not wilfully offend god for all the kingdoms of the earth; and in this plentifull efusion of gods grace you continu thirsty and very hungry, desirous still of more; and through the humility of your mind thinke yourself in poverty whill you are indeed truly rich . . . I know you will be ofended at the comendations I bestow upon you but truly I canot help it for I am so mouch convinced of the thing that I coud not avoid speaking of it to the glory of god; if you answer not my carecter endeaver to doe it: this panegyricke will serve for precepts and if you are not com to what I describ I hope you will in time: blesed be god you are further gon in your jurney then two year ago you could have thought.[37]

[36] Ibid., SG to MB, 'thursday 6 a clock' [16 Apr. 1674].
[37] Ibid., MB to SG, 'friday 6 a cloke' [c.May 1674]

Godolphin read this letter, which he called the best he had ever received from her, with 'teares of joy & thankfulnesse' running down his face.[38] Although their marriage might still be postponed until Margaret's portion was paid and his own finances were established, they seem to have accepted that from now on their future lay together.

Meanwhile the involvement in public affairs which had sustained Evelyn's constant presence in London for three years was dwindling. With Clifford gone he lost what little impetus he still had to finish his history of the Dutch war. He did reluctantly bestir himself in the winter at the King's request to produce a much shorter piece of propaganda, 'A succinct but full deduction of his Majesties indubitable Title to the Dominion and Sovereignty of the British Seas, and consequently the Fishery and Duties thereunto', making the best of an argument he could not privately agree with; but before it could go to press the peace was signed and it had to be withdrawn.[39] Wanting to salvage something from his labours, he decided on his own initiative to publish the completed introduction on navigation and commerce, the only part of the history in which he had taken any satisfaction. But this work, which Clifford had thought too favourable to the Dutch, was now complained of by their ambassador as too critical of a friendly power and the King had to have it officially suppressed. Although he assured Evelyn privately that he approved of it, the order to the Stationers' Company reproved him for having 'intermeddled with certain matters of state beyond what becomes him or belongs to him'.[40] His lack of political sense, and above all his failure to finish the whole work when it would have been of use to the government, meant the end of his undistinguished career as its historiographer.

The attendance at the Council of Trade and Plantations which had provided the occasion for his Tuesday meetings with Margaret was also becoming very intermittent. Without the influence over policy which it had pretended to in the beginning, the Council was taken up more and more with particular disputes, especially those of the African Company and the planters over the cost of supplying negroes to the West Indies. Meanwhile salaries went unpaid and debts were allowed to mount up. John Locke, brought in by Shaftesbury as secretary, soon found that his most pressing task was to negotiate with the upholsterer who had supplied their furnishings for payment in instalments. Shaftesbury himself was increasingly at loggerheads with Danby and the court, and it was quite clear to Evelyn by this time that

    [38] Ibid., SG to MB, 'saturday morning' [May 1674].
    [39] JE, *Diary*, iii. 30; HMC Pepys MSS, 267; *PF*, 136–7: JE to Pepys, 19 Sept. 1682.
    [40] Keynes, *JE*, 203–4; *CSP Domestic 1673–1675*, 332: Charles II to the Stationers' Company, 12 Aug. 1674.

trade would continue to be carried on 'more by antient Methods, and the sedulitie of Private Men, than by any publique Encouragement'. Long before the Council was formally wound up at the end of the year it was apparent that its days were numbered.[41]

Even Sayes Court was no longer a haven to him. During the previous year Sir Richard Browne's brother-in-law and former trustee William Prettyman, from whom Evelyn had purchased the property more than twenty years before and who was now in financial difficulties, began a Chancery suit to recover money which he claimed was still owing to him from Browne's years in exile. Any hope of settling this dispute would depend in turn on the settling of Sir Richard's debt from the crown. Despite his long acquaintance with Danby, Evelyn, along with everyone else, was finding the new Lord Treasurer brusque and high-handed to deal with. Even his routine business at the Treasury was an ordeal and it was clear that he could expect no favours in this long-standing affair. Yet without it the lawsuit was likely to drag on for years, undermining their peace and possibly in the end swallowing up most of the family's fortune with its costs. Evelyn blamed himself fruitlessly for not making use of Clifford's friendship while he could, but the anxiety bore hardest on Sir Richard, whose health now began to give way. All Mary Evelyn's time not taken up with her 'little flock of girls' was devoted to nursing and cheering him.[42] Jack still moped about the house, undecided about his future. More and more Evelyn withdrew from this comfortless family circle into his private devotional life. Mrs Evelyn rather forlornly described their situation during this bitter winter for Glanville's benefit: each member isolated from the other and herself as the only link; 'My father . . . is at present in bed, but not very ill. We have our workmen still, but hope a little time will finish all. Your brother [Evelyn] watches and prays still. Jack studies and ruminates, the girls make a noise, and I lend a little of my time to any one that seems to want it.'[43]

The workmen were building a new study for Evelyn at the east end of the parlour.[44] To this 'little cell or cabinet' he could retreat from the noise of his children and sit up late into the night, not just to 'watch and pray', but to write. It is likely that he sometimes slept there as well; he told Margaret that

[41] Library of Congress, Phillipps MS 8539: Journal of the Council of Trade and Plantations, 1673–4, *passim*; Charles M. Andrews, *British Committees, Commissions, and Councils of Trade and Plantations 1622–1675* (Baltimore, 1908), 111–12; R. P. Bieber, 'The Plantation Councils of 1670–4', *English Historical Review*, 40 (1925), 106; K. H. D. Haley, *The First Earl of Shaftsbury* (Oxford, 1968), 259–65; *PF*, 140: JE to Pepys, 19 Sept. 1682.

[42] BL Add. MSS 78615: papers relating to the Prettyman lawsuit, 1673–4; 78539: ME to Bohun, 19 Nov. [1677]; JE, *Diary*, iii. 14, 20.

[43] Bray, iv. 39–40: ME to Glanville, 31 Dec. 1673.   [44] JE, *Diary*, iii. 37.

he and his wife would now often agree to sleep separately so that he could 'vacate to holy and solemn Offices'.[45] At the beginning he had taken the dominant role in the friendship, but now the balance of power had shifted to her. In works of charity especially he was no more than her follower. One day in December he recorded that they dined together and 'thence to an Almeshouse, where was prayers, & reliefe, some very sick & miserable: . . . it was one of the best daies I ever spent in my life'.[46] He castigated himself bitterly that she was so far in advance of him in her dedication to God; 'that I should be such a wretch, & so unhappy, as to be able to give him only the Evenings, how have I spent my morning, & my mid day & almost my whole day; when I consider what you have don; oh how I abhore & despise my selfe, & fall down on my knees to deplore the time I have lost, & that I have begun so lately to live'. But he had no doubt now that his salvation must be through her:

to whom am I more obliged that I live than to my sweete friend . . . day & night I praise God for you, & I hope I shall recover the steps which I have lost & pursue you till I over take . . . but who shall procur all this heape of of mercys for me, o it must be my praying friend; it is a favour you can do me above all the saints that I know in this world, for I am perswaded most infinitly that you are a blessed creatur, beloved & greatly favour'd of God.[47]

All his intellectual as well as his emotional life was now focused on Margaret. He took up various unfinished literary projects, not to complete them as originally conceived, but to recycle and transform their matter into a highly-wrought sequence of devotions for her on the theme of the creation, one for each major festival of the church year and one for each day of the week. They made use yet again of the passages already taken over from his 'Rational Account of True Religion' into his treatise on navigation and commerce, on the 'divine Oeconomy' of the rivers and coastline; while the rapturous celebrations of plants and flowers from *Sylva* and the 'Elysium Britannicum' were transformed into a meditation on the wonders of botanical generation and growth; only now, in his preoccupation with Margaret's future, the close and passionate observation of the natural world which gave his writing its greatest attractiveness was apt to be interrupted with fantasies of virgin nymphs rising to prepare for their nuptials:

We will now Walk into yonder parterre, and Observe how these small and despicable Atomes of the flowry rudiments, are cast into their cold and expos'd Beds, and

[45] BL Add. MS 15950, fo. 109: JE, 'Oeconomics to a Newly Married Friend', [1676], p. 81.
[46] JE, *Diary*, iii. 28.
[47] BL Add. MS 78307, fo. 32: JE to MB (draft), [winter 1673–4].

rotting (in appearance) under the damp mould, should yet at last . . . put forth their
pretty and extravagant rootes, serpenting in the Earth . . . peeping out first with a
small, pale thried, tip'd with faint enamell, and mantl'd in their greene scarfs, which
by degrees they explaine, discovering the raies of a long conceil'd, but admirable
beauty in the leaves, bud and flower, which they delicately unfold, unplaiting their
tresses, and modestly un-vailing their virginal blushes . . . with what infinite delight,
and satisfaction, do we in our Gardens behold some of these modest Nymphs open
their chast and fragrant boosomes, at the first dawning of the fresh morning! Some
we may see half dress'd . . . some that ye would take to be clad in White Sattin, or
figur'd Snow: some in Velvet and cloth of tissue: They are pink't, plaited, cham-
bletted, embroidred, pennach'd and chammarr'd with gold; others again have the
resemblance of soft mother of pearle; they hang their little bells of flexible Saphyrs,
and pendents of rubie, others open their painted cups, pretty paniers, and boxes lin'd
with crimson, and incarnadine damasks; vasetts of Chrystal . . . vein'd and streak'd
with Colours Celestial, flaming and radiant, and all of a gemmy lustre; all of them
blooming, all of them faire . . . They peepe out of their Vergin buds, as out of so
many eyes, trickling into teares of joy, and turning themselves into a thousand varieties, some are erect, others reflex'd, arch'd, round, spiral, pyramidal, wreath'd,
jagged, escalop'd and indented; some are single, others double, and curl'd, tufted,
truss'd-up and pursh'd, deck'd with plumes of plush, and feather'd tops, crown'd and
adorn'd as a royal Bride for the day of her Nuptials . . . If there be a heaven upon
Earth, it is when holy Soules contemplate these wonders of their Maker, and
Celebrate his Praises, when at every step they tread upon Miracles, and Converse
with the purest, most innocent and most abstracted of earthly delights.[48]

The late hours in the solitude of his study devoted to this work became the
climax of his day; 'My child I am doing good things for us both', he wrote to
Margaret, '& indeed I delight when evening comes because then I have time
to converse with my friend . . . & my sole delight.'[49]

Yet Margaret's mind was no longer chiefly on the friendship, but on her
own future. She thanked him for the latest meditation, which he anxiously
felt might not be sufficiently devout and moving, assuring him that it was 'the
most entertaining, instroctive plesent thing I ever read and so far from not
being very devout and moving that it made me admire the works of gods creation more then ever I did in my life'.[50] But there were none of the spontaneous outpourings of love and friendship of the previous year. Instead, with
the renewed understanding between her and Godolphin, she began to show

[48] BL Add. MS 78379, fos. 5ᵛ–15ᵛ: 'Tuesdays Meditation', Apr. 1674; Hiscock I, 133–4. For
comparable passages, see *The History of Religion*, ed. R. M. Evanson (1850), i. 27–8; *Navigation and
Commerce: Their Original and Progress* (1674), in Upcott, 629–31; *EB*, 399–400; *Sylva* (1670), 245–6.
[49] BL Add. MS 78307, fo. 32: JE to MB (draft), [winter 1673–4].
[50] Ibid., fo. 34: MB to JE, [Apr.–May 1674].

uneasiness about those she had already sent. In May she asked Evelyn to return all her letters; not, he said later, 'that she could be Conscious of having ever Writen that to me, which might not have pass'd the Severest Eye'; but in case they might 'fall into hands that profane every thing, the most Innocent & Vertuous'.[51] In the event she singled out only six letters which she wanted to retain and destroy. But these, with their declarations of love and acknowledgements of what she owed him for the transformation of her devotional life, were now his most treasured possessions and he protested vehemently that he could not bear to give them up. Margaret replied that she must give them back to him if he insisted, but that she had 'some undenigh-able reasons' why she did not want to do so; 'I don't know that ever I write any leter to you in my life, that did not assuer you of my prayers for you: and in which I did not aknowledg how much I have bin beholding you upon religious accounts . . . remember an english proverb of much adoe about nothing, and se if your case is not like it.' She reminded him that he could always take copies in his own hand of the passages he most valued, 'without putting any marke upon them whose they were'. Although their authentic-ity was a large part of their value to him, she briskly dismissed this as 'an idle fansey' and in the end he had to comply.[52] Even though he had never tried to influence her seriously against marriage, the futile sense that he and Godolphin were competing for her would constantly resurface; he had to tell himself not to take her request for the letters as a sign that she intended to break off their relations, 'as Ladys us'd to do with Unfortunate Rivals'.[53] She did what she could to soften the blow by assuring him that she was as much his friend as ever, and that she kept Tuesdays dedicated to his prayers and meditations even when they were unable to meet. But it was painfully clear to him that the period when the friendship had been as important to her as it was to him was over. Taking it as a sign that her marriage must now be very close, he offered to release her from her promise of binding friendship.[54]

Meanwhile the elite residents of London were preparing to disperse for the summer: the court to Windsor, the Berkeleys and Margaret with them to their mansion by the river at Twickenham. This was a Tudor house of turrets and vanes, lying end-on to the river and linked to its landing stage there by a

[51] *Life*, 57.

[52] BL Add. MS 78307, fos. 41, 45–6: MB to JE, Friday 26 June [1674] and n.d [1674]. Writing ten years later in the *Life*, 57, Evelyn dates this episode at the time of her marriage in May 1675, but the sequence of letters clearly places it in the preceding year; see further Appendix B.

[53] *Life*, 58.

[54] BL Add. MS 78307, fos. 34–5, 37: MB to JE, [May 1674], [1674?]; *Life*, 58: MB to JE, [May–June 1674?].

short tree-lined avenue.[55] Unlike the wide reach of the Thames at Deptford, with its tidal ebb and flow, cloud-reflecting water, and seagoing traffic, this upstream stretch of the river moved placidly. Only barges and wherries passed slowly to and fro and the river, divided here and there by small, lush islands, took its colour from these and from the tree-lined banks, which cleared at intervals to allow glimpses of the neighbouring riverside mansions and ornamental villas. It was in this house in the last years of Elizabeth that Francis Bacon had thought of founding a scientific college, 'since I experimentally found that place much convenient for my philosophical conclusions'.[56] In the following reign Lucy Harington, Countess of Bedford, the patroness of Jonson, Drayton, and Donne, had laid out the great garden there, whose structure still remained: concentric circles of lime and birch around a grass centre, perhaps representing the Copernican universe, all revolving about Lucy Harington herself, 'the brightness of our sphere'; with the four quadrants marked out in rosemary and box.[57] Here during another such spring, John Donne had come to walk with her in the garden:

> And at mine eyes, and at mine eares
> Receive such balmes, as else cure every thing

It promised to be the perfect paradisal retreat where Margaret could practise her meditations undisturbed. 'But O, selfe traytor', Donne had continued,

> I do bring
> The spider love, which transubstantiates all,
> And can convert Manna to gall,
> And that this place may thoroughly be thought
> True Paradise, I have the serpent brought.[58]

Margaret seemed also to have brought the serpent into paradise, for at Twickenham she was again thrown into a turmoil. The immediate cause is not clear, but the general one, for all her renewed understanding with Godolphin, was the continuing insecurity about her own future. Even in this place there could be disturbing encounters. One of the riverside houses a little upstream belonged to Lord Berkeley's widowed sister, Mrs Jane Davies, 'a very temperate, healthy old lady' who had surrounded her house with

---

[55] Alan C. B. Urwin, *Twickenham Parke* (Twickenham, 1965), 70–7, reproducing a bird's-eye view of 1635; the layout is still recognizable on John Rocque's cartographic survey of 10 miles around London, 1741–5.

[56] R. S. Cobbett, *Memorials of Twickenham* (1872), 226–9,

[57] Roy Strong, *The Renaissance Garden in England* (1979), 120–3.

[58] 'Twicknam Garden', in *The Metaphysical Poets*, ed. Helen Gardner (Harmondsworth, 1972), 66; cf. R. C. Bald, *John Donne: A Life* (Oxford, 1970), 173–7.

cherry orchards, a fruitful walled garden, and vegetable plots, and eccentrically chose to live on their produce, 'without animal food'.[59] In the visits to and fro Margaret found unexpectedly that she had something important in common with this 60-year-old royalist gentlewoman. Thirty years before, as Jane Berkeley, she had been betrothed to Sidney Godolphin's uncle and namesake, 'as perfect and as absolute a piece of virtue as ever our nation bred', who had been killed in an inconsequential skirmish in the early days of the Civil War. It had happened while he was under Berkeley's command, pursuing a parliamentary force with a party of horse across Dartmoor. In a bitter winter's dawn they rode into an ambush in the village of Chagford. Godolphin, who had refused to accept military rank because he was not trained for it, was riding alongside his cousin as a volunteer. Since their troop was too small to stand and fight, they made a dash through the town, and as they did so he was hit by a random musket shot 'from an undiscerned and undiscerning hand', fell from his horse and died within moments.[60] 'There is not any vertue that disposeth a man, either to the service of God, or to the service of his Country, to Civill Society, or private Friendship, that did not manifestly appear in his conversation,' Thomas Hobbes wrote, 'not as acquired by necessity, or affected upon occasion, but inherent and shining in the generous constitution of his nature.'[61]

In his will Godolphin had left his 'dear cousin Mrs Jane Berkeley' £1,000, and it was she who preserved the verses which had circulated privately in his lifetime but were never published. 'He loved her exceedingly', John Aubrey noted, 'afterwards she married one Mr Davys who I think is now dead.'[62] Why had she and Sidney Godolphin never married? Both were in their early thirties at the time of his death; there was no financial obstacle and the family was much intermarried already: Sidney's sister Penelope to Jane's eldest brother; his brother Francis to her cousin Dorothy. Yet it seems that neither was eager to do so.[63] Sidney Godolphin had sought promotion at court and in the diplomatic service and been well received; but he was also, his friend Clarendon noted, 'inclined somewhat to melancholy, and to retirement amongst his books', and so easily deterred by perceived difficulties that he would allow even minor ones to deprive him of pleasures he had eagerly

[59] Cobbett, *Twickenham*, 211–13; it was on the site of the present Orleans House.
[60] Mary Coate, *Cornwall in the Great Civil War* (Oxford, 1933), 47–9.
[61] *Leviathan*, ed. W. G. Pogson Smith (Oxford, 1929), 3.
[62] Sidney Godolphin, *Poems*, ed. William Dighton (Oxford, 1931), pp. xv–xxviii; Anthony Wood, *Athenae Oxonienses*, ed. Philip Bliss (1813–20), iii. 46.
[63] A later copy of 'Sydney Godolphin's Verses to Miss [*sic*] Davies', beginning 'Cloris it is not thy disdayne', is printed in Julia Longe, *Martha Lady Giffard: Her Life and Correspondence* (1911), 89, and suggests reluctance on Jane Berkeley's side.

looked forward to.[64] In his verse he meditated on the nature of human desire and how it might be affected by consummation:

> Vaine man, borne to noe happinesse,
> but by title of distresse,
> Alli'de to a Capacitie
> of Joye, only by misery;
> whose pleasures are but remidies
> and best delights but the supplies
> of what he wantes, who hath no sence
> but poverty and indigence:
> Is itt not paine still to desire
> and carry in our breast this fyer?
> is it not deadnesse to have none
> and satisfyed, are wee not stone?
> Doeth not our Cheifest Blisse then lie
> Betwixt thirst and satiety,
> in the midd way? which is alone
> in an halfe satisfaction:
> and is not Love the midle way,
> att which, with most delight wee stay?
> desire is totall indigence,
> But Love is ever a mixt sence
> of what we have, and what wee want,
> and though it bee a little scant
> of satisfaction, yet wee rest
> in such an halfe possession best.
> A halfe possession doeth supply
> the pleasure of variety,
> and Frees us from inconstancy
> by want causd, or satiety.[65]

Margaret must have heard something of this story and may even have been given the verses to read; there was a curious echo of them in one of her later letters to Evelyn.[66] Something of this withheld-ness, this fondness for 'half satisfaction' and wariness of satiety, seemed to have been passed to the poet's nephew. From Windsor Godolphin came and went on occasional visits, but there was still no sign when their marriage could take place. Even if they should marry, a complete severance from the court would still be years in the future. It was not a place which fostered confidence in the marriage bond and

[64] Edward Hyde, 1st Earl of Clarendon, *Life . . . in which is Included a Continuation of his History* (Oxford, 1857), i. 43.
[65] Godolphin, *Poems*, 4–6.   [66] BL Add. MS 78307, fo. 94: MB to JE, [1678].

at times their long-drawn-out betrothal made each of them lose confidence in the other. 'My deare I can't goe to sleep till I have ask'd you what it is that makes you weep soe grievously', Godolphin scribbled in an undated note, 'indeed it grievs my heart to see you soe sad, & I hope in God I shall never doe or omitt any thing that may bee the cause of soe much trouble to you, if I had the whole world I would give it to make your life comfortable to you.' It must have been some suspicion or jealousy on her part which caused this crisis, for he added, 'indeed I promise you I will never seek to please soe much as my eye with any body else as long as I live, I don't know why I say this to you for I am sensible the danger is of the other side & have too much reason to fear you will not love me very long, don't bee angry with mee my deare, I mean this in no ill sence to you, God knowes I beg of him every day that he would reward all your love to me.'[67]

As Margaret traced Lucy Harington's concentric paths and looked out from the pavilions she could take no satisfaction in its universal patterns and geometric precision, for everything was uncertain in her own life. Would she find herself, like Jane Berkeley, in a perpetual state of betrothal which never led to marriage? 'Thus she Continu'd at Twick'nam, (as it were in probation)', Evelyn says, 'for the most part Retir'd, and sometimes in Conversation: He came often to Visite her, and that broke her Heart; If he abstain'd from Coming, she was still Uneasy.'[68] She was plunged again into the 'torment of suspense' from which she knew only one escape; 'how blesed shall we be when once we com to love nothing but god, thinke of him always', she wrote to Evelyn, '. . . I beg of him with many tears that I may love nothing but him, ah that he would hear me: he will in tim[e] . . . and when he thinks fit he will help and deliver me.'[69] Should they not after all do as she had first proposed, and as Jane Berkeley and her cavalier poet had evidently decided: agree not to put their love for each other to the final test, but serve God asunder?

Meanwhile there were signs that Margaret's stay with the Berkeleys would not last much longer. On the opposite bank of the river were the remnants of Richmond Palace, where the Duke of York's children lived. There was much coming and going there with the court at Windsor and even talk of some entertainment in the winter for which Margaret might be summoned back to take part. Berkeley, still intriguing for a further public appointment, was quite prepared to make his paradise a stake in the game. In June Francis Godolphin came over from Dublin, where he was serving under the Lord

[67] BL Hammick Papers: SG to MB, 'munday night'.   [68] *Life*, 50–1.
[69] BL Add. MS 78307, fo. 39: MB to JE, 'Saterday past 2 a clok' [June 1674].

Lieutenant, called to pay his respects to his cousins, and afterwards wrote to warn his master that Berkeley was working to supplant him and had promised to let the Duchess of Portsmouth have Twickenham Park if she could bring it about.[70] Francis Godolphin's presence in the house was a source of tension in itself; it seems to have been understood by the Berkeleys that he too was in love with Margaret.[71] Some difficult encounter or a combination of all of them brought matters to a head. Margaret returned abruptly and prematurely from Twickenham to London, as determined as when she had resigned from court to put an end to her suspense and take her future into her own hands.

All this while she had continued to correspond with Dean Benson at Hereford and at some point he offered her the refuge she wanted: a place in or near his own household in the cathedral town. It seemed the perfect solution. She would not be in a remote country parish but in a centre of religious life where her aspirations would be understood; well away from all her court acquaintance but still in a community of friends. Benson's son, a young court chaplain, was already well known to her, and the families of the Dean and the Bishop, Sir Herbert Crofts, 'a warm devout man' who did not hesitate to criticize the King's conduct from the pulpit, were closely linked.[72] For companionship she would have Evelyn's little daughter Betty, as they had agreed. Her plan was to go north on the pretext of a month's visit to her sister in Yorkshire and then, instead of returning to London, to travel on to Hereford. There she was sure she could live as she had always wished, 'in perfect Freedom, without Formes; Frugaly; without Contempt . . . At distance from the Bussle of the World, Where I shall forget and be forgott'n: Be Arbitresse of my own time, and Serve God Regularly'. She would remember Godolphin only in her prayers.[73]

Evelyn, coming up to London to meet her on this new alarm, was thoroughly concerned at her state. She was thin and pale and plainly overwrought. The Hereford plan did not commend itself to him at all. In fact he had more reason to be jealous of Benson's influence over her than of Godolphin's; it would take her even more completely out of his sphere than marriage, and in a community of clerics she would have no need of any other spiritual mentor. And it was still not clear that she would be content there. If

[70] Osmund Airy (ed.), *Essex Papers*, Camden Society, new ser., 47 (1890), i. 240–2: Francis Godolphin to Lord Essex, 16 July 1674.

[71] BL Add. MS 78308: Lady Berkeley to JE, 9 Sept. [1676].

[72] Gilbert Burnet, *History of his own Time*, ed. M. J. R[outh] (Oxford, 1833), i. 474; Pepys, *Diary*, viii. 131. Crofts and Benson died within a few months of each other in 1691 and are buried side by side in Hereford Cathedral quire, their memorial brasses linked by joined hands and with the shared inscription, 'In vita conjuncti. In morte non divisi' ('joined in life, in death not divided').

[73] *Life*, 39–40, 68.

the distance of Spain and France had made no difference to her love for Godolphin, he asked her, how could she expect Hereford to do so? He begged her to reconsider and to consult further with her friends. 'Your advice I like and all you say upon both subjects', Margaret replied, 'yet I am still wher I was, wishing to live alone, I can't but think it most suitable to my humer and the nearest way to heaven.' But she did promise him, as she had the previous year, to make no final resolution until she had consulted with Godolphin, 'and not leave—untill *he* giv[e] me free leav to do it'. In the meantime, acknowledging that marriage was still in prospect, she undertook to take care of her health and her looks, 'sleep 8 hours and then drinke red cow's milke . . . eat my meat hartely', so that if she did go away she would not be thought to do so unwillingly; and if she did marry, 'I ought more to take caer of myself that I may not be disagreeable in his eyes'. But she still wished that she 'were setled wher I need use non of these complacences: but might atend on god night and day with fasting and prayer'. She consoled herself that it would not be 'above three months at the furthest I shall need to doe this (unless it becoms my duty by being maryed) and then endeed I shall be always worldly, but if not then by the end of the sumer I shall be at liberty, non will consider my looks nor I shall not need to caer if they doe being so far off from them'.[74]

Although Evelyn told her that he resigned her to God, he was no more able to keep himself detached from her than she was from Godolphin. In his next letter he broke into such passionate lamentations at any prospect of their parting that Margaret first reproached him for having so little regard to their ultimate religious aims, and then hastened to comfort him: 'when we are weak God is strong, he raised you up a frind of nothing, and he can comfort you without that frind . . . do you believe I shall not be broken at parting . . . weep perpetually when I think of you . . . pray for you night & day, and will labour to inspire my Betty with all the love and duty imaginable for you'. Nothing in fact was really settled. Having presumably spoken to Godolphin by this time, she was already temporizing about her journey; 'that is', she added, 'in case of the cruell separation I speak of, but who knows it may be God has better things in store for us.'[75]

It was Lady Berkeley who decided the matter. As soon as she heard of the Hereford plan she adamantly refused to part with Margaret for more than a month's visit to her sister, telling her that 'she never did think hardly of my going without tears, and that she loved me as her heart, and how could I resolv to leav her, and why would I be so mad to go by myself'. Margaret was

---

[74] Ibid., 48–50; BL Add. MS 78307, fos. 41–2: MB to JE, 26 June [1674].
[75] BL Add. MS 78307, fos. 43–4: MB to JE, [June–July 1674].

touched and gave way readily enough: 'now I think sens God has been pleased to aford me such a frind and many opportunities of seeing my best frind [Evelyn], I shall not do wisely to run into a chang unles for a best frind [Godolphin], which can't be yet of many years I fear . . . I began to consider that . . . I was very young to live all alone: without ever seing my best frind . . . that I hopt I took the middle way if at least I stayd some time longer.' Evelyn was now convinced that if she was not already married she must be very close to it. Yet she told him again, 'I am not so near that state of life as you imagin nor may be shall never venture. I have quite other thoughts but I am gods, let his will be done on me in me and by me: your frend will be hapey: how so ever or wher so ever I be disposd of.'[76]

It is not quite clear if it was marriage itself, or simply a married life separate from the court which Margaret envisaged as being so many years in the future. Evelyn, though more disposed than most to find the couple's religious aspirations compelling, was puzzled by now at their constant deferral of commitment. Their financial uncertainties were an excuse rather than a sufficient reason. Once Godolphin had restrained his gambling, they would have a modest competence in the present and the promise of better things to come. The 'great work' of his repentance was complete to Margaret's satisfaction. Sincere as her vocation was, real as the problems of Godolphin's way of life were, there was and is a suggestion that both were still hesitating before the irrevocable commitment. 'If he or I should both repent—', Margaret blurted out to Evelyn in an unguarded moment.[77] Their complete freedom only made it more difficult. There was no higher authority, no parental presence to defer to, no succession of property to safeguard; only their personal choice. While they remained as they were, Margaret knew that she held an equal and independent, sometimes a dominant position, and that once she married she would lose this entirely. Godolphin clearly had his share of his family's caution in the face of marriage. In their way these exchanges between a long-betrothed couple, though conducted in terms of religion, fell into a traditional pattern of 'courtship crises', part of the protracted and complex private negotiation by which a woman especially, on the brink of lifelong commitment, would repeatedly appear to spurn a well-established suitor and defer marriage, in order to test the strength of his attachment to her and maintain her own position, while she reconciled herself to the final step.[78]

---

[76] Ibid., fos. 43–4, 48, MB to JE, [June–July 1674].   [77] *Life*, 40.
[78] Sara Mendelson and Patricia Crawford, *Women in Early Modern England* (Oxford, 1998), 116; Amanda Vickery, *The Gentleman's Daughter* (New Haven, 1998), 53. For warnings of the risks and disadvantages of marriage, though largely from the man's standpoint, see Alan Macfarlane, *Marriage and Love in England: Modes of Reproduction 1300–1840* (Oxford, 1986), 169–72.

Meanwhile Margaret still chafed at the disruptive way of life in Berkeley House and Twickenham and cast about for some alternative; not in Yorkshire or Hereford now, but closer at hand. One of her thoughts was to rent a small house of her own at Greenwich, which she knew well from her summers with the Howards. This plan did not appeal to Evelyn either: 'I thought it Inconvenient for a Lady so Young and who was allready dispos'd to a more than Ordinary Reserv'dnesse, to indulge the humour.' If Dean Benson could offer her a refuge, so could he. He proposed that instead she should come to board with them at Sayes Court, a small household but one where her vocation would be respected.[79] In mid-July he received a sudden and cryptic summons from Margaret to London 'upon an unjust report'.[80] He says no more than this in his diary, but the likelihood is that Lady Berkeley had got wind of this plan as well and made her disapproval very clear. Margaret's companionship was useful to her. Whether or not she blamed Evelyn for her companion's intermittent resolutions against marriage, she certainly opposed them, and in his household Margaret would be quite outside the family sphere. There could be no question of her offending her future husband's most powerful relations and so this project was also dropped without further ado. 'My best Friend', Margaret wrote tactfully, 'As to my being in your Family it was Almost, and ah! that it had not been almost but altogether!'[81]

He evidently still felt that she was detaching gradually herself from the friendship, for she reassured him that 'what ever you think, it is hard for one to describe how sorry I am, to be thus far from so deare a Friend; and you don't know that I have given over severall other Proposals of settling myself, when that Thought comes into my head, that I shall be a greate way from you unless I continue where I am'. At the same time she gently discouraged him from focusing his life so exclusively on her. She wanted him to enjoy the 'pleasant hours' of summer at Sayes Court with his wife; 'it is my daily prayer that God will not only continue but still more and more increas your hapenes in her who is I daresay everyway perfectly good and excelent'. She took his resignation of her 'to our lord beter than anything you can doe for me, it shows you are the best christian and frend in the world', and when he urged her to encourage him in his religious duties, she replied, 'alas what can I say: ther is for you prais that coms not from man but god: ther is for you an eternal exceeding great reward. You serve your maker and redeemer and asist his poor servant: after this what can anything that I speake signify to you.'

---

[79] *Life*, 51.   [80] JE, *Diary*, iii. 37.   [81] *Life*, 51–2: MB to JE, [summer 1674].

She prayed that God would give him 'such comforts as will make you forget all others'.[82]

Just as this episode was over and she was reconciling herself to staying with the Berkeleys 'at least for some months, till God is pleased to dispose of me, one way or other',[83] she again found herself drawn back into the court, not just for the Christmas festivities but for a celebration of its glories on an unprecedented scale. ❧

[82] BL Add. MS 78307, fos. 39, 48: MB to JE, 'Saterday past 2 a clok' [1674], 2[?] July [1674?].
[83] *Life*, 52: MB to JE, [summer 1674]

8

ঙ্কু

The Marriage Masque

AT Windsor during the summer of 1674 there was a full residence of the court for the first time since the Restoration. With Arlington preparing to take charge of the household above stairs, the passion for Continental magnificence which had transformed his own great houses was turned to an ambitious cultural programme of enhancement of the glory of the English monarchy.[1] Circumstances were more favourable to this than at any time since the beginning of the reign. England had withdrawn from the expensive Continental war and Parliament was not due to meet again until the following year. With the Treasury under Danby's rigorous management, income for the first time began to succeed expenditure.[2] At court a lively younger generation was making its presence felt: the new Duchess of York and her household; the Duke's daughters, now old enough to leave the nursery and join the public life of the court; and the King's illegitimate children, especially his eldest daughter by Barbara Villiers, Lady Anne Fitzroy, whose marriage to the Earl of Sussex took place at Windsor in August, and the Duke of Monmouth, who had declined his usual summer service in the French army in deference to Danby's policies.[3] In July and August accounts began to arrive at Windsor of the grand fête being staged at Versailles to celebrate Louis XIV's conquest of Franche-Comté.[4] Charles II and his circle turned their minds in similar directions.

---

[1] Political studies have not done justice to the significance for Restoration court culture of Arlington's appointment as Lord Chamberlain; but see Katharine Gibson, 'The Decoration of St George's Hall, Windsor, for Charles II', *Apollo*, 147, pt 2 (April–June 1998), 32.

[2] C. D. Chandaman, *English Public Revenue 1660–1688* (Oxford, 1975), 235; Ronald Hutton, *Charles II* (Oxford, 1989), 322.

[3] G. S. Steinmann, *A Memoir of Barbara, Duchess of Cleveland* (1871), 147, and *Addenda*, 6–7; PRO: PRO 31/3/130: dispatches of the French ambassador, 14/24, 16/26 Mar. 1674.

[4] Peter Burke, *The Fabrication of Louis XIV* (New Haven, 1992), 78.

In the water meadows between the north front of the Castle and the river the earthworks of a mock fortress were raised, on the same Continental model as Evelyn had seen at Tilbury. There in August Monmouth treated the courtiers to a re-enactment of Louis XIV's siege of Maastricht, in which he had taken part the previous summer. News-writers represented this as a worthy exercise: 'of great use for the training up of the young soldiers in military affairs'.[5] Evelyn, who had been uneasy about the real fortress at Tilbury, responded with a virtuoso's uncomplicated delight to this demonstration of the new science and display of military engineering, with its exotic terms and rituals:

There was approches & a formal siege, against a Work with Bastions, Bulwarks, Ramparts, Palizads, Graft, hornworks, Counterscarps &c in imitation of the city of Maestrict newly taken by the French: & this being artificialy design'd & cast up in one of the Meadows at the foote of the long Terrace below the Castle, was defended against the Duke of Monmouth . . . Who with the Duke of York attaqu'd it with a little army, to shew their skill in Tactics: so on Saturday night, They made their approches, opened trenches, raised batteries, took the Conterscarp, Ravelin, after a stout Defence. Great Gunns fir'd on both sides, Granados shot. mines Sprung, parties sent out, attempts of raising the siege, prisoners taken, Parties . . . & what is most strange, all without disorder, or ill accident, but to the greate satisfaction of a thousand spectators, when being night it made a formidable shew, & was realy very divertisant.[6]

As this suggests, the affair was much more than a training exercise; it was a theatrical spectacle; a showcase for the King's dashing son and a kind of *son et lumière* of military tactics and conquest. Charles II might have made peace with the Dutch Republic, but he was very willing to use this means of re-enacting its humiliation at the hands of the Sun King.

At the castle itself, now grown 'exceedingly ragged and ruinous', a gigantic rebuilding programme was set going under the direction of Evelyn's friend Hugh May, and these renovations were also designed to make a 'formidable shew'. Within the austere fortress, magnificence in the most opulent European manner was to be given free rein. In the course of the next four years Antonio Verrio, whose first work in England had been for Arlington at Euston, covered the staircases, walls, and especially the ceilings of the new state apartments with vast glamorous paintings: vistas and domes opening on illusory spaces of luminous sky and billowing clouds, through which heroic allegorical figures and classical deities descended in rapturous celebration of the glory of the restored monarchy and church. In the Guard Chamber Jupiter and Juno were enthroned with Mercury in attendance; in the King's Presence Chamber Mercury displayed a portrait of the King 'with

---

[5] HMC *LeFleming MSS*, 112–13: newsletter, 18 Aug. 1674.   [6] JE, *Diary*, iv. 42.

Transport, as it were' to the four corners of the world; in the Privy Chamber the Church of England was restored in allegory; in the Queen's apartments Catherine as Britannia was drawn towards the temple of Virtue, and in the Great Bedchamber suppliant figures of the four Continents brought homage to Charles II, elevated among the clouds.[7] It was the scenery painting for state theatre, and while the designs for it were being drawn up, another scheme was devised for realizing the very same images of glorified sovereignty on stage, this time in the Hall theatre in Whitehall. It was announced that the centrepiece of the coming Christmas festivities would be a great masque representing the 'Splendour & Grandeur of the English monarchy',[8] and inaugurating a new programme of lavish court entertainments.

The masque was an ambitious, idealizing genre with a long history, intended to promote the reputation of the court and aristocratic society. In the hands of Ben Jonson and Inigo Jones it had been raised to a cultural form of intellectual and theatrical importance, in which the spectacle of dazzling costumes, stage machinery, and high-born performers was used to 'lay hold of more remov'd mysteries'.[9] Intermittently, at Shrovetide celebrations ever since the Restoration, there had been minor revivals of the form,[10] but what was now planned was on a far more lavish scale; the masque would be combined with a play or opera with pastoral interludes, and professional singers and dancers as well as amateur court performers would take part.

The new Duchess of York was credited with the idea, and certainly there were Italian as well as French elements in the hybrid entertainment.[11] But there was far more to it than the personal taste of a 16-year-old girl, whose inclination, when she was not confined to her apartments by pregnancy, in any case seemed to run more to the sideshows of Bartholomew Fair than to courtly entertainments.[12] The point was not just to imitate Continental models, but to demonstrate that English ones could equal or surpass them. The court now had, or thought it had, at its command a number of professionals in the performing arts of European standing. Evelyn thought Mary Knight, who had 'the greatest reach' of any English female singer, much

[7] JE, *Diary*, iii. 560; Howard Colvin, *The History of the King's Works*, v (1976), 322–3; David Esterly, *Grinling Gibbons and the Art of Carving* (1998), 66; Edward Croft Murray, *Decorative Painting in England* (1962), i. 240–2.

[8] Quoted in Andrew Walkling, 'Masque and Politics at the Restoration Court: John Crowne's *Calisto*', *Early Music* (Feb. 1996), 55, n. 9.

[9] David Lindley (ed.), *The Court Masque* (Manchester, 1984), 1–15.

[10] Peter Holman, *Four and Twenty Fiddlers: The Violin at the English Court* (Oxford, 1993), 359–66.

[11] James Anderson Winn, *'When Beauty Fires the Blood': Love and the Arts in the Age of Dryden* (Ann Arbor, 1992), 236; Walkling, 'Masque and Politics', 51–2.

[12] HMC *Rutland MSS*, ii. 27: Lady Chaworth to Lord Roos, 7 Sept. 1675.

improved by her period of training in Italy. The composer Nicholas Staggins was said to give his countrymen 'hopes of seeing in a very short time a Master of Musick in England equal to any France or Italy has produced'. Robert Streeter, the King's Serjeant Painter who was claimed by his countrymen as the equal of Michelangelo and Rubens and would work alongside Verrio at Windsor, would be responsible for the scenery.[13] 'Thou shalt in all my noblest arts be skilled', Europe promises Britannia at the beginning of the masque. The whole performance was intended to demonstrate that England no longer lagged behind Europe; that the best of Continental achievement was now as fully naturalized in court culture as Evelyn had sought to make it in architecture and gardening.[14]

It would also be the coming-out of the King's eldest niece. After her father, Mary of York was in direct line of succession to the throne. If the child her young stepmother was already carrying proved to be a son, he would of course take precedence over his half-sisters, but whether or not this happened, Mary was still the eldest 'daughter of England'. To the great unease of the French ambassador, her likely match with her cousin William of Orange was discussed throughout this year, as a natural outcome of Danby's policies.[15] The foreign ambassadors always formed an important constituent of the audience of court entertainments.[16] Mary, although deplorably ill educated, was pretty and graceful and had been an accomplished dancer from an early age; she and her sister Anne loved performing and made little impromptu plays part of their summer picnics at Windsor.[17] This masque would display them to best advantage. Both girls in fact were to be brought forward on to the public stage as the instruments of European alliances by which (as Dryden was to put it in his epilogue) the peace-loving king would bind his friends and disarm his foes. The masque would usher in not just a new cycle of court entertainments, but a new age of diplomatic relations between England and the continent of Europe.

The supporting players from the court's circle of 'little young ladies' were chosen in advance. The other speaking parts were to go to the newly married Lady Sussex; to Lady Mary Mordaunt, whose parents headed the Duke and Duchess of York's household; to Lady Henrietta Wentworth, an heiress of the

[13] JE, *Diary*, iv. 49; Holman, *Four and Twenty Fiddlers*, 369; Murray, *Decorative Painting*, i. 44–5; Eleanor Boswell, *The Restoration Court Stage* (Cambridge, Mass., 1932), 150–1, 208–11.

[14] For the importance of this to the King, see Holman, *Four and Twenty Fiddlers*, 362–4.

[15] PRO: PRO 31/3/130: dispatches of the French ambassador, 29 Jan./8 Feb., 9/19 Feb, 19 Feb./1 Mar. 1674.

[16] Lindley (ed.), *Court Masque*, 10; Walkling, 'Masque and Politics', 30.

[17] Pepys, *Diary*, ix. 507; Margaret Toynbee, 'An Early Correspondence of Queen Mary of Modena', *Notes and Queries*, 193 (1948), 293

much-ramified court clan of the Mordaunts and the Careys; and to Sarah Jenyns, the liveliest of the Duchess of York's new maids of honour. The amateur dancers would include Carey Frazier, daughter of the King's physician and on her mother's side another of the Carey–Mordaunt cousinhood; the Duke of Ormonde's newly wedded granddaughter Lady Derby; her friend Katherine Fitzgerald, married as a child for the sake of her Irish estates to the 9-year-old grandson of the Lord Privy Seal; the Duchess of Portsmouth's younger sister, whose match with the Earl of Pembroke was imminent and her soon-to-be-sister-in-law Lady Katherine Herbert, herself a Villiers on her mother's side and therefore a cousin of Lady Sussex.[18]

None of these girls was more than 14 or 15 and all were friends and relations, drawn from the same close-knit court circle. The player who did not belong was Margaret Blagge. Why was she, the one reluctant and conspicuous adult in the whole proceedings, to be brought back to court for this unlikely occasion? Apparently just because she had acted successfully with the royal children before. This was not to be one of their informal 'little plays'. It was a long, expensive affair which could easily be spoilt, as at least one recent court performance had notoriously been, by too many unskilled amateurs.[19] Margaret did not dance or sing in any notable way, but she was accomplished in speaking parts. 'It was not possible, to leave her out', Evelyn says, 'who had upon the like Solemnity formerly, (and when a Maid of Honor) acquitted herselfe with so universal Applause & Admiration.'[20] He was of course disposed to admire anything Margaret did, but what confirmed the court's desire for her participation was that the one practical difficulty was so readily solved. While the other amateur players were expected to provide their own costumes, Margaret's was to be paid for out of the Great Wardrobe.[21]

But Margaret had gone through even the earlier entertainment with gritted teeth; 'go not to the Dutchesse of Monmouth, above once a Weeke, except we dresse to Rehearse', she admonished herself, 'and then Cary a Book with me to reade, when I don't Act and so come away before Supper'. Having now left the court ostensibly to marry, to be obliged to return to it so publicly with her future still undecided was 'to put a Mortification upon her, that Cost her, not only much reluctancy, but many Teares'.[22] Someone, Bab May or John Hervey perhaps, must have suggested to Godolphin that her

---

[18] John Crowne, *Dramatic Works* (Edinburgh, 1873), i. 327–33; George Edward Cokayne, *The Complete Peerage* (1887–98), under Derby, Pembroke, Sussex, and Wentworth of Nettlestead; Allan Fea, *The Loyal Wentworths* (1928), 37–9; Therese Muir Mackenzie, *Dromana: Memoirs of an Irish Family* (Dublin, 1906), 124–31.

[19] Pepys, *Diary*, ix. 23.   [20] *Life*, 52.   [21] Boswell, *Restoration Court Stage*, 215.

[22] *Life*, 16, 52.

willing participation would be the best means of prompting the payment of her marriage portion, now eighteen months overdue and needing the King's personal authorization before it could be paid out of the Treasury. Knowing the ways of courts well enough herself, Margaret realized that she would have to comply if she expected it to be paid at all.[23]

Her one comfort was that willingness might be all that was necessary. For so conspicuous a relaunch of the Stuart monarchy, the task of writing the libretto should rightly have fallen to the poet laureate, John Dryden. Instead, supposedly as a slight to him, the commission was thrust on a young and relatively untried playwright, John Crowne. Yet there was no hint of resentment in the graceful epilogue Dryden contributed, or in his readiness to offer Crowne advice.[24] It is much more likely that he was glad to evade a commission which had to be carried out under impossible constraints of time and casting; for Crowne was given only a few hours to submit a suitable 'fable' for approval and only a few weeks to adapt it for the stage, with the additional stipulation that it must provide speaking parts for seven female performers, 'no more and no less', with dancing roles for a further group of both sexes. Resolving to choose the first 'tolerable story' he could find, he turned to a well-used and fruitful source, Ovid's *Metamorphoses*, and chose one from the second book: Calisto, daughter of the King of Arcadia and one of the attendant nymphs of the virgin huntress Diana, is raped by Jove in the guise of the goddess herself; she gives birth to a son, is changed by an angry Juno into a bear, and both are finally transformed by Jupiter into a constellation. Having had the choice of subject approved (in itself surprising enough), Crowne then had barely a month for the composition, including the extended allegorical prologue and entr'actes. It looked doubtful whether such an elaborate work could be written and learnt by amateur performers, the music composed, the dances arranged, the costumes made, and the sets constructed, all in less than four months.[25]

While she was still hoping that the whole project would be stillborn, Margaret was invited to spend part of the summer with the Duchess of Monmouth at Moor Park. The Duchess loved balls and amateur theatricals and in other circumstances might have been one of the masque players herself. But as a child she had fallen while dancing and dislocated her hip. Several agonizing attempts to reset it failed and she was lamed for the rest of her life. Despite the handicap she had matured into an impressive, though somewhat volatile and extravagant personality: 'one of the wisest & craftiest of her sex',

[23] Ibid. 53.

[24] Crowne, *Dramatic Works*, i. 221, 241–2; Boswell, *Restoration Court Stage*, 179.

[25] Crowne, *Dramatic Works*, i. 236–7.

Evelyn observed, and seen as quite capable of being the power behind her handsome, erratic husband.[26] She had already borne him two sons and by the summer of 1674 was expecting another child. But it was already clear that Monmouth was well beyond his wife's control. He was soon disputing possession of one of the new maids of honour, Mary Kirk, with two rivals, and setting another, Eleanor Needham, up in her own household where she would eventually bear him four children.[27] His Duchess, betrayed as publicly as the Queen, could only maintain her dignity and her punctilious religious observance. Margaret's presence would be a comfort to her during her summer in the country, and in return she promised to speak to the King about the payment of her portion.[28]

Having formerly kept Godolphin at a distance, Margaret was now reluctant to put herself out of his reach: 'will you be willing to have me go for a month when presently after you are to go to Winsore? I hope you won't, I have not promised therefore you may stay me.' But Godolphin's first priority was the pleasing of his powerful cousins: 'in the first place what say's my lady Berkeley', he replied, 'I reckon she is to bee consider'd in this matter something.' But for the Duchess of Monmouth's sake he favoured the visit; 'I love her well', but 'not too well neither', he added, bearing in mind Margaret's anxieties, '& you would surely bee a great comfort to her, & a very charitable thing in her condition besides . . . she is a very good woman but I believe she may be better & nothing more like to make her soe'.[29] In fact after Twickenham Lady Berkeley required Margaret's attendance at Tunbridge Wells before she would let her go, and so Margaret found herself spending another summer at her beck and call, 'mightily disturbed in mind by thes perpetuall hureys that I am in, never at rest nor peace'.[30]

When she finally reached Moor Park she found herself in what had been, in its heyday, one of the most beautiful of all Renaissance gardens, 'the perfectest figure of a garden I ever saw . . . at home or abroad', according to the connoisseur Sir William Temple, who had spent his honeymoon there. Twenty years on it still retained much of its grace. Set on a gently sloping hillside, the house opened on a terrace 300 yards long, set with standard laurels and with a summer house at each end. From this level stone staircases

---

[26] Christopher Clay, *Public Finance and Private Wealth: The Career of Sir Stephen Fox* (Oxford, 1978), 279; JE, *Diary*, iv. 6; John Sheffield, Duke of Buckingham, *Works* (1726), ii. 20.

[27] [A. W. Thibaudeau (ed.)], *The Bulstrode Papers* (1897), 303; John Sheffield, Duke of Buckingham, *Works*, ii. 22; Elizabeth D'Oyley, *James, Duke of Monmouth* (1938), 98.

[28] BL Add. MS 78307, fo. 47: MB to JE, 25 July [1674].

[29] BL Hammick Papers, MB to SG, 'friday 6 a cloke'; SG to MB, 'saturday morning' [May–June 1674].

[30] BL Add. 78307, fo. 50: MB to JE, 1 Sept. [1674].

descended to the next: a parterre, divided by gravel walks into quarters, ornamented with fountains and statues and flanked with stone-arched cloisters, as 'walks of shade'. From the centre of this level descended a curved double staircase, framing a grotto embellished with figures of shell rock-work and waterworks, and at the lowest stage was a 'wilderness', penetrated by green walks and adorned with rough rock-work and fountains. But this was not a paradise of prelapsarian innocence. It was an arcadian garden, peopled with numinous pagan beings and disturbing transformations. Ovid was a source much plundered by gardeners as well as poets. On the walls of the grotto, copied from Italian models Evelyn had seen at Pratolino, were Ovidian scenes of 'that mighty love to the creature', the unruly, procreative, transforming, and destructive passion from which Margaret in some moods had prayed to be freed: Jupiter in the shape of a bull, the embodiment of untrammelled sexual desire, bore off Europa; Diana's virgin nymphs discovered that their companion Calisto had also succumbed to him and was about to bear his child; and the nymph Daphne fled from his son Phoebus, her upraised arms sprouting leaves and her feet rooted in the soil as she was transformed into a laurel tree to make her escape, while on the terrace above stood ranks of laurels signifying virtuous love and chastity.[31]

Evelyn had composed a prayer for the success of Margaret's business: 'that being by thy Providence supply'd with decencies for the comfortable support of Life [she] may have also wherewithall to assist & refresh those in want';[32] but the Duchess of Monmouth's influence was not powerful enough in this case. Danby was paying off the fleet by putting a stop on court pensions and salaries and the King was in no hurry to exempt a former maid of honour whose services might still be required at court. 'Where I least Expected Difficultys, I find the greatest,' Margaret told Evelyn, 'The King says nothing to my Lord Treasurer, Nor my Lord to him: So that for ought I perceive, 'tislikely to depend thus a long time.' Worse still, Crowne, with prodigies of facile effort, had produced, in barely a month, a libretto for an entertainment in five acts, complete with allegorical prologue, dances, and pastoral interludes. The Hall theatre was being refitted, and the play was to go ahead; 'I am Extremely heavy; for still I would be free from that Place, have nothing to do with it at all; but it will not be . . . Deare Friend, I beg your Prayers this Clowdy Weather; that God would endow me with Prudence and Resignation.'[33]

---

[31] Roy Strong, *The Renaissance Garden in England* (1979), 141–6; John Dixon Hunt, *Garden and Grove: The Italian Renaissance Garden in the English Imagination* (1986), 42–58, 130–3. For the survival of the garden after the Restoration, see Bodleian Library, MS Carte 35, fos. 528, 537: Edward Cooke to Ormonde, 5, 19 July 1667.

[32] BL Add. MS 78392: JE, prayer, [1674].   [33] *Life*, 53: MB to JE, 22 Sept. [1674].

Margaret's response to the second anniversary of the friendship was therefore decidedly less rhapsodic than the first. In her present mood the meditations Evelyn continued to press on her seemed little more than self-conscious
literary exercises. Snappishly she asked him why he still expected praise for
them when she had already given him so much, and reminded him rather
sharply that he ought to take less credit to himself and attribute more to God:
'forgiv me this wrong but you desierd to be told of your faults, and for ought
I know this is non of them, but judging you by my self, I fear that som tims
ther may be self love in thos things wherin we imagine we only intend gods
glory'. But then she relented and went on to make the acknowledgement
which meant so much for him:

least I injuer you by judging thus hardly of you I will comply with your desier and
acknowledg to almighty god wherin I have bin edefyd by you his servant: in the first
place you have given me beter notions of god then ever before I reseavd from any:
secondly you have acquainted me with many holy truths of which I was ignorant;
thirdly you have asisted me exceedingly, nay to only you I owe the sweetnes of my
devotions: ther order and method, their fervensey and zeal, ther softnes and love:
most if not all the holy thoughts of god his love and providence: the dignity of our
union with christ, the plesuer of solitud and abstraction from things below.

Torn between secular and sacred fulfilments, her moods were now
thoroughly confused and erratic; at times she was 'les weary of the world
and of my life then I was and yet more willing to leav all and be with Christ'.
She did not reject Evelyn's prayer for their temporal happiness, but added that
'if the greatest blessings upon earth would rob us of but one spark of his
devine love, I did beseech him for Jesus christ his sake, to strip us even of
cloths and let us wander naked through the world: indeed with nothing but
his love stript of all ornaments but grace, and better were it for us doutles
dear frind'. Yet as her return to court drew closer she found herself more
often 'cold and wandering in my prayers, peevish to my servants, vain in my
thoughts, backward to holy duties, apt to relaps and grow worldly'. She
berated herself for being either too merry or drearily depressed; 'yet not to
mak[e] my self beter than I am, tis not so eager a thirst after things devine as
a wearynes of all things I se here: wether that proceed from my loving god or
no I daer not determin, but I fear it dos not: for it is not all days alike'. But
she still turned to the friendship as a relief: 'Dear Mr Evelyn you will have
litle reason to like my leters I fear, for of late they are rather complaints than
frindly leters; but the liberty you have given me you know and I take it.'[34]

---

[34] BL Add. MS 78307, fos. 43, 54–7: MB to JE, 16 Oct. 1674, [summer 1674], 'monday night'
[autumn 1674].

In November the masque went into rehearsal three times a week. Combined with the fitting of costumes and the learning of parts, it left her very little time for her devotions, except what she could snatch by retreating into a corner of the tiring room with a book, 'under pretence of conning her next Part'.[35] But this was nothing to her dismay when she realized what she would have to act on stage. Crowne claimed that what had attracted him about the fable was 'the exact and perfect character of Calisto'—to be played by Mary—'which I thought a very proper character for the princess to represent'. Obviously it was appropriate to make clear to the foreign ambassadors that this potential bride for the princes of Europe was uncontaminated by the laxity of her uncle's court. His main difficulty with the story was 'greater than the invention of the Philospher's Stone . . . to write a clean, decent, and inoffensive play on the story of a rape'; and not just a rape, but one with lesbian overtones; for not only were all the players female, but Jupiter assumed the guise of Diana to carry out the seduction of Calisto. There was a limit to what the most hardened courtier would consider proper for these well-born girls, one of them no older than 9, to perform in public, or what the girls themselves would agree to. Crowne had either to remove the rape scene altogether, 'and so my story would be no story', or 'by keeping to it, write what would be unfit for Princesses and Ladies to speak'.[36] His solution was to alter the story so that it turned on Calisto's successful resistance. To fill out the action and accommodate the other players he plundered Ovid's more sinister and violent fable of Diana and Actaeon for the names of two additional nymphs: Calisto was given a sister Nyphe and a rival nymph Psecas, envious of her superior virtue, who would use Mercury's passion for her to plot the downfall of the goddess and her entourage. Nyphe was to be played by Lady Anne; Jupiter by Lady Henrietta Wentworth, Juno by Lady Sussex, Psecas by Lady Mary Mordaunt, and Mercury by Sarah Jenyns. The presiding role of Diana went to Margaret. There were mean jokes at the aptness of her taking the role of virgin goddess, but 'you know I am to turn the other Cheeke', she wrote to Evelyn, 'nor take I notice of it'.[37] Although the first public performance was not until February, the later dress rehearsals were public events in themselves, attended by the King and the court. Evelyn was in the audience for one of these in December and able to see for himself.[38]

---

[35] *Life*, 54. [36] Crowne, *Dramatic Works*, i. 237–8

[37] *Life*, 53–4: MB to JE, 22 Sept. [1674].

[38] JE, *Diary*, iv. 49–50. The following account is based on the libretto printed in Crowne, *Dramatic Works*, i. 241–324 (although the work as performed might not have conformed to it exactly), and details of sets and costumes in Boswell, *Restoration Court Stage*, 205–25, 303–43.

The new red, blue, and white striped curtain rose first on the prologue. This was the masque proper, celebrating the plenty and glory of an England at peace while war still ravaged Europe. On a stage billowing with radiant clouds like one of Verrio's ceilings, the nymph of the Thames (Moll Davies, one of the King's many incidental mistresses) was disclosed, leaning on an urn, with Somerset House in the background: a tableau which was perhaps suggested by the famous fountain on its Thames frontage depicting the rivers of England,[39] and perhaps also by the site of this royal house on a curve of the river, symbolically linking the opposed vistas of the court and the City, for their reconciliation was the theme of the masque. Peace and Plenty (Mary Knight and Charlotte Butler in silver and gold watered silk, copiously laced and ribboned, bearing as their respective emblems an olive branch and a cornucopia) then enter to reassure the nymph, who has been frightened by the cries and lamentations of Augusta (an old name for the City) and the neighbouring countries still at war which waft from the wings. Then the four quarters of the world enter with their offerings to her: Europe ('thou shalt in all my noblest arts be skill'd') fringed, laced, and beribboned in gold and silver, with a jewelled and spangled Roman helmet; Asia ('my jewels shall adorn no brow but thine') with turban and flashing scimitar, sky-blue vest, and scarlet breeches encrusted with multicoloured glass gems and spangles, and over all a cloak of pink and gold silk; America ('thy lovers in my Gold shall shine') in a cloak made up of 6,000 coloured swan's feathers and scarlet silk hose; and Africa ('thou for thy slaves shalt have these Scorched sons of mine') in black satin, trimmed with gold and scarlet, black silk hose, a black wig, and a black and gold cap topped with feathers. All the labour, truck, hazard, and brutal traffic which made up England's trade with its plantations and colonies, and which Evelyn had seen laid out in all its naked reality at the Council table week after week, was thus rendered in one shimmering, seductive, slightly absurd tableau of ease, love, art, and adornment.

But Augusta, amid all these riches, continues to lament, and in response the nymph of the river sings the one show-stopping song of the performance, 'set extreme pleasantly for a treble voice', giving the court's view of the perennially discontented City, 'though none so fair, so rich, so great as she':

> Augusta is inclin'd to fears.
> Be she full or be she waining,
> Still Augusta is complaining:
> Give her all you can to ease her,
> You shall never, never please her.

---

[39] Boswell, *Restoration Court Stage*, 208; Strong, *Renaissance Garden*, 87–90.

The Genius of England enters and is reassuring: 'Europe only should lament . . . this sweet isle no monster can invade'; its protectors are two heroes of the King's family who have already come to the aid of Europe and won renown. Representations of the Dukes of York and Monmouth duly appear, the first as a naval hero, in a green silk costume puffed around the bottom 'in the form of a shell', attended by sea-gods and tritons; the second, in a plumed helmet and armour of gold and silver silk, bringing 'beauty, youth and love' along with him. While sea-gods and warriors dance, the cloud scenery is drawn back to reveal the Temple of Fame, a translucent structure of varnished silk, lit from behind by stepped ranks of candles. Figures representing the King and Queen come forward—'Chaste beauty in her aspect shines, | And love in his does smile'—and all do homage to them:

> Pleasure, arts, religion, glory
> Warm'd by his propitious smile,
> Flourish there and bless this isle.

In a restoration of Arcadian bliss, Peace calls up a dance of water-nymphs and rural gods (the latter in ingenious Pan-like costumes of close-fitting pink 'bodies', with breeches and hose of worsted fringe, garnished with bunches of grapes and parchment vine leaves), and tells them to enjoy their loves. Then, with one final cleverly devised entry of carpenters, in laced red waist-coats and grey breeches, the scene is shifted to Arcadian woodland in readiness for the main 'fable'.

'I neede not Inlarge upon the Argument of the Poeme', Evelyn wrote later, 'which you may be sure . . . was exactly Modest, and Suitable to the Persons, who were of the first Rank, and most Illustrious of the Court.'[40] Crowne had not only modified Ovid's original story to remove the rape; he had made further alterations when his first draft was pronounced still too coarse, and more after the first public performances in February, both to improve the quality of the hastily written original and because the girls were still reluctant to perform some of the more explicit scenes. The only version we now have is this much amended one, the result of several processes of 'softening'.[41] Evelyn admittedly was writing in retrospect and in an idealizing mode; Margaret seemed to him in memory 'a Saint in Glory abstracting her[self] from the Stage'.[42] Yet by no conceivable extension of the term could even this much bowdlerized version of the fable be described in words or action as 'exactly Modest'.

[40] *Life*, 54–5.
[41] Crowne, *Dramatic Works*, i. 237–8; BL Add. MS 78307, fo. 60: MB to ME, [bef. 13 Apr. 1675].
[42] *Life*, 54.

The first act opens with Jupiter (Lady Henrietta Wentworth) and Mercury (Sarah Jenyns) searching the groves of Arcadia for two of Diana's nymphs, Calisto and Psecas, with whom they have fallen in love, and talking frankly of Jupiter's indiscriminate sexual appetites:

> We know what pleasure love affords,
> To heavy beasts and mettled birds;
> Here and there at will we fly,
> Each step of nature's perch we try;
> Down to the beast, and up again
> To the more fine delights of man:
> We every sort of pleasure try;
> So much advantage has a deity.

At this point Margaret as Diana makes her entry with her train of nymphs, including Mary and Anne as her adoring favourites Calisto and Nyphe, and Lady Mary Mordaunt as the glowering Psecas.

The classical deity Artemis/Diana had been the archetype of virgin power and militant chastity. She was also '*dea silvarum*', the personification of wildernesses and groves: not their ordered horticultural simulacra, but the numinous, dread-inspiring, unexploited forests of the golden age, the groves 'which had never felt the axe', celebrated in Evelyn's *Sylva*. Ovid's other fable of Diana illustrated the mercilessness with which the goddess preserved her inviolate nature; the hunter Actaeon, having broken in upon her privacy while she was bathing at a grotto in her sacred grove, was transformed into a stag and torn to pieces by his own hounds.[43] The Elizabethans had taken this manifestation of Diana very seriously. In a famous grotto at Nonesuch Palace Actaeon's fate was made into a moral tableau, a warning to curb the sensual passions.[44] But after the Restoration this high seriousness was rapidly deflated. Court women in masquerade or sitting for their portraits would be decked with the emblems of the virgin goddess, in deliberate appropriation or knowing parody of the myth.[45] The only insignia of Diana borne by Margaret Blagge were a bow and a quiver of arrows. Otherwise this virgin huntress roaming the sacred groves of Arcadia was decked out in a very elaborate form of court dress: a habit and petticoat of heavy gold brocade, sewn with bands of gold and silver

[43] Terry Castle, *Civilization and Masquerade* (Stanford, Calif., 1986), 312; Camille Paglia, *Sexual Personae* (Harmondsworth, 1991), 75–81; Robert Pogue Harrison, *Forests: The Shadow of Civilization* (Chicago, 1992), 20–5; JE, *Sylva* (1670), 225.

[44] Strong, *Renaissance Garden*, 68.

[45] See for example the portraits of Nell Gwyn and the Duchesse Mazarin as Diana in Catharine MacLeod and Julia Marciari Alexander (eds.), *Painted Ladies: Women at the Court of Charles II* (2001), 170–1, 176.

lace and draped with yards of the finest 'point d'Espagne' and further ornamented with thousands of pounds worth of diamonds and pearls lent for the
occasion by the Queen's groom of the stole, Lady Suffolk. Topping it all was
an immense, nodding headdress of white and red ostrich plumes.[46]

As Crowne's fable continues, Diana lavishly praises Calisto and Nyphe,
who have renounced the life of royal privilege, 'ease and loves', while Psecas
looks on jealously and says in an aside that there is no point in wasting her
youth practising chastity if others are to get all the credit for it. She resolves
to encourage Mercury's passion for her, and in the process to discredit the
whole band of nymphs by exposing their chastity as a pretence:

> I'll swear we are dissemblers all
> From men we only seem to fly,
> To meet 'em with more privacy.

Meanwhile, abandoning earth and heaven to slide into anarchy, Jupiter also
resolves to devote himself to the pursuit of love. Despairing of overcoming
Calisto's virtue by an overt seduction, he decides to appear to her in the guise
of her goddess. 'The nymph will all Driana does allow', he declares in a couplet intended to raise a snigger in his audience, 'Nay think she liv'd in some
mistake till now'. The act ends with a dance of nymphs and shepherds and the
recommendation to all lovers to abandon groves and forests, which encouraged only solitary self-possession and melancholy meditation, and follow
love; not just with the joyous irresponsibility of the god, but for the preser-
vation of mankind. 'Kind lovers, love on', sing the nymphs and shepherds,

> Lest the world be undone,
> And mankind be lost by degrees
> For if all from their loves
> Should go wander in groves
> There soon should be nothing but trees

---

[46] Boswell, *Restoration Court Stage*, 323–4; *Life*, 54–5. A portrait by Jacob Huysmans in the Tate
Gallery (T901) of a young woman in masquerade costume as Diana has sometimes been identified
as Margaret Blagge (it is reproduced as such in Walkling, 'Masque and Politics', 49) and does have
some facial resemblance to known portraits of her. However the hairstyle indicates a date in the
1660s, and in the Witt Library of the Courtauld Institute of Art there are photographs of two other
versions of this portrait, in which the sitter resembles Queen Catherine (as an added complication
the inscription calls her the Duchess of Monmouth, although she was much younger in the 1660s
than the subject appears to be). The similarity between the headdress assigned to Margaret Blagge
in the *Calisto* costume accounts and that in the Tate portrait is suggestive, but this kind of headdress
was a common 'prop' of court portraits and the subject wears a simple white dress very different
from the elaborate silver and gold costume described in the accounts. I am indebted to Tabitha
Barber of the Tate Gallery for discussion about this painting, which illustrates the difficulties of
Restoration female court portraiture. It seems best to leave it out of any account of Margaret Blagge
and *Calisto*, although it is not impossible that her features were added to an existing portrait-type.

In the second act Jupiter demonstrates his powers of disguise to Mercury, revelling in his cynicism and the power of appearances—'No vice but for a virtue may escape, | If it be acted in a holy shape'—and in his Hobbesian ability to make and unmake moral categories: 'No action is by nature good or ill; | All things derive their natures from my will.' He then appears in the guise of Diana before Calisto as she rests in a grove and confesses to her

> a strange uncommon flame:
> A kindness I both fear and blush to name;
> Nay, one for which no name I ever knew,
> The passion is to me so strange, so new!

The bewildered Calisto frantically fends off the advances of her lovesick 'goddess': 'Stand off, or I shall be infected too'. 'That is the reason why I press so nigh', Jupiter urges,

> To cure me you must be as sick as I . . .
> In this necessity you must submit;
> It will be only one tempestuous fit,
> And we shall both be well—you must, you shall—.

It was not until Calisto threatens to kill herself with one of her own darts that he draws back and instead tries to appeal to her ambition by revealing himself in his true form. But she still adamantly refuses him. At his command she is borne off captive by the winds, a spectacular group of dancers in costumes of silver silk, deeply fringed and with trailing 'longets' of gold and silver and wings of wired gauze.

Crowne might have omitted the rape as such, but his seduction scene was sufficiently prolonged and explicit to recall the lesbian components of some male erotica.[47] What is not clear from the stage directions is how the transformation of Jupiter to Diana and back again was brought about on stage. There could have been no costume changes in so short a time. The obvious solution would have been for Margaret as Diana to come forward to replace Lady Henrietta Wentworth as Jupiter (who perhaps disappeared behind the shutters of boscage or by means of the trapdoor which was newly built for the performance), speak his lines and carry out the attempted rape of Calisto. If so, Margaret's distaste for the role must have been redoubled and only the most determined blindness to what was happening on stage could have persuaded Evelyn that modesty was being preserved.

---

[47] Winn, '*When Beauty Fires the Blood*', 239–40; Lillian Faderman, *Surpassing the Love of Men* (1985), 23–30.

In the third act the jealous Juno enters to lament a wife's subordinate situation and the disreputable, subversive power of mistresses in a society which condoned male promiscuity:

> We with reproaches mistresses defame,
> But we poor wives endure the greatest shame.
> We to their slaves are humble slaves, whilst they
> Command our lords, and rule what we obey.

Meanwhile Psecas, renouncing Diana and chastity altogether, yields to Mercury and together they resolve to combat all 'rebels against nature's laws'. He promises her that Calisto would be disgraced and she herself crowned. When Juno challenges Jupiter, he declares again that to pursue love 'Is greater glory than to reign above'. But Calisto persists in maintaining her chastity as superior to all:

> All kinds of love to me are so impure
> I hate the marriage bed, which you endure
> Nor would exchange my virtue for [th]y power
> A virgin is a Queen's superior.

Even when Jupiter finally acknowledges her autonomy and departs for heaven with Juno, Calisto is still left distraught and contaminated:

> For I am enough dishonour'd, and asham'd
> To breathe, but in the air where love is nam'd.
> But be disgrac'd with an attempt so foul
> I hate this place, the world, the gods, my soul.

In Ovid's version, depicted in the grottos of Pratolino and Moor Park, Calisto conceives Jupiter's child and Diana's other nymphs, in a dramatic and explicit scene, discover her condition when they all undress to bathe. In Crowne's version Psecas brings about this denouement in Act 4 by denouncing Calisto and Nyphe falsely to Diana, but when the goddess confronts them, they show how staunchly they have defended their virtue by assuming that she is Jupiter returned in disguise and attacking her with their darts. In the last act Psecas's falsity is revealed, and in a spectacular finale Calisto and Nyphe are paraded under a canopy made of yards of multicoloured avinion, gauze, and tinsel ribbon. The scenery is then rolled back to discover 'an open heaven' with gods and goddesses enthroned amidst massed clouds, against the backdrop of a 'glory', a screen with taffeta stretched across it and backlit like the Temple of Fame. Jupiter descends, retracts his design to transform Calisto and Nyphe into stars, and leaves them on earth so that they can experience the pleasures of human love before ascending to heaven:

With each of you I can oblige a throne . . .
On that design you here shall still remain.

And with this the curtain was finally brought down.

   The difficulty Charles II and his circle faced in recreating the glory of the early Stuart masques and rivalling the state theatre of Louis XIV was that in the last resort they could not command the taste or the talent to do so. For all its huge expense the project was sleazy and makeshift from the first. With no one capable of recreating the elaborate stage machinery of the earlier court theatre, the spectacle depended entirely on the costumes and scenery. On these the greatest expense was made, and it was generally agreed that they, and the dancing, were effective. But none of the other elements matched them. Apart from one or two catchy tunes, the music by Staggins was thin textured and short-winded, some of it scarcely adequate for public perform-ance.[48] The want of Dryden's talent was very evident. Crowne admitted that to execute the work in time he had kept the verse 'flat and brisk', simply a vehicle for moving along the story, and this was only too obvious to his hearers. He was also inexperienced in coordinating the disparate elements of the play and the last act in particular was so inordinately long that it must have been a serious ordeal to the spectators; the first public performance did not finish till one o'clock in the morning.[49] The involvement of the royal chil-dren kept public criticism muted, but the lukewarm or privately disparaging comments of those who knew what such entertainments could be at their best spoke volumes. Mary Evelyn was being kinder than most when she commented to Bohun that while the staging was 'extraordinary of the kind', it far exceeded 'the Poets industrie or geneous'.[50]

   Crowne's masque had done little to fulfil its original purpose of glorifying the monarchy and aristocratic society. The unruly, cynical, promiscuous Jupiter bore what appeared to be a quite intentional resemblance to the King. Calisto's only reward for her heroic chastity was an earthly crown in a world which had lost all sense of 'removed mysteries' and was concerned only with the pursuit of 'ease and loves'. Mary Evelyn for one was not surprised by this; she had already remarked that the tough-minded, disillusioned mode of the Restoration theatre was utterly inhospitable to the idealizing and illusion of an earlier generation. The tinsel and painted scenery of the masque were now

---

   [48] Holman, *Four and Twenty Fiddlers*, 371.
   [49] Crowne, *Dramatic Works*, i. 237; Boswell, *Restoration Court Stage*, 189; BL Add. 40860, fo. 84: Anglesey's diary, 16 Feb. 1675.
   [50] BL Add. MS 78539: ME to Ralph Bohun, 24 Feb. 1675; *Life*, 54–5, for Evelyn's claim that the play was modest, '*however defective in other particulars*' (my italics); Walkling, 'Masque and Politics', 56, n. 29.

seen for what they were, effective props by candlelight, but shabby and artificial in the light of day, retaining no aura of the mysteries they had once represented. But she was still prepared to relish the new drama as amusing and perceptive, and 'the more the Originalls being Extant';[51] and Crowne had certainly dramatized with some acuteness the situation of young women players, who all had to choose between the chastity which was still the chief virtue publicly required of them and 'nature's law' of sexual attraction, in a courtly society which had lost faith in the marriage bond and was ready to believe all virtue merely an untrustworthy appearance. Within a few years Lady Sussex would become Ralph Montagu's mistress in Paris; Lady Mary Mordaunt would be first married to, then separated from, and finally divorced amid much public scandal by Arundel's great-grandson; and Lady Henrietta Wentworth would become Monmouth's last mistress, both of them convinced that their relationship was more genuine in the eyes of God than his long-standing marriage.[52] While the rehearsals were still in progress Lady Derby and Lady Pembroke were discovering that they had acquired great titles at the cost of being tied to brutal and drunken husbands, and as soon as the last performance was over Katherine Fitzgerald appealed to the church courts to have her child marriage dissolved so that she could choose her own lover.[53] Sarah Jenyns was the only one who fared well in marriage. Her performance as the handsome youth Mercury, 'sparkling in glory brighter than the day', dazzled many, including the 9-year-old Lady Anne and a young army officer, Colonel John Churchill, newly returned from service in France in the company of her brother-in-law George Hamilton. Their courtship, begun at this time, was to become the most famous and successful love match of their generation; but at this early stage Churchill was still chiefly notable for his love affair with Lady Sussex's mother, and before he could be free to marry he had to extricate himself from a match his parents were arranging for him with an heiress who was already marked out as 'none of the most virtuous' before she was out of her teens.[54]

Mary Evelyn was mildly, though not unkindly amused to see 'Mrs Blagge's severity' constrained to make one of this company,[55] but for Margaret herself

---

[51] BL Add. MS 78539: ME to Bohun, 23 June 1668; cf. Jeremy Taylor, *The Whole Works* (1847), ix. 313; Charlotte Fell Smith, *Mary Rich, Countess of Warwick* (1901), 337.

[52] Andrew Browning, *Thomas Osborne, Earl of Danby* (Glasgow, 1951), i. 286–7; JE, *Diary*, iv. 112; v. 393–4; Cokayne, *Complete Peerage*, under Norfolk; Fea, *Loyal Wentworths*, 128–33, 255.

[53] Cokayne, *Complete Peerage*, under Derby and Pembroke; Mackenzie, *Dromana*, 124–31; BL Add. MSS 40860, fos. 85–6, and 18730, fo. 8ᵛ: Anglesey's diary, 25, 27 Mar, 14 Apr. 1675, 24 Mar. 1676.

[54] Frances Harris, *A Passion for Government: The Life of Sarah, Duchess of Marlborough* (Oxford, 1991), 17–23; JE, *Diary*, iv. 13.

[55] BL Add. MS 78539: ME to Bohun, 24 Feb. 1675.

the experience was deeply humiliating. As soon as the last performance was over she slipped away 'like a Spirit' to Berkeley House, not staying to share in the supper prepared for the players. There Evelyn saw her fall on her knees at her oratory, thanking God that she was delivered from her ordeal. Her prolonged public exposure and the jests about her withdrawal from court with the intention of marrying and 'living now so long neere it, without proceeding any-farther' made it a turning point.[56] One purpose had at least been served. Between the first public performance in February and the second in April, she at last received out of secret service funds a payment of £600 in settlement of half of her portion as maid of honour, and the other half must have followed shortly after.[57] There was no longer any need for her to linger on at the margins of the court; she was free to choose her own future.

It was clear in any case that she could no longer continue as she was. Just before the last performance of the masque Lord Berkeley was named ambassador to Nijmegen.[58] It would be a prolonged appointment; his wife and family would go with him and his houses would be shut up. Unless Margaret was prepared to leave England she must find a refuge elsewhere. Godolphin, Lady Berkeley, and Evelyn, by their several means, had managed to dissuade her from her Hereford plan twice before. This time she had much more reason to be in earnest. Godolphin might still have no married home prepared, but if he wanted to keep her from going out of his reach they must marry without further delay. The masque, with its atmosphere of heightened sexuality and coupling, its message that chastity might be powerful but was also life-denying, probably played its part in overcoming the last scruples and hesitations on both sides.

The scrupulous would still avoid marrying in Lent, but on Ascension Day, 16 May 1675, the clerk of the Temple Church made an entry in his register: 'Mr Lake married a Cupple . . . their names I doe not knowe.' Later he inserted the names on a separate slip: 'Sidney Godolphin Esq. one of the Grooms of the Bedchamber to his Majesty' and 'Mrs Margarett Blague one of the Maids of Honour to the Queen'.[59] Margaret's 'torment of suspense' was over; God had disposed of her in marriage and after the ceremony they sealed their vows by taking communion together. The clergyman, Edward

---

[56] *Life*, 55–6.

[57] BL Add. MS 28080, fo. 14: secret service accounts, 23 Mar. 1675 (I am grateful to Andrew Walkling for this reference). Dorset RO, Ilchester MSS, Box 267: account book of Sir Stephen Fox, for 1660–75, p.9, records an investment of £1,200 for Margaret Blagge in 1675.

[58] [Thibaudeau (ed.),] *Bulstrode Papers*, 279.

[59] Sir Tresham Lever, *Godolphin* (1952), 289; for the allowed periods for marriage in the church calendar, see David Cressy, *Birth, Marriage & Death: Ritual, Religion and the Life Cycle in Tudor and Stuart England* (Oxford, 1997), 298–9, 305.

Lake, was a west country man and a friend of both of them; once attached to the household of Godolphin's patron the Earl of Bath and now chaplain to Mary and Anne at St James's. Yet outwardly there was no change at all in Margaret's circumstances. The Temple Church was chosen not just because it was well away from the court, but because it was a freehold belonging to the lawyers (Godolphin's brothers Francis and Charles amongst them) and 'a royal peculiar', not a parish church, and so the bans did not have to be read. The ceremony was as unobtrusive as possible; Lady Berkeley and Margaret's maid Beck were the only witnesses and as the clerk's note indicated, the little party did not even make themselves known beforehand to the church officials.[60] Godolphin said nothing to his brothers and sisters and Margaret was expected to observe the same secrecy. Evelyn, who had returned to Sayes Court the day before, knew nothing of it. When the ceremony was over Margaret returned to Berkeley House and Godolphin to his Whitehall lodgings and his attendance on the King.

There was only one hint of what had happened. Two days later Evelyn and his wife were summoned from Deptford to a collation, at which they found Margaret, her sister Lady Yarburgh (in London with her husband for the meeting of Parliament), Mrs Howard, Lady Berkeley, and other friends. But if his intermittent suspicions were revived at the time, as they were in retrospect, by this gathering he chose to say nothing, 'assuredly knowing, (and as afterwards I learn'd) that this nicenesse could not possibly proceede from her-selfe; but from some other Prevalent Obligation; and I ever esteem'd it an Impertinence to be over-Curious, where I found there was a designe of Concealment'.[61] Afterwards, in halcyon weather, Margaret came to spend a week with the Evelyns at Sayes Court. Mindful of her changed status, she was careful as she walked in the garden with the diffident Mrs Evelyn to represent herself simply as a family friend and in no way a rival to her long companionate marriage; and she took special pains with the ailing and plaintive Sir Richard Browne, sitting with him and entertaining him for hours.[62] Mary Evelyn, who liked the girl and respected her piety, met these overtures readily, even making allowance for the clumsiness and insensitivity with which her husband encouraged them. 'I believe she is sincerely yours', he wrote to her after Margaret had gone,

and being so, you have the greatest jewell in the world, and at my heart I am glad you love her, for indeed she will make you love God, and our blessed Saviour above all things in this world, and so more and more indeare you to me . . . she is now yours

[60] David Lewer and Robert Dark, *The Temple Church* (1997), 62; *Life*, 57.
[61] JE, *Diary*, iv. 63–4; *Life*, 59.   [62] *Life*, 100.

in spirit and the bond of friendship as she is mine, and how can I be happier? for if (as you pronounce) there were never two more alike in our way, and inclination, it is not possible you should long converse together, but you must contract something of that which in her resembles me, and so of necessity I must love you more, since resemblance is the motive of all affection; Be but like her, and you are perfect, make her like you and she will be so; you both want something of each other, and I of you both, and I hope in God we shall all be the better for one another, and that this three-fold cord shall never be broken.[63]

Margaret for her part asked Evelyn why he should want a friend when he had so good a wife, and told him prudently that from now on her letters would be intended for them both, 'sense you are all one and I to you both a true frind and humble servant'.[64] Godolphin had come to visit her at Sayes Court, but still nothing whatever was said of the marriage. Instead Margaret broke the startling news to the Evelyns that she was shortly to go abroad with the Berkeleys, not to Nijmegen but to Paris, for Lord Berkeley's appointment had been altered at the last moment on the death of the ambassador in post. In fact this did more than anything else to disperse Evelyn's suspicion that she was already married, and despite the prospect of indefinite separation he was almost inclined to welcome the news; it would at least mean that there would be no impulsive flight to Hereford in the foreseeable future.[65]

Secret marriages, sometimes not disclosed for months afterwards, were not at all uncommon at this time. Of the *Calisto* players, Carey Frazier and Sarah Jenyns had the same start to their married lives as Margaret. A common practical reason, when parental disapproval was not a factor, was simply that the couple had nowhere to set up house together and receive the formal visits which would follow the public announcement of a marriage. Godolphin's Whitehall lodgings would need major alteration before they could be fit for a married household and he had made no attempt to do this in advance, possibly because he still regarded their future at court as uncertain. He had originally been talked of for Berkeley's post in Paris and might have hoped that this would allow him to announce his marriage and take Margaret with him in a proper style.[66] His other choice was to join his brothers and sisters in Cornwall, where they had all gathered for the summer. Having never shown much attachment to his family home, he probably had no thought of settling there; the journey to and from London could take days if not weeks, the erratic posts were an exasperation, and the tin miners who made up much of the population unnerving to live among, 'a mad people without fear of God

[63] BL Add. MS 78431: JE to ME, 7 July 1675.
[64] BL Add. MS 78307, fo. 72: MB to JE: [*c.* July 1675].
[65] *Life*, 59.   [66] [Thibaudeau (ed.),] *Bulstrode Papers*, 301.

or the world', who would plunder any ship which was wrecked on the coast and strip the survivors unless Sir William and the neighbouring gentry could turn out in time to prevent them.[67] But Margaret would at least have her wish of seeing the place and they might spend their honeymoon there while he explored the possibility of some post which would not tie him so closely to the court. Neither of these plans came to fruition. Godolphin was objected to by the French as too 'little a man' and too hostile to their interests to be a suitable ambassador,[68] and he would only contemplate the journey to Cornwall if there was to be no meeting of Parliament in the winter. But by the end of August the court was preparing to move itself from Windsor to Whitehall and it was certain that Parliament would meet. Everybody, Godolphin wrote to his brother, was 'putting on their busy face'; 'this news I suppose may hasten your coming hither, as well as hinder my coming to you which I did certainly intend'.[69]

Evelyn conjectured afterwards that since the couple had nowhere to live together, they thought it best, out of 'a singular and extreame nicenesse', to keep entirely apart and that Margaret's journey to Paris was their solution to this problem.[70] In fact there was really no reason why Godolphin could not have taken married lodgings of some kind in London if there had been nothing else to take account of. The deciding factor, as before, seems to have been Lady Berkeley, who was not yet ready to part with Margaret, married or not. It was her first visit to Paris, while Margaret had lived there as a child, was fluent in the language, and would be an ideal companion. She was not accustomed to being gainsaid, as Margaret and Evelyn had already discovered, and the young couple were in her debt for accommodating Margaret for so long. Godolphin ('what says my Lady Berkeley?') was always concerned to please her, and now that Margaret was married she had no choice but to comply with both of them. She was finding herself even more tied to the Berkeleys after marriage than before.

But she was deeply unhappy at having to go and made no attempt to conceal this from the Evelyns, though she could not explain the main reason for it in so many words: 'you will say why doe you go: why only becaus I thinke it is fit for me to doe it, and for no other reason'. For a brief time she had thought herself happy in her marriage, but now she began to see it as yet another unsatisfactory aspect of the human condition; that she of all people

[57] H. R. Coulthard, *The Story of the Ancient Parish of Breage* (Camborne, 1913), 72–3, 79; James Whetter, *Cornwall in the 17th Century* (Padstow, 1974), 59–81.

[68] [Thibaudeau (ed.),] *Bulstrode Papers*, 301.

[69] BL Add. MS 28052, fo. 73: SG to Sir William Godolphin, 4 Sept. [1675].

[70] *Life*, 60, 63.

could not be content, 'who realy am soe much at my ease, who can if I can not live without croses, who have no children servants master father mouther'—her careful omission of a husband from this list was perhaps intended as a clue for them to pick up—'things that though they are blesings yet often they prove otherwais and the best of them have days in which one thinkes one could live without them: but yet I am not hapey absolutly nor never shall [be] I find in this life'.[71] In this first experience of the constraints of marriage she turned to Mary Evelyn especially, with her long and patient experience of a wife's subordinate role. Evelyn told his wife that Margaret wanted to visit again before her departure, 'that she may (as she says) kisse & weepe over you: for she is inwardly extreamely sad'. She was not being entirely disingenuous when she told them that they were the only ones in whom she could really confide.[72]

Then at the end of October, on the very eve of his departure, Berkeley suddenly collapsed as he was coming out of the council chamber into the gallery at Whitehall. He was nearly 70 and it was assumed that this reminder of mortality would make him put all thoughts of the embassy aside. Yet within the fortnight he was insisting that he was as ready as ever to set out, though, Evelyn says, 'in most mens opinions not so perfectly restor'd to his other Intellectuals & abillitys' as he claimed, and with the prospect that he might at any time have a second and fatal seizure. It made his wife cling even more vehemently to Margaret, who felt that it was now quite impossible to deny her; she 'tells me, I breake her heart, if I forsake her', she told Evelyn, 'and you see what Condition her Lord is; and (poore Woman) what would become of her, if he should die, and she have never a friend by her?'[73]

By this time Evelyn had another and entirely self-interested reason for not being sorry for Margaret's journey, for it was giving him the opportunity of sending his wayward son abroad under cheap and reliable supervision and with the prestige of being attached to an ambassadorial household. Margaret had promised to see that he kept to his studies, and even offered the use of her maid to wash his linen. 'We shall be infinitely obliged to my dear friend and that family,' Evelyn told his wife, 'I cannot devise how we shall deserve it.'[74] In fact, like Margaret, he soon found himself required to pay a heavy price for accepting any favour from the Berkeleys. During his time in Ireland Berkeley had been badly cheated by the steward he had left to look after his affairs and he now wanted a more reliable substitute. And so Evelyn found himself importuned by Margaret to undertake yet another trusteeship, 'which was to

[71] BL Add. MS 78307, fo. 58: MB to JE, [July 1675].
[72] BL Add. MS 78431: JE to ME, [Oct. 1675].   [73] JE, *Diary*, iv. 77; *Life*, 60–1.
[74] BL Add. MSS 78307, fos. 58–9: MB to JE, [July 1675]; 78431: JE to ME, 7 July 1675.

receive his Rents, looke after his Houses & Tennants, solicite for Supplies from the Lord Tressurer &c: [and] Correspond weekely with him'; in effect to be an almost full-time but unpaid factotum. To Berkeley's face he claimed to embrace the role as an honour which needed no reward, but privately he grumbled that it was 'more than enough to employ any drudge in England: but what will not friendship & love make one do!'[75]

On 10 November Evelyn and his son set out from Deptford to join Berkeley's great train of coaches, wagons, and horses as it passed through New Cross, and kept it company as it crawled in slow stages, 'my Lord but valetudinarie yet', to Dartford, Sittingborne, and Canterbury. There Evelyn and Margaret went to prayers in the Cathedral and afterwards walked together in the precincts. Margaret continued to insist that it was only for Lady Berkeley's sake that she was going, and 'if ever I Returne againe, and do not Marry; I will still Retire; & End my Dayes among you'. It was the only time, Evelyn said later, 'that in her whole life, she ever prevaricated with me'. At Dover that evening she gave him her power of attorney, of doubtful legal validity now, since it was signed 'Margarit Blagge'. The next morning, Sunday and a 'glorious day', Evelyn received his last instructions from Berkeley and took his seal, keys, letters of attorney, and will into his custody. Margaret was now in floods of tears, distressing and mystifying him to the point of exasperation at what he could only interpret as a perverse insistence on indefinitely prolonging the torment to herself and her lover:

I believe there is one you realy love, and that 'tis mutual: How is it then you thus go from him & he from You? This is a strange Proceeding, 'tis Spiritual! 'tis high! 'tis Mysterious & Singular; but find it a name if you can, for I Confesse, I understand it not: Nothing is in Nature so repugnant as Love, and Absence, when nothing forbids the Object to be present . . . Since I know of no Ingagement you have to go from your Friends, and those whom you professe to Love: Go back, Go back then and be happy both; or this Course, will weare ye both out; if realy you love him . . .

Unable to explain that this was no spiritual refinement, that she was a married woman and had no choice, Margaret only sobbed, 'For goodness Sake, do not break my breake my heart . . . You see I am ingag'd.' From the beach the coaches carried the party a little way into the sea, from where they clambered into small boats and were rowed out to the royal yacht which waited for them. Its captain, Christopher Gunman, was the Evelyns' old acquaintance from Greenwich. As the boat hoisted sail it was given a cannon salute from the Castle and answered with its own, 'according to Forme'. Evelyn watched as the white puffs of smoke from the guns dispersed and the boat stood off for the French

---

[75] JE, *Diary*, iv. 77–8.

coast, then turned back to the town to go to church and pray for its safe crossing. His agent there for the sick and wounded seamen put him up for the night,
and next day by way of Canterbury and Rochester he returned home.[76]

Godolphin had not come to Dover to say goodbye, Evelyn said afterwards,
because he was of the same 'relenting nature' as Margaret, 'and durst not trust
his Passion'.[77] But back in London Lady Sunderland berated him about
the separation, and with a great deal more justification than Evelyn had
for blaming Margaret. Apparently with no thought that he might have acted
differently, he simply offered his acceptance of these reproofs to Margaret as
evidence of his devotion: 'she does nothing but chide me all day long about
you, and indeed I love her for it with all my heart, I hope my deare that is a
signe I deserve it but little'. He assured her that he thought of her perpetually, that he had no pleasure except in corresponding with her, and that
he gambled very little now that Berkeley was gone, 'scarce ever at all but at
tennis'. But he seemed curiously light-hearted in accepting the uncertainty
about when they would see each other again, even sending her a 'foolish
song' of his own composing on the subject; 'I beleive you will laugh at me for
my pains', he added, 'but I send you this my deare not as anything worthy of
you but only as a mark of my own unquietnesse':

> How cruell is absence to hearts that are joyn'd
> & with truest love to each other inclind
> how they sigh & complain that the object they lov'd
> is from their fond eyes such a distance remov'd
> yett were the time fix'd though it did long appear
> twere a pleasure to think it drew daily more near
> but alas how it adds unto true lovers pain
> to bee so uncertain of meeting again
> your image my fairest is still in my thoughts
> each houre, each moment to my fancy tis brought
> by some thing that either I doe or I see
> nor has darknesse the power to hide you from me
> for when nights sable curtains are over me drawn
> your Idea still opens them ere the light dawn
> & if by chance sleep does my sences surprize
> even then tis more welcome than rest to my eys

The only sign of real uneasiness he showed was when she commented favourably on the religious communities in France: 'pray, my dear, remember what
you said to me on that subject, or rather what I said to you'.[78]

---

[76] *Life*, 61–3; BL Add. MS 78307, fos. 73–4: power of attorney, 31 Aug. 1675; JE, *Diary*, iv. 79.
[77] *Life*, 61.   [78] BL Hammick Papers: SG to MB, 25 Nov. [1675].

This further period with the Berkeleys was hateful to Margaret from the first. Since she could not declare herself a married woman she had to keep away from the court, 'where the Virtues of Strangers, did not allways protect the Sex from inconveniencys'. More than ever she found she had to be 'perpetually dedicating' herself to other people. When she was not at the shops with Lady Berkeley, 'which I think I live in', there was the social life of the household, made even more burdensome than before by her role as interpreter: the ritual of formal dressing, 'then to pub[lic] prayers: then din[e], then talk: then at three pray publikly again, then talk: god knows till 6 a cloke, then pray for you and som more, then play at cards till bedtim[e], oh pity me'. The only respite came late in the evening, when Jack Evelyn and the household chaplain, Dean Benson's son Samuel, came to her chamber for an hour's congenial company before she went to bed.[79] What made it all worse than Berkeley House or Twickenham was the sense of being cut off from her faith. Lord Berkeley, who had sometimes attended the Roman Catholic chapel at St James's, was now obliged by his position to observe Protestant worship, but his secretary Sir Ellis Leighton was a Catholic sympathizer and Lady Berkeley had acquired a new companion: Frances Hamilton, the elder sister of Sarah Jenyns and a Catholic convert. Margaret's discontent with her situation must have been obvious by this time—her status as a married woman, though it was a secret between her and Lady Berkeley, had subtly altered her sense of dependency—and she soon felt herself supplanted as favoured companion by the more amenable Lady Hamilton. With nothing but 'cold respect' between her and Lady Berkeley, she had to warn Evelyn not to convey any business information in his letters to her, since the family did not want her to know anything of their concerns. She felt thoroughly alienated and disoriented. 'Dear frind,' she wrote to him, 'pray hartily that if it be gods will I may be restored to my own peeple, god and nation: for though god be every wher I can not call upon him as I can at home.'[80]

An added difficulty was the situation of Jack Evelyn. In her homesickness he was a real comfort to her, 'so good and so very even and cheerful in his temper, and maks me laugh when somtims I am ready to cry, for people can have spleen in Paris, let them talk what they will of the aire, that I asuer them well'. But he was still a hopeless sloven in his dress and bearing, a poor rat, as he bitterly called himself, and quite unfit to be an ornament to an ambassadorial household. Margaret ordered him a suit of fashionable clothes and engaged a dancing master to improve his bearing and confidence, but they

---

[79] *Life*, 63–6; BL Add. MS 78307, fos. 75, 81–2: MB to JE, 13 Dec. 1675, 4 Feb. 1676.

[80] BL Add. MSS 78300: ME to JE, 1 Feb. 1676, quoting a letter from their son; 78307, fos. 81, 83–4: MB to JE, 8, 14 Feb. 1676.

made little difference. Berkeley quickly decided that he was not worth troubling with and except at family meals ignored him. Jack, who had been encouraged by his father to hope that he would be introduced to the business of the embassy, was left in his garret room next to the footmen, 'with bare walls, without Table, stool, shelf, tack or candlestick', until in his loneliness and humiliation he chose to move into a *pension* with a transient population of young English travellers.[81] It is not quite clear what the rights of the situation were. Jack chiefly blamed James Fraser, the Berkeley children's Scots tutor and major-domo of the household, who had been recommended to the post by Evelyn. Yet in his letters Fraser praised Jack's virtuous temper and advantageous use of his time and offered him introductions to men of learning and the use of his own collections. The chaplain Benson also reported well of 'his parts, industry and great integrity and honesty', although he did admit that he thought himself slighted by Berkeley and Leighton.[82] What they both seem to have been trying to make clear tactfully to Jack's father was that he was forcing a young man of real ability but no social graces into a public milieu for which he was quite unfit. Berkeley himself was insensitive and preoccupied with his own affairs, but his summing up of Jack was not unkind or unjust: 'he will never dance, nor make a legg well, nor have his perriwig or cravate in good order, or be a la mode, but he will be an honest sollid and judicious man, and be very good company'.[83]

His father's contacts in Paris were long outdated or otherwise unsuitable. When he recommended Jack to engage the mathematics master who had once taught his mother, Jack conscientiously tracked down the old man and found that he could teach him nothing he did not already know. He was given an introduction to the savant Henri Justel, 'but his house is always frequented by graver people then my knowledge & experience can fit me to keep company with'. He did not dare to open his mouth, which only served to depress his confidence further.[84] Margaret could do little to improve his standing in the household, because her own relations with the family had grown so cool. Although she tried to cheer him by keeping him company in his studies, she was quite unequal to tutoring a young man who was already far more advanced than herself. But to Jack she was simply the one being who lightened a dark time. On New Year's Day he left a poignant set of verses in her pillow:

[81] BL Add. MSS 78307, fos. 75–6: MB to JE, 13 Dec. 1675; 78300: ME to JE, [Feb. 1676]; 78301: JE jun. to his father, 10 Dec. 1675, 27 Mar. 1676.
[82] BL Add. MS 78317: Benson and Fraser to JE, 4/14, 5/15 Feb. 1676.
[83] BL Add. MS 78308: Berkeley to JE, 27 May 1676.
[84] BL Add. MS 78301: JE jun. to his father, 15 Feb. 1676.

As this day is bright and clear
Which begins the infant year
May you to me than light more dear
Ever fair and young appear . . .
May fresh happinesse attend
On every minute that you spend
May all your wishes have their end
May you never want a friend.[85]

If it were not for her, he told his father, 'I should dye with melancholy in a little time . . . I am become most desperately her humble servant. That man is too happy who is to be master of such a treasure.' His parents might well feel that the greatest danger was of his adding to his unhappiness by falling seriously in love with her, but his mother assured Margaret that they both had complete faith in her as far as Jack was concerned; they were not afraid of her charming him and confident that he had a 'perfect respect' for her.[86]

Evelyn put the best face on his son's situation that he could: ''tis sufficient he has the honor of being in a family the very Genius of which is enough to finish him with great Improvements'; but Mrs Evelyn told him that he was being too obsequious; 'my Lord should not be faithfully served and complemented by you for slighting your sonne'.[87] In fact Berkeley was treating Evelyn himself with little enough courtesy, complaining if his letters did not come regularly or he failed to send the gazettes, and employing him like a servant to send over 'half a dozen bamboo canes' and the spectacles he had left behind.[88] Years later Evelyn could still resentfully enumerate 'my Journeys to his Tenants, Accompts with his Baillife & receivers; Clamors of Workemen and Mechanics for their Arreres & Bills: Reckoning with servants, Inspection of his Houses, gardens &c to the very Scavengers of the streets', accounts of which were as rigorously exacted from him 'as if I had ben his Factor, nay his Bailyf at Twickenham, so . . . That in my Life I never went through greater toile'.[89] But by far his most formidable task was to dun the Lord Treasurer for the payment of Berkeley's 'extraordinaries', a matter which, to Danby's disgust, filled the ambassador's dispatches as well. In fact he made no attempt to conceal his contempt for Berkeley, saying publicly that the King might as well save the whole cost of maintaining him at Paris, since he did not discharge even the basic duty of regular correspondence

[85] BL Add. MS 78456: verse commonplace book of JE jun.
[86] BL Add. MSS 78301: JE jun. to his father, 25 Mar. 1676; 78437: ME to MG, [Jan. 1676].
[87] BL Add. MS 78300: ME to JE, 31 Jan. 1676.
[88] BL Add. MS 78301: JE jun. to his father, 10 Dec. 1675.
[89] BL Add. MS 78299: JE to Lady Sylvius, 4 Nov. 1688.

adequately.[90] The Lord Treasurer always respected Evelyn in his own areas of expertise, consulting him as Arlington had about his library and garden,[91] but in this matter he shrewdly realized that Evelyn was allowing himself to be exploited. When he attended the Treasury to relay yet more importunate demands, Danby asked him contemptuously if he were my Lord Berkeley's steward.[92]

What Danby could not know is why Evelyn let himself be put in this position; 'what will not friendship & love make one do!' In his letters to Lady Berkeley he was still light-heartedly sending 'a little of my love to St Marguerite', as if she were the adolescent protégée of the early days at Berkeley House;[93] but his letters to Margaret herself were shot through more than ever with the anxiety of a lover who doubts whether his devotion is returned. He had understood her, mistakenly as she afterwards protested, to say at parting that once a month was sufficient for him to write. He worried that his letters were too frequent, too long, not religious enough, and 'if my wishes to see you, my delight to heare from you, my continual thoughts of prayers for you be symptoms of love, I cannot helpe it'. Every Tuesday he renewed their 'Sacrament of perpetual Friendship' by saying the office of the communion of saints, and welcomed 'the return of that day, as if it were the lords'. For he was still struggling to transform his love for her into a sense of saving grace and to remind himself that God and not Margaret herself should be its object: 'I protest you are the joy of my heart, and I have thoughts above this world as I consider your glorious progresse . . . Go on excellent creature in the holy path and lead me after you'; though so much younger, she was 'nearer home & to that repose by much than I . . . quicken me then that I may mend my pace, or rather O Lord do thou quicken me'. He was tormented with the thought that they might not see each other again, and if they did, 'I am still in danger of losing you againe: therefore ah, how I often think to be where we may meete and here part for ever, & clasp you in the boosom of our lord'.[94]

Like Godolphin he was disturbed by her approving comments about the religious orders and, perhaps with her cousins the Warners in mind, cautioned her against taking any extreme step. 'What doe you mean by doeing extrodinary [sic] things', she replied rather waspishly, 'I could content my self with any thing I thinke now so I were at home again.'[95] With Lady

[90] PRO SP 78/141: Berkeley's dispatches, 1, 5 Feb. 10 Apr. 1676; Longleat, Coventry MSS 33 (BL M.863/24): Sir Ellis Leighton to Henry Frederick Thynne, 6 Apr. 1676.

[91] JE, *Diary*, iv. 126,130–1.					[92] BL Add. MS 78299: JE to Lady Sylvius, 4 Nov. 1688.

[93] BL Add. MS 78298: JE to Lady Berkeley, 13 Apr. '1675' [1676].

[94] BL Add. MS 78307, fo. 84ᵛ: draft by JE on the back of MB's letter of 14 Feb. 1676.

[95] Ibid., fo. 81ᵛ: MB to JE, 8 Feb. 1676.

Hamilton taking her place as interpreter and companion, the main reason for her presence in Paris was at an end, but she could not travel back unescorted. It was not until March that the Earl of Bath's brother passed through Paris on his return from a diplomatic mission to the Duke of Savoy, and Margaret, 'with a world of fine petticotes' in her baggage, could attach herself to his train.[96] Still giving no hint of being married, she asked Evelyn and Lady Sunderland in advance to have her bed transferred from Berkeley House to the lodgings of her cousins Dr Edward Warner and his wife in James Street Covent Garden.[97] She landed at Dover on 3 April and Evelyn saw her again for the first time at Lady Sunderland's. Ten days later they both came with the Howard sisters to dine at Sayes Court.[98] ❧

[96] *Life*, 66; BL Add. 78440: JE jun. to ME jun., 16 Apr. 1676.
[97] *Life*, 66, 267–8; BL Add. MSS 15889, fo. 13: Lady Sunderland to JE, 1 Apr. 1676; 19154, fos. 212ᵛ–213, genealogical table of the Warner family.
[98] JE, *Diary*, iv. 88.

9

Godly Housekeeping

MARGARET continued to live with the Warners as a single woman for several more weeks. Even to Godolphin's sisters she still only hinted at being married. Writing to her sister Frances in Cornwall of a round of visits she had just made with 'Mrs Blagge', Jael Boscawen added that Margaret had told her something in the course of it 'that has increased our familiarity, but you are not to make much reply to this nor imagine by it, a marriage, for I don't think tis soe yet, & these are ill times to set up with upon their foundation'.[1] There was more to this than the congenital caution of the family in such matters. Outwardly the fifteen-month prorogation of Parliament which began in November 1675 seemed a period of profound political tranquility, but Danby knew that he had covert opponents to deal with. 'I always thought the Court of no good complexion towards your Lordship', his brother-in-law warned him, 'and that if such small things as Bab May, Chiffinch, Godolphin and others had had influence enough with their master to have removed you, it had been long since effected.'[2] In the interval between parliamentary sessions he set about clearing the ground of potential rivals with a will. Sir Stephen Fox was dismissed as paymaster in January, not for any malpractice but because his monopoly of government undertakings with the City merchants made him too powerful for the Lord Treasurer's peace of mind. Margaret wrote anxiously from Paris about the investments Evelyn had made with Fox on her behalf, 'the little stock I have in his hands being of so great moment to me in this orphan condition and independent as I am from Whitehall'.[3] In

---

[1] BL Add. MS 28052, fo. 73: Jael Boscawen to Frances Godolphin, 25 Apr. 1676.
[2] HMC *Lindsey MSS*, 376–7: Earl of Lindsey to Danby, 25 Aug. 1675.
[3] Christopher Clay, *Public Finance and Private Wealth: The Career of Sir Stephen Fox* (Oxford, 1978), 102–5; BL Add. 78308: postscript by MG (copied in JE's hand) to a letter from Lady Berkeley, [Jan. 1676].

April the Chancellor of the Exchequer Sir John Duncombe followed Fox into the wilderness, another loss to feel personally, since he shared the same network of Suffolk cousins as the Godolphins and the Blagges. Even in the harmless post of Lord Chamberlain Arlington was still regarded as a rival. Talk of the King's spending a single night at Euston was enough to make Danby uneasy, and other names were named, on no better grounds than that 'my Lord Treasurer, who is here look'd upon as omnipotent, does not mightily like any of them'; and this time Godolphin's was amongst them. 'You heare poor Sir John Duncome is out of his place', Jael Boscawen continued to her sister, 'my Lord of Ormonde, My Lord Chamberlain, Mr Secretary Coventry, Mr May & my brother Sid said to follow him speedily.'[4] To be thought worthy of Danby's hostility in this company was another indication that Godolphin was ceasing to be one of the 'small things' of the court. He was spared dismissal, but Danby did block his path in other directions. His cousin Sir William, the ambassador at Madrid, also held the Exchequer office of Auditor of Wales, which he performed by means of a deputy. When he petitioned the King to be allowed to surrender it to his cousin Sidney, who proposed to qualify himself to execute it in person, the request was summarily refused as being 'contrary to His Majesty's rules made by my Lord Treasurer's advice'.[5]

Margaret did share the secret of her marriage with her own sisters, however, and at the end of the month one of them, probably Lady Yarburgh, finally broke the news to Evelyn. Whether she blurted it out by accident or was asked to do so to spare Margaret the awkward moment of revelation is not clear. In its usual reticent style his diary only says of this bombshell: 'Din'd with [pentacle]; discovered her Marriage by her sister.'[6] It must have been clear to him at once that the marriage, however secret, had had witnesses and that he was not one of those trusted, even though Margaret had once assured him that she would ask him to take a father's role and give her away. He was told the full truth, that the marriage had taken place a year before and not after Margaret's return from Paris, as was generally assumed. He remembered the scene at Dover at which he now saw she had deliberately misled him. He says only that he took the concealment 'a little to heart'; in reality he must have been deeply hurt and disappointed in her. But her guilt and distress were plain; she protested that 'she had ben so afflicted in her selfe for it; that, were

[4] Andrew Browning, *Thomas Osborne, Earl of Danby* (Glasgow, 1951), ii. 37: Danby to his wife, 8 Apr. 1676; Harry Ransom Humanities Research Center, University of Texas: newsletter to Bulstrode, 1 May 1676; BL Add. MS 28052, fo. 73: Jael Boscawen to Frances Godolphin, 25 Apr. 1676.

[5] *CSP Domestic 1676–77*, 534; *CTB 1676–79*, 85.   [6] JE, *Diary*, iv. 89.

it to do againe, no Consideration in the world, should have prevaild on her to breake her Promise, as some had don, to her regrett'. 'Some', it was clear, resolved itself into Godolphin, presumably supported by Lady Berkeley. Evelyn, who strongly believed in a husband's authority, therefore put aside his hurt feelings and sensibly accepted that her silence had been excusable, especially considering the 'singular temper & gravity' of the husband, with whom after all he had no friendship which would justify his being let into so intimate a secret. Less than a week afterwards he was visiting and praying with her as before.[7]

But it was a sharp reminder that Margaret was no longer at her own disposal and this only made it more urgent for him to establish how the friendship was to be continued once she began to live as a married woman. With little property of his own for a marriage settlement, Godolphin left his wife's fortune in her own hands and so she would at least still need a trustee. Burdened as he continued to be with tasks for the Berkeleys, Evelyn undertook this role willingly, negotiating an extension of the crown lease at Spalding which she had inherited from her mother, securing the money she had in Sir Stephen Fox's hands and arranging to invest £1,000 for her as an interest-bearing loan to the Sunderlands, who were always short of ready money. There were numerous small negotiations and payments on behalf of her sisters as well.[8] But he made sure at the same time that she understood the reciprocal obligation: 'not to think any new Condition, or Circumstance of Life of force to absolve you from the many solemn, & holy protestations you have made of the inviolable Esteeme, which my sincerity & the pious Affection I have constantly borne you, might pretend to merite of you'.[9] Margaret's acknowledgements were rather glib and perfunctory at first; but as the tasks mounted up she became conscience-stricken and a little uneasy: 'I am in amaze at your persisting thus to oblidge me so many ways, I now thinke if I could have foreseen how great a toyl I was like to have proved to you I would never have employd you for tis a stark sham[e] to put you to all this pains, God may reward you but I am certain I never can'.[10]

At the end of June the Godolphins at last announced their marriage publicly, and began to live together as man and wife. There was no further

---

[7] *Life*, 67; JE, *Diary*, iv. 90; the public version was that the marriage had taken place in April or May 1676; see Harry Ransom Humanities Research Center, University of Texas: newsletter to Bulstrode, 14 July 1676.

[8] JE, *Diary*, iv. 93; *Life*, 68, 71; Dorset RO, Ilchester MSS, Box 268: Sir Stephen Fox's ledger 1672–9, fos. 311, 314, 326, 330, 334, interest payments to JE on MG's behalf, Oct. 1675–Nov. 1676; BL Add. MS 78307, fo. 79: MB to JE, [1676].

[9] BL Add. MS 78386: JE, 'Oeconomics to a Newly Married Friend', [1676], p. 1.

[10] BL Add. MS 78307, fo. 87: MB to JE, [May 1676].

talk of Cornwall. Margaret received her visits of congratulation not at the Warners' or Whitehall, but at Berkeley House. Empty apart from Evelyn's visits of inspection and a few servants, it was vulnerable to burglary and so the offer of part of it to the young couple as a temporary home was to everyone's advantage.[11] As long as Evelyn's laborious duties on the Berkeleys' behalf continued, he would never lack legitimate reasons for visiting the Godolphins there.

As she embarked on 'this Adventure and the new-world' of married life, Margaret asked him for guidance on how she should conduct herself. There was a long tradition of advice books concerning the purpose and conduct of the household, from the classics (Aristotle's *Oeconomica* and Xenophon's *Treatise of an Household*), to the humanists (Erasmus' *Matrimonii Institutio Christiani* and Vives's *Instruction of a Christian Woman*), and after the Reformation a succession of examples from the Protestant married clergy, of which William Perkins's *Christian Oeconomie*, Robert Cawdrey's *Godly Form of Household Government*, and William Gouge's *Domesticall Duties* were the best known. Their common basis was the importance of the married state and the private household both politically and spiritually.[12] Evelyn was familiar with them all and fully agreed about the significance of the subject; but was not satisfied that any of them had treated it adequately.[13] He had already produced his own 'Instructions Oeconomique' for his wife on their marriage; but this was no more than a sketch. She had been a child, and he, for all his readiness to instruct her, completely without practical experience as *paterfamilias*. Now Margaret's request gave him the opportunity to make his definitive contribution, not just to the literature on marriage but to the subject which engrossed him even more and which had certainly not been dealt with adequately by clerical writers: the theory of friendship and its relation to the married state. He put aside the cycle of meditations and devoted his nightly labours to this new project. The result was a treatise of nearly a hundred pages, entitled 'Oeconomics to a Newly Married Friend'. Closely written in his neat, fluent book-hand in a quarto notebook with rough paper covers, and embellished with the pentacle symbol and the familiar motto, 'Un Dieu Un Amy', it survives much as he presented it to Margaret in the first summer of her married life.[14]

---

[11] *Life*, 68; BL Add. MS 78308: Berkeley to JE, 26 Aug. 1676.

[12] F. L. Powell, *English Domestic Relations 1487–1653* (New York, 1912), 111–39; William and Malleville Haller, 'The Puritan Art of Love', *Huntington Library Quarterly*, 5 (1941–2), 245–7; Margo Todd, *Christian Humanism and the Puritan Social Order* (Cambridge, 1987), 96–117; Anna Bryson, *From Courtesy to Civility: Changing Codes of Conduct in Early Modern England* (Oxford, 1998), 38.

[13] BL Add. MS 78298: JE to Samuel Hartlib, 4 Feb. 1660.

[14] BL Add. MS 78386: 'Oeconomics', [1676].

It was a long time since Evelyn had written to Robert Boyle that there was not on earth a friendship comparable to marriage. The first nineteen pages of this treatise on the married household, almost a quarter of the whole, were devoted to an extended parallel between friendship and marriage, ostensibly to help Margaret understand her new relationship, but really all tending to persuade her of what he had already suggested when they made their pact: that the former was the higher state. Of course his aim was to keep his place in her life, to convince her that their friendship was still valuable and marriage no obstacle to it, and also (with her husband in mind) that neither was it a threat to her marriage. But this did not make the arguments less interesting; certainly it was a bolder and more ambitious treatment of the subject than could be found in any clerical treatise, which simply subsumed friendship into the unequal relationship between man and wife.

He began by citing the numerous examples of notable friendships amongst the men and women in the early Christian Church, and passages from later writers to confirm it, most notably the declaration of Francis Bacon that 'the nuptial Love indeede continues Mankind; but it is friendly Love which onely perfects it' (p. 3). It was this emphasis on the innate perfectability of friendship, in contrast to the fallen world of sexual love, to which Evelyn constantly returned; 'I cannot better represent the perfection of the new Relation you are enter'd into, than by Comparing it to a perfect Friendship', he concluded, 'in whatever it falls short of that, it is defective' (p. 8). But the most important respect in which marriage differed from friendship was of course in permitting the full physical expression of love. When Evelyn called this the 'very poorest circumstance, and the meanest', he was not just displaying a residual puritan distrust of the pleasures of the flesh. It was neoplatonic doctrine that the 'commerce incident to flesh and blood' tended to corrupt the perfection of love, which Evelyn claimed to have confirmed by his own experience was sustained by the noble senses of seeing and hearing 'as nearest the residence of our soules'; whereas the lower senses, smell, touch, and taste (those involved in kissing, embracing, and intercourse itself) all tended to debase it (p. 5). Friendship, being perfectible, would also last '& accompany us to the other World, when all the tyes of Flesh and Blood, yea and of Marriage it selfe shall cease' (p. 8).

Then he moved on to his most compelling argument for the superiority of friendship in their society: that marriage and all family and household relationships were unequal and subject to law and contract. Margaret had already experienced the subjections of married life in her enforced journey to Paris and marriage manuals, with their catalogues of permissions and prohibitions, were their clearest manifestations. Even the most biddable female reader could perceive that they all served to maintain her subordinate position. Friendship by contrast, Evelyn reminded her, was free and spontaneous. There was no binding contract and no innate inequalities. It was sustained only by the mutual virtue of the participants, and being innately virtuous, it tended more to a state of grace than marriage. It was the only thing, he added as evidence of this, 'which next our Love to God' could admit of no excess, 'whereas all Love else must still be kept in fetters; Yea, that betweene the Married; so as Friendship seemes implanted by God alone, our Loves by Passion; and yet there's Love in Friendship, and Passion too; but 'tis without disorder' (p. 11). But this, if not disingenuous, was too reassuring a version of his own experience. In the end he would have to admit, at least to his own conscience, that there was no such easy separation of passion and friendship. For the present however he was concerned to define the ideal: 'Friendship is not made by Interest, or riches; divertisement and pleasure of the Sense, which are all of them corporeal appetites and of the inferior Man, which being obnoxious to detriment and change, determine with their Causes; but it is a complication of all that's Vertuous & holy; Goodnatur'd, obliging, and Gratefull; and a true Friend is another Parent, the most trusty Guide; the truest Oracle, the sacred'st Repository, Dilligent Advocate, and most faithfull Steward in the World.' 'In a Word', he concluded, recalling himself to his ostensible subject, 'Friends should thus be qualified, and so should Husbands' (pp. 9–10). He knew very well that their generation was no longer hospitable to this kind of idealism, that it was liable to be dismissed 'as a pretty speculation onely', when it was not actually laughed at. Yet he insisted that it could certainly have its 'real existence, and is practicable in all its dimensions', and that even if it was imagined more often than found, there was still value in defining and describing it, so as to 'draw as neere after the original as we can' (p. 12).

It was his most sustained, most cogent, and indeed most moving statement of what he aimed at in his friendship with Margaret Godolphin. It set his contribution to the conduct literature about marriage apart from its predecessors and gave it a real and hard-won distinction. What marred and contradicted it was his repeated claim that she was in fact as much bound to him as she was to her husband: through her promises in her letters (which he had preserved and now quoted at length), through her obligations to him for his practical help, and through what he now legalistically chose to call the 'Instrument' of their friendship, the drawing of the altar which she had signed 'between jest and earnest' when she made her vow of friendship. Forgetting that he had himself offered to release her from her binding promises when her marriage seemed imminent, he now insisted that she could not claim that marriage absolved her from these 'many solemn & holy protestations', since at the time she made them she had anticipated it: 'did you not Calculate for all events . . . and were you not then as fully determin'd to make him yours and give him the Possession of your person, as well as your heart?' (p. 17)

These exactions were of course born of Evelyn's insecurities and his depth of feeling for her; his nagging consciousness of his own failings, and his sense, as he became ever more dependent on the friendship, that Margaret was no longer as fervent, and would never be again, as she had been in its first rapturous year. He admitted to her that such friendship was rare, almost always remaining an ideal only, precisely because 'the Virtues which are the bond of it are so imperfect and hard to find in most persons; that unless we accommodate and conforme ourselves to the mutual Infirmities of each other, the Friendship does not last, and prosper to that degree which so exalts it above other Relations'. This was what made him anxious, since 'there is no Creature living knows more of my Imperfections than your selfe'. Hence his poignant appeal: 'reproove not the intercession which I so passionately use with you; not to despise the Imperfections of your Friend; so his Friendship be intire', his constant references to what he had done to prove this, and his harsher reminder that 'whatever Circumstances may (thro my defects) happen sometimes to suspend the sense of this Continu'd Fervor', he was entitled to expect it 'by a right of some prescription as well as promise' (p. 18).

Evelyn was trying to make it clear to Margaret that despite her marriage to a worthy husband, he still had something to offer with his friendship which it could not supply. Yet even while he congratulated her on having found a husband who was also a worthy friend, there was a strong suggestion that he was, as he put it, 'magnifying his office' and competing with Godolphin. He therefore moved on to the practical issue which most preoccupied him: the future relations between the three of them. 'But you will object', he prompted Margaret, that 'since Friendship (as I describe it) can onely be betweene Two Persons (for Wife & Husband are no more) what becomes of Yours and Mine? I'le tell you faithfully. Just where it ever was.' There followed some rather specious juggling with numbers: that all good friendships should have a third member: 'indeede the Graces (reckon'd the Patronesses of Friendship) were Three'; that it was 'a number of Perfection, sacred to Conversation'; or somewhat contradictorily, that since she and her husband were united by their marriage, the one-to-one nature of the friendship was not really altered (p. 13). But he did not really consider at this stage that her marriage had extended the intimate friendship to her husband. What he wanted to make clear, not just to Margaret but to Godolphin (who he must assume might read the treatise) was that the continuance of the friendship posed no threat to him; that 'the Identity and samenesse, which formes the Union of Friends dos not in the least violate or divide the Conjugal & Matrimonial; because it is onely spiritual, and in the soule, which constitutes our very forme & essence'. In a classic definition of seraphic love and spiritual friendship he repeated what he had so often said in his letters and prayers to her: that 'so long as God alone is the sourse and Object of it, the spiritual Life our Hope and the End, and summit of it', it would remain 'a sincere, holy, and unblameable Conversation' (pp. 13–14). In fact the more conventional advice manual which followed was offered expressly as a token that he wished for her happiness and fulfilment in her new state.

His general precepts to Margaret about family and household, when he did finally address himself to them, had a good deal in common with his earlier 'Instructions Oeconomique' and with the many published manuals on the subject. There was the same basic premiss, deriving ultimately from St Augustine, that 'In Truth the master himselfe is of original right Priest of his Family . . . he has in effect Cure of soules under him; for even Private Families, the Husband & Wife, being the first Politiq & Society in the World, are the seminaries both of Church and State' (p. 33). Yet even here there was a more personal tone; an intense, even voyeuristic following of the godly married couple through their daily and nightly rituals, their dressing, their household duties, dining, visiting, discussing the events of the day and retiring together. In fact his idealizing imagination was already transforming Margaret and Sidney Godolphin into an archetypal, almost a prelapsarian couple. He did not, he said, insist on mid-afternoon prayers in a small private household, 'because they are so subject to being interrupted by People's coming in and out', but he recommended that whenever possible the husband and wife should both retire together for prayer and devout reading in the early evening, 'it is a conversation with your heavenly Maker as was that in Paradise in the coole of the day, before sin had enter'd in to disturbe it' (p. 21). Sexual relations should be conducted in the same spirit: after commendations to God; 'this is truely to tast the innocent sweetes, the heavenly and chast Mysteries of the Married Life; which thus order'd is rather Angelical, than anything we ordinarily see . . . true pleasure (even that of the most sensual) consists not in wanton transports, which ends in bitternesse & satiety; but in those sweete & chast moments, which are attended with the peace of Conscience, and after which they awake refresh'd, and thus repeate and nourish their loves without sin, & disorder'. But there was a sudden and startling lapse from the idealizing tone when he added that a married couple should always meet and part, 'as full of respect, as Affection; without that clownish slabbering & vulgar fondnesse, by which some thinke to recommend their kindnesse to their Wives & Husbands, & to which they often add a ridiculous Gibberish, nick-names, & apish toying' (p. 23). This sharp revulsion at the thought of the moments of casual physical intimacy permitted to a married couple but utterly prohibited between himself and Margaret was perhaps the one sign he allowed to escape him of the repression of these impulses towards her.

Next would normally have come the care of children, but since Margaret had none as yet, and was 'a mistress before she is a mother', Evelyn turned to relations with servants. His advice, clearly based on his own experience and practice, was admirably sensible and humane: the guiding principle that 'neither nature nor law made servants, but such as freely make themselves so'; the reminder of the duty of mutual respect and affection and the wisdom of refraining from humiliating rebukes and bearing with small mistakes. In conclusion, very much in the manner of Gouge's *Domesticall Duties*, he listed the 'positive duties of servants and masters', drawn chiefly from Scripture (pp. 26–34). Margaret was then firmly reminded, as Mary Evelyn had been before her, that 'the chiefe care of all things within the house' was 'especially and by Apostolicall precept' her concern. She must keep accounts and inventories, learn something of still-room and dairy work, and 'not despise the knowledge of herbs & their vertues, because it is not only pleasant in the contemplation, but very useful & profitable'. Again there followed the formal permissions and prohibitions of her role in the marriage: she might go to church and receive the sacrament and take care of her family 'by positive right' and without her husband's leave. But she might not take vows, 'discipline herself by rigorous penances (for her body is not her own)', or give alms without his permission, unless she had (as Margaret did) money of her own to dispose of (pp. 35–40).

At this point there is a gap in the manuscript. Ten pages, evidently devoted to procreation and the nurture of children, have been cut out (by Evelyn himself, as we shall see) and are now lost, and when the treatise resumes (on p. 51) the children are at an age to be educated. This last was a topic on which Evelyn could always expand, although he was also ready to acknowledge ruefully that most of the rules parents set themselves in advance for bringing up their children were likely to prove unworkable in practice. But before he set these out he could not resist again giving friendship the privileged place: parents should make their children their 'first friends', since 'the name of friend alone is of much neerer alyance than that of blood, and it produces greater indearments, and more good offices than any tie of nature'. Then there followed a compendium of (mostly) conventional opinions about the education of boys and girls. For the former he was not in favour of public schools or of sending them abroad in their late teens; travel should take place, if at all, about the ages of 9 or 10, when they would be more docile and learn languages more readily. The most interesting recommendation was in favour of trade as a profession, despite the traditional gentry prejudice against it. As for social accomplishments, both sexes might be taught to dance courants, sing in tune, and play the lute or harpsichord acceptably, 'but 'tis not necessary they should Compose, play at first sight, or daunce like Comedians'. Drawing and painting in miniature was 'a sweet diversion and entertains the fancy usefully, and disposes it to order in other things'. Otherwise daughters needed only to be taught a little arithmetic and to write a legible hand, and their reading beyond devotional works should be carefully regulated; 'it were better that our Daughters read the Lives of the Saints & holy Martyrs, that they duly observ'd the hours of prayer and employ'd the rest of their time with the Needle, or in learning something which might come to be usefull when they come to be housekeepers, & have families'. And again there followed a list of the 'positive duties of parents and children' which had scriptural warrant (pp. 51–66).

Thus far Evelyn had cast his guidance to Margaret in terms which might apply to any newly married young woman. Now he turned to matters particular to her. Better than anyone he knew that before her marriage she had had recurrent doubts about its compatibility with a fully realized religious life. Although she was to all appearance a happy wife and he could see no sign that these 'Melancholy & despondent thoughts' continued to haunt her, 'yet I would have so excellent a Christian as you are, assur'd in all you do, as far as I am able to contribute to it' (p. 67). And so he turned again to the arguments in favour of marriage which he had once rehearsed for Robert Boyle's benefit and later for Margaret herself in the first year of their friendship: that it was first instituted in Paradise ('all other Ordinances were appointed by Men or Angels; this by God alone'); that it had been consecrated by the first miracle of Jesus; that 'all the saints now in heaven have ben the Fruits of holy Wedlock; yea, and even those who most declam'd against it'. St Paul's famous pronouncement in favour of a celibate life, he repeated, was a recommendation for early persecuted Christians only and not of general application. Then he moved on to Margaret's personal situation, arguing that her early understanding with Godolphin had effectively been a betrothal, and in that case to have put off her marriage until she had 'pass'd her prime' would have been 'undecent, & perhaps Un-just'. He admitted that her religious vocation made her something of a special case, and in view of it, 'if your Affections had never been engag'd' and if 'the Customes, and provisions of your Country made the Retreate decent', perhaps the choice of a virgin life would have been best for her. But there were no Protestant convents, and more to the point, Margaret had been a young woman in love and therefore at risk in remaining single. There was nothing startling in making this point; the argument for marriage as a protection against sexual temptation was a commonplace of post-Reformation treatises of this kind.[15] 'The single life is more sublime', was Evelyn's version of it, 'but tis also more perilous; the fall is higher, and if there be burning or a flame inkindl'd, as dangerous as a fire without a chimney to preserve the house; for if the virgins be not pure in spirit as well as in body, 'tis an unhappy state; and what circumspection is requir'd to the first, those who have try'd can best resolve, and many by sad Experience; whilst the Married have provision and need not disquiet themselves' (pp. 67–9).

As for Margaret's fear that married life and the care of a household would not allow her time for religious observance, he could point to many 'holy Matrons', 'excellent wives and mothers in antiquity and since; Lady Falkland, that saint, my excellent Grandmother (twise married), my owne deare and scrupulously pious Mother', who had lived with a dedicated piety equal to any virgin state:

What Prayers! what teares! what reading! what hearing! Receiving! holy Conference! Charities to the poore! Almes-giving! Visiting of the Sick and those in bonds; yea in what indefatigable Labours of Love did these holy Matrons exercise themselves almost continualy; and yet they had very great Families to looke after, and liv'd honorably in them; because they did all things in order (p. 70).

With some justification he could even offer himself as proof that domestic responsibilities were no impediment to a full devotional life; had he not composed the whole series of prayers and meditations for her, despite 'the solicitudes of no inconsiderable family, and many external Employments'? With his lurking contempt for the professional cleric, he could not help adding that 'those who study Divinity for bread and the Cure of Soules, do not spend much more time un-willingly in their Labours then he professes to do willingly & cherefully to serve you'. In itself this was a retort to those who claimed the active life was inconsistent with the contemplative, and proof that his own choice had been legitimate. 'Let this then be for your Encouragement also', he added to Margaret, 'as not to scruple whither you have don well or ill in Marrying; so not to desist from your holy & Religious Course' (p. 71).

His final summing up of their long debate about relative virtues of marriage and the virgin life was sensible and even-handed: morally both were

---

[15] Powell, *English Domestic Relations*, 120; Haller, 'Puritan Art of Love', 265–6; Anthony Fletcher, 'The Protestant Idea of Marriage in Early Modern England', in A. Fletcher and P. Roberts (eds.), *Religion, Culture and Society in Early Modern Britain* (Cambridge, 1994), 177–8.

neutral states, 'as being both of them natural forms of living and none of them enjoyn'd or prohibited'. Social usefulness was one means of judging between them; so was what would most conduce to the happiness and safety of particular individuals. Those who could not control their sexual impulses by temperance, caution, and prayer were called to marriage under penalty of incurring mortal sin. For those who ran no such danger, 'and whose affections were not engag'd', it might well be easiest, 'and yet still perhaps not best', to live single. For all his celebration of friendship, he had never denied that marriage could also be a spiritual state; at its most ideal, as he envisaged it for Margaret, it was not just an earthly union, but in itself the shadow of a higher reality. Echoing the words of the marriage service, he told her that 'there is in Marriage, Union, Society & Mysterie, and such a Mysterie as is made to represent the most bright and happy state of a Glorified Creature; even our Union with Christ, & his Church' (pp. 72–3).

The main treatise ended at this point; but there was originally a second part of about ten more pages, conceived as a further exploration of Margaret's personal situation. Much later, when Evelyn retrieved the manuscript with thoughts of revising it, he evidently realized that he had already dealt with some of these matters in the first part and planned to incorporate the whole of the second part in the same way. He cut out the pages, apparently intending to insert them earlier in the text, but never completed the process, and in course of time some of these loose leaves became separated and lost. As it now survives, the second part begins by recounting the beginning of their friendship; how Margaret, in a state of depression, had asked for Evelyn's help and how he set out to make her devotional life less rigorous. Then (on p. 74) the manuscript breaks off, with all the remaining pages apparently missing. But in fact only four of them (75–8) are lost altogether; another six (79–84) were removed by the nineteenth-century collector, William Upcott, who plundered the Evelyn archive, and preserved as a separate fragment.[16] When this resumes Evelyn is dealing in detail with the subject of Margaret's sexual relations with her husband. These are evidently the passages which he intended to insert in place of those on the same subject which he cut out of part 1.

In the chapter entitled 'Of mutual society' in his 'Instructions' to his 13-year-old bride, he had not dwelt on this subject in great detail, confining himself to the conventional advice that she should not refuse her husband's 'lawfull embraces' except in the case of illness; but neither should he make excessive demands on her, and that there might also be sexual abstinence at times of 'special mortification' for religious reasons. His advice to Margaret

---

[16] BL Add. MS 15950, fos. 108–110.

was much more detailed. Although he was prepared to admit that sexual pleasure was legitimate, he did so at first rather grudgingly; arguing that God had made the act more enjoyable than any other 'because the Circumstances accompanying it are otherwise so contemptible, poore, & inconvenient, that the whole species would certainly be lost without them'; indeed all satisfying of bodily appetites was 'of so meane & low a progeny (compar'd with other actions of our lives) that meere necessity and some delight of the sence extraordinary had neede be a great ingredient to render them tollerable & competent to Creatures so refin'd, and reasonable'. To stimulate sexual pleasure 'by impure objects, unnatural provocation, fancy, & studied artifices merely to prolong the pleasure of sense only, other than such as is consonant to the order of Nature' was 'against the reverence of the Body, much more of the soule & spirit of a Christian'. But orgasm in the woman was believed to be essential to conception, and therefore to avoid it was 'not onely impossible, but a stupidity, and impediment to the chiefe End'; and so 'holy Guides (whatever some pretend) have justified the mutual liberties of this mysterious state'; and he cited the 'Songs of Solomon', with their 'chaste endearments of love & Union, even to Excesse': 'rejoice with the Wife of thy Youth; Let her be as the loving Hind, and pleasant Roe: Let her Breasts satisfy thee at all times, and be thou perpetualy ravish'd with her Love' (p. 79).

So far the advice was little different from what he was to give his son on marriage a few years later, and quite in keeping with the readiness of some clerical writers of post-Reformation conduct manuals to encourage sexual fulfilment and pleasure as legitimate aspects of marriage.[17] Its main significance for Evelyn's relations with Margaret was to show quite clearly that for all his tendency to 'magnify his office' as a platonic friend, he was also concerned to promote her married happiness. For she had not just had doubts about marriage as a distraction from her devotional life; she had had scruples about sacrificing her virginity at all. He remembered that she had once pointed out to him a passage in the writings of Jeremy Taylor, 'which seem'd exceedingly to straiten the limites' of what was permitted sexually even to a married couple, and he had just strongly hinted to her himself that sexual relations were a debasement of perfect spiritual love. Aware that this could do more than anything else to destroy the harmony between a married couple, making 'many otherwise excellent wives (who have fond husbands) timerous, doubtful peevish and ungratefull companions, as believeing no expression of affection can be chast, or warrantable but what a statue may pretend

---

[17] Edmund Leites, 'The Duty to Desire: Love, Friendship and Sexuality in Some Puritan Theories of Marriage', *Journal of Social History*, 15 (1982), 388–9; Fletcher, 'Protestant Idea of Marriage', 174–9.

to, unlesse in order to propagation', he emphasized that sexual pleasure was not just legitimate; it should be sought.

Since it was a creation of the mind and not just of the body, it was quite possible, he told her, 'so to estrange and divert the Imagination . . . that the duty of marriage passes without much sense of satisfaction on either part; for tis not fullnesse so much as fancy which warmes the bloud, inclines and excites the desires of sexes by sending forth from the braine . . . those ungovernable spirits and that flower of the body'; but 'devout abstraction' of this kind was only to be practised 'where we find a proneness to excesse . . . distracting us from other duties'. Otherwise 'a natural satisfaction within the protection of this sacred Institution' was to be encouraged. Moderation might in theory be best, 'for so neither will nature be oppress'd or God offended', but excess was not grounds for agonizing and self-castigation; it should be 'humbly and yet confidently asked pardon for', and so he added with psychological acuteness, 'shall you slepe, and rise with holy thoughts, and often with greater alacrity at your very prayers than when you have been the most abstinent & spiritual' (pp. 81–3).

Margaret might now be instructed in the conduct of a marriage and household, but she still had no home of her own. Godolphin's attempts to find an alternative to his bedchamber post had so far failed. For all the insecurity of his position at court and Margaret's desire to detach herself from it altogether, they therefore decided to renovate his Scotland Yard lodging, putting off the prospect of a country retirement till the indefinite future. Evelyn described this as 'an house, or rather an appartment, which had all the conveniences of an house';[18] the lower floor was in separate occupation and there were no grounds apart from the adjoining courts and yards. It might not be ideal, but accommodation of any kind in Whitehall was much sought after, and despite being in the service area of the palace this was quiet and convenient enough. In August 1676 permission was obtained from the Lord Chamberlain and Wren, as Surveyor, was ordered to put the work in hand.[19] In practice it was devolved on his colleague Robert Hooke, and Evelyn, who heartily welcomed this development because it would keep Margaret within his orbit, offered to supervise.[20]

Hooke was a curious, unprepossessing, even rather sinister figure, skeletally thin and crooked, with pale sharp features and long lank hair hanging about his face. He moved like a spider, 'stooping and very fast', and from his constant round of public business in committee rooms, laboratories, coffee

[18] JE, *Diary*, iv. 98; *Life*, 68. [19] PRO LC 5/141, p. 452: warrant, 1 Aug. 1676.
[20] JE, *Diary*, iv. 98–9.

houses, and building sites, would withdraw to the private world of his rooms above Gresham College and a secret and incestuous relationship with his niece and ward. But he was also one of the most brilliant men of his day. This conversion of Godolphin's lodgings was a trivial job compared with the public and private work he already had on his hands. Having collaborated with Wren in the rebuilding of the City churches after the Great Fire, he was now engaged simultaneously on Bethlehem Hospital in Moorfields, the Royal College of Physicians, a great mansion in Bloomsbury in the French style for Ralph Montagu, and a house in the Privy Garden of Whitehall for the Earl of Oxford. And architecture itself was only his secondary interest. As curator of experiments at the Royal Society he was almost single-handedly responsible for the distinction of its early experimental programme, and by his *Micrographia*, illustrated with his own remarkable engravings, he was also a pioneer of the new world laid open by the microscope.[21]

Yet for all his achievements he felt himself to be beset with scoffing and belittlement. The court wits, taking their cue from the King himself, had made a butt of the Royal Society almost from the beginning, 'for spending time only in weighing of ayre, and doing nothing else since they sat'. Its defenders had always known that these jibes could do it more harm than all their 'severe and frowning and dogmatical adversaries', who only accused it of slighting traditional authority and fostering atheism.[22] During this summer, partly out of boredom and want of other occupation, the mockery reached its climax. It was a long, hot, and thunderously close season, and with Windsor under reconstruction the court had nowhere to go for its summer recess. The theatre was a distraction, and the most successful play of the season was undoubtedly Thomas Shadwell's *The Virtuoso*, a clever and undemanding farce with a good helping of sex, whose primary purpose was to debunk the Royal Society. Its chief character, Sir Nicholas Gimcrack, had all those attributes of the 'rare mechanic philosopher' which were guaranteed to reduce the court wits to tears of mirth: the battery of microscopes and telescopes, the indiscriminate and credulous enthusiasm for all natural phenomena from ants, maggots, and spiders to the geography of the moon, the cellar full of bottled air, the hare-brained experiments in swimming and flying, the cruel and pointless exercises in vivisection, the revolting advocacy of putrid phosphorescent meat as a source of light, and the naive conviction that it was all for the sake of knowledge and not for any use or benefit to mankind. Unfairly the brunt of this attack fell not on the gentleman amateurs of the

[21] Richard Westfall, 'Robert Hooke', in *Dictionary of Scientific Biography* (1970–80), vi. 481–8.
[22] R. H. Syfret, 'Some Early Critics of the Royal Society', *Notes and Records of the Royal Society*, 8 (1951), 42–6.

Society, who partly deserved it, but on Hooke, the genius of useful instru-
mentation and the very embodiment of the scientific professional. 'Damned
Doggs. *Vindica me deus.* People almost pointed,' he snarled in his diary, after
he had braved one performance to see for himself.[23]

Margaret had predicted that with marriage she would grow worldly.
Certainly the interval between the ceremony and the setting up of her own
household was an awkward and unsettling one. Lady Yarburgh was still in
London and in her company Margaret overcame her scruples so far as to go
and see the play, and was all the more startled to learn shortly afterwards that
Sir Nicholas Gimcrack was to be the architect of her new home. Evelyn's
explosion of indignation when she taxed him with it must also have taken her
aback. In fact his attendance at the Royal Society had flagged in recent years,
not just because of the demands on his time but because he could not help
seeing that it was failing to fulfil its ambitious early programme. But he was
not prepared to concede this to its detractors and he also felt personally stung
by Shadwell's attack. He had always feared being 'brought on the stage' to
be made fun of,[24] and the elaborate speeches of encouragement from
Gimcrack's crony, Sir Formal Trifle, were too close to his own style for
comfort: he, the author of one of the most useful of all the Society's publications, who was about to devote the preface of the third edition of *Sylva* to
answering 'those few Ignorant and Comical Buffoons' who, 'with Insolence
suitable to their Understanding [are] still crying out, and asking, What have
the Royal Society done?' Now he found Margaret, who had been the occasion of so much of his distraction from worldly affairs and who had never
concerned herself with such matters until now, parroting the same question,
having learned to do so at just the kind of 'scandalous Interlude (for it wholy
degenerates from the antient & genuine Comedy)', which he had always
warned her against. On 18 July, the same day he met Hooke at Scotland Yard
to begin the work on her lodgings, he sent her a long letter of explanation,
defence, and reproof.[25]

'Next the actual service of God & those few offices which I endeavor to
do my friends', he began with a pointed reminder of how much his time was
occupied in her affairs, 'I have learned more profitable and useful things from
some hours conversation in that Meeting than ever I have done from the
quintessence and sublimest rapture of those empty casks whose noise you so
admire at court'; the Society's only purpose was 'the investigation of Truths,

---

[23] Thomas Shadwell, *The Virtuoso*, ed. M. H. Nicolson and D. S. Rodes (1966), pp. xii–xxv;
Robert Hooke, *Diary*, ed. H. W. Robinson and W. Adams (1935), 243.

[24] BL Add. MS 78298: JE to James Hamilton, 27 Apr. 1671.

[25] Ibid.: JE to MG, 18 July 1676.

& discovery of Errors & Impostures . . . without any Offence or provocation to anybody'. They did not aim 'to raise a new Theorie of Philosophy, but to collect a plenty of Materials by new & joint Attempts for the Work'. Even so they had produced many useful inventions, including watches, cranes, pumps, and mathematical instruments. As for the theatre, he went on with heavy sarcasm, 'I would not have you think me so vaine and singularly ridiculous as to fancy my selfe borne to correct and reforme the Age, which were to be more ridiculous than a fellow of the Royal Society.' He admitted that he went to the playhouses himself from time to time, had even tried his hand at writing one, and was perfectly willing to 'say as much for plays as that diversion would honestly bear, to gratify an innocent conversation'. But when he spoke 'upon a serious and religious Account' and 'to a holy & extraordinary friend', he added, recalling Margaret to her former situation, his judgement, supported by 'the whole current of Divines & Religious men (some very few of our modern carpet priests excepted)' was to condemn 'the Trade of Mocking and Jeasting & disguising the Person, exposing the modest Sex, the pompous expense, & other voluptary arts accompanying it' as 'not agreeable to Christian & Evangelical perfection & time which is given us to make our calling & election sure'.

Soon the lodgings were ready to be fitted out and they could find common occupation again in these practicalities. They crossed the river together in September to visit Gerrard Weymans's 'magazine of marble' at Lambeth to buy chimney pieces, to the Duke of Buckingham's glassworks in search of mirrors, and to the East India warehouses at Blackwall to look at 'Indian Curiosities'.[26] Far from repining at still being confined to the court, in her usual anniversary letter on 16 October Margaret poured out her gratitude:

I thank Almighty God, who has ben so Infinitly Gratious to me this Yeare: for he has brought me back into my owne Native Country in Safty & honorably: Prosper'd me in my Temporal Affaires, above my Expectation: Continu'd my Health, & my Friends: Deliver'd me from the Torment of Suspense: Given me an Husband, that above all men living, I value: In short, I have little to Wish, but a Child; and to Contribute something to my Friends hapynesse (which I most Impatiently desire).[27]

In fact by this time she did believe herself to be expecting a child.[28] When Godolphin travelled with the court to Newmarket in October she stayed under Mrs Evelyn's wing at Deptford, and as the snowbound winter set in she lived almost 'secretly' at Berkeley House, while her husband drove the

[26] JE, *Diary*, iv. 98–9.
[27] *Life*, 70: MG to JE, 16 Oct. [1676] (incorrectly dated 1677 by JE).
[28] BL Add. 78308: Lady Berkeley to JE, Aug. 1676.

Duchess of York's sled in St James's Park and was in the thick of the Christmas festivities at Whitehall.[29] As a New Year's gift Evelyn presented her with another devotional tract, headed 'Oeconomical, Conjugal and Domestick Offices: fitted for the devouter Married Persons & Housekeepers', a sequence of prayers almost all in anticipation of her motherhood. But Margaret must have mistaken her condition or miscarried, for when the Scotland Yard lodgings were ready to move into in March of 1677 there was still no sign of a child. Instead she devoted herself to mastering the practicalities of housekeeping.

The Godolphins, even as a childless couple setting up house for the first time, would have no less than six servants: Margaret's maid Beck, who was also to act as housekeeper, and her husband's manservant, two housemaids, a footman, and a groom. Margaret had £500 a year to manage with, from which she had to equip her lodgings and keep the whole household in food, clothing, and transport. She had been at court almost since childhood and her mother was long dead. She turned to the Evelyns again; not to Evelyn himself this time, but to his 'Martha', who knew very well what it was like to turn from her higher aspirations and learn to govern a house, and whose judgement, as Margaret told Evelyn, 'no disprais to you I would as soon rely on as yours . . . As to our litle family, aight is the number we are to have nor more nor les, three dishes of meat at diner we would willingly have, and no supers at all, no coach doe we entend to keep but he has always two riding horses . . . now what derections you pleys to bestow shall be very wellcom to me.'[30]

The two women were now good friends in their own right; Mary Evelyn was painting a picture as a house-warming present for her husband's 'seraph-ick', 'who deserves that and any thing a thousand times better'.[31] She now responded with a practical manual, compiled with great care and thoughtfulness and detailing the whole annual housekeeping expenses for a family of eight; 'as many as were in the Ark'. These were calculated by the week and centred on the three-course dinner: one dish of butcher's meat, one of fish, rabbit, or fowl, and one of dessert. The only exception was Fridays, when there would be no meat, but only 'pottage maigre' and one dish of fish, 'of what sort ordinary (fresh or salt) you please, for it will else goe but a little way with Servants; Fasting-days being of all other (I find) most troublesome in a Family'; supplemented by oatmeal, eggs, frumetie, herb tarts or quaking

---

[29] BL Add. MS 28052, fo. 86: Charles to Sir William Godolphin, 28 Sept. 1676; JE, *Diary*, iv. 100; *Life*, 69; HMC *Rutland MSS*, ii. 34: Lady Chaworth to Lord Roos, 25 Dec. [1676].

[30] BL Add. MS 78307, fo. 86: MG to JE, 11 May 1676 (date endorsed by JE).

[31] BL Add. MS 78540: ME to Ralph Bohun, 19 Nov. [1677].

pudding. Expenses for bread, beer, butter, eggs, fruit, fuel (sea-coal for the kitchen and washing cauldrons, wood for the chamber fires), candles, soap, starch, and washing were also detailed. All this came to £4 12s. a week or £244 4s. a year. Annual expenses included clothing: £66 for Margaret's, 'you being already so plentifully stock'd', and £40 for her husband's; £38 for servants' wages; £30 for keeping the horses; and £26 more for coach and chair hire. This left £40 a year for Margaret's charities and pocket-money, and £20 over for unforseeable expenses, 'little enough considering Sicknesse, Physicians, and innumerable Accidents that are not to be provided against with any certainty'.

There was no allowance for furniture and fittings, 'you already having so nobly & handsomly furnish'd your Lodgings & Rooms of Reception'. What the young couple chiefly needed were household durables, and Mrs Evelyn went on to estimate the outlay on these under their several headings: linen, plate, pewter, tin, copper and brass, iron, wood, wicker, glass, and earthenware. The largest expense was silver at £197, enough 'to serve your owne Table all in plate, than which nothing is more cleanly & honorable', but 'rather plain then wrought; there being so much lost in change of the other when the fashion alters'. Of household linen, there were to be four pairs of sheets for their own bed and two each for all of the others, copious towels, napkins and tablecloths for everyday use, 'a suit of fine Diaper & an other of Damask' for special occasions, not forgetting 'Dish-clouts, 6 yards at first, afterwards old Linnen will be found soon enough to supply'. And so on, through kitchen utensils of all kinds. 'So things will multiply', she ended, 'and in a little time you will have all complete for your Family & Designs: Curiositys are infinite; and I have heard wise people affirme that what is more than usefull is Burden & Lumber not Houshold-stuff.'[32]

Margaret applied herself conscientiously to her new role. She soon found that she had to attend to everything herself, since Beck proved quite incompetent as a housekeeper, but an urban household was after all a small responsibility compared with Mary Evelyn's; she did not have to learn the skills of the stillroom, the brewhouse, or the dairy. She kept the household accounts,

[32] *Life*, 223–30. Evelyn retrieved the original after Margaret's death, then passed a copy on to Samuel Pepys; it is now Pforzheimer MS 35H, Harry Ransom Humanities Research Center, University of Texas; see *PF*, 160–1. The date, 13 Apr. 1675, given there and in the catalogue of the Pforzheimer Library, *English Literature 1475–1700* (New York, 1940), iii. 1215, must be incorrect. The letter to Evelyn in which Margaret requests these instructions (see n. 31 above), and to which Mrs Evelyn refers in her own covering letter, is endorsed 11 May 1676 (confirmed by a reference in it to Jack Evelyn's return from Paris). Mary Evelyn habitually dated her letters in a tiny hand which can be difficult to decipher; the correct date for the household instructions is probably April 1677.

Evelyn noted approvingly, making them up every Saturday, and managed all the household consumption 'with an hardinesse & masculine Virtue . . . None knew better than she, to Buy, & to choose what was fit, Tempering a discreete Frugality, with a generous hand, and a large Heart.' If she was extravagant in anything, he still thought, it was in her charity.[33] Now that she had a home of her own she took in an orphan child, a little girl probably from the Westminster tenements, whom she tended 'with all the Circumstances of a most carefull Nurse'.[34] She and Evelyn still prayed together regularly and in September he received a letter from her, as passionate and spontaneous as any she had written in the first year of their friendship, acknowledging how much she still owed to him for the enhancement of her devotional life and reaffirming her commitment to it: 'Is not one day with god worth ten thousand with the greatest men in the world: oh tis; and we are wors then made [*sic* for mad] when we despise so real a pleasuer that may so cheaply be had to persue thos that are so hard to com by, and so very trivleing when possesed'. Above all he had the satisfaction of seeing her, alone of all the *Calisto* players, happy and settled, both in her marriage and in the house he had contrived for her:

When this day I considerd my hapines in having perfect health of body, chearfulnes of mind, no disturbance from without nor grife within, my time my own, my hous quiat, sweet and prity, all maner of conv[en]iance for serving god in publicke and in private, how hapey in my frinds, husband, relations, servants, credite and non to wait or atend upon but my dear and blesed God from whom I reseive this, what a melting joy ran thrugh me at the thought of thes mercies.[35]

In November, when Evelyn became a trustee of their first formal marriage settlement, the Godolphins seemed the perfect Christian couple he had envisaged: 'never were Two so fram'd for one-anothers Dispositions; Never liv'd paire, in more peace & harmony'.[36] By this time, at the urging of his publisher, he was preparing another edition of *Sylva* and to 'sweeten the toil' he conjured up a sentimental pastoral fantasy of their consulting it when he was long dead. One day they would have country house and a garden of their own, 'and then my Calendar would be call'd for'. While Margaret was 'knitting a Chaplet or culling a Sallad for a Philosophic Supper', she would call to mind her old friend, 'and perhaps pay a Teare to his Memorie and the Pearly-Drop raise a new Flower . . . and they would call it Amarantha, but I Electra'.[37] In the meantime, although they were

---

[33] *Life*, 79–80, 98–9.   [34] Ibid. 70.
[35] BL Add. MS 78307, fos. 91–2: MG to JE, 22 Sept. 1677.   [36] *Life*, 98.
[37] BL Add. MS 78307, fo. 120: JE to SG, 17 Oct. [1679].

still confined to the court and the city, Evelyn pictured them as making their own Eden; their prayers 'a Conversation with your heavenly Maker as was that in Paradise in the coole of the day, before sin had enter'd in to disturbe it'.[38]

In November 1677 one of the predictions of *Calisto* was fulfilled. Under Danby's auspices Mary of York was married to her cousin William of Orange and returned with him to The Hague. The Duke of York acquiesced, hoping the Protestant match would reassure his opponents that his religion was a purely private matter. William's European coalition had fought on against Louis XIV after England had withdrawn from the war. Now the marriage brought a new offensive alliance with the Dutch in its train and England once more prepared to send troops to the Continent. Godolphin remained as much opposed to the power of France as he had been in the summer of 1672, when he had followed as a junior envoy in the wake of Louis's invasion of the Low Countries. In Parliament he supported Danby's policies and associated himself closely with Sunderland, now a rising man at court. This explains why, less than two years after he had been spoken of as one of the 'little people' marked for dismissal when Danby swept the court clean of his opponents, the Lord Treasurer was now ready to employ him as confidential envoy to the Prince.

It was a thankless task however. Although a majority in England now wanted to see Louis XIV brought low, the King's affinities remained with his cousin at Versailles and there was too much mutual distrust and hostility to bring it about. Deeply corrupted and divided by bribery (both Danby's and the French ambassador's) the Cavalier Parliament had reached the end of its useful life. Williamson warned Godolphin at the outset that 'wee are againe fallen into the old circle of the King's askeing to be enabled to act, and their insisting to have him act before they have enabled him, so as, God knowes, things looke but very awkwardly as to a warre, and such a warr as this ought to bee'.[39] The envoy's first task in January 1678 was to negotiate the cession of Ostend as a bridgehead for operations in Flanders. Then he was to attend William, concert with him the operations of war, and carry messages to and fro which were too secret to be sent by dispatch. Between January and April he made the round trip between England and Holland no less than four times at the most turbulent season of the year, spending days at a stretch tossed or becalmed at the mercy of winds and tides in the Dutch coasts and rivers, and staying so briefly in any one place that his letters could not keep up with

---

[38] BL Add. MS 78386: 'Oeconomics', [1676], p. 21.
[39] Browning, *Danby*, ii. 603: Williamson to SG, 17 Mar. 1678.

him.[40] The court at The Hague, where he came intermittently to rest, was young, sociable, cosmopolitan, and full of familiar company, but Godolphin took no pleasure in it, shutting himself up to write letters rather than go to supper with the Princess and her ladies.[41] Inevitably he found himself ground between two millstones. The peace party in Holland blamed the divisions in England for their sufferings at the hands of the French and took this grievance out on the nearest representatives to hand. But when there was talk of recalling him because he would be more useful in the House of Commons than as envoy, the prospect of facing the court's opponents there was even less inviting.[42] By May it was quite clear that no effective war could be waged on England's part. To the Lord Treasurer's despair the King signed a secret treaty with France, promising neutrality and disbandment of those troops which had been raised in return for a renewed subsidy. Danby wrote to William to make what peace he could.[43] 'Sure you are all mad in England,' Godolphin wrote bitterly to his sister, 'is it possible else that all sides could conspire to be so fatally in the wrong.'[44]

His only cheer came from Margaret. She now knew for certain that she was expecting a child. Amid news that Parliament had voted the disbandment of the army and he would soon be recalled, she buoyantly relayed the latest scraps of court gossip: Carey Frazier, who had never made any secret of her ambition to be a royal mistress, 'was finer then any body on the King's birthday and the King said he thought ther would need more fools then one to maintain that bravery upon which one said they believed his Majesty would supply the want'. The Earl of Bath's son was married but having to endure a delay before he could cohabit with his bride; 'the other day he went to se[e] her and saw her as he thought run quit[e] undresd into a darke closet from him: he persued her and fell so violently upon her that the lady cryd out for the love of god my lord forbear tis the mouther not the daughter: upon which he left of[f] and found his mistake to the great disatisfaction of the lord and vainety of the lady for she brags of it to every body living'; at dinner with the Sunderlands there had been a skirmish between the two distinguished

[40] SG's instructions and correspondence with Williamson in BL Add. MS 10115 and Bodleian Library, MS Firth b1/1, *passim*; see also Longleat, Coventry Papers 41 (BL M.863/32), fos. 325, 335, 341: SG and Hyde to Coventry, 10/20, 19/29 Mar. 2/12 Apr. 1678; Sir Tresham Lever, *Godolphin* (1952), 32–6; C. L. Grose, 'The Anglo-Dutch Alliance of 1678', *English Historical Review*, 39 (1924), 349–72, 526–51.

[41] BL Add. MS 78530: SG to Jael Boscawen, 20/30 May 1678.

[42] Longleat, Coventry Papers 41 (BL M.863/32), fos. 404, 454: SG to Henry Frederick Thynne, 9/19 May, 22 May/3 June 1678.

[43] Browning, *Danby*, ii. 334–432.

[44] BL Add. MS 78530: SG to Jael Boscawen, 20/30 May 1678.

French guests about rival court beauties. When the Marquis de Saint-Évremond at first failed to recognize Margaret in her matronly condition, Sunderland told him that 'he did thos[e] things on porpos to make sacrifice to Madam Mazerin'; on which the Marquis de Ruvigny (one of the negotiators of the secret treaty with France) 'was much deverted, for he is all for Mrs Middleton and was glad to find one that had forsaken her so treated'. 'You se[e] what stuf I picke up for you rather then give over,' Margaret ended; 'My dear good by, I love you as my life and do long to se[e] you, oh how glad I shall be.'[45]

By the end of June Godolphin was back in Whitehall. The experience had left him ashamed for his country and with renewed doubts and scruples about his public role, 'of which', as he told Evelyn much later, 'I never did speak to any body but one, whom I was never weary of speaking to of them, or she to heare me'.[46] But whatever passed between him and Margaret in private, the reality was that only a man with long-term ambitions would have accepted such a post at such a time. Far more than his appointments under Arlington, this marked the real beginning of his public career. He had established a good rapport with William, far better than that of the resident ambassador Laurence Hyde. His association with Hyde and Sunderland was also strengthened, and for the first time he found himself working alongside John Churchill, the young colonel from the Duke of York's household who had been sent over to concert the military detail, and who had just made his own secret marriage with *Calisto*'s dazzling Mercury, Sarah Jenyns.[47] In this forging-place of European alliances the two young men were able to test their own and each other's mettle and lay the foundation of their lifelong partnership. On his return Godolphin completed the transaction he had been negotiating with Hyde for months: the sale of his bedchamber post to purchase Hyde's office of Master of the Robes. This was not just professional courtiers' bartering, but part of the jockeying for position amongst the group of ambitious men who were to be the next generation of ministers. The sale was intended to further Hyde's elevation to the secretaryship of state, and it was carried through determinedly in the face of the opposition from Ralph Montagu, who wanted the secretaryship for himself, and Halifax's brother Henry Savile, who wanted the Robes.[48] It gave Godolphin a clear income of £500

[45] BL Hammick Papers: MG to SG, 31 May [1678].

[46] BL Add. MSS 78530: SG to Jael Boscawen, 20/30 May 1678; 78307: SG to JE, 26 Jan. 1679.

[47] Bodleian Library, MS Firth b1/1, pp. 281–331: correspondence of Williamson with SG and John Churchill, Apr. 1678; Sir Winston Churchill, *Marlborough* (1947), i. 133–4.

[48] *Life*, 56–7; *CSP Domestic 1678*, 302; Harry Ransom Humanities Research Center, University of Texas: newsletter to Bulstrode, 24 July 1678; Bodleian Library, MS Carte 103, fo. 228: newsletter, 5 Aug. 1678; Browning, *Danby*, ii. 344–5.

a year and freed him from the constant duty of 'waiting', but still left him very much involved with the day-to-day life of the court. Margaret was well aware of the negotiations and did not oppose them.[49] After three years of marriage both seemed, for all their private scruples, to be well assimilated into the life of the court.

During this summer Evelyn seemed more restored to himself. The return of the Berkeleys freed him at last from his demeaning stewardship. Instead of suffering Danby's jibes, he now found himself invited to breakfast and his advice sought about the gardens and library at the newly bought Wimbledon.[50] It was a mark of his standing at the Royal Society that in the absence of the president he was invited to take the chair for a demonstration of experiments with the microscope, 'particularly the motions of certaine particles, or rather Animaculs in Milk, & another in Bloud upon which some excellent discourses'; and later he marvelled as Dr William Croone described how freezing water 'shoots into the shape of branches infinitely multiplied . . . resembling the veines in the leaf of a vegetable' and how snow 'by accression did grow when falling, & shot like a tree . . . besides the Stellifying of every individual atome of it'.[51] His diary, sparse in the time of the most intense friendship, began to fill again with descriptions of pleasures and curiosities, as if his eyes had been newly opened to them: Robert Hooke's new Bethlehem hospital, 'magnificently built & most sweetely placed in Morefields'; at the Mint an equestrian statue of the King 'a Yard high', cast in dazzling silver by Roettier the engraver, 'who emulates even the Antients in both mettal & stone'; at Windsor, where the renovations were now far advanced, 'the rare Worke of Virrio, & incomparable Carving of Gibbons'. Even the army drawn up on Hounslow Heath and so much a bone of contention between the King and Parliament was a sight to be relished, the new grenadiers in their 'furr'd Capps with coped crownes like Janizaries' and their uniforms, 'py bald yellow & red', seeming at once fierce and fascinatingly exotic.[52]

In a spell of perfect weather, 'bright & temperate', in late August, he allowed himself the pleasure of a sight-seeing ramble through Surrey. At Weybridge he admired the rich parqueting of cedar, yew, and cypress at the Duke of Norfolk's extravagantly renovated house, pried curiously into the priest holes, stood entranced before a painting of Tudor courtiers dancing ('such amorous countenances & spritefull motion did I never see expressed'), and managed to persuade the Duke to donate what remained of Arundel's great collection of books and manuscripts to the Royal Society, seeing 'how

[49] BL Hammick Papers: MG to SG, 31 May [1678].   [50] JE, *Diary*, iv. 126, 130–1.
[51] Ibid., iv. 128, 146.   [52] Ibid., iv. 134, 136–8.

negligent he was of them, in suffering the Priests & every body to carry away & dispose of what they pleased'. Then he took in the paper mills at Byfleet, where he watched the rag pulp being dextrously turned out of its sieves like thin pancake, pressed dry, and hung up like 'linnen in the Laundry'. Finally there was the series of ravishing villa gardens on the Thames: Lord Lisle's within the enclosure of the former Carthusian monastery of Sheen, where one of the remaining 'solitary Cells' could still be seen; Sir William Temple's, stocked with the fruit trees and vines which he had brought home with him from his years of diplomacy, the orange trees on their stone pedestals and fruit on the south wall 'most exquisitely nailed & applied, far better than in my life I had ever noted'; nearby the old timber house of Essex's brother Sir Henry Capel at Kew, with its terrace walk, yew hedges, and 'the Choicest fruite of any plantation in England'; and most beautiful of all, Ham House, newly renovated by the Duke and Duchess of Lauderdale, 'which is indeede inferior to few of the best Villas in Italy itselfe . . . Parterrs, flower Gardens, Orangeries, Groves, Avenues, Courts, Statues, Perspectives, fountaines, Aviaries and all this at the banks of the sweetest river in the World', the ideal princely garden of his 'Elysium Britannicum' made manifest.[53]

His relations with Margaret as she faced motherhood seemed calmer, more like the settled friendship with his first Electra, Lady Mordaunt; and he encouraged the two to become better acquainted. When Anne Howard, now a beautiful 20-year-old, attracted a passionate middle-aged suitor, the Prince of Orange's major-domo Sir Gabriel Sylvius, whose feelings she could not reciprocate, Evelyn had sufficient detachment to see the parallel with his own situation: 'I that have a natural pitie for sufferers (as having myself experienced that Bitter-Sweete) could not abstain from compassionating his condition . . . Lovers are only happy when he who loves is lov'd agen—which rarely hapning in the Creature, and when attain'd the feare of loosing what we love is so tormenting: let us endeavour to place it upon God when 'tis onely perfect & permanent & whom we can never love too much'.[54] On her wedding anniversary in May Margaret came to dine at Sayes Court with the new Lady Sylvius and her sister Dorothy. Then, as a last outing before she became too unwieldy to leave her house, Evelyn took all the women to see the botanic garden and private museum called 'The Ark' in south Lambeth.[55]

This was a curious and rather melancholy survival. Fifty years before it had been founded by the Tradescants, father and son, the most distinguished

---

[53] Ibid., iv. 140–4, 576.   [54] BL Add. MS 78298: JE to Anne Howard, 22 June 1677.
[55] JE, *Diary*, iv. 134–5, 138–9.

plantsmen of their generation, and opened to the public as one of the sights of London. But John Tradescant the younger had died in 1662 with no surviving heir, having conveyed his collections by deed of gift to the herald and antiquary Elias Ashmole. The settlement was then bitterly contested by his widow, who claimed that Ashmole had tricked her husband into signing it while he was drunk. When her life interest was confirmed in law, Ashmole promptly took possession of the property next door, in order, she claimed, to keep watch and oppress her. A few months before Evelyn's visit she had been found face down in a pond in the garden, drowned, and Ashmole moved immediately to acquire the lease of the house and garden. But he had none of the Tradescants' genius as a gardener and what had been one of the famous paradises of London was now in decline. It was chiefly the curiosities Evelyn and his party had come to see, and these were still a virtuoso's feast: the birds' eggs; the beaks, horns, and hooves of strange creatures 'not found in any Author'; the shells, insects, corals, and fossils; the 'Outlandish Fruits'; the tiny miraculous carvings, a set of chessmen in a peppercorn 'turned in ivory', a cherry stone with a dozen wooden spoons in it; the exotic weapons; the 'King of Virginia's habit all embroidered with shells', woman's breeches from Abyssinia, and night-caps of grass from the West Indies; a Roman lamp; and 'a steel-glasse that showes a long face on one side and a broad on the other'.[56] When they had browsed and exclaimed sufficiently over these, they mounted to one of the turrets of the house, which Ashmole grandly called his 'Tower of Speculation', with its vertiginous views across the Lambeth flats to the city, 'not discovering any house about the Country'. This eyrie was hung with mathematical instruments and stacked with books of astrological schemes and nativities. Evelyn, who had little time for astrology, dismissed these as the trappings of Ashmole's ego. He had risen by industry and advantageous marriages from a saddler's family to the office of Windsor Herald and Evelyn was prepared to recognize him as an industrious student and collector, but he wanted to be thought a great magus, a master of the occult, and 'I believe him as much a Conjuror as my-selfe'. Anne Sylvius also refused to be impressed, interrupting the explanations of his art with: 'come, leave off your Giberish, & tell us our fortunes: Here's a Lady with a Greate Belly: Shall she have a Boy?' Ashmole, amiably accepting the role of the popular fortune-teller, assured them that she would, 'a brave Child, be assur'd of it madame', and so passed on to Dorothy and her sister, 'which created a great deale of Innocent Mirth'. But as they all went downstairs, Mary Evelyn quietly bringing up the rear, Ashmole whispered to her 'with some concern' that he had not wanted

---

[56] Prudence Leith-Ross, *The John Tradescants* (1998), esp. 86–92, 118–162, 233–51.

to worry the company, but 'something makes me wish, that Lady may have a hapy delivery'. Back at Sayes Court she passed this on to her husband, but he pooh-poohed it as mere guesswork, pointing out that Ashmole had not constructed any horoscope for Margaret which could give it a basis in his art, and they both put it out of their minds.[57]

In the last weeks of her pregnancy Margaret's mood changed. Very unwieldy now, she seldom left her house except to attend service at the Chapel Royal. But it was a withdrawal in mind as well as body. The same restlessness and dissatisfaction with all the circumstances of her life overtook her as before her marriage, but she no longer saw a devotional retreat as the full solution. What she longed for was to be 'perfectly at repose and sin no more':

which endeed I long for more then for all the satisfactions of this world, for ther is no plesuer of this world to be chosen for it self. Eating is to satisfy the pain of hunger, sleep to eas wearynes, and devertiments are to take off the mind from being too long bent upon things that it cannot always atend without great inconvenience to the facultys of it: then retyerment again is to ease it of thos burthens and stains it has sustaind and contracted by being in company, so that our wholl life is, in my opinion, a search after remedys, which doe often if not always, exchange rather than cuer a diseas.[58]

Conscious of seeming melancholy and ill-humoured, she told Evelyn that he could always be sure of her friendship, 'let the apearances of the contraery be what they will'.[59] They were the last lines he ever received from her. He continued to call each Tuesday and encouraged his wife and Lady Mordaunt to visit as well, thinking that she would have more comfort from these older women with their long experience of childbirth. When they did so, they found her red-eyed and solemn. She explained that she had been doing 'a Sad; Yet (to her) a Pleasing thing', writing a letter to be given to her husband in the event of her death, containing her last requests and bequests, so that 'in Case I be to leave this World, no Earthly thing may take up my thoughts'. Fears and premonitions in pregnant women were common, but what made Margaret's case unusual was that she seemed to welcome the prospect. She told them she was sure she would not survive the birth, that she wanted to leave her husband one child as a 'Pledge of her intire Affection' and after that 'seem'd to thirst after nothing more, than to be with God'.[60]

At the end of August Godolphin left to join the court at Windsor. On Sunday 1 September Margaret took communion. On the following Tuesday morning Evelyn made his usual visit, found that her labour had come on in

---

[57] JE, *Diary*, iv. 138; *Life*, 72.
[58] BL Add. MS 78307, fo. 94: MB to JE, [1678], endorsed by JE, 'written a little before her death'.
[59] Hiscock I, 184–5.   [60] *Life*, 71–3, 79.

the night, and stayed to await the outcome. Her husband had been sent for, but would not, any more than Evelyn, have been allowed into the darkened and exclusively female domain of the birth chamber even if he had been in the house. The midwife was with her, and so were the group of friends whom she had chosen to sustain her during her labour, Anne Sylvius and her sisters-in-law, Jael Boscawen and Penelope Godolphin, the latter apparently an exception to the normal rule that only married women should attend a birth. They reassured Evelyn that Margaret had gone through her labour well, and within the hour Anne Sylvius came out to tell him that she was delivered of a son. Shortly afterwards he was allowed in to see the child, first in the midwife's arms and then laid by its mother. Margaret's first words to him were, 'I hope you have given Thanks to God for his infinite Mercy to me.' The baby was sturdy and thriving and Margaret's fears that she would not come through the birth had not been realized. The child was put in the care of the wet-nurse, and the friends and family thought only of 'Rejoicing, and Praising-God, Auguring a thousand Benedictions'.[61] Later that day Godolphin arrived from Windsor. Godparents were chosen: his brother Sir William, his court mentor John Hervey, and Lady Berkeley. On Thursday the chaplain who officiated in the family, perhaps Edward Lake who had married them, baptized the baby, following a growing though still rather controversial fashion, in the mother's bedchamber. In the family tradition he was given the name of his paternal grandfather: Francis. Mrs Evelyn came up from Deptford to congratulate and together she and her husband returned home, 'as full of Joy and Satisfaction, as we could be'.[62]

Then on the following Sunday morning, while they were at morning service in Deptford church, a note, minutely folded and shakily written, was handed to Evelyn by a messenger:

My poore Wife is fall'n very Ill of a Feavour, with lightnesse in her head: You know who says, The Prayers of the faithfull, Shall Save the Sick: I humbly beg your Charitable Prayers for this poore Creature, and your distracted Servant: S.G.

Evelyn never forgot the physical pang of acute anxiety and foreboding which shot through him as he took in the contents of the scrap of paper: 'Oh! how was I transfix't with this, as with a Dart!'[63] High fever in a woman who had recently given birth was the most ominous of symptoms. He and his wife hurried back to Whitehall, and there found Margaret 'in all the Circumstances of Danger'. Although she was still able to recognize them, she

---

[61] Ibid. 75. For childbirth customs and male exclusion, see David Cressy, *Birth, Marriage & Death: Ritual, Religion and the Life-Cycle in Tudor and Stuart England* (Oxford, 1997), 55–9.
[62] *Life*, 75. [63] BL Add. MS 78307, fo. 95: SG to JE, [8 Sept. 1678]; *Life*, 76.

was intermittently delirious and rambling in her speech. With the weather still as hot as high summer London was unhealthy, and their first thought was that she had succumbed to the prevailing 'malignant fever'. By the end of the day her fits of delirium were so violent that she had to be forcibly restrained in bed and afterwards she sank back in utter lassitude and exhaustion. But Mary Evelyn learned that she had continued to bleed ever since the birth, and when an inflamed rash began to spread rapidly over her back and breast it became quite clear that this was no seasonal fever but a complication of childbirth, 'some Accident, in which the Midwife was Concern'd; and might perhaps not performe her part skillfully'.[64]

Two of the court doctors, Thomas Short and Richard Lower, the latter a pioneering anatomist and physiologist, had been called in, but in Margaret's weakened state would prescribe nothing but blisters and cordials to sustain her strength. On Mary Evelyn's advice Hugh Chamberlen, of the famous Huguenot family of 'man-midwives', was also sent for. When he could not be found by the evening and seeing that Margaret now seemed a little calmer, she returned to her own children at Sayes Court and at nine o'clock Evelyn also retired to his King's Street lodgings a few hundred yards away. Then at about eleven at night Chamberlen arrived and Evelyn was sent for again to consult with him. It was common for male surgical practitioners to be summoned to a birth when the midwife's normal methods of delivery had failed. Usually their task was to extract the foetus surgically in order to save the mother's life; obstetric forceps were the closely guarded secret of the Chamberlens' success. He agreed with the Evelyns that 'the Midwife (to whom I perceiv'd he was no friend) had left something behind that might be the cause of these malignant Vapours'.[65] It was now clear in fact that in Margaret's case the final stage of labour, the delivery of the placenta, had not taken place in the normal way shortly after the birth. This meant that it had to be extracted manually and Chamberlen's examination evidently showed that the midwife had not succeeded in doing so completely. The continued bleeding meant that Margaret was already weakened as she faced the main onslaught of her illness. For at some point the midwife had unknowingly (for a carrier might be asymptomatic) introduced the virulent infective agent which must have been familiar in its outward signs to all the medical men present. The fiery inflammation of erisypelas spreading rapidly over Margaret's upper

---

[64] *Life*, 76; JE, *Diary*, iv. 148. For the high mortality in this year from epidemic ague or intermittent fever, see Mary J. Dobson, *Contours of Death and Disease in Early Modern England* (Cambridge, 1997), 415.

[65] Hiscock I, 186: JE to ME, [8–9 Sept. 1678]; Adrian Wilson, *The Making of Man-Midwifery* (1995), 47–57.

body was an unmistakable symptom. From the site where it had been introduced the infection quickly spread through the bloodstream to produce high
fever and generalized septicaemia. The doctors did yet not call it by its later
name 'puerperal sepsis', and the agent responsible, *Streptococcus pyogenes*, was
not to be identified for several more generations. They could only speak of
'malignant Vapours' spreading from the womb, but they must have known from
experience that there was absolutely no effective treatment. Once the infection had taken hold, as it clearly had in Margaret's case, death was inevitable.[66]

To try to contain and distance his anguish Evelyn began a letter to his wife,
adding to it 'by snatches, being continualy call'd away upon some occasion or
other'. He and all those at the bedside were frantic at the unwillingness of the
doctors to attempt any significant treatment. Chamberlen did say that he
'would have don something', but not without consultation with the other
medical men. By this time they were into the early hours of Monday morning. Lower and Short would not return until daybreak. The only physician
Evelyn could prevail upon to come immediately was his old friend Gasper
Needham, who had attended his son's deathbed and was now in failing health
himself. As soon as he saw Margaret he agreed that there was 'no safe
medling', 'the malignancy of the distemper being (as he sayd) so high & dangerous . . . so as besides a Frontal of Red rose cake, Vinegar & nutmeg; they
would direct no more'. Then they left, saying that they would attend again in
the morning.[67]

Margaret's family and friends watched and ministered to her as best they
could for what remained of the night, with 'a Resolution of attempting
something at Adventure' if she lasted till morning. Very early Lower and
Short called again and found the rash had spread as far as her waist, 'as thick
& fiery as you can possibly imagine'. Having ordered the blisters to be
changed, they left again 'without anything at all don', but agreed to return to
meet Needham and Chamberlen for a last consultation at eleven. Margaret's
pain and delirium were by this time so violent that her shrieks could be heard
'to the farther part of Whitehall'. Those at her bedside could hardly bear to
be present, 'and yet without great strength & company, there is no keeping
her in the bed'. At intervals between convulsions she sank back exhausted,
her pulse so feeble that it could scarcely be felt, 'and in one of these I feare she
will go away', Evelyn wrote to his wife, 'so as I can see very small hopes from

---

[66] Irving Loudon, *Death in Childbirth: An International Study of Maternal Care and Maternal Mortality 1800–1920* (Oxford, 1992), 49–84; although this relates to a later period, the stages of the puerperal infection it describes exactly correspond with those recounted by Evelyn of Margaret's deathbed.

[67] Hiscock I, 186–8: JE to ME, [8–9 Sept. 1678]; JE, *Diary*, iii. 209; iv. 183.

any Crisis, but rather that she grows worse & worse'. Godolphin, prostrate and beside himself, begged him to stay and deal with the doctors since he could not do so coherently. Evelyn had already given Needham and Chamberlen each their two guineas, and in the calm of hopelessness wrote to his wife, '& now at the 3d consultation (which I presume will be the last) we shall see their utmost resolution: the case I find being desperate'.[68]

All the schools of medical practice had attended Margaret; the midwife with her traditional functions, the new 'man-midwife', the two experimental physicians, and Needham of the older school. All agreed that conventional remedies were useless. In their desperation her friends turned to what Evelyn would otherwise have dismissed as quackery: the alchemical elixir of life, claimed to derive its authority 'from Hermes himself immediately after the Flood', gold in liquid form: *aurum potabile*. Evelyn had been acquainted with this long before by its Parisian manufacturer, Claude Rousselle. Now a Scandanavian physician, Dr Albert Otto Faber, was promulgating the remedy in England and claimed one cure already from within Evelyn's family.[69] He had a further devotee in the ailing Lady Mordaunt, and it was she who now sent a quantity of it, with the encouragement that it had been known to perform 'great matters' in desperate cases. Lower and Short, the 'Methodist Physitians', as Evelyn now called his Royal Society fellows dismissively, shook their heads and refused to authorize the administering of it, sending their apothecary away with another prescription of their own, 'which was onely a forme'. Margaret's agonizing convulsions grew ever more frequent, until 'the good man himselfe, no longer able to heare or beare it; with the silence, tho' (I cannot say) consent of the doctors, gave way that the famous (I must now call it something else) *Aurum potabile*, was given her'. Having swallowed two or three spoonfuls, she seemed to grow quieter, but then her convulsions returned and this time she was too far spent to sustain them. Tears flooded from her eyes and she sank into unconsciousness.[70]

The clergyman who had christened the child had remained in the background, as much to sustain the family as Margaret herself, and now came forward to speak the last rites. As he did so Evelyn and Anne Sylvius, holding her by either hand, felt her pulse cease and knew that she was 'deliver'd from all earthly miserys'. It was a little after one o'clock in the afternoon on

---

[68] Hiscock I, 186–8: JE to ME, [8–9 Sept. 1678]; *Life*, 76–8.

[69] JE, *Diary*, iii. 86; Faber, *De auro potabilia medicinali* (1677), a promotional pamphlet, claiming (p. 2) amongst others a cure of Lady Lewkenor, whose sister was the widow of Evelyn's brother Richard and afterwards courted by William Glanville. For alchemy and *aurum potabile*, see Keith Thomas, *Religion and the Decline of Magic* (Harmondsworth, 1973), 271.

[70] Hiscock I, 188–9: JE to ME, [8–9 Sept. 1678]; *Life*, 78, 201–2.

Monday 9 September, six days after she had given birth. In her delirium she had not made the 'good death' for which her whole life had seemed to prepare her. There had been no final communion, no consoling blessings and farewells. The only comfort Evelyn could find to record was that 'in all this disorder of Phancy (& almost distraction) she utter'd not one Sylable or Expression, that might in the least offend God, or any Creature about her ... which Shew'd how blessed a thing it is to live holily & carefully as this Innocent did: Persons that are Delirious usualy uttering Extravagances which discover their worst Inclynations'. And as her features relaxed he had a last glimpse of her, 'Lovely in death, & like an angel'. 'My teares suffer me to say no more,' he wrote to his wife, and '... I truely cannot say enough to describe a losse, that is not to be express'd; for I am in sorrow unspeakable.'[71]

Yet it was he who still had to sustain the burden of the traumatized household, for the servants as well as family and friends were all left prostrate with shock and exhaustion. 'There is no Creature in the House who either gos about anything,' Evelyn told his wife, 'or I thinke minds what is necessary to be don; either with the Corps, or the poore Child, or any thing else.' Yet the heat of the season and the manner of Margaret's death meant that there must be no delay. It fell to him to pay off the doctors and apothecaries and as quickly as possible have the body prepared for burial. He asked his wife to come up the next day if she could, to see that the baby was being properly cared for; 'I am for my owne part confounded also, & begin to be weary & to desire solitude, that I may also bemoane my selfe a little, before my time also come'. He assured her that for all his watching and grief he was well, but stalwart and enduring as he was, a weariness to death with this unrelenting burden of practicalities descended on him: 'ah that I were where my Friend is, for she is hapy, her part is finish'd'. 'Do what you think fit', he added desolately, 'for we are sad Creatures. Never was there such a Tragedy on the suddaine.'[72]

His wife, though a little more distanced, was herself deeply saddened by the loss: 'I cannot work off perpetual regrets and whilst I live shall lament the losse of so worthy a creature, I dayly think of her, the first thing when I wake the whole day and last when I go to sleep ... it is some years since any thing has touched me so neerly.' Her chief concern was for his welfare; 'I can [not help being] in paine [that you] are hourly among the afflicted and [though you may] be usefull to them in doing the part of a friend yet you may hurt your selfe by continuing the cause of your sorrow'; and when he was not with

---

[71] Hiscock I, 189: JE to ME, [8–9 Sept. 1678]; *Life*, 77–8; JE, *Diary*, iv. 151; cf. Ralph Houlbrooke, *Death, Religion and the Family in England 1489–1750* (Oxford, 1998), 28.
[72] Hiscock I, 189–190: JE to ME, [8–9 Sept. 1678].

them he had only his bleak lodgings as a refuge, 'without a servant or friend to eat with'. But his preoccupation with Margaret to the exclusion of his family made her tentative in offering him consolation: 'Deare make use of christianity and beare up against this severe attaque, remember all are not gon that loves you and you have some who require your care for them, they would be comforts to you would you receive them so.' She could only urge him conventionally to 'strive against excessive griefe, it is unjust to wish her in this unsteady world, from a place where questionlesse she is happy and at rest'.[73] But to Ralph Bohun she spoke more freely:

I declare from the bottom of my heart I never saw so much witt prudence good nature virtue generosity equity piety and charity joined to so pleasing and beautiful a person. She had the graces of a Court and the sincerity, innocency and zeale of a primitive Christian, never desirous of long life infinitly grateful to God for the bless-ings she enjoyed, in all her expressions owning she had fulfilled all her desires as to husband, fortune, friends, and last of all in the gift of this child which like Rachell cost her her life, well she is gone a miracle of a woman, her example cannot but work upon all that knew her, I rejoice to have bin in her esteme and tho not in the first rank of her friends yet infinitly obliged to her growing kindnesse . . . she is happy, happier than conquering princes who seek matter for future glory.[74]

In his overwhelming sense of loss Evelyn could find no such consolation, only punishment for his own failings. 'I know the part you will bear in this affliction', he wrote to Lady Mordaunt, 'but what is that whilst I still am mis-erable, & see no end of it . . . Her soul was precious to God, and he will have her ours no longer because the happinesse was too great: too greate for me indeede, unworthy sinner.'[75] The condolence which probably gave him the most comfort came from Lady Sunderland at Althorp. Just beforehand, knowing nothing of Margaret's situation, she had written to him to ask his help in ordering her tangled financial affairs. As soon as she heard what had happened she wrote again, an unexpected tribute from so worldly a courtier to Margaret's influence and their ideal of friendship:

the part I have in this great loss of ours can never be comprehended but by thos who have had their share in the comforts I have received from her tender friendship and rare example, yourself being one . . . I do with all my soul mourn with you and for you and beseech almighty god to enable you to bear this great afliction and beg you will oftener remember poor sinfull mee in your prayers then ever as being a slothfull creature to all good and now lord help mee that have lost so pious an exhorter that never failed to put me in mind of my duty by her councell and example, how

---

[73] BL Add. MS 78300: ME to JE, [*c*.9 Sept. 1678].
[74] BL Add. MS 78539: ME to Bohun, 10 Sept. [1678].
[75] BL Add. MS 78309: JE to Lady Mordaunt, Monday [9 Sept. 1678].

unspeakable are the obligations I have to her and for ever shall her memory be dear to mee . . . Good sir let mee have the benefit of your prayers and help by your advice for besids the perticular esteeme and valewe I have for your piety the friendship my dear frend had for you and which none knows better then my self, that I say must ever make you and all your concerns my own, my unworthy prayers you shall never faile of whilst I live, lord make us all fitt to meet that blessed saint in the happy place she is gone to, I can say no more, God of his infinit mercye comfort you.[76]

The letter Margaret had written in the last days of her pregnancy, to be delivered to her husband 'in case of mortal accidents', was now opened and read. It concerned Evelyn, since it fell to him as Margaret's trustee to execute some of its bequests. As he recorded it, it was an uncannily prescient document, assuming as a certainty what in fact happened: that she herself would die but the child survive: 'In the first place, my Deare, Believe me; That of all Earthly-things, you were, and are the most deare to me; and I am Convinc'd, that no body ever had a better, or half so good an Husband.' She went on to beg his pardon for her failings: her inexperience as a housekeeper and being 'oftener Melancholy & Splenetick more than I had Cause to be: I was allways asham'd of my-selfe, when I was so . . . and I hope it will come into the number of faults that I could not help.' She asked him to be kind to the child she left behind, 'for my Sake, who Loved you so well: But I neede not bid you: I know you will be so'; but assuming that he would eventually remarry, she asked him to let his sisters bring it up, 'for it may be, tho' you will love it, my Successor may not be so fond of it, as They I am sure, will be'. There were some bequests: money for her servants; her share of the Spalding lease to be divided between her two unmarried sisters; £100 for an impoverished cousin; a diamond ring for Lady Sylvius and customary mourning rings for Godolphin's five sisters. But to Evelyn's great distress there was no mention of him except as her trustee and the distributor of her charity. He could only reconcile himself to this by reflecting that she had made no mention of her brothers-in-law either, or of any male relation; that she had often in her lifetime expressed a wish to do him service; and above all that he still had her picture and her letters acknowledging the value of their friendship, 'which I preserve & Value above all she Could else have bequeathd me'.[77]

Margaret's last and probably least expected request was that her body should be taken to Cornwall, 'where I have had such a mind to go my-selfe', to be buried with Godolphin's ancestors in Breage church; 'I believe if I were Caryed by Sea, The Expense would not be very greate'; but she added, 'I don't Insist on that Place, if you think it not reasonable: Lay me where you

[76] Ibid.: Lady Sunderland to JE, [2], 14 Sept. 1678.   [77] *Life*, 79–83.

please.' 'Now, my Deare, God b'uy', she ended, 'Pray God blesse you, and keepe you his Faithfull Servant for ever: In him be all your Joy & delight, Satisfaction and Comfort; and do not grieve too-much for me; since I hope, I shall be Hapy, being very-much Resigned to Gods-Will, and leaving this World with (I hope in Christ-Jesus) a Good Conscience.' Then she added the blessing which concluded the communion service: 'The Peace and God which passeth all Understanding, keepe your heart & Mind In the Knowledge & Love of God, & of his Sonn Jesus Christ our Lord: And the Blessing of God Almighty, The Father, the Sonn & the Holy Ghost, be with Thee and remaine with Thee Ever & Ever Amen.'[78]

The transportation of a corpse long distances to an ancestral home for burial was an expensive business, normally undertaken only for territorial magnates.[79] Since the deaths of their parents three of Godolphin's brothers and sisters had died, Francis in Dublin and two of the unmarried sisters, one of them not far from home, and none had been taken back to Godolphin for burial. Yet it was immediately decided that Margaret's wish should be carried out. Perhaps as a kind of expiation for never having given her the retreat from court which she had longed for, Godolphin decided that the long journey should be taken, not by sea but by road, as an almost penitential procession of her family and servants. The Scotland Yard lodgings would be dismantled and sold to meet the costs, which even without undue ostentation amounted to several hundred pounds. When Mary Evelyn learnt this she asked Evelyn to retrieve the picture she had painted for Margaret, so that it would not be dispersed amongst the rest, and added 'if upon the sale of the goods there were any th[ing] of use in our way I should esteeme it doubly and purchase it for that reason'.[80]

Evelyn had already taken care of the first preparations. Margaret's body was embalmed and encased in a lead coffin, essential when there was to be a long interval before burial. On the lid he had soldered a brass plate, engraved with his own Latin inscription. This gave the details of her parentage and marriage and was perhaps intended as a guide for the memorial tablet at her burial place, but he had also added, as he had done so often before, the pentacle sign and the motto, 'Un Dieu Un Amy', so ensuring that these insignia of their friendship would be buried with her. Then, 'being so full of sorrow and tir'd with it', he at last returned home for two days' respite at Sayes Court, leaving the rest of the funeral arrangements to her family. On 16 September he returned to accompany the procession on its first stage out of London. By

---

[78] Ibid. 81.
[79] Clare Gittings, *Death, Burial and the Individual in Early Modern England* (London, 1984), 131–2; Houlbrooke, *Death, Religion and the Family*, 267.
[80] BL Add. MS 78300: ME to JE, [*c*.9 Sept. 1678].

Margaret's wish and from the need to keep the cost within bounds it was 'without the least pomp'. The hearse with six horses was accompanied by Sir William, two more of the brothers, Henry and Charles, the three unmarried sisters, Penelope, Katherine, and Anne, and for the first stage at least, by twenty or so more of her relations and servants.[81] Godolphin, unable to contemplate the slow journey with his wife's body, remained behind in London to follow later, as did Jael Boscawen, who was nursing a sick child.

From its first stopping-place at Hounslow the procession with its smaller escort went on in slow stages through the western counties, past Salisbury, down to Exeter, and into Cornwall. Each night the coffin was set up in an inn or house with tapers burning and servants watching by it.[82] As they drew closer to the foot of the county the countryside took on its characteristic appearance, bleak and barren, sculpted by sea-winds, with 'pared hedges and dwarf-grown trees', stone houses built low for shelter from storms, and the landscape scarred by tin workings: quarries, pits, stamping-mills, and 'blowing houses', where the ore was dug, crushed, and smelted. At last, after miles of stony road, they passed over an open heath, turned in at a gate and along an avenue of sycamore and ash, and came up to the low granite pile of Godolphin House in its grove of ancient misshapen oaks. It was a traditional Tudor house standing four-square round its courtyard. Only the entrance façade, added by Godolphin's father in the first flush of his inheritance, was unexpected in such a remote place: decorative crenellations above a Tuscan portico, looking for all the world 'like one of Inigo Jones's fairy castles for a masque at the Stuart court'.[83]

The original walled garden lay to the west, still known as the King's garden from the fact that Charles II, as Prince of Wales, had stayed a night in the house during his escape from England after the Civil War. To the east on rising ground was the more recent 'great garden' of nine compartments, bordered with hedges, the furthest and highest containing a piscina and bowling-green. The upper floors of the house had been modernized, but the lower one still had the traditional screened hall 'after the old collegiate manner'.[84] There the coffin was probably set up as a last resting place. If anyone present

---

[81] *Life*, 114; JE, *Diary*, iv. 151. When the coffin was discovered during a repair of the church in the late 19th century, it was identified by Evelyn's coffin-plate; see S. J. Wills, 'Discovery of the Coffin of Margaret Godolphin in St Breage Church', *Antiquary*, 25 (Jan.–June 1892), 202.

[82] JE, *Diary*, iv. 151.

[83] Richard Carew, *The Survey of Cornwall*, ed. F. E. Halliday (1953), 85; BL Add. MS 78512: 'Iter Occidentale': journal by JE's grandson, 1702; Roy Strong, 'A Week in the Country', *Country Life*, [*c.*1994–5] (from a cutting not precisely dated).

[84] Peter Herring, *Godolphin, Breage: An Archaeological and Historical Survey* (Truro: Cornwall Archaeological Unit, 1998), 67–9, 187–237; BL Add. MS 78512: 'Iter Occidentale', 1702.

wrote an account of the burial ceremony to Jael Boscawen in London, it has not survived. But a Godolphin homecoming always filled the hall with company, and it is likely that the neighbouring families, the Penroses, the Pennecks, the Orchards, the Paynters, the Sparnons, and the St Aubyns of Clowance and the Mount, were invited to receive the usual presents of black gloves and mourning rings and to follow the coffin the last three miles to Breage church, where the lanes and hedges would have been lined with the tin workers and cottagers Margaret had hoped to live among.[85] On 27 September, ten days after they had set out from London, the bell was tolled for her and the local clergyman spoke the burial service. The family vaults beneath the south aisle of the church had last been opened ten years before to receive Godolphin's parents. With difficulty one more space was found for Margaret's coffin, in a shallow grave only a foot beneath the floor. There must have been a dearth of local stone carvers, for just as the graves of Sir Francis and his wife had been left unmarked, no slab or memorial inscription was added to show her burial place.[86]

Godolphin now arrived to join his brothers and sisters. A few days later one of the unmarried sisters, the chonically ailing Katherine, became ill 'more than ordinarily' and died, of what seems to have been epilepsy. So, back in London, did Mrs Boscawen's daughter 'little Peggie', who had probably been Margaret's goddaughter, since Godolphin wrote that he was 'more than ordinarily concern'd for that child'. Jael Boscawen was the closest to him of all the sisters and to her he was able to express something of the admonitory meaning for him of all these deaths: 'God Almighty is able to send us Comforts equall to those he takes from us if he sees fitt, but tis better not to have our portion in this life; people are too apt in prosperity to forgett to whome they owe it. Affliction is easier to beare & keep one's duty. I hope you and I shall always endeavour to doe ours & I pray every day that wee may succeed in it, I doubt not but you doe so too.'[87]

From a distance he continued his negotiations to dispose of the Scotland Yard lodgings, relying on the Boscawens to accommodate him when he

---

[85] The guidebook by Patrick Thorne, *Breage and St Breaca's Church* (Breage, 1996), reproduces a seating plan of the church in 1666 with the names of the Godolphins' fellow parishioners; see also BL Add. MSS 28052, fo. 12, and 78531: Lady (Dorothy) Godolphin to her children, 2 Feb. 1667, 21 Mar. 1668, and Frances Godolphin to Jael Boscawen, 10 June [167–?]; Houlbrooke, *Death, Religion and the Family*, 282–9; Wills, 'Discovery of the Coffin of Margaret Godolphin', 201.

[86] Wills, 'Discovery of the Coffin of Margaret Godolphin', 201; BL Add. MS 78307: Francis Godolphin to JE, 5 July 1690. Cf. in general Julian Litten, *The English Way of Death: The Common Funeral since 1450* (1991).

[87] BL Add. MS 78530: SG to Jael Boscawen, 2, 5, 13 Oct. 1678; cf. Houlbrooke, *Death, Religion and the Family*, 222.

returned. By the second week of October he was on his way back to London, where he told his sister, 'I shall bee glad to see you & very few people besides.'[88] A retreat in Cornwall was not to be his solution in Margaret's death, any more than in her life. He had fulfilled her last wish and now he had to decide about his own future; whether to become an urban recluse like his elder brother or to give himself over, for all his misgivings, to the public career which was just opening to him. ❧

---

[88] BL Add. MS 78530: SG to Jael Boscawen, 6 Oct. 1678.

Epilogue

MARRIAGE with the prospect of childbearing always entailed risk for a woman. Longevity had been one of the advantages of a virgin life which Evelyn had mentioned to Margaret. Yet he never, in the light of the catastrophic outcome of her marriage, regretted helping to persuade her to take the conventional course. His belief in a divine providence governing the lives of men, which they both shared, offered no grounds for doing so. God, she had said, would dispose of her one way or other, and he had disposed of her in marriage. Some of her fears in advance had related to childbirth; not just of the event itself, but of having more children than could be provided for or of having none; but once she was married she longed for a child. Although the manner of her death had been inexpressibly harrowing, she had sometimes seemed to embrace the prospect of it in advance as a release from the conflicts which beset her in life. It remained for the survivors not to wish it otherwise, but to draw their own lessons from it.

In the immediate aftermath it had been useless for Godolphin's family to offer him conventional exhortations against excessive sorrow. In Margaret's last hours he had been 'allmost dead with griefe', in Evelyn's words to his wife, '& lying for the most part flat on the boards, which he drownes with his teares'; 'when the torrent will abate, I do not see', he added to Lady Mordaunt, 'for this has broaken all our measures to pieces'.[1] But to most people it appeared that after this first collapse he recovered his composure very quickly. Even close friends were kept at a distance. 'For the advise, it would be well for me I think if I needed itt,' Godolphin replied to a friend who wrote to him in Cornwall, urging him not to give way to his grief, 'but my temper which you mistake is sufficiently proofe agaynst all melancholly impressions how reasonable soever, and I ought to be asham'd of letting you see when I come to town agayn how little I have been wrought upon by soe great a Cause of affliction as you very well know I have had.'[2] He put his baby son in the care

[1] Hiscock I, 187: JE to ME, [8–9 Sept. 1678]; BL Add. MS 78309: JE to Lady Mordaunt, Monday [9 Sept. 1678].

[2] Longleat, Coventry MSS: SG to Henry Frederick Thynne, 8 Oct. 1678, quoted in Sir Tresham Lever, *Godolphin* (1952), 47.

of his sisters as Margaret had wished, took up temporary lodging in the Boscawens' house, and resumed his life at court as if his marriage had never been. 'The ladies' intelligence' was that he would be 'easily comforted'.[3]

Evelyn also had to go on living. 'He who loses his friend, loses half himself, is dead whilst alive, because half of him was in his Friend,' he wrote in his commonplace book; 'I am sensible (says St Augustine . . .) that my soule & that of my friends is but one soule in two bodys, therefore I hated life because I liv'd but halfe & therefore I also feared to die, least he should wholy die, whome I so lov'd.'[4] Having turned back from Margaret's funeral procession at Hounslow, he went not to Deptford but to Whitehall and spent the next afternoon with Godolphin, who was clearing the Scotland Yard lodgings of all traces of his married life. Together they went through Margaret's papers: prayers, meditations, sermon notes, letters, and resolutions for the conduct of her life, 'so pertinently digested, as if she had ben all her life a student in Divinity'. A sealed packet which Evelyn thought contained her confessional exchanges in cipher with Dean Benson was burnt at her request without being read. Godolphin put the rest of the papers into Evelyn's hands to sort and take out what he chose, as materials for the memorial life which he now proposed.[5] A funeral sermon was the commoner memorial in such cases, but Margaret's would be preached, if at all, in a remote parish where she was a complete stranger. The shared task broke down the barriers between them. Before they parted Evelyn offered to take Godolphin into Margaret's place in his friendship. When he returned to Sayes Court on 19 September, he repeated the offer by letter.[6]

Godolphin had certainly been aware of Evelyn's friendship with his wife, but chiefly as a kind of lay version of Dean Benson's spiritual mentorship. He had played no part, knowingly at least, in its intensities, Margaret had burnt all Evelyn's letters, some of which might have given a husband pause, and retained only the prayers and meditations. There is no suggestion that Godolphin suspected Evelyn of encouraging her reluctance to marry, but equally he had not regarded the friendship as sufficiently important to include him in the secret of their marriage when it did take place. Yet since that time they had both accepted considerable practical help from Evelyn, not just as Margaret's trustee but in the renovation of their Whitehall lodgings, and most of all in his support of the whole family during her catastrophic last days; and it must have been clear that he was as much devastated by her loss as any of her family. In the circumstances her failure to mention or

---

[3] Henry Hyde, 2nd Earl of Clarendon, *Correspondence*, ed. S. W. Singer (1828), ii. 31.

[4] BL Add. MS 78328, pp. 153–4: commonplace notes concerning friendship and MG.

[5] *Life*, 83, 93–4; JE, *Diary*, iv. 152.

[6] The letter does not survive, but its contents are clear from the following correspondence.

leave any bequest to him in her last letter was an omission which had to
be remedied. Godolphin gave him a memorial ring and assured him that
Margaret had often regretted not being able to repay her obligations to him
in any substantial way.[7] But he did far more than this, and probably very much
to Evelyn's surprise; he grasped the offer of friendship not just as a matter of
polite form, but as if it were a personal lifeline.

He began by begging Evelyn to compose a meditation for him to use every
Monday, the day of his wife's death, and sent a prayer of his own, 'that seeing
my first thoughts & sense upon this Affliction you may bee the better able to
follow & improve them for me'. Then he followed this with a long, deliberate, formal letter which Evelyn carefully preserved, inaugurating an independent spiritual friendship between them: 'I lay hold (to the great joy &
Comfort of my spirit) of the promise of your friendship & kindnesse; I lay
hold of it in the manner you offer it to me, I desire to fill the place that
she held with you & O if it were the will of the Almighty that I might doe it
worthyly'; it was the greatest consolation he could have, 'a beame of God
Almighty's countenance, & an earnest of his future care & protection of me'.
He promised 'most faithfully and inviolably' to keep Evelyn's letter as long as
he lived as a pledge of their friendship and to look on him from now on 'as
the Depository of all my concerns spirituall & temporall, to be wholly guided
& directed by you in the former, to have always a great regard to your opinion in the latter'. In contrast to the reticence he maintained with everyone
else, he confessed that he was 'divided, & almost rent between the submission
that I owe to God Almighty, & the ease that I seeke (& for the present
perhaps should find) in giving the rein to my griefe'; but his most pressing
anxiety, to which he was to return again and again in the coming weeks, was
that Margaret's influence over him, which had caused him to reform his way
of life, would gradually grow less with time, 'as wee see all impressions of
this nature are in most people', that his sense of spiritual regeneration would
gradually fail him, and 'I have no patience to think it shall be soe'. He sought
Evelyn's friendship as the best means of continuing it: ''tis that which I want,
'tis that which I would have wish'd of all earthly things'. 'And now', he added,
'you see I have putt you just in the place of her I have Lost.'[8]

A month later, after his return from Cornwall, Evelyn saw him again on
the routine business of making up his annual accounts as Margaret's trustee.[9]
Godolphin asked him to continue the same function for the benefit of the
little boy on whom her fortune was now settled, and he also made it quite

---

[7] *Life*, 82–3.   [8] BL Add. MS 78307: SG to JE, 22 Sept. 1678; *Life*, 5–6.
[9] JE, *Diary*, iv. 155.

clear that his earlier letter had not just been a passing mood in the aftermath of his loss. When Evelyn returned to Sayes Court, intending to stay there for some days, Godolphin's anxious letters followed him: 'if I should stay soe long without sometimes giving vent to those thoughts, I am fearfull that by degrees time would weare out the impressions of them in mee, & I am not able to contain myselfe in that thought'. Seeing that Evelyn was diffident at first, he confirmed their friendship and its function more vehemently than ever: 'when will you leave off making excuses for writing to me often, when I tell you as often, & will ever repeat it, that nothing now in the world gives me soe much satisfaction as hearing from you, & hearing a hundred things to continue mee the Vertue & Excellence of that Creature who is gone before us'. In his desperate need to extract some meaning from the loss and retain the sense of Margaret's saving grace, he added that he was 'almost come to that passe, as to blesse & admire the goodnesse & mercy of Almighty God even in taking her from me . . . whom nothing lesse than an Affliction of such Astonishment could restrain from consuming the greatest part of my time in folly & Vanity & sin'. He was convinced that he would not live long himself, and 'I doe not care to live for any reason but that I may be more fitt to die'; 'O that I had lived soe that I were prepared to meet it tomorrow.' 'This great affliction was necessary to take my thoughts wholly off from this world & fix them upon heavenly things,' he reiterated, 'I pray you therefore my deare Friend to beare with me in this thing, for I must vent it some way or other.'[10]

Since he found it easier to express his sense of what the friendship meant to him in writing than face to face, after each of their London meetings the letters would follow Evelyn to Sayes Court: 'I find myselfe often (especially after having been some time alone) soe full of what I owe you not only from the Effects of your Kindenesse to her that is gone, but also for your Continuance of it to mee, that tho unwilling to presse your modesty in speaking of it, while you are with me, I can't refuse my selfe the ease of letting you see my sense of it when you are absent.' He wanted to feel that the friendship was given not just for Margaret's sake but for his own,[11] and Evelyn was only too glad to respond. He still could not take comfort from the thought that Margaret was now at peace or enjoying the rewards of an exemplary life. He continued to be tormented by visions and fantasies of her and could only stave off mortal depression with the prospect of being reunited with her after death.[12] In the meantime his only comfort was in

[10] BL Add. MS 78307: SG to JE, 29 Oct. 1678.
[11] Ibid., 21 Nov., 31 Dec. 1678.
[12] BL Add. MS 78307: JE to SG, 9 Sept. 1679 (draft).

Godolphin's compensating friendship. To Philip Packer, his Middle Temple friend of years before, he confided, 'I confess this late loss has touched me nearly, and were it not for the consolation of that worthy person (her dear husband) I would not care at all to live: 'tis long that he has let me into his friendship and brotherly affection.'[13]

In the meantime the government was descending into a crisis which forced itself on everyone's attention. While Godolphin was still in Cornwall, a disreputable clergyman, Titus Oates, had laid before the Privy Council his fabricated tale of a Jesuit plot to assassinate the King and bring his brother to the throne. The general climate of uneasiness about Roman Catholicism ensured him a receptive hearing and two specific events seemed to confirm his tale: the discovery that the Duke of York's former secretary Edward Coleman, whose papers were seized at Oates's suggestion, had certainly harboured treasonable designs, and the violent death of Sir Edmund Godfrey, the magistrate before whom Oates had sworn his depositions. On 21 October, just as the alarm was about to spread, Parliament met. The 'Popish Plot' was the one thing capable of giving this corrupt and divided body common cause and purpose: 'nothing was don but in order to finding out the depth of this', Evelyn wrote in his diary, '. . . Oates was encouraged, & every thing he affirm'd taken for Gospel.'[14] Godolphin, appointed to the Commons committee for translating Coleman's papers, told Evelyn that 'there are strange things in them & like to bee attended (I veryly believe) with strange Consequences'.[15] By the first week in November the Duke of York had been barred from attending the Council and a bill was drawn up to exclude other Catholics from court and Parliament. Evelyn noted that on the birthday of the Queen, whose Roman Catholic physician was another of those implicated by Oates, 'I never saw the Court more brave, nor the nation in more apprehension.'[16] Soon the turmoil engulfed the whole government. Under threat of impeachment himself, Ralph Montagu had revealed to the Commons letters which showed Danby to have been involved in the procurement of subsidies from Louis XIV at the same time as he was asking them for supplies to make war against France. The Commons failed to force the Lords to commit him immediately for treason, but 'between you and I', Lady Sunderland wrote to Evelyn, 'I fear he will find he is ill-advised if he thinks to carry it with a high hand; for I believe he will prove a wounded deer and be very unserviceable to the King in the place he is in . . . I am told they mean to move him an enemy to the country, and that they will never give

---

[13] BL Add. MS 78298: JE to Philip Packer, 16 Dec. 1678.   [14] JE, *Diary*, iv. 154.
[15] BL Add. MS 78307: SG to JE, 29 Oct. 1678.   [16] JE, *Diary*, iv. 157.

money while he has the managing of it.'[17] To try to save his chief minister the King prorogued Parliament. 'As you may imagine peoples apprehensions are not a little encreased by itt,' Godolphin wrote to Evelyn, 'My Lord Mayor was sent for to the Councell to day & the King has assur'd him he will disband the army with all speed, that he will prosecute the plot, & secure the religion established, Amen I say, & soe says all England I believe.' A week later, when the prorogation had become a dissolution, he hoped that 'the new parliament will set all right',[18] but soon it was clear that there must be new ministers as well. In February Lady Sunderland let Evelyn know that her husband had accepted the post of Secretary of State; 'I pray God direct my lord and prosper him to the good of his country and to Gods glory. Pray for him and mee, and love mee I beg of you'; in a postscript she added, 'be so charitable as to furnish me with some prayer particular to the occasion'.[19]

Even at the height of his bereavement Godolphin had taken care not to sever his links with the court. His Cornish journey had coincided exactly with the King's departure for Newmarket and he timed his return for the meeting of Parliament. While he was away Laurence Hyde had continued to send him news of public affairs and he had even sent off letters by the foreign post, probably to William of Orange who was using him as intermediary for the payment of his wife's dowry.[20] His stay in his sister's household was only temporary. Before long he moved back to Whitehall to lodge with the Sunderlands.[21] Lord Sunderland was already in high office and when Danby should go, as it was clear he soon must, Laurence Hyde had ambitions to fill his place. They were both young and untried men at a time of great difficulty and danger and Godolphin was their closest associate and had long been marked for advancement. It was inevitable that he would soon be pressed to come in with them.

Despite all his pangs of conscience and memories of Margaret's strictures, his old way of life at court, the Christmas festivities and especially the gaming tables, began to draw him back. 'I am afrayd you use me too gently & are too kind a friend,' he wrote guiltily to Evelyn in December, 'I wish you would tell mee sometimes wherein I don't doe well, & don't fancy I should not like it, for indeed I deceive my selfe if I should not take it very kindly from you.' He had just suffered one of his recurrent attacks of stone in the kidneys,

---

[17] Bray, iii. 252–3: Lady Sunderland to JE, 25 Dec. 1678.
[18] BL Add. MS 78298: SG to JE, 31 Dec. 1678, 5 Jan. 1679.
[19] BL Add. MS 15889, fo. 21: Lady Sunderland to JE, 11 Feb. 1679.
[20] BL Add. MS 78530: SG to Jael Boscawen, 2, 5 Oct. 1678; Lever, *Godolphin*, 47.
[21] BL Add. MS 78530: SG to Jael Boscawen, 13 Oct. 1678, 6 Oct. 1679 (referring to his bed at the Sunderlands).

and 'I have need enough of the sharpest remembrances to keep me close to my duty, & from swerving after the world.' But he added, just as he had once protested to the sceptical Margaret, that this 'swerving' was not from his own choice; 'at this time I can hardly keep from concerning myselfe in matters that perhaps doe but little belong to me, in which all the Comfort I have is that I am here whether I will or noe'; if he could follow his own mind, he assured Evelyn, he would 'quickly be out of a place where I have such continual pretexts for the careless life that I lead'. Then came the familiar appeal: 'You must pardon me in this thing, for if I should not sometimes give my selfe the ease of venting my grievances to you what an uncomfortable condition were I left in, & indeed I find great support in being able to speak to you as to a man whom I know both soe capable & soe desirous of giving me the best Counsell & assistance, & of these things which I now trouble you I never did speak to any body but one whom I was never weary of speaking to of them, or she to heare me.'[22] What lay behind all this was that the King was now planning to put the Treasury into commission; Laurence Hyde was to be one of its members, and Godolphin was proposed as another. Unable to wait until Evelyn came to town, he set out on foot to Sayes Court to talk over his dilemma. The Sunderlands, recognizing Evelyn's influence over him, enlisted his aid to overcome Godolphin's scruples and persuade him to accept.[23]

Margaret had been quite clear that her ideal was their complete departure from the court. When Godolphin told her that he stayed only out of a sense of duty or because he had no alternative, she was quite ready to accuse him of affectation. For Evelyn this was a much less straightforward matter, as Godolphin must have known quite well. He had repeatedly acknowledged his debt to Evelyn on his own and Margaret's account and promised to repay it with his patronage. In the most unequivocal terms he urged Evelyn to 'dispose of mee I beg you & of my endeavours to serve you in anything as freely as she might doe were she still alive . . . that she was wanting in this particular, was (I think) the only regrett she Left this World with, she as often recommended to me the supplying of it'.[24] This to Evelyn was too much the answer to a prayer to be ignored. The family was descending at an alarming rate into what he called a retrograde condition. The Prettyman lawsuit had now lasted for six years. The legal costs alone were crippling and there was still no prospect of a settlement. He was hastening the marriage of his son so as to have the dowry to clear their immediate claims, but in return he would

[22] BL Add. MS 78307: SG to JE, 5, 26 Jan. 1679.
[23] BL Add. MS 78298: JE to Lady Sunderland, [15 Mar. 1679].
[24] BL Add. MS 78307: SG to JE, 6 Dec. 1678.

have to settle the Sayes Court estate on the young couple, and soon his eldest daughter and then her two sisters would be marriageable and must have portions of their own. Evelyn needed a profitable office urgently, or failing that, one for his son or even his wife. Prettyman's claims had always been bound up with the long-standing debt owed to Sir Richard by the crown, and the settlement of Sayes Court made the extension of the crown lease again a live issue, especially as there were rumours that others were trying to obtain the reversion after the Evelyns' term of years should expire. With Godolphin at the Treasury he would have a better friend at court in all these matters than he had had since Clifford's death. As Godolphin trudged over the frosty riverside paths to Deptford he must have known perfectly well that Evelyn would be unlikely to advise him to refuse the prospect which was being held out to him.

Still, there was more to this than a ritual of pretence on the one hand and self-interest on the other. Evelyn's more worldly friends sought his advice and made him their conscience because they trusted his humanity, his judgement, and his capacity to reconcile opposing forces, and because they knew that in the last resort he would not let material considerations outweigh spiritual or moral ones. When Godolphin had once told Margaret that a life of country retirement would be 'too solitary' for him, he was trying to explain to her how necessary the occupations of public life and the easy, accepting social life of the court were to him. Even with her companionship he could not survive in contented reclusiveness, observing public affairs from a safe distance and filling his time with the amateur study of theology and medicine. To try to do so now that he was alone would be to court mortal depression. Yet the memory of Margaret's aspirations and the lessons her death seemed to have reinforced put him so much at odds with himself that when his friends urged him to join them in government he needed all Evelyn's reassurances that he would not simply be returning to 'vanity, folly and sin'. Evelyn, who had been exercised all his life by this debate between public and private virtue, compromising action and passive contemplation, understood his dilemma better than Margaret could. Even the diversions of the court, which he was willing to condemn in general, were a matter for indulgence in this case. His opinion of Godolphin's situation, as he summed it up a year or two later, was formed at this time and it was acute and humane:

You are perpetually in public business, and I am glad you are so, because you are else too much Soule, that is (according to Des Cartes) in continual Thought, which is prejudicial to you; and this would I have by any means diverted . . . Tis I assure you on this account that I often justifie all your other Recreations (which some are pleas'd to judge less favourably of) because I am assur'd you preserve your heart intirely to God: give him as much of your time as you can, and often think of that blessed saint, who allways pray'd you might do so.

He reassured Godolphin that to take public office when it was offered as a duty was no betrayal of his religious aspirations, 'such a worthy & able persone as you are knowne to be in spight of all your modestie and humble thoughts'. 'Who knows', he added, 'whether you are not come into the court for such a time as this?'[25]

Then just as Godolphin's appointment to the Treasury commission was settled Evelyn received another scrawled note from him, very like the one put into his hands in Deptford church at the onset of Margaret's illness. His youngest sister Anne, to whom all the family were devoted, had contracted smallpox; 'God Almighty send her & us patience, howsoever it bee his will to dispose of her,' Godolphin wrote; 'Wee have this comfort that there has not lived a Creature of more Innocence & sincerity of heart, nor better fitted for the next World . . . now you know our Condition pray for us.'[26] She died a few days later. The loss of another pious and unworldly young woman seemed once again to make all his intrigues and ambition meaningless. At her husband's urging Lady Sunderland begged Evelyn again to recall Godolphin to his public duty. Evelyn tried to do so; but 'the truth is', he reported, 'the sense of this late repeated affliction has at present so intierely possessed him, that he does not willingly entertain any mention of business, & this evening being appointed for the burial of the sister he loved, puts me out of all hopes of being able to perswade him to endure the court'.[27]

But it was not just bereavement which made Godolphin reluctant to accept public office by this time. A new set of country gentry was now assembling at Westminster, bitterly hostile to the court, demanding that the Duke of York be excluded from the succession, and likely to be suspicious of every aspect of the ministerial conduct. When Sunderland's appointment as Secretary of State was announced his wife wrote frankly to Evelyn, 'I cannot think it worth rejoicing much at it, as times now are.'[28] It did not help that Arlington, in the eyes of the new Parliament men a prime representative of the discredited court, had been the King's first thought to head the new Treasury commission. Yet Evelyn fully agreed that public occupation was more necessary for Godolphin now than ever; he would 'intirely resigne himselfe to Thoughts which will certainly consume him, if the Importunity of Friends & some Buisness forc'd as it were upon him, do not interpose'. But to insist that he must make it his personal decision in his present state would only force him deeper into paralysing depression; he must really be convinced that he had no choice. Evelyn's advice was that the King should simply announce the appointment and present it to Godolphin as an unavoidable duty. Only then would it cease to conflict with his religious scruples and he would feel free to 'receive his M's favour with all readiness'.[29] It turned out just as he predicted; Godolphin accepted his place on the Treasury commission without further demur. When at the eleventh hour the King appointed the Earl of Essex, a man of solid ability and credit with the opposition, in Arlington's place, this did much to reconcile Godolphin to his post as well.[30] His long and distinguished public career was to be punctuated with such episodes and Margaret was certainly not the last to suggest that they were an affectation. He 'constantly refused every thing that he was sure would be forced upon him', an opponent commented sarcastically years later. Only Evelyn and a few others closest to him, the Sunderlands and later John Churchill, understood how necessary these rituals were to him and why.[31]

Godolphin assured Evelyn that his greatest satisfaction in the appointment was that it might 'one time or other furnish me with means of doing you some little service', and that he would neglect no occasion 'consisting with my duty & the trust I am to discharge'; but the timing, he added, must be up to him.[32] He still sought Evelyn's company and advice, spending hours *tête à tête* with him in his study or walking in Greenwich Park. As the spring came on Lady Sunderland and Mrs Boscawen begged a 'play day' for him from the Treasury and brought him down with them to see the garden. Evelyn presented him with a copy of the latest enlarged edition of *Sylva*, with the hope that 'when Mr Godolphin shall be sated with the Splendor & Pomp of courts . . . he will (when I am dead & gon) betake himselfe to the Country, Contemplate these Rusticities with more solid delight, and tast the Pleasures of Life, the next of kin to happinesse of any on this earthly Stage'.[33] When the news came that first Catherine Talbot in Dublin and then Lady Mordaunt in Paris had died, Evelyn reminded him how Margaret, if she had lived, would also have missed them; 'it seems to me as if God had cald her first . . . and sent for the rest, to accompany & rejoice her . . . do not you find something that does greatly refresh us both as oft as we think of it, that at

[29] BL Add. MS 78298: JE to Lady Sunderland, [15 Mar. 1679].

[30] BL Add. MS 15889, fo. 33: Lady Sunderland to JE, 28 Mar. 1679.

[31] Gilbert Burnet, *History of his own Time*, ed. M. J. R[outh] (Oxford, 1833), v. 8, Dartmouth's note; Lever, *Godolphin*, 82.

[32] BL Add. MS 78307: SG to JE, 27 Mar. 1679.

[33] BL Add. MSS 78431: JE to ME, 29 Apr. 1679; 78307: JE to SG, 17 Oct. [1679]; 15889, fo. 35: Lady Sunderland to JE, 14 May 1679.

our migration when we depart from hence, we shall all be restor'd to our deare Friends, never more to be separated from one another?'; but with so many gone, he added, 'how happy I am that God has spared me you'. More diffident now about writing on personal matters, he added, 'do not reproach a Confidence which your own goodness has created, for be assured I will use it modestly'.[34] Godolphin responded as warmly as before. 'Mr Godolphin is exceedingly kind to me,' Evelyn wrote to Anne Sylvius, '& these topics are our often Entertainment; & if his signal Friendship to me, ded not in some measure supply my losse beyond what I ever expected, I should be very miserable: He says, & writes the same to me; but in the meane time we are both miserable Comfortees.'[35]

What laid an impossible burden on the friendship and mutual dependence was the issue of patronage which Godolphin himself had raised. Evelyn's wife and father-in-law irritated him with their naive expectations that everything they desired concerning the lawsuit would now be granted as a matter of course. He knew that these were complex issues with myriad conflicting interests and snappishly wished Sir Richard had sufficient health to bestir himself on his own account and not lay the whole burden on him; 'if you expect I should do wonders upon my score of acquaintance (as you seem to do) . . . you lay a thing on me which I cannot promise you to succeed in . . . I cannot force great men to do what we wish'. In fact it was soon clear that for all Godolphin's genuine goodwill, no quick return could be expected from his patronage. At the Treasury he was still very much a junior partner. Supernumerary offices throughout the government were to be retrenched and experienced candidates for all essential posts were at a premium. He told Evelyn that he was finding it difficult to place even his young brother Charles 'in something worth his time'; only 'very meane Unprofitable offices' presented themselves, unsuitable for Evelyn or his son.[36]

Although Evelyn was a respected figure in his own field, his perception of himself as capable of being 'considerable' in government was an additional problem. Although Godolphin could not say so outright, at almost 60, with limited qualifications and a notorious reluctance to adapt to court ways, he would be even more difficult to provide for than before. Godolphin could only hint at the re-establishment of Council of Trade and Plantations, and even in that case the fact that Evelyn had no parliamentary connections would now be a disadvantage.[37] Evelyn himself continued to hanker, quite

[34] BL Add. MS 78307: JE to SG, [May 1680].
[35] BL Add. MS 78299: JE to Lady Sylvius, May 1679.
[36] BL Add. MS 78431: JE to ME, 29 Apr. 1679.   [37] Ibid.

unrealistically, for a place on one of the Revenue or Navy boards. In case Godolphin's junior status should be a handicap, he tried to enlist Sunderland's aid as well. Lady Sunderland, whom he was helping with her garden and the renovation of her Whitehall lodgings, assured him that 'my lord does not need any solicitation for I have many times of his own thought heard him say that twould be of very great satisfaction to him if he could do you any service'.[38] But the first anniversary of Margaret's death came and went with no change in Evelyn's circumstances.

'She's continually with me, ever before me, always in my thoughts, and with unaffected sincerity I can affirme it that there has never pass'd a day, seldome an hour in a day, wherein I have not remembrance of her,' Evelyn wrote to Godolphin on the anniversary, 'I place her in the calendar of Saints, and call this *Her Day*, I doubt not with as just a merite as any that has been canonized among the Apostles, Blessed Martyrs & Confessors . . . I lost in that happy Creature all Relations. She was neither Wife, Mother, nor Sister to me, but she was something which was above them all, but which has no name in this world.' As if accepting that their ways would inevitably part, he added, 'go you still on & leave me to mourne this losse which is verily your Crowne . . . that there is a Saint in Heaven who continually prays for you'.[39] Yet Godolphin, whose taciturnity was now becoming a byword at court, still responded warmly and at length, in terms that could leave Evelyn in no doubt that their personal friendship was as important to him as ever. He had thrust his grief aside at first, he admitted, but only because he could not dwell on it and keep his sanity:

to this houre were I only to Consider myselfe, I should bee of the same opinion & nothing could relieve me at all but the assurance I have of the felicity of that excellent Creature who was too precious for any place but that which by the mercy of God in Christ Jesus I trust she is now possess'd . . . Deare Mr Evelyn, there is nothing I take so much comfort in, nor value so much as the Continuance of your kindnesse & assistance in all the occasions of my life & thereafter Lett me beg of you that whenever your thoughts are so kind as to prompt you to say any thing to me upon this or any other subject what so ever, that you would not lett yourselfe be discouraged from it, either by any apprehension of my want of kindnesse or Leisure to entertayne it as I ought, or by any other yett more slender pretence which your own modesty may perhaps suggest to you, but bee assured . . . wherever I am & whatever becomes of me in the world, you & any thing that comes from you shall always bee most welcome to me.[40]

[38] BL Add. MS 78309: Lady Sunderland to JE, 7 July [1679].
[39] BL Add. MS 78307: JE to SG, 9 Sept. 1679 (draft).
[40] Ibid.: SG to JE, 11 Sept. 1679.

Hitherto Danby's place as first minister had been supplied by a partnership of elder statesmen, the Earls of Essex and Halifax and Sir William Temple. But when the King prorogued his new Parliament in the summer of 1679 and would not allow its successor, even more hostile to the court, to meet, Essex resigned from the Treasury and Halifax and Temple retreated also. In Essex's place as First Lord rose the difficult, hot-tempered, but extremely able and hard-working Laurence Hyde. He and Sunderland then drew in Godolphin as a third member of their ministerial group. On these young men, rather contemptuously dubbed 'the chits', now devolved the direction of the King's business and all the turbulence of the coming Exclusion crisis.[41] There was talk of Godolphin's intended remarriage, something which Evelyn himself was quite prepared for, but which Lady Sunderland was convinced would never happen, now or in the future.[42] And she was quite right. Godolphin buried himself in his Treasury business, his only relaxations being the breeding of racehorses, which his increased income now let him indulge in, and periodic visits to Jael Boscawen's household to see his little son; 'he grows infinitly fond of him', she noted, and when he let more than a day or two pass without a visit, added dryly, 'he has enough to doe of all conscience and makes his new mares . . . wait six, seven, nay eight hours at a time without ever minding them'.[43] Evelyn and Lady Sunderland joined the family in a kind of joint guardianship over 'our little boy', and Jael Boscawen became if anything more devoted to him than to her own children; so that when he came safely through smallpox Lady Sunderland thanked God not only for his sake, but for hers, 'whose life I thinke, I'm sure her comfort is bound up in him'.[44]

With the encouragement of the anniversary letter Evelyn continued to write; though not as often, he assured Godolphin, as he was urged to do by 'the Importunities of those who are told I have some Interest in you'. He passed on the concerns of the Whig MPs who were not allowed to meet: 'they tell me nothing can secure the Nation, or satisfy the People in any sort, but such a settlement of the Protestant Religion as may leave no more place or cause for future jealousy,' but he addressed Godolphin as 'my dearest friend' even more tentatively now, as 'a compellation of greater familiarity'

---

[41] J. P. Kenyon, *Robert Spencer, Earl of Sunderland* (1958), 21–42.

[42] Henry Sidney, *Diary of the Times of Charles the Second*, ed. R. W. Blencowe (1843), i. 209: Lady Sunderland to Henry Sidney, 16 Dec. 1679.

[43] BL Add. MS 78531: Jael Boscawen to her sister [Penelope?], 13 Nov. [1680].

[44] BL Add. MS 15889, fos. 34, 36, 38, 54, 56, 96: Lady Sunderland to JE, 28 Mar, 14 May, 11 June 1679, 27 Sept., 29 Dec. 1680, 29 June [1689]. In revising a list of his papers at Wotton [*c.*1702], Evelyn added the words 'son to me' above a reference to Francis Godolphin (Add. MS 78639); Hiscock characteristically added a note drawing attention to this.

than might be consistent with his new ministerial status. Godolphin replied promptly and kindly, but still without any specific favour to offer.[45]

What abruptly and completely changed their relations, shortly before the second anniversary of Margaret's death, was the fate of a petition of Sir Richard Browne to the Treasury concerning the lease of Sayes Court, asking again that he should be granted the lands in freehold, the cost to be deducted from 'the grand arrear' of his crown debt. It was refused flatly, as contrary to Treasury rules.[46] Evelyn was shocked and incredulous. His friend Sir Stephen Fox had now been added to the Treasury commission, and he and Godolphin had both agreed in principle beforehand that the petition was not unreasonable. Blaming Hyde's severity, Evelyn unwisely demanded that Godolphin reverse the decision: 'it is Certainely in your power to Revive it yet & fix it by going to Mr Hide . . . I am sure the thing is just, & proofe against all Apprehentions. In a word, remember I am your Friend, you mine, and now do like a Friend.'[47] Godolphin was clearly embarrassed, but it was also clear that he was quite unprepared to jeopardize his relations with his senior colleague by doing any such thing. The succession of intimate letters came to an abrupt end.

The event profoundly affected Evelyn's standing in his family. Neither Sir Richard nor his daughter could understand how his powerful friends could have given them such a rebuff. His own instinct was always to see such mortifications as a punishment for his moral failings. At a deeper level the episode made him question, probably for the first time, the whole basis of his friendship, not just with Godolphin, but with Margaret. With his sixtieth birthday approaching, he took himself right away from Sayes Court and his family and went up for a week to his London lodgings; not for any reason of business, but in order to be alone and engage in a long process of self-examination. It took him several days and his confessional notes, in minute, heavily abbreviated Latin, still survive. In parts they are not easy to decipher, but they include many references to Margaret Blagge and his 'excessive' attachment to her.[48] It appears that he could now acknowledge for the first time that their friendship, instead of being one stage in an ascent towards

[45] BL Add. MSS 78298, 78299: JE to SG, 12 Mar. '1679' [1680]; '9 Sept 1680' (but must have been written earlier in the year, shortly after his son's marriage).

[46] *CTB 1679–80*, 795; BL Add. MS 78614: William Harbord's report to the Treasury, 1 Apr. 1680.

[47] BL Add. MS 78307: JE to SG, draft 13 Aug. [written over Sept.] 1680.

[48] JE, *Diary*, iv. 223–4; Hiscock II, 126 and frontispiece; though it is not clear that the notes reproduced by Hiscock are those made at this time, since they contain entries up to 1688 with no obvious change of hand and refer back to the 'solem examinat.' of November 1680. For the original see BL Add. MS 78392, and for its content see further Appendix B below.

divine love, to be gradually transformed as he moved forward, had become
for him an end in itself. Partly from a love which he could not help and partly
from a conviction that she was his means of salvation, he had clung to her too
obsessively. Margaret herself had often tried to warn him of this and gently
encouraged him to detach himself. She had now gone beyond his reach and
he had to make his way alone. He resolved to dedicate the remainder of his
life to God.

But the family's parlous financial state continued and his wife and
father-in-law continued to make him feel that he was not doing enough to
safeguard their interests. In December 1681, when a further Test Act had
created some vacancies in government posts, he suppressed his hurt feelings
and approached Godolphin again: 'who can meditate on those tendernesses
of yours to me, and call in question your being as intirely mine as the most
sacred Friendship can make you?' He set out their circumstances: that he still
urgently needed a salaried post to provide portions for his daughters; that his
daughter-in-law's £3,000 had all gone to pay for the costs of the lawsuit; that
at 60, he was not seeking office for his own sake, but only at the prompting
of his family who could not understand why he made 'so little progresse in
the world'; 'they tell me of the Faculties you have to oblige in the Chequer,
the Customs, the Farms, the Navy, the Wardrobe, and a thousand more that
streame from the Ocean of the Ld Treasurers of most of which they can
wholly dispose of; nor can I wholly contradict them'. But his chief grievance
was still that 'having a small request, grounded upon a solemn obligation
under his Majesties own hand & seales, to passe a long lease (of no crowne
demesnes) into Inheritance upon a fair discount of a stated and acknowledged Debt, I could not obtaine that little Justice.'[49]

The breakdown of a friendship which had sustained him at the height
of his bereavement had evidently been as distressing to Godolphin as to
Evelyn. In the midst of this public crisis he took the opportunity to reply
frankly and at length, and assure Evelyn that 'there is no time (I think) since
I have knowne you, but where I have had the power or the prospect to doe
you any service, I would [not] have embraced the Occasion with more will-
ingnesse then any whatsoever'. He agreed that there were many places at the
Treasury's disposal, but repeated that few were suitable for Evelyn and whenever these arose he found them already disposed of by his colleagues. He
agreed that the claim to the Sayes Court lease was grounded on former royal
promises and 'those promises very well merited by reall services', but the
refusal 'was only to preserve a rule which hitherto has not been broken, & but

---

[49] BL Add. MS 78307: JE to SG, 19 Dec. 1681.

for such rules, Wee our selves must have been broken long agoe considering the dayly hardships Wee are forced to suffer, if not to doe'. For Evelyn to show any resentment of Hyde (who had now been raised to a peerage) would only make it more difficult to do him any service in the future. 'For my owne part in the matter', he added ruefully, 'don't think that I shall bee lesse mindfull of it now, than when you thought best of me.'[50] The following year he did at last have a prospect to hold out. A hospital for disabled soldiers was being planned at Chelsea and Evelyn would be an ideal candidate for the governorship. He embraced the offer at once: 'it suits with my Yeares, my Genius, my Formalitie, and the greate disposition I have to be usefull to brave men'. He readily undertook to surrender Sayes Court to his son's family and go with his wife to live there. But the drawback was that it was at least two or three years in the future, '& that's a very long day in my Kalendar', and so he still pressed unrealistically for an immediate appointment in the revenue administration; 'make one harty attempt for your old friend', he urged, '& defer it not'.[51] There was no further response Godolphin could make, and except for brief letters from Evelyn on the anniversaries of Margaret's death, their correspondence lapsed.

All this explains why Evelyn's project for a memorial life of Margaret had made little progress. Godolphin had never objected to it as such: 'I would not restraine you from the satisfaction & the entertainment of it: I would not bar myself from the profit and delight of itt.' He seems even to have suggested that they might collaborate in it, or at least that he would revise and add to it; but he urged Evelyn to do nothing hastily.[52] Occasionally Evelyn referred to the project in his anniversary letters—it was in progress, or needed another year's work, or was being transcribed—but it is clear that very little, if anything, had actually been done and Godolphin never pressed him about it. It was left to Anne Sylvius, on a visit to England in the winter of 1683/4, to urge Evelyn not to let the plan lapse, saying that Margaret's friends wanted it to keep the example of her life before them. With this prompting he settled to the task in earnest. Perhaps he incorporated some of his earlier drafts, but the bulk of the text was certainly not composed until the spring or summer of 1684; it was addressed throughout to Lady Sylvius and referred fondly to 'those innocent moments, and the Sweete Conversation which fifteen-yeares since wee enjoyed', when the Howards had first come to Deptford in 1669. It was to her that he presented the finished text, fair copied in a scribal hand, in August of that year.[53] As a further sign of the distance between himself and Godolphin,

---

[50] Ibid.: SG to JE, 24 Dec. 1681.
[51] Ibid.: JE to SG, 19 Nov. 1682.
[52] *Life*, 6: SG to JE, 22 Sept. 1678.
[52] *Life*, 7, 18–19; Hiscock II, 134; JE, *Diary*, iv. 429.

he made no attempt to consult him at any stage or even to send him a copy of the finished text (although he did introduce the work with a copy of the letter of September 1678 which showed that he had not disapproved of the project). All he did was to compose a curious letter, a kind of codicil to his will, to be given to Godolphin after his death. In it he bequeathed him the portrait by Matthew Dixon which Margaret had given him, mentioned that an 'essay' for her life was in the hands of Lady Sylvius, and again reproached him obliquely for not keeping up, or allowing him to feel any benefit from their friendship.[54]

Even if he had wanted to present Godolphin with a copy of the 'Life', he was not in any state to receive it. Contemporaries had commented on how little he seemed to be affected by his wife's death at the time. It was only to Evelyn that he explained that he had done all he could to avoid dwelling on it, 'from the apprehension I had that scarcely was it to be borne without distraction'. Now both his unresolved grief and his deep-seated guilt at his return to public life seemed to have returned to take their revenge. In the spring of 1684 he was transferred from the Treasury to the more lucrative and demanding office of Secretary of State. But he had held it for only a few months when he suffered a major physical and psychological breakdown. Something of it could be attributed to the stresses of his public life, but the letters Jael Boscawen wrote to Evelyn suggest that really the cause went much further back, to his marriage and its harrowing end. Although he believed himself to be mortally ill, she and the doctors were sure that his symptoms presented no real danger. The chief trouble was a crippling depression, 'a most inveterate spleen, which methinks gets ground of us dayly', as she described it. Godolphin would not move from his darkened room at Windsor; 'said he had a great mind to receive the sacrament' but could not do so because he was 'unworthy of so great a blessing & for that reason was rendered incapable of doing it'. He gave her the keys to his cabinet in London, telling her that there were papers there 'which he would have noe body see but myself & that I must see them because I might burn them'; they were 'papers of my wife's', he added, 'some of hers to me & some of mine to her'.[55] In his sense of being cast away, of having failed Margaret's hopes for him utterly, he wanted to destroy all trace of the correspondence in which she had recalled him to God.

Eventually he struggled back to some kind of normality. He surrendered the secretaryship of state but returned to the Treasury, this time with a peerage,

---

[54] BL Add. 78307: JE to SG, 8 Aug. 1684. This letter is present in a draft and a copy, with the endorsement by JE, 'take out this leafe & place it at the end of Electra's [letters]'.

[55] BL Add. MS 78307: Jael Boscawen to JE, 5, 6 July 1684.

to replace Hyde as First Lord. In November Evelyn thought that he still looked 'exceedingly ill', though he went about his public business as usual.[56] Putting aside his sense of grievance, he resumed his regular visits, consulting Godolphin about the interminable lawsuit, but also trying to persuade him again that his crippling guilt and religious scruples were unfounded. When Charles II was suddenly stricken with mortal illness in February 1685, Evelyn wrote grimly that 'a World of atheisme, Prophaneness, Uncharitableness, & ingratitude requir'd this severe Rebuke, & you know I have long apprehended it'; but reassured Godolphin that he was 'safe in the Arke'.[57] James II peacefully succeeded his brother; Hyde, now Earl of Rochester, took over as sole Lord Treasurer; Sunderland remained in ministerial office; but Godolphin, probably from personal choice, was relegated to the minor ceremonial post of Lord Chamberlain to the Queen. He purchased Cranbourn Lodge in Windsor Park, and when Jael Boscawen was widowed later in the same year, set up house there with her and their combined family of children. Although the most important part of his career was still ahead of him, for the next three years he effaced himself from public life almost without trace.

During this time Evelyn's circumstances also changed radically. In the first year of the new reign two of his daughters, first Mary and then Betty, died of smallpox, the latter after having eloped with the nephew of one of the dockyard officials in order to escape the desolation of her parents' house after her sister's death.[58] At a terrible personal cost, more crippling to his wife even than to himself, Evelyn's financial responsibilities were much reduced. Then in the autumn of that year he at last achieved the public office he wanted, being appointed one of the commissioners of the Privy Seal while the Earl of Clarendon, who held the office, was in Ireland. Two years later both Sir Richard Browne's debt and the Prettyman lawsuit were settled by a complex and mutually dependent transaction in which Godolphin must have played a part. Even Jack Evelyn was found minor Treasury jobs and eventually made a commissioner of the Irish revenue, and finally Evelyn was given, not the governorship of Chelsea, but the treasurership of Greenwich Hospital. Godolphin had at last kept his and Margaret's promises.

It was time for the Evelyns to detach themselves from Sayes Court and they did so without much reluctance. The repeated refusal to grant them the inheritance of the lease meant they could not regard themselves as more than sojourners there in any case. The 'villa' was now almost overwhelmed by the town and the Yard and Evelyn never forgave the dockyard officials who had

[56] BL Add. MS 78431: JE to ME, Nov. 1684.
[57] BL Add. MS 78298: JE to SG, 11 Feb. 1685.
[58] JE, *Diary*, iv. 420–31, 460–4; BL Add. MS 78539: Elizabeth Evelyn to Bohun, 2 June 1685.

been aware of his daughter's liaison and had failed to warn him. Between
1683 and 1685 the gardens which he had invested with so much meaning
were devastated by a succession of bitter winters and drought-ridden summers. Always resilient, he set to work to repair and simplify them, to reduce
the cost of maintenance and establish greenhouses, but the numinous air they
had once had was dissipated, and ''tis late for me to begin new paradises'.
What he now regarded as the excessive pride he had taken in his house and
garden became a matter for confession and self-castigation.[59]

In London he found the gardens of Berkeley House where he had walked
with Margaret being parcelled into building lots. The city, 'by far too dispro-
portionat already to the Nation', had almost doubled in size in his lifetime.[60]
It was time to seek the deeper country retreat, and his thoughts turned back
to Wotton. His brother George had two sons, but by 1691 both had prede-
ceased him, leaving Evelyn the next heir in the male line. Three years later he
and his wife left Sayes Court for good and moved to an apartment at Wotton
to save the cost of separate housekeeping. After four more years of intermittent wrangling about the settlement George died, leaving John in possession
of what had always been 'his most cherished place on earth'.[61] The restless
unsatisfied striving of his middle years had burnt out, and in old age an elus-
ive contentment at last came to him. He and his wife found themselves able
to enjoy each other's company, he wrote, more than in fifty years past.[62] With
the final demise of the dynasty of Hyams, Ralph Bohun was even restored to
them as rector of the parish. It was true that the woods at Wotton, the 'onely
best and proper Husbandry the Estate is capable of', were sadly depleted,
having been over-exploited, destroyed by storms, or felled to pay debts, so
that the place was left 'naked, and ashamed almost to own its name'. But it
was not too late for Evelyn to set about repairing the damage. Industrious to
the last, he made this a labour of love; and with his characteristic sense,
sharper now at the end of his life, that it was a spiritual as well as a physical
one: '[I] shall if God protract my years and continue health be continually
planting,' he wrote at the end of his last edition of *Sylva*, 'till it please him to
transplant me into the glorious regions above, the celestial Paradise, planted
with perennial groves and trees bearing immortal fruit.'[63]

[59] *PF*, 151–2; JE to Pepys, 31 July 1685; JE, *Diary*, iv. 364–5, 384, 446; Upcott, 692–6: JE to the
Royal Society, 14 Apr. 1684; Douglas Chambers, 'John Evelyn and the Invention of the Heated
Greenhouse', *Garden History*, 20 (1992), 201–5; BL Add. MSS 78431: JE to ME, Nov. 1684; 78539:
ME to Bohun, 3 June 1685; 78392: JE, confessional notes, 1680s.
[60] JE, *Diary*, iv. 380–1.   [61] Hiscock II, 159–217,
[62] Helen Evelyn, *The Evelyn Family* (1915), 78: JE to William Wotton, 18 Jan. 1697.
[63] JE, *Memoires*, 17; *Sylva* (1706), ed. John Nisbet (1908), ii. 260. For the deforestation of
Wotton, see P. F, Brandon, 'Land, Technology and Water Management in the Tillingbourne
Valley', *Southern History*, 6 (1984), 91–9.

Godolphin, who had returned reluctantly to the Treasury under William III, was by this time at the height of his power as Queen Anne's prime minister and of his long personal and political partnership with the Churchills, now Duke and Duchess of Marlborough. Evelyn had marked his accession to power by retrieving Lady Sylvius's copy of 'The Life of Mrs Godolphin' and making a version of it in his own hand for presentation. It was clearly out of the question now to think of publishing it, 'nor indeed; is this Race of Scorners, worthy of it'.[64] Otherwise their contacts were infrequent and entirely formal. Yet Evelyn still nursed one last ambition in fulfilment of the friendship. He had once told his wife that if he had a granddaughter and £10,000 to bestow on her, he would seek to marry her to Margaret Godolphin's son; 'pardon this excess of fondness to that excellent soul'.[65] In fact Francis Godolphin was already marked out for the eldest Churchill daughter, but it was not long before Evelyn began to conceive of another dynastic possibility. Jack Evelyn's life, never a good one, had already come to an unhappy and premature end, but his son, a third John, throve and was the apple of his grandfather's eye. When it came time to think of a match for him, there were Jael Boscawen's two daughters, with whom Francis Godolphin had been raised virtually as a brother. Evelyn lived just long enough to see his grandson's marriage to Anne Boscawen and the inauguration of a long Indian summer of fruitfulness and prosperity for their joined families.

In the 1690s Godolphin had made one attempt at remarriage, withdrawing at the last moment for reasons which cannot now be traced.[66] After this his private life became increasingly bound up with the Marlboroughs; not just with John Churchill, but with Sarah, now a formidable beauty who held not only her husband and Godolphin, but also the Queen in thrall. She was a passionate Whig supporter, but Godolphin's natural Tory allegiances did not affect her regard for him as 'the truest friend to me & all my family that ever was, & the best man that ever lived'. 'Hee never cared for any party but as they were absolutely necessary to preserve the queen & country,' she added, 'hee liked to employ those that were capable of doing servise & had good characters of any side, and encouraged the torys as long as they would support the queen; hee was bred a high churchman & had certainly more true religion then ever I knew any man have in my life, as well as all the appearance of it.'[67] In fact this was the legacy not just of his high church

[64] *Life*, 4.　　[65] Hiscock II, 141–2.

[66] Cornwall R.O, Godolphin Papers 319: draft articles on SG's 'intended marriage' to Barbara, Lady Mauleverer (who later married Thomas Herbert, 6th Earl of Pembroke). Evelyn heard rumours of this and congratulated Godolphin prematurely; see Hiscock II, 159, and Lever, *Godolphin*, 297.

[67] Bodleian Library, MS Add. A.191, fo. 5: Duchess of Marlborough to Burnet, 25 Sept. 1712; BL Add. MS 61118, fo. 21: her notes about SG.

upbringing, but of his long dead wife, whose letters he still preserved and who had taught him, as he once told Evelyn, all he knew of God. The process by which he parted company with his natural Tory allies and forged an alliance with the Whigs who would support the European war was a painful one, during which he found himself denounced by intemperate high church men as an enemy of the Church. When the Archbishop of York met with the Lord Treasurer at this time in the House of Lords and asked him how he did, Godolphin made the unexpectedly cold answer: 'as well as a poor man could be, that was run down by them whom he endeavoured to oblige'. The Archbishop sought him out in private and managed to exculpate himself, and 'after all', he recorded in his diary, 'we parted very friendly, and he said, he hoped in his distress he might have recourse to me, or words to that effect. He was often as I thought, in a great concern, and very near weeping.'[68] Even at the height of his power there could still be glimpses in moments of stress of the young man who had read Margaret Blagge's letters with tears running down his face.

'They do best, who, if they cannot but admit love, yet make it keep quarter, and sever it wholly from their serious affairs and actions of life,' Francis Bacon had written in his essay on the subject, 'for if it check once with business, it troubleth men's fortunes, and maketh men that they can no ways be true to their own ends.'[69] *Calisto* had in its way celebrated this unruly, subversive power. Both Godolphin's and Evelyn's love for Margaret Blagge had the same troubled quality. It disrupted their worldly ends, the active public lives which their education and background enjoined on them, and neither of them had been able to make it 'keep quarter'. In fact their relationship with her was something quite apart from the sphere of masculine means and ends; a manifestation of the longing for 'something yet to come, and more than all this world contains' which Evelyn saw as the strongest evidence of man's religious nature. Because of her refusal to be content with worldly pleasures and her passionate surrender to divine love, and because she had been taken away from them so early, the young woman 'who had outgrown them all in her dying'[70] never lost her power over them. Her beauty and spirituality took on the aspect of a higher reality of which she remained their most compelling evidence. As old men they each preserved her letters as their best intimation of salvation.

[68] Thomas Sharp, *The Life of John Sharp, Archbishop of York* (1825), i. 368–9.
[69] Francis Bacon, *Essays*, ed. B. Vickers (Oxford, 1999), 23.
[70] Sylvia Townsend Warner, *The Corner that Held Them* (1988), 219.

Note on Sources

I. The Evelyn Papers (now British Library Add. MSS 78168–78693)

These descended in the ownership of Evelyn's family, largely intact with the notable exception of a substantial number of items removed by the early nineteenth-century collector William Upcott. Some of these were purchased by the British Museum when Upcott's collections were sold at auction in 1846; others were bought back by the family and restored to the archive (see Theodore Hofmann et al., *John Evelyn in the British Library* (1995), 64–71). Between the late 1940s and 1995 it was on deposit at Christ Church, Oxford, where it was available for research, although accessibility was limited by the lack of a catalogue. In 1995 it was bought by the British Library and full cataloguing and conservation are now well advanced.

The archive contains records of the Evelyn and related families from Tudor times until the nineteenth century, although the papers of John Evelyn the diarist form the core of it. In addition to the manuscripts of his diary, his letter-books, and his incoming correspondence, it includes the range of his commonplace books and library catalogues, the manuscripts of his unfinished literary and scientific projects, a very large collection of devotional material, and records relating to his public offices, finances, and estates.

The most important components of the archive for the present study are the Evelyn–Godolphin correspondence (Add. MS 78307) and the devotional material (Add. MSS 78360–92). There are about fifty letters from Margaret Godolphin, of which four are copies made by Evelyn (in circumstances discussed below). She destroyed all of his letters, but a few drafts and copies were retained by him. The devotional material includes a small quantity of Margaret Godolphin's papers and a large number of prayers and formal 'meditations' written by Evelyn for her use. These were given back to him by Sidney Godolphin after her death, as material for the life he intended to write. Several more of Margaret's letters and devotional papers, including the rules for her conduct at court, were transcribed by Evelyn into the 'Life', but the manuscript originals no longer survive. Otherwise he preserved her letters carefully; they are mentioned in several of his lists and inventories of his papers in Add. MS 78639 and in *Memoires for my Grand-son*, 64–5, at the end of his life, sometimes in connection with an unfulfilled plan to make a fair copy of the whole sequence of Godolphin letters. Most of them carry his endorsements in the form of crossed-out numbers and other comments, probably representing his attempts to establish the chronological order. No further correspondence between Evelyn and Margaret Godolphin is known to exist elsewhere, although his

Devotionarie Book, which is associated with her, passed into the ownership of the Boscawen family and was published from that source in 1936.

Margaret Godolphin's letters date between 1673 and 1678. Few are fully dated, but precise or approximate dates can be assigned to many of them on internal evidence with reasonable certainty, at least so as to make the sequence clear. Most of the manuscript originals have pencilled dates added by the Deputy Librarian of Christ Church, W. G. Hiscock, but a number of these are unreliable (to give just one neutral example, a letter which clearly refers to the death of their friend James Hamilton in a naval battle in June 1673 is dated '1674' by Hiscock); for Hiscock and the Evelyn Papers see Appendix B following.

II. The *Life of Mrs Godolphin*

Evelyn declared in Margaret Godolphin's lifetime that he would write the history of their friendship, but the work he began at this time, 'The Legend of Philaretes and the Pearle', now survives only as a fragment (BL Add. MS 78379) covering his marriage and earlier platonic friendships. The posthumous *Life of Mrs Godolphin* is of course the basic document for any study of their friendship, although, as indicated in the Introduction, it is not a biography in the modern sense and its essentially devotional purpose must be borne in mind. There are two manuscripts of the 'Life', both now in the Houghton Library, Harvard University (MSS Eng. 992 and 992.1). The earlier of the two, a fair copy in a rather clumsy scribal hand, was originally presented by Evelyn to Anne (Howard), Lady Sylvius, in 1684, retrieved by him later, and used as the basis for the autograph version which he presented to the Lord Treasurer Godolphin in 1702. The 1684 manuscript remained in Evelyn's family until the nineteenth century, when it came into the hands of his great-great-grandson, Edward Venables Vernon-Harcourt, Archbishop of York, who made it available for publication by Samuel Wilberforce, Bishop of Oxford. The first edition of 1847 and all subsequent impressions and editions up to and including that published by Sir Israel Gollancz in 1904 derived from this text. The second manuscript presumably descended in Godolphin's family, was sold by Puttick and Simpson in 1861, and passed through the hands of several private collectors before it was acquired by the Houghton Library in the 1950s. In 1939 an admirable edition based on this later manuscript (then owned by A. S. W. Rosenbach of Philadelphia) was published by an American scholar, Harriet Sampson. The whereabouts of the 1684 manuscript, thought mistakenly to be in Evelyn's hand, were unknown to her (it remained in the Wilberforce family until 1956), but she provided a detailed collation with the nineteenth-century editions which were based on it (provenance documents for both manuscripts are preserved with them at the Houghton Library; see also Keynes, *JE*, 247–50, where the binding and opening pages of the second manuscript are reproduced). The present work relies chiefly on the Sampson edition, though I have also consulted both manuscripts and all the earlier editions. Apart from its other content, the *Life* remains an essential primary source because Evelyn included in it several excerpts from Margaret Godolphin's letters and devotional papers for which no manuscript originals now survive.

III. British Library, Hammick Papers

This archive, which contains the papers of the nineteenth-century clergyman, Sir St Vincent Love Hammick, 2nd Bart., also preserves as a chance survival the courtship letters of Sidney and Margaret Godolphin. All are originals as sent. All are unsigned, but are identifiable from the (partially obliterated) address on two of them to 'Mrs Blagge', from the handwriting, and from internal evidence. There are eighteen letters in all, sixteen dating from late 1672 or early 1673 to 1674 and two after their marriage; most can be dated with reference to external events mentioned in them or to other letters in the sequence. Margaret Blagge's letters were preserved by Godolphin. His were initially preserved by her; they may be those referred to by Evelyn in the *Life*, 58, as having been 'choicely reservd' (presumably she kept them in some special container). After her death the two groups came together in Godolphin's possession and were probably the same correspondence ('papers of my wife's, some of hers to me & some of mine to her'), which he asked his sister to destroy if he failed to recover from a major illness in 1684. At his death in 1712 the correspondence must have passed to their only child, Francis, 2nd Earl of Godolphin, and then been given by him to his eccentric companion and physician Dr Messenger Monsey (1693–1788), as suggested in the Prologue, since this can be the only explanation for their present whereabouts. Monsey's papers were in turn inherited by his daughter and only child, Charlotte, wife of William Alexander, and so eventually merged with the papers of Sir St Vincent Love Hammick, who married Mary, daughter of Robert Alexander, of a younger branch of the family.

W. G. Hiscock, John Evelyn, and Margaret Godolphin

When the Evelyn manuscripts were placed on deposit at Christ Church in the 1940s, they came into the custody of its Deputy Librarian, W. G. Hiscock. Esmond de Beer's edition of the diary was in progress at the time, but carried on entirely outside the context of the rest of Evelyn's archive (in fact this is the only shortcoming of an otherwise definitive work). Hiscock was the first person for several generations outside Evelyn's family to have unrestricted access to his papers. He had already published a number of short works based on discoveries in the college library and archive. In 1952 he followed these with *John Evelyn and Margaret Godolphin*, published by John Murray, drawing extensively on the unpublished letters and devotional papers. Its argument was that Evelyn's friendship with Margaret Godolphin had been a great deal more suspect and complex than his *Life of Mrs Godolphin* indicated, that far from trying to overcome her scruples about marriage, as he there claimed, he had secretly encouraged them; that the relationship had been a kind of seduction in which he was effectively a rival to her husband, and that one of the purposes of the *Life* was to conceal this from him after her death. Evidently in response to criticisms of his book's lack of scholarly apparatus, Hiscock followed it three years later with *John Evelyn and his Family Circle*, this time published by Routledge: a more sober and contextualized study, which he claimed in the Preface contained 'all other relevant Evelyn material'. It was more systematically footnoted and included a bibliography and a summary account of Evelyn's manuscripts. It also contained one important new piece of evidence: confessional notes in minute, abbreviated Latin which referred several times to his 'excessive affection' for Margaret Godolphin (represented by the pentacle symbol). Hiscock reproduced these as his frontispiece and on the dust-jacket.

The manuscript evidence Hiscock brought to light certainly suggested that there was more to the friendship than was revealed in the *Life* and some reviewers found the case persuasive. It fell to Esmond de Beer, who had made the proofs of his edition of the diary available to Hiscock, to point out in a series of articles in *Notes and Queries* (June, July, Aug. 1960, pp. 203–6, 243–8, 284–6) that there were obvious weaknesses in his modes of argument: his placing too much weight on negative evidence, his tendentious interpretation of documents which were capable of other and simpler readings, his errors of fact (such as the misplacing of Arlington House, which was actually on the site of the present Buckingham Palace, adjacent to Berkeley House, to support the claim that Godolphin had taken up residence there to watch

Evelyn's comings and goings). To these he might have added examples of misinter-
pretation of the seventeenth-century idiom; when Margaret protested to Evelyn in
an early letter that 'when I looked contracted I was never nearer dissolving', Hiscock
took this to refer to the breaking off of her engagement with Godolphin (I, 31).
In fact it is clear from adjacent letters that Margaret was simply excusing herself
for apparent rudeness by saying that when she appeared gloomy and unwelcoming
('contracted'), she was actually nearer 'dissolving' into tears; for she goes on to add
(in a passage Hiscock mistranscribed), 'so you see you are not skild in my face though
you are in my soul'.

De Beer never attempted to consult the Evelyn Papers at Christ Church, all access
to which was through Hiscock himself, but he did remark that 'I find Mr Hiscock's
handling of his sources and general habits of argument, in that part of his account of
Evelyn where his sources are readily accessible, such as to prevent my accepting his
account of those parts of Evelyn's life for which his sources are less readily accessible.' If he had been able to examine all the relevant documents for himself, he would
have realized that Hiscock had suppressed the evidence of several, of which he was
certainly aware, because they did not support his version of events. In the marriage
manual, 'Oeconomics to a Newly Married Friend' (Add. MS 78386), Evelyn not only
encouraged Margaret in her acceptance of marriage but asked her always to 'remember and if neede be, acknowledge, how solicitous I have ben in all occasions (and not
seldome amidst doubtfull resolutions) that the Worthy, and excellent Person (now
your Husband) might be in Possession of the Blessing God had reserved for him', a
statement which would have been unaccountable if both of them had known that it
was grossly untrue. More significantly, the letters Godolphin wrote to Evelyn after
Margaret's death, which Hiscock dismisses with a passing mention as belonging
more properly 'to a study in patronage' (I, 194), make it clear that he was so far from
being suspicious or disapproving of the friendship between Evelyn and his wife, as
Hiscock suggested, that he begged repeatedly to be taken into Margaret's place.

Hiscock replied briefly to De Beer (*Notes and Queries* (Dec. 1960), 476–7), resting
his case on six points. Since these provide a useful summary of it, I will say something
here to each.

1. *The letter in which Margaret writes to Evelyn (in early 1673), 'as for my being married
you know you won't let me resolve'.* This was Hiscock's trump-card and probably the
germ of both his books. But the likelihood is that Margaret's meaning was exactly
the opposite of his reading. Evelyn's letter in which he debates the pros and cons of
marriage with Margaret survives in a manuscript fair copy clearly dated '27 February
1672/3'; but in the *Life*, 43–6, he summarizes its contents in the context of events in
the following year, and on these grounds Hiscock suggests that the copy of the letter
must have been deliberately misdated by Evelyn in retrospect (I, 84–90). There is
in fact no good reason to reject the date on Evelyn's letter, which is supported by
the sequence of other letters at this time. The paraphrase at a later point in the *Life*
simply indicates that he was not concerned with strict chronological accuracy in that
source; the debate over marriage was after all a recurrent one between him and
Margaret and the letter provided a convenient summary. If one accepts the date

which appears on Evelyn's letter, it becomes clear that Margaret's words, 'as for my being married you know you won't let me resolve', refer back specifically to Evelyn's words in that letter, 'nor . . . ought you to resolve *not* to change your condition' (my italics); that is, Margaret was acknowledging that Evelyn had urged her not to resolve *against* marriage, as she showed signs of doing; not that he had himself tried to persuade her against marriage. This reading agrees with the evidence of 'Oeconomics to a Newly Married Friend', quoted above.

2. *Evelyn's confessional notes, admitting, amongst many other failings, to twelve occasions when he indulged in 'excessive affection' (Affect Nim') for Margaret Godolphin*. This import-ant document, which Hiscock discovered in time for his second book and which he claimed as proof of his case, certainly confirmed that Evelyn privately acknowledged the friendship as more intense and ambivalent than he was prepared to admit pub-licly. This is not after all very surprising, but it does not follow that he tried to seduce Margaret and prevent her marriage. Hiscock's statement (II, 126) that the confession mentioned 'excessive affection for Margaret Blagge and many indecipherable failings; including—*we must believe*—the falsehood that he advised her to marry' (my italics) is highly tendentious. Although parts of the confessional notes are hard to decipher, the gist is clear enough. They range over the whole of Evelyn's life; his religious observance, his relations with his family, his excessive pride in his house and garden, and his conduct in public life. Occasions of untruthfulness or equivocation (a staple of confessions) are certainly mentioned, but nothing which can be identified as a reference to Margaret's marriage. The confession in fact undermines Hiscock's case in a different way. He suggested that the meditations Evelyn presented to her, urging that human love should never be allowed to come into competition with the divine, were deliberate attempts to undermine her love for Godolphin, but in the light of his awareness of his own 'excessive affection', they can be seen as exhorta-tions to himself as much as to her.

3. *That Margaret destroyed Evelyn's letters as soon as they were read*. This is not neces-sarily evidence that they were incriminating, only that they were private; Evelyn says that she 'disposed of' a number of Godolphin's courtship letters as well (*Life*, 57).

4. *That she recalled her own letters from Evelyn and refused to return six of them*. This episode enabled Hiscock to suggest that evidence to support his version of events had once existed but had been suppressed by this means. However, when Evelyn protested at Margaret's keeping the letters she suggested that there was nothing to prevent his taking copies, 'without putting any marke upon them whose they were' (BL Add. MS 78307, fo. 45). In fact four of Margaret's surviving letters are copies in Evelyn's hand and two other long letters in which she discussed her relations with Godolphin are preserved only in transcript in the *Life*, 30–1, 40–1. With her marriage impending, these are precisely the letters which she might have been most uneasy about. Certainly there is no other obvious reason why Evelyn should have taken the copies and failed to keep the originals, and once he had transcribed the two letters into the *Life* there would have been no reason for him to keep his earlier loose copies. The episode is therefore quite consistent with existing documentation and does not prove that significant 'incriminating' evidence was destroyed by this means.

5. *That Margaret married in secret and lied to Evelyn about it afterwards out of fear, saying 'maybe I shall never venture'*. Secret marriages were very common at the time for a variety of reasons (see David Cressy, *Birth, Marriage and Death* (Oxford, 1997), 316–32) and in this case not only Evelyn but Godolphin's family were excluded from the secret. But the letter in which Margaret says 'maybe I shall never venture' almost certainly dates from 1674, the year before her marriage. Hiscock was understandably misled by an endorsement by Evelyn on one of the letters in the same sequence, dating it shortly after her marriage in May 1675. But this endorsement must have been made in retrospect (in 1675 he did not of course know of the marriage) and is itself incorrect. The recall of the letters certainly made Evelyn suspect, though wrongly at this stage, that she was secretly married, for Margaret responded (truthfully at this stage): 'I am not so near that state of life as you imagin, nor may be shall never venture. I have quite other thoughts, but I am gods, let his will be done on me in me and by me' (Add. MS 78307, fo. 48). The endorsement was probably made when Evelyn looked through the letters much later in writing the *Life*, where he makes the same mistake in dating (*Life*, 58). The actual date is fixed by Margaret's covering letter sent with the returned letters, clearly dated by her 'Friday 26 June [1674]'. It seems likely that Evelyn, reading the whole series of (largely undated) letters nearly ten years later, confused the sequence of events in his mind, or simply thought that chronological accuracy was less important at this stage than a coherent narrative.

6. *That 'the equivocal Life of Mrs Godolphin' contains even more instances than Hiscock had cited 'of Evelyn's brightening of Margaret's halo'*. As the Introduction sets out, the *Life* was written after Margaret's death at the request of her friend Anne Sylvius, specifically as a devotional aid and using the models of hagiography and 'exemplary lives'. But Evelyn's 'brightening of Margaret's halo' was not confined to the public document of the *Life*; it is also to be found in his private tribute to her in his commonplace book (Add. MS 78328, p. 154) and appears to have come from a sincere conviction, shared by other friends who knew her well (including Lady Sunderland and Mary Evelyn), that Margaret Godolphin had exceptional spiritual gifts, was in effect a saint.

To sum up: it was a considerable achievement on Hiscock's part to have recognized and brought to light this complex episode from a mass of confused and undated documentation, but in the process he fell into the familiar errors of someone with an over-mastering theory to prove and only fragmentary and ambivalent data to work with: he placed more weight on the evidence he had than it would bear and accommodated all other matters accordingly. His preoccupation with Evelyn's unruly sexual feelings and his tendency to see Margaret Godolphin's spiritual aspirations as neurotic tell us at least as much about himself as them. More seriously, he never gave sufficient consideration, either personally or in the wider historical context, to the passionately held religious convictions of Evelyn, Margaret, and Sidney Godolphin, and their importance in determining the lives of all three.

Select Bibliography

MANUSCRIPT SOURCES

British Library, London

Additional MSS 10115 (Sir Joseph Williamson papers); 10117 (Restoration news-letters); 15858, 15889, 15948, 15950 (Evelyn papers); 18220 (Restoration verse); 18730 and 40860 (Lord Anglesey's diary); 19095, 19118, 19154 (Davy's Suffolk collections); 28052, 28071 (Godolphin papers); 28080 (secret service accounts); 33065 (Newcastle papers); 34326 (petitions to the Council of State); 36916 (Restoration newsletters); 36755 (Sir Henry North, 'Eroclea'); 36989 (Gawdy letters); 47131 (Egmont papers); 57861 (Coningsby letters); 61118, 61453 (Blenheim Papers); 75376 (Savile letters); 78168–693 (Evelyn Papers); Hammick Papers (not yet numbered).

Egerton MS 2539: Restoration newsletters.

Harleian MS 6828, fos. 510–23: Mary Beale's 'Discourse on Friendship'.

King's MSS 43–4: surveys of the royal dockyards.

Stowe MS 562: ordinances for the household of Charles 11.

Microfilm 636/23–4: Verney letters, 1669–71.

Reserved Photocopy 5460: letter from Evelyn to Lord Clifford, 23 Nov. 1670.

Public Record Office

Lord Chamberlain's Department (LC), warrant books: 5/139–41.

Auditors of the Land Revenue (LR), Catherine of Braganza's jointure: 5/68–95.

Gifts and Deposits (PRO), transcripts of the French ambassadors' dispatches: 31/3/130–2.

Probate Records (PROB) 11: 309/114; 325/132; 337/129; 358/121: Blagge and Godolphin wills.

State Papers (SP), Domestic Series, Charles II: 29/25, 47, 62, 97, 98, 240.

State Papers (SP), Foreign Series, France: 78/126–41.

State Papers (SP), Foreign Series, Spain: 94/59.

Bodleian Library, Oxford.

MS Add. A.191: letters to Gilbert Burnet.

MSS Carte 34–6: letters to the Duke of Ormonde; 103: Restoration newsletters.

MS Film 293: Restoration newsletters.

MS Firth b1/1: Sir Joseph Williamson's papers.

MS Malone 44: Privy Purse accounts of Charles II.
MS Rawlinson D. 78: memoirs of Lady Elizabeth Delaval.

Dorset Record Office

Ilchester MSS, Boxes 267 and 268: ledgers of Sir Stephen Fox.

Cornwall Record Office

Rogers MSS: RP 1, letters to John Rogers of Penrose.
Godolphin MSS: GO 1–860, estate and financial papers.

Lincolnshire Record Office

Worsley MSS: Privy Purse accounts of Catherine of Braganza.

National Library of Scotland

Advocates MS 31.1.22: warrant book of Lord Chamberlain's servants, Restoration period.
Additional MS 3420: Godolphin letters.

Sheffield University Library

Hartlib Papers.

Longleat

Coventry Papers 33, 41: letters from ambassadors in Paris and The Hague (British Library Microfilm 863/24, 32).

Library of Congress, Washington, DC

Phillipps MS 8539: Journal of the Council of Trade and Plantations, 1670–4.

Harry Ransom Humanities Research Center, The University of Texas at Austin, Texas

Pforzheimer Library MS 103c: newsletters addressed to Sir Richard Bulstrode, 1676–8

Houghton Library, Harvard University

MSS Eng. 991: Evelyn letters.
MSS Eng. 992: John Evelyn, 'Life of Mrs Godolphin', [*c.*1702].
MSS Eng. 992.1: John Evelyn, 'Life of Mrs Godolphin', [*c.*1684].

PRIMARY PRINTED SOURCES

AIRY, OSMUND (ed.), *Essex Papers*, Camden Society, new ser., 47 (1890).

ANON., *A Sketch of the Life and Character of the Late Dr Monsey* (London, 1789).

AULNOY, MARY CATHERINE, Baronne d', *Memoirs of the Court of England in 1675*, ed. G. D. Gilbert (n.p., 1912).

AUSTEN, RALPH, *A Treatise of Fruit-Trees . . . togeather with Spirituall Use of an Orchard* (Oxford, 1653).

BACON, FRANCIS, *Essays*, ed. Brian Vickers (Oxford: Oxford University Press, 1999).

BOYLE, ROBERT, *Works*, ed. Michael Hunter and Edward B. Davis, 7 vols. (London: Pickering & Chatto, 1999).

—— *Robert Boyle by Himself and his Friends*, ed. Michael Hunter (London: Pickering, 1994).

BROWNE, SIR THOMAS, *Works*, ed. Simon Wilkin, 4 vols. (London: Pickering, 1836).

—— *Works*, ed. Geoffrey Keynes, 4 vols. (London: Faber, 1964).

BRUCE, THOMAS, 2nd Earl of Ailesbury, *Memoirs*, [ed. W. E. Buckley], Roxburghe Club, 2 vols. (1890).

BRUNET, FRANÇOIS, 'A French Traveller in Charles II's England', *Cornhill Magazine*, new ser., 20 (Jan.–June 1906), 660–74.

BURNET, GILBERT, *History of his own Time*, ed. M. J. R[outh], 6 vols. (Oxford: Oxford University Press, 1833).

CAREW, RICHARD, *The Survey of Cornwall*, ed. F. E. Halliday (London: Andrew Melrose, 1953).

CASTIGLIONE, Baldesar, *The Book of the Courtier*, trans. George Bull (Harmondsworth: Penguin, 1967).

CATHERINE OF BRAGANZA, 'Establishment of her Majesty Queen Catherine', 1671–2, *Catholic Record Society*, 38 (1941), pp. xxix–xxxii.

CAUSSIN, NICOLAS, *The Holy Court*, trans. Sir T[homas] H[awkins] (London, 1650).

CAVE, WILLIAM, *Primitive Christianity: or The Religion of the Ancient Christians in the First Ages of the Gospel* (London, 1673). (Evelyn's copy, British Library Eve.a.86.)

CAVENDISH, MARGARET, Duchess of Newcastle, *Plays never before Printed* (London, 1668).

CHAMBERLAYNE, EDWARD, *Angliae notitia* ([London], 1669, 1671–4).

CHRISTIE, W. D. (ed.), *Letters . . . addressed to Sir Joseph Williamson*, Camden Society, new ser., 8, 9 (1874).

CLARKE, J. S. (ed.), *The Life of James the Second*, 2 vols. (London: Longmans, 1816).

CROWNE, JOHN, *Dramatic Works*, 4 vols. (Edinburgh: Paterson and Sotheran, 1872–4).

DEFOE, DANIEL, *A Tour through the Whole Island of Great Britain*, ed. Pat Rogers (Harmondsworth: Penguin, 1971).

DELAVAL, ELIZABETH, 'Notes from a Delaval Diary', *Proceedings of the Society of Antiquaries of Newcastle upon Tyne*, 3rd ser., 1 (1903–4), 149–53.

—— *The Meditations of Lady Elizabeth Delaval*, ed. D. G. Greene, Surtees Society, 190 (1978).

EVELYN, JOHN, *Sylva*, 2nd edn. (London, 1670), 3rd edn. (London, 1679).

—— *Numismata* (London, 1697).

—— *Miscellaneous Writings*, ed. William Upcott (London: Henry Colburn, 1825).

—— *The Life of Mrs Godolphin*, ed. Samuel Wilberforce (London: Pickering, 1847).

—— *The History of Religion*, ed. R. M. Evanson, 2 vols. (London: Henry Colburn, 1850).

—— *Diary and Correspondence of John Evelyn*, ed. William Bray, 4 vols. (London: 1859).

—— *Sculptura*, ed. C. F. Bell (Oxford: Clarendon Press, 1906).

—— *Sylva* (1706), ed. John Nisbet, 2 vols. (London: Arthur Doubleday, 1908).

—— *Memoires for my Grandson*, ed. Geoffrey Keynes (London: Nonesuch Press, 1926).

—— *A Devotionarie Book*, ed. Walter Frere (London: John Murray, 1936).

—— *The Life of Mrs Godolphin*, ed. Harriet Sampson (London: Oxford University Press, 1939).

—— *Diary*, ed. Esmond de Beer, 6 vols. (Oxford: Clarendon Press, 1955).

—— *Writings*, ed. Guy de la Bédoyère (Woodbridge: Boydell, 1995).

—— *Acetaria: A Discourse of Sallets*, ed. Christopher Driver (Totnes: Prospect Books, 1996).

—— *John Evelyn's Translation of Titus Lucretius Carus De rerum natura*, ed. Michael M. Repetzki, Münsteraner Monographien zur englischen Literatur, 22 (Frankfurt: Peter Lang, 1997).

—— *Elysium Britannicum*, ed. John Ingram (Philadelphia: Pennsylvania University Press, 2001).

—— and MACKENZIE, GEORGE, *Public and Private Life in the Seventeenth Century: The Mackenzie–Evelyn Debate*, ed. Brian Vickers (New York: Scholars' Facsimiles & Reprints, 1986).

—— and PEPYS, SAMUEL, *Particular Friends: The Correspondence of Samuel Pepys and John Evelyn*, ed. Guy de la Bédoyère (Woodbridge: Boydell, 1997).

FABER, OTTO, *De auro potabilia medicinali* (London, 1677).

FIENNES, CELIA, *Journeys*, ed. Christopher Morris (London: Cresset Press, 1947).

G., E., *A Discourse of Friendship* (London, 1676).

GARDNER, HELEN (ed.), *The Metaphysical Poets* (Harmondsworth: Penguin, 1972).

GASSENDI, PIERRE, *The Mirrour of True Nobility & Gentility, being the Life of the Renowned Nicolaus Claudius Fabricius*, trans. William Rand (London, 1657).

GODOLPHIN, SIDNEY, *Poems*, ed. William Dighton (Oxford: Clarendon Press, 1931).

GOUGE, WILLIAM, *Of Domesticall Duties* (London, 1622).

GRANVILLE, DENIS, *Remains*, ed. G. Ormsby, Surtees Society, 47 (1865).

HAMILTON, ANTHONY, *Memoirs of the Count de Grammont*, trans. and ed. Horace Walpole (London: Swann Sonnenschein, 1911).

HANMER, SIR THOMAS, *Correspondence*, ed. Sir H. Bunbury (London, 1838).

HERBERT, GEORGE, *Works*, ed. F. E. Hutchinson (Oxford: Clarendon Press, 1953).

HERVEY, S. A. H. (ed.), *Horringer Parish Registers* (Woodbridge, 1900).

HISTORICAL MANUSCRIPTS COMMISSION (for full details, see HMSO Sectional List 17), *Third, Fourth, Seventh, Eighth and Thirteenth (App. VI) Reports; Beaufort MSS, Buccleuch MSS (Montagu House), Kenyon MSS, LeFleming MSS, Lindsey MSS, Portland MSS, i–iii, Pepys MSS, Rutland MSS, ii; Various Collections.*

HOBBES, THOMAS, *Leviathan*, ed. W. G. Pogson Smith (Oxford: Clarendon Press, 1929).

HOOKE, ROBERT, *Diary*, ed. H. W. Robinson and W. Adams (London: Taylor and Francis, 1935).

HOWARD, THOMAS, Earl of Arundel, *Remembrances of Things Worth Seeing in Italy Given to John Evelyn 25 April 1646*, ed. J. M. Robinson, Roxburghe Club (1987).

HYDE, EDWARD, 1st Earl of Clarendon, *A Collection of Several Tracts* (London, 1727).

—— *Life . . . in which is Included a Continuation of his History*, 2 vols. (Oxford: Oxford University Press, 1857).

—— *Calendar of the Clarendon State Papers*, ii (for 1649–54), ed. W. Dunn McCray; iv (for 1657–60), ed. F. J. Routledge (Oxford: Clarendon Press, 1869, 1932).

HYDE, HENRY, 2nd Earl of Clarendon, *Correspondence*, ed. S. W. Singer, 2 vols. (London, 1828).

LINDENOV, CHRISTOPHER, *The First Triple Alliance: The Letters of Christopher Lindenov; Danish Envoy in London 1668–1672* ed. W. Westergaard (New Haven: Yale University Press, 1947).

LORD, GEORGE DeF. (ed.), *Poems on Affairs of State: Augustan Satirical Verse 1660–1714*, 5 vols. (New Haven: Yale University Press, 1963–75).

MAGALOTTI, LORENZO, *Travels of Cosmo III, Grand Duke of Tuscany through England during the Reign of King Charles II* (London: J. Mawman, 1821).

—— *Lorenzo Magalotti at the Court of Charles II*, ed. W. E. Knowles Middleton (Waterloo, Ont.: Laurier University Press, 1980).

MANLEY, DELARIVIERE, *New Atalantis*, ed. Ros Ballaster (London: Pickering, 1991).

MARVELL, ANDREW, *Complete Poetry*, ed. George deF. Lord (London: Everyman, 1984).

MONCONYS, BALTHASAR, *Les Voyages de M. de Monconys en Angleterre* (Paris, 1695).

MORDAUNT, JOHN, Viscount, *Letter-book 1658–1660*, ed. Mary Coate, Camden Society, 3rd ser., 69 (1945).

MUNDY, PETER, *Travels*, ed. R. C. Temple and L. M. Anstey, Hakluyt Society, 2nd ser., 5 (1936).

NORTH, ROGER, *Examen* (London, 1740).

—— *Lives of the Norths*, ed. A. Jessopp, 3 vols. (London: Bell, 1890).

—— *General Preface and Life of Dr John North*, ed. Peter Millard (Toronto: University of Toronto Press, 1984).

OVID, *Metamorphoses*, trans. Mary M. Innes (Harmondsworth: Penguin, 1955).

PATRICK, SIMON, *The Christian Sacrifice: A Treatise Shewing the Necessity, End, and Manner of Receiving the Holy Communion* (London, 1672). British Library Eve.c.19 (with Evelyn's notes).

—— *Works*, ed. A. Taylor, 9 vols. (Oxford: Oxford University Press, 1858).

PEPYS, SAMUEL, *Diary*, ed. Robert Latham and William Matthews, 11 vols. (London: HarperCollins, 1995).

PHILIPS, KATHERINE, *The Collected Works of Katherine Philips, the Matchless Orinda*, ed. Patrick Thomas, 3 vols. (Stump Cross: Stump Cross Books, 1990–3).

RERESBY, SIR JOHN, *Memoirs*, ed. A. Browning (Glasgow: Jackson, 1936).

RIMBAULT, EDWARD (ed.), *The Old Cheque Book . . . of the Chapel Royal 1561–1744*, Camden Society, new ser., 3 (1872).

RUSSELL, RACHEL, Lady, *Letters*, ed. Lord John Russell, 2 vols. (London, 1853).

SALES, FRANCIS DE, *Introduction to the Devout Life*, trans. Michael Day (London: Everyman, 1961).

SAVILE, GEORGE, Marquess of Halifax, *Complete Works*, ed. J. P. Kenyon (Harmondsworth: Penguin, 1969).

—— *Savile Correspondence*, ed. W. D. Cooper, Camden Society, 70 (1858).

SCHELLINCKS, WILLIAM, *The Journal of William Schellincks' Travels in England*, ed. M. Exwood and H. L. Lehmann, Camden Society, 5th ser., 1 (1993).

SHADWELL, THOMAS, *The Virtuoso*, ed. M. H. Nicolson and D. S. Rodes (London: Edward Arnold, 1966).

SHEFFIELD, JOHN, Duke of Buckingham, *Works*, 2 vols. (London, 1726).

SOPHOCLES, *Electra*, trans. C[hristopher] W[ase] (The Hague, 1649).

SORBIÈRE, SAMUEL DE, *A Voyage to England* (London, 1709).

STANHOPE, PHILIP DORMER, 2nd Earl of Chesterfield, *Letters* (London: E. Lloyd, 1829).

TAYLOR, JEREMY, *The Whole Works*, 9 vols. (n.p., 1847).

THIBAUDEAU, A. W. (ed.), *Catalogue of the Collection of . . . Alfred Morrison*, 6 vols. (London: privately printed, 1883–92).

—— *The Bulstrode Papers* (n.p., 1897).

THOMPSON, E. M. (ed.), *Correspondence of the Family of Hatton*, Camden Society, new ser., 22 (1878).

VERNEY, MARGARET M., *Memoirs of the Verney Family from the Restoration to the Revolution* (London: Longmans, 1899).

WILMOT, JOHN, Earl of Rochester, *The Rochester–Savile Letters*, ed. J. H. Wilson (Columbus, Oh.: Ohio State University Press, 1941).

WILSON, J. H. (ed.), *Court Satires of the Restoration* (Columbus, Oh.: Ohio State University Press, 1976).

WOOD, ANTHONY, *Athenae Oxonienses*, ed. Philip Bliss, 4 vols. (London: Rivington, 1813–20).

—— *The Life and Times of Anthony Wood*, ed. Andrew Clark, Oxford Historical Society, 1 (1891).

SECONDARY SOURCES

ACKERMAN, JAMES, *The Villa: Form and Typology of Country Houses* (London: Thames and Hudson, 1990).

ALMOND, PHILIP, *Adam and Eve in Seventeenth Century Thought* (Cambridge: Cambridge University Press, 1999).

ANDREWS, CHARLES M., *British Committees, Commissions and Councils of Trade and Plantations 1622–1675* (Baltimore: Johns Hopkins University, 1908).

BALDWIN, ANNA, and HUTTON, SARAH (eds.), *Platonism and the English Imagination* (Cambridge: Cambridge University Press, 1994).

BARBER, TABITHA, *Mary Beale* (London: Geffrye Museum, 1999).

BARNES, A. S., 'Catholic Chapels under the Stuarts', *Downside Review*, 20 (1901), 158–65, 232–49.

BATTIGELLI, ANNA, *Margaret Cavendish and the Exiles of the Mind* (Lexington, KY: University Press of Kentucky, 1998).

BEER, ESMOND DE, 'Evelyn and Col. Herbert Morley in 1659 and 1660', *Sussex Archaeological Collections*, 78 (1937), 176–83.

—— 'John Evelyn: Mr W. G. Hiscock's Account of him', *Notes and Queries*, 205 (1960) 203–6, 243–8, 284–6.

BIEBER, R. P., 'The Plantation Councils of 1670–4', *English Historical Review*, 40 (1925), 93–106.

BOSWELL, ELEANOR, *The Restoration Court Stage* (Cambridge, Mass.: Harvard University Press, 1932).

BRANDON, P. F., 'Land, Technology and Water Management in the Tillingbourne Valley', *Southern History*, 6 (1984), 75–103.

BRETT-JAMES, NORMAN, *The Growth of Stuart London* (London: Allen and Unwin, 1935).

BROWNING, ANDREW, *Thomas Osborne, Earl of Danby*, 3 vols. (Glasgow: Jackson, 1951).

BRYSON, ANNA, *From Courtesy to Civility: Changing Codes of Conduct in Early Modern England* (Oxford: Clarendon Press, 1998).

BUCHOLZ, ROBERT, *The Augustan Court: Queen Anne and the Decline of Court Culture* (Stanford, Calif.: Stanford University Press, 1993).

BURKE, PETER, *The Fabrication of Louis XIV* (New Haven: Yale University Press, 1992).

—— *The Fortunes of the Courtier: The European Reception of Castiglione's 'Cortegiano'* (Oxford: Polity, 1996).

CASTLE, TERRY, *Civilization and Masquerade* (Stanford, Calif.: Stanford University Press, 1986).

CHALKLIN, C. W., *Seventeenth Century Kent* (London: Longmans, 1965).

CHAMBERS, DOUGLAS, *The Planters of the English Landscape Garden* (New Haven: Yale University Press, 1993).

—— 'John Evelyn and the Invention of the Heated Greenhouse', *Garden History*, 20 (1992), 201–5.

CHANDAMAN, C. D., *The English Public Revenue 1660–1688* (Oxford: Clarendon Press, 1975).

CHARLESWORTH, MICHAEL, 'A Plan by John Evelyn of Henry Howard's Garden at Albury Park, Surrey', in T. O'Malley and J. Wolschke-Bulmahn (eds.), *John*

Evelyn's Elysium Britannicum and European Horticulture (Washington, DC: Dumbarton Oaks, 1995), 289–93.

CLARK, RUTH, *Anthony Hamilton* (London: John Lane, 1921).

CLAY, CHRISTOPHER, *Public Finance and Private Wealth: The Career of Sir Stephen Fox* (Oxford: Clarendon Press, 1978).

CLOAKE, JOHN, *Palaces and Parks of Richmond and Kew*, 3 vols. (Chichester: Phillimore, 1995–6).

COAD, JONATHAN, *The Royal Dockyards* (Aldershot: Scolar, 1989).

COATE, MARY, *Cornwall in the Great Civil War* (Oxford: Clarendon Press, 1933).

COBBETT, R. S., *Memorials of Twickenham* (London: Smith, Elder, 1872).

COKAYNE, GEORGE EDWARD, *The Complete Peerage*, 8 vols. (London: Bell, 1887–98).

COLLINSON, PATRICK, '"Not Sexual in the Ordinary Sense": Men, Women, and Religious Transactions', in *Elizabethan Essays* (London: Hambledon, 1994), 119–50.

COLVIN, HOWARD, *The History of the King's Works*, vol. v (London: HMSO, 1976).

COULTHARD, H. R., *The Story of the Ancient Parish of Breage* (Camborne: Camborne Printing Co., 1913).

CRAWFORD, PATRICIA, *Women and Religion in England 1500–1720* (London: Routledge, 1993).

CRESSY, DAVID, *Birth, Marriage & Death: Ritual, Religion and the Life Cycle in Tudor and Stuart England* (Oxford: Clarendon Press, 1997).

DAVIES, KATHLEEN M., 'Continuity and Change in Literary Advice on Marriage', in R. B. Outhwaite (ed.), *Marriage and Society* (London: Europa, 1981), 58–78.

DENNY, MARGARET, 'The Early Program of the Royal Society and John Evelyn', *Modern Language Quarterly*, 1 (1940), 481–97.

DOBSON, MARY J., *Contours of Death and Disease in Early Modern England* (Cambridge: Cambridge University Press, 1997).

DODD, A. H., 'The Tragedy of Col. John Bodvel', *Transactions of the Caernarvonshire Historical Society*, 6 (1945), 1–22.

D'OYLEY, ELIZABETH, *James, Duke of Monmouth* (London: Geoffrey Bles, 1938).

DUFFY, EAMON, *The Stripping of the Altars: Traditional Religion in England* (New Haven: Yale University Press, 1992).

EALES, JACQUELINE, 'Samuel Clarke and the "Lives" of Godly Women in Seventeenth Century England', in W. J. Sheils and D. Wood (ed.), *Women in the Church* (Oxford: Blackwell, 1990), 365–76.

—— *Women in Early Modern England 1500–1700* (London: UCL Press, 1998).

EDMOND, MARY, 'Nicholas Dixon, Limner, and Matthew Dixon, Painter', *Burlington Magazine*, 125 (1983), 611–12.

—— 'Bury St Edmunds: A Seventeenth Century Art Centre', *Walpole Society*, 53 (1989), 106–18.

ELLIOT, HUGH, *The Life of Sidney, Earl of Godolphin* (London: Longmans, 1888).

ESTERLY, DAVID, *Grinling Gibbons and the Art of Carving* (London: Victoria and Albert Museum, 1998).

EVELYN, HELEN, *The Evelyn Family* (London: E. Nash, 1915).

FADERMAN, LILLIAN, *Surpassing the Love of Men* (London: Women's Press, 1985).

FALK, BERNARD, *The Berkeleys of Berkeley Square* (London: Hutchinson, 1944).

FEA, ALLAN, *The Loyal Wentworths* (London: John Lane, 1928).

FERGUSON, GEORGE, *Signs and Symbols in Christian Art* (New York: Oxford University Press, 1961).

FLETCHER, ANTHONY, 'The Protestant Idea of Marriage in Early Modern England', in A. Fletcher and P. Roberts (eds.), *Religion, Culture and Society in Early Modern Britain* (Cambridge: Cambridge University Press, 1994), 161–81.

—— *Gender, Sex, and Subordination in England 1500–1800* (New Haven: Yale University Press, 1995).

FOLEY, HENRY, *Records of the English Province of the Society of Jesus*, 7 vols. (London, 1875–83).

FORNERON, HENRI, *Louise de Kéroualle, Duchesse de Portsmouth* (Paris, 1886).

FRASER, ANTONIA, *The Weaker Vessel: Woman's Lot in Seventeenth-Century England* (London: Methuen, 1984).

—— *King Charles II* (London: Mandarin, 1993).

FULTON, J. F., *A Bibliography of the Honourable Robert Boyle*, Oxford Bibliographical Society, 3 (London, 1932–3).

GIBSON, KATHARINE, 'The Decoration of St George's Hall Windsor for Charles II', *Apollo*, 147, pt 2 (Apr.–June 1998), 30–8.

GITTINGS, CLARE, *Death, Burial, and the Individual in Early Modern England* (London: Croom Helm, 1984).

GOMBRICH, E. H., *Symbolic Images* (London: Phaidon, 1972).

GREER, GERMAINE, *Slipshod Sybils: Recognition, Rejection and the Woman Poet* (London: Viking, 1995).

GREGG, EDWARD, *Queen Anne* (London: Routledge, 1980).

GROSE, C. L., 'The Anglo-Dutch Alliance of 1678', *English Historical Review*, 39 (1924), 349–72, 526–51.

HALEY, K. H. D., *The First Earl of Shaftesbury* (Oxford: Clarendon, 1968).

HALLER, WILLIAM, and HALLER, MALLEVILLE, 'The Puritan Art of Love', *Huntington Library Quarterly*, 5 (1941–2), 235–72.

HARLEY, J. B., *Music in Purcell's London* (London: Dennis Dobson, 1968).

HARRIS, FRANCES, *A Passion for Government: The Life of Sarah, Duchess of Marlborough* (Oxford: Clarendon Press, 1991).

—— '"The Honourable Sisterhood": Queen Anne's Maids of Honour', *British Library Journal*, 19 (1993), 181–98.

—— 'The Letter-books of Mary Evelyn', *English Manuscript Studies* (1998), 204–13.

HARRISON, ROBERT POGUE, *Forests: The Shadow of Civilization* (Chicago: University of Chicago Press, 1992).

HARTMANN, C. H., *La Belle Stuart* (London: Routledge, 1924).

—— *Clifford of the Cabal* (London, Heinemann, 1937).

—— *The King's Friend: A Life of Charles Berkeley, Viscount Fitzhardinge, Earl of Falmouth* (London: Heinemann, 1951).

—— *The King my Brother* (London: Heinemann, 1954).

HENSLOWE, JOYCE, *Anne Hyde, Duchess of York* (London: Werner Laurie, [1915]).

HERRING, PETER, *Godolphin, Breage: An Archaeological and Historical Survey* (Truro: Cornwall Archaelogical Unit, 1998).

HERVEY, MANNERS W., *Annals of a Suffolk Village* (Cambridge: Cambridge University Press, 1930).

HILL, BRIDGET, 'A Refuge from Men: The Idea of a Protestant Nunnery', *Past and Present*, 117 (1987), 107–30.

HISCOCK, W. G., *John Evelyn and Margaret Godolphin* (London: John Murray, 1951).

—— *John Evelyn and his Family Circle* (London: Routledge, 1955).

—— 'John Evelyn' [a reply to Esmond de Beer], *Notes and Queries*, 205 (1960), 476–7.

HISTORY OF PARLIAMENT, *The House of Commons 1660–1690*, ed. B. D. Henning, 3 vols (London: Secker & Warburg, 1983).

HOLMAN, PETER, *Four and Twenty Fiddlers: The Violin at the English Court* (Oxford: Clarendon Press, 1993).

HOUGHTON, W. E., 'The English Virtuoso in the Seventeenth Century', *Journal of the History of Ideas*, 3 (1942), 51–73, 190–219.

HOULBROOKE, RALPH, *Death, Religion and the Family in England 1489–1750* (Oxford: Clarendon Press, 1998).

HUNT, JOHN DIXON, *Garden and Grove: The Italian Renaissance Garden in the English Imagination* (London: Dent, 1986).

—— 'Evelyn's Idea of a Garden', in T. O'Malley and J. Wolschke-Bulmahn (eds.), *John Evelyn's Elysium Britannicum and European Horticulture* (Washington, DC: Dumbarton Oaks, 1995), 269–88.

HUNTER, MICHAEL, *Establishing the New Science* (Woodbridge: Boydell, 1989).

—— *Science and Society in Restoration England*, 2nd edn. (Aldershot: Gregg Revivals, 1992).

—— 'John Evelyn in the 1650s', in *Science and the Shape of Orthodoxy* (Woodbridge: Boydell, 1995).

HUTTON, RONALD, *Charles II* (Oxford: Clarendon Press, 1989).

—— *The Triumph of the Moon: The History of Modern Pagan Witchcraft* (Oxford: Clarendon Press, 1999).

HYATTE, REGINALD, *The Arts of Friendship: The Idealization of Friendship in Medieval and Early Renaissance Literature* (Leiden: Brill, 1994).

IMPEY, OLIVER, and ARTHUR MCGREGOR (eds.), *The Origins of Museums* (Oxford: Clarendon Press, 1985).

JOHNSON, B. H., *Berkeley Square to Bond Street* (London: John Murray, 1952).

JORDAN, W. K., *The Charities of London 1480–1660* (London: Allen and Unwin, 1960).

JUSSERAND, J. J., *A French Ambassador at the Court of Charles II* (London: T. Fisher, 1892).

KEEBLE, N. H. (ed.), *The Cultural Identity of Seventeenth Century Woman: A Reader* (London: Routledge, 1994).

KELLY, JOAN, *Women, History and Theory* (Chicago: Chicago University Press, 1984).

KENYON, J. P., *Robert Spencer, Earl of Sunderland* (London: Longmans, Green, 1958).

—— *The Popish Plot* (Harmondsworth: Penguin, 1974).

KETTON-CREMER, R. W., *Norfolk Portraits* (London: Faber, 1944).

KEYNES, SIR GEOFFREY, *John Evelyn: A Study in Bibliophily, with a Bibliography of his Writings*, 2nd edn. (Oxford: Clarendon Press, 1968).

KIRCHBERGER, C., 'Elizabeth Burnet', *Church Quarterly Review*, 148 (1949), 17–51.

KNIGHTS, MARK, *Politics and Opinion in Crisis 1678–1681* (Cambridge: Cambridge University Press, 1994).

KUGLER, ANNE, 'Constructing Wifely Identity: Prescription and Practice in the Life of Lady Sarah Cowper', *Journal of British Studies*, 40 (2001), 291–323.

LAIRD, MARK, 'Parterre, Grove and Flower Garden: European Horticulture and Planting Design in John Evelyn's time', in T. O'Malley and J. Wolschke-Bulmahn (eds.), *John Evelyn's 'Elysium Britannicum' and European Horticulture* (Washington, DC: Dumbarton Oaks, 1995), 171–220.

LAKE, PETER, 'Feminine Piety and Personal Potency: The Emancipation of Mrs Jane Ratcliffe', *Seventeenth Century*, 2 (1987), 143–56.

LAURENCE, ANNE, *Women in England 1500–1760: A Social History* (London: Weidenfeld and Nicolson, 1994).

LAVERY, BRIAN, *Building the Wooden Walls* (London: Conway Maritime Press, 1991).

LEFTWICH, B. R., 'The Parish of St. Nicholas Deptford', *Ecclesiological Society Transactions*, new ser., 1 (1942–7), 199–224.

LEGG, J. WICKHAM, *English Church Life from the Restoration to the Tractarian Movement* (London: Longmans, 1914).

LEITES, EDMUND, 'The Duty to Desire: Love, Friendship, and Sexuality in some Puritan Theories of Marriage', *Journal of Social History*, 15 (1982), 383–408.

LEITH-ROSS, PRUDENCE, 'A Seventeenth Century Paris Garden', *Garden History* (Winter, 1993), 150–7.

—— *The John Tradescants* (London: Peter Owen, 1998).

LEVER, SIR TRESHAM, *Godolphin* (London: John Murray, 1952).

LEVINE, JOSEPH M., 'John Evelyn between the Ancients and Moderns', in T. O'Malley and J. Wolschke-Bulmahn (eds.), *John Evelyn's 'Elysium Britanncium' and European Gardening* (Washington, DC: Dumbarton Oaks, 1998), 57–78.

LEWER, DAVID, and DARK, ROBERT, *The Temple Church* (London: Historical Publications, 1997).

LINDLEY, DAVID (ed.), *The Court Masque* (Manchester: Manchester University Press, 1984).

LITTEN, JULIAN, *The English Way of Death: The Common Funeral since 1450* (London: Hale, 1991).

LONGE, JULIA, *Martha Lady Giffard: Her Life and Correspondence* (London: George Lane, 1911).

LOUDON, IRVING, *Death in Childbirth: An International Study of Maternal Care and Maternal Mortality 1800–1920* (Oxford: Clarendon Press, 1992).

LOVE, HAROLD, *Scribal Publication in Seventeenth Century England* (Oxford: Clarendon Press, 1993).

LUCKETT, RICHARD, 'Exotick but Rational Entertainments: English Dramatick Operas', in Marie Axton and Raymond Williams (eds.), *English Drama: Essays in Honour of Muriel C. Bradbrook* (Cambridge: Cambridge University Press, 1997), 123–41.

LYNCH, KATHLEEN, *The Social Mode of Restoration Comedy* (New York: University of Michigan, 1926).

—— *A Congreve Gallery* (Cambridge, Mass.: Harvard University Press, 1951).

McGOLDRICK, TERENCE A., *The Sweet and Gentle Struggle: Francis de Sales on the Necessity of Spiritual Friendship* (Lanham, Md.: University Press of America, 1996).

MACKENZIE, THERESE MUIR, *Dromana: Memoirs of an Irish Family* (Dublin: Sealy, 1906).

McKITTERICK, DAVID, 'Women and their Books in Seventeenth Century England: The Case of Elizabeth Puckering', *Library*, 7th series 1 (2000), 372–8.

MacLEOD, CATHARINE, and ALEXANDER, JULIA MARCIARI (eds.), *Painted Ladies: Women at the Court of Charles II* (London: National Portrait Gallery, 2001).

MARSH, F. G., *The Godolphins* (New Milton: privately printed, 1930).

MARTZ, LOUIS B., *The Poetry of Meditation* (New Haven: Yale University Press, 1954).

MAY, PETER, *The Changing Face of Newmarket 1660–1760* (Newmarket: Peter May Publications, 1984).

MENDELSON, SARA HELLER, *The Mental World of Stuart Women* (Brighton: Harvester, 1987).

—— and CRAWFORD, PATRICIA, *Women in Early Modern England* (Oxford: Clarendon Press, 1998).

MILLAR, SIR OLIVER, *Sir Peter Lely* (London: National Portrait Gallery, 1978).

MILLER, JOHN, *Popery and Politics in England 1660–1688* (Cambridge: Cambridge University Press, 1973).

—— *James II* (London: Methuen, 1989).

MINTZ, SAMUEL, *The Hunting of Leviathan* (Cambridge: Cambridge University Press, 1962).

MURRAY, EDWARD CROFT, *Decorative Painting in England 1537–1837*, 2 vols. (London: Country Life, 1962).

NETHERCOT, A. H., 'John Evelyn and Colonel Herbert Morley in 1659–60', *Huntington Library Quarterly*, 1 (1938), 439–46.

OLLARD, RICHARD, *Clarendon and his Friends* (London: Hamilton, 1987).

PAGLIA, CAMILLE, *Sexual Personae: Art and Decadence from Nefertiti to Emily Dickinson* (Harmondsworth: Penguin, 1991).

PANOFSKY, ERWIN, *Studies in Iconology* (New York: Oxford University Press, 1939).

PARRY, GRAHAM, 'John Evelyn as Hortulan Saint', in Michael Leslie and Timothy Raylor (eds.), *Culture and Cultivation in Early Modern England* (Leicester: Leicester University Press, 1992), 130–50.

PHILLIPS, PATRICIA, *The Scientific Lady: A Social History* (London, Weidenfeld and Nicolson, 1990).

PLATT, COLIN, *The Great Rebuildings of Tudor and Stuart England* (London: UCL Press, 1994).

POWELL, F. L., *English Domestic Relations 1487–1653* (New York: Columbia University Press, 1912).

PREST, JOHN, *The Garden of Eden: The Botanic Garden and the Re-creation of Paradise* (New Haven: Yale University Press, 1981).

PRINCIPE, LAWRENCE M., 'Style and Thought of the Early Boyle: Discovery of the 1648 Manuscript of *Seraphic Love*', *Isis*, 85 (1994), 247–60.

RANDALL, DALE B. J., *Gentle Flame: The Life and Verse of Dudley, 4th Lord North* (Durham, NC: Duke University Press, 1983).

REDFORD, BRUCE, 'Evelyn's Life of Mrs Godolphin and the Hagiographical Tradition', *Biography*, 8 (1985), 119–29.

RICHARDSON, C. F., *English Preachers and Preaching 1640–1670* (New York: Macmillan, 1928).

ROBERTS, DAVID, *The Ladies: Female Patronage and Restoration Drama* (Oxford: Clarendon Press, 1989).

ROBERTS, GARETH, *The Mirror of Alchemy* (London: British Library, 1994).

ROBERTSON, ALEXANDER, *The Life of Sir Robert Moray* (London: Longmans, 1922).

ROBINSON, C. B., *History of the Priory and Peculiar of Snaith* (London: Simpkin Marshall, 1861).

SHAPIN, STEVEN, *A Social History of Truth* (Chicago: University of Chicago Press, 1994).

SHARP, THOMAS, *The Life of John Sharp, Archbishop of York*, 2 vols. (London, 1825).

SHAW, J. J. S., 'The Commission for Sick and Wounded and Prisoners 1664–1667', *Mariner's Mirror*, 25 (1939), 306–27.

SMALL, CAROLA, and SMALL, ALASTAIR, 'Evelyn and the Garden of Epicurus', *Journal of the Warburg and Courtauld Institute*, 60 (1997), 198–202.

SMITH, CHARLOTTE FELL, *Mary Rich, Countess of Warwick* (London: Longmans: 1901).

SMITH, HILDA L., *Reason's Disciples: Seventeenth-Century English Feminists* (Urbana: Illinois University Press, 1982).

SOMERVILLE, SIR ROBERT, *The Savoy Manor, Hospital, Chapel* (London: Duchy of Lancaster, 1960).

SOMMERVILLE, C. JOHN, *Popular Religion in Restoration England* (Gainesville, Fla.: University Presses of Florida, 1977).

SOMMERVILLE, MARGARET R., *Sex and Subjection: Attitudes to Women in Early Modern Society* (London: Edward Arnold, 1995).

SPURR, JOHN, *The Restoration Church of England* (New Haven: Yale University Press, 1991).

—— *England in the 1670s: 'This Masquerading Age'* (Oxford: Blackwell, 2001).

STARKEY, DAVID, et al. (eds.), *The English Court from the Wars of the Roses to the Civil War* (London: Longmans, 1987).

STEINMANN, G. S., *A Memoir of Barbara, Duchess of Cleveland* (n.p., 1871).

STEVENSON, DAVID, 'Freemasonry, Symbolism, and Ethics in the Life of Sir Robert Moray', *Proceedings of the Society of Antiquaries of Scotland*, 114 (1984), 405–31.

—— *The Origins of Freemasonry* (Cambridge: Cambridge University Press, 1988).

STEWART, STANLEY, *The Enclosed Garden: The Tradition and Image in 17th Century Poetry* (Madison: Wisconsin University Press, 1966).

STRANKS, C. J., *Anglican Devotion: The Spiritual Life of the Church of England from the Reformation to the Oxford Movement* (London: SCM Press, 1961).

STRICKLAND, AGNES, *Lives of the Queens of England*, 12 vols. (London: Henry Colburn, 1840–8), viii.

STRONG, ROY, *The Renaissance Garden in England* (London: Thames and Hudson, 1979).

STUART, J. DOUGLAS, *Pin-ups or Virtues: The Concept of the 'Beauties' in Late Stuart Portraiture*, William Andrews Clark Memorial Library Seminar (Los Angeles, 1974).

SUNDSTROM, ROY, *Sidney Godolphin: Servant of the State* (Newark, NJ: University of Delaware Press, 1992).

SURVEY OF LONDON, XIII, XIV, *The Parish of St Margaret, Westminster (Neighbourhood of Whitehall)*, i and ii (London, 1930–1).

SYFRET, R. H., 'Some Early Critics of the Royal Society', *Notes and Records of the Royal Society*, 8 (1951), 20–64.

TAYLOR, F. SHERWOOD, 'The Chemical Studies of John Evelyn', *Annals of Science*, 8 (1952), 285–92.

THOMAS, KEITH, *Religion and the Decline of Magic* (Harmondsworth: Penguin, 1973).

—— *Man and the Natural World: Changing Attitudes in England 1500–1800* (Harmondsworth: Penguin, 1984).

THORNE, PATRICK, *Breage and St Breaca's Church* (Breage: Breaca Books, 1996).

THURLEY, SIMON, *The Lost Palace of Whitehall* (London: Royal Institute of British Architects, 1998).

—— *The Whitehall Palace Plan of 1670*, London Topographical Society Publication, 153 (1998).

—— 'A Country Seat Fit for a King: Charles II, Greenwich and Winchester', in Eveline Cruickshanks and David Starkey (eds.), *The Stuart Courts* (Thrupp: Sutton, 2000), 214–26.

TODD, MARGO, *Christian Humanism and the Puritan Social Order* (Cambridge: Cambridge University Press, 1987).

URWIN, ALAN C. B., *Twickenham Parke* (Twickenham, 1965).

VEEVERS, ERICA, *Images of Love and Religion: Queen Henrietta Maria and Court Entertainments* (Cambridge: Cambridge University Press, 1989).

VICKERY, AMANDA, *The Gentleman's Daughter: Women's Lives in Georgian England* (New Haven: Yale University Press, 1998).

WALKLING, ANDREW, 'Masque and Politics at the Restoration Court: John Crowne's *Calisto*', *Early Music* (Feb. 1996), 27–62.

WALMESLEY, ROBERT, 'John Wesley's Parents', *Proceedings of the Wesley Historical Society*, 29 (1953–4), 51–7.

WARNER, MARINA, *Alone of all her Sex: The Myth and Cult of the Virgin Mary* (London: Weidenfeld and Nicolson, 1976).

WEBSTER, CHARLES, *The Great Instauration: Science, Medicine and Reform 1626–1660* (London: Duckworth, 1975).

WENDORF, RICHARD, *Elements of Life: Biography and Portrait-Painting in Stuart and Georgian England* (Oxford: Clarendon Press, 1990).

WESTFALL, RICHARD, 'Robert Hooke', in *Dictionary of Scientific Biography* (New York: Scribner, 1970–80), vi. 481–8.

WHETTER, JAMES, *Cornwall in the 17th Century* (Padstow: Lodenck Press, 1974).

WILL, S. J., 'Discovery of the Coffin of Margaret Godolphin in St Breage Church', *Antiquary*, 25 (Jan.–June 1892), 200–3.

WILSON, ADRIAN, *The Making of Man-Midwifery* (London: UCL Press, 1995).

WINN, JAMES ANDERSON, *'When Beauty Fires the Blood': Love and the Arts in the Age of Dryden* (Ann Arbor: University of Michigan Press, 1992).

WYNNE, SONYA, 'The Mistresses of Charles II and Restoration Court Politics', Ph. D. thesis (Cambridge, 1997).

ZAGORIN, PEREZ, *Ways of Lying: Dissimulation, Persecution and Conformity in Early Modern Europe* (Cambridge, Mass.: Harvard University Press, 1990).

Index